OUR JERUSALEM

New Edition
including about 80 pictures
most of them published for the first time
and Epilogue

BERTHA SPAFFORD VESTER

OUR
JERUSALEM

AN AMERICAN FAMILY
IN THE HOLY CITY
1881-1949

THE AMERICAN COLONY, JERUSALEM
ARIEL PUBLISHING HOUSE, JERUSALEM

Horatio Spafford

Anna Spafford

Frederick and Bertha Vester and Children

FOREWORD TO THE NEW EDITION

"Our Jerusalem", originally published in 1950, was written by my mother, Bertha Spafford Vester, as a record of an American family's life in Jerusalem. Arriving in Jerusalem at the age of three, she remained there until her death at the age of ninety.

Her parents, Horatio and Anna Spafford, a devout and well-to-do Chicago couple, came to the Holy Land in 1881, seeking consolation in a simple religious life after a series of personal tragedies, recorded in the book. Joined by a number of like-minded Americans and, later, by a large group of villagers from Sweden, they founded a religious community which came to be known as the American Colony.

Leading a simple communal life and frequently one of difficulty and hardship, they supported themselves by various enterprises: a small farm, a butchery, a bakery, a smithie, a souvenir shop and a photographic business. They never attempted any missionary work but, through their friendship with all sections of the strange and wonderful people of Jerusalem's varied community, became involved in teaching and philanthropic work.

It has been decided to re-publish the book, now out of print, on account of the great historical interest of the period it records. This new edition is a facsimile of the

1950 first edition. An epilogue and more than eighty pictures, taken from the albums of the American Colony, have been added. Many of them were taken by American Colony photographers and are now published for the first time.

The pictures cover about sixty years, from the end of the last century to 1948. Together with the story, they illustrate not only the history of the American Colony, but also the major events in this dramatic period, through the collapse of the Ottoman Empire, the first World War and subsequent British Mandate, up to the time of the creation of the State of Israel.

Anna Grace Lind
Jerusalem 1988

This book is dedicated to
Father's and Mother's nine grandchildren

APPRECIATION

Life in the American Colony of Jerusalem during the last decade was tranquil although surrounded by political turmoil. Our consuls were friendly. Religious leaders understood us better. Perhaps we had become less of an enigma, and perhaps Jerusalem had changed. Modern Jerusalem accepted us at our value. The old stories cropped up now and then, but were turned aside with oh-that-used-to-be looks, which hurt worse than accusations when one thought of the robust Christianity of the Colony's founders which allowed "no room for selfpity," as Mother expressed it, at the most crucial moment of her life.

It was during this time that I began work on the record of my parents' experiences in Jerusalem and elsewhere which would serve as a record for my children and grandchildren. I have taken five years writing it, part of which was done while we were under fire in the recent war against the partition of Palestine. Preceding this I had worked for fifteen years gathering material incorporated in its writing, and for such contributed data, letters and memoirs, newspaper accounts and testimonials, legal, ecclesiastical and historic, I am indebted to more friends in the United States, the Holy Land, and England than I have space to acknowledge, but whose kindness and interest have contributed greatly to this account of our lives in America and Jerusalem.

I should like to express my public appreciation to Mr. Lowell Thomas, author, lecturer, and radio commentator, whose friendship over many years has meant much to the American Colony in Jerusalem and to me, and who was the first to suggest that I turn into a book my private family record by which others might see the Holy City as it has seemed to us for nearly seventy years.

To Dr. Millar Burrows, Winkley Professor of Biblical Theology at the Divinity School of Yale University and late Director of the American School of Oriental Research in Jerusalem,

I am deeply grateful for whole-hearted encouragement and advice.

My gratitude is also extended to the Rev. Charles T. Bridgeman, at present connected with Trinity Church, New York, formerly Canon of St. George's Cathedral in Jerusalem, who has given unstintedly of his twenty years' experience in Palestine, particularly in church matters.

I also wish to thank Miss Evelyn Wells for her help.

BERTHA SPAFFORD VESTER

INTRODUCTION *By Lowell Thomas*

For years my wanderings took me to many parts of the
world. In the course of these travels I met a fair proportion
of the unusual personalities of our time—statesmen, explorers,
soldiers, scientists, missionaries, writers, mining men, merchants,
and artists. When a traveler thinks of mountain ranges, certain
peaks stand out in his mind—Kinchinjunga in the Himalayas;
Aconcagua in the Andes; Saint Elias and McKinley in Alaska;
Demavend in Persia; Chomolari in Tibet; Rainier in the Puget
Sound country; Mount Washington in New England, and a
dozen more in various lands. Looking back on the people I have
met, a few are like the mountains I have mentioned. One of
these is the author of this book.

Of all the remarkable personalities I have known, Bertha
Vester is one of the few that I have envied.

To me Jerusalem is the most dramatic of the cities of this
earth, more so even than Athens, Rome or Paris. And Bertha
Vester is the only outstanding person who has lived there, both
as an observer and a participant in events, under the Turkish
sultans, through World War I, the period of the Mandate,
a second world war, and finally the period of the return of the
Children of Israel. What a panorama!

Since the days when Dr. John Finley, famous editor of the
New York *Times*, and I, first met her in Jerusalem, I have been
urging her to write the story of her life. For thirty years I have
conducted this campaign, in person and by correspondence.
Always she was too busy with her social-service work in the
Holy City, too involved with her educational problems and
with trying to save children from disease and starvation. She is
a modern Florence Nightingale, with a more colorful and romantic story. Through three generations she has been a central
figure in the life of the city that is sacred to three great religions, Judaism, Christianity, and Mohammedanism.

It was a sheet from one of her hospital beds that provided

ix

the white flag used at the surrender of Jerusalem when, in 1917,
a Christian army entered the Holy City for the first time in nearly
a thousand years. Although called the City of Peace, Jerusalem
has nearly always been a city of violence. As one of the few
Protestants in Jerusalem, she has had a unique opportunity to
watch the pageant of history unroll. Nearly all other prominent
personalities who have spent any time at all in that city atop
the Judean Hills "aloof, waterless, and on the road to nowhere,"
have been on either one side or the other in some bitter struggle.
As a social-service worker, Bertha Vester has been unique in
the sixty-five years of her life in the Holy City.

I haven't read her manuscript. Therefore I know little of
her attitude toward recent events. But I do know that in times
when emotions run high partisans on either side invariably say:
"Well, if you are not *for us*, you must be *against us*." However,
that sort of charge should never be made about either an honest
reporter or social worker.

During the hottest part of the recent fighting between the
Jews and the Moslem inhabitants Mrs. Vester found herself
in a dilemma. One of the elderly members of the American
Colony had died during the night. The battle was raging across
the road between Mrs. Vester's home and the cemetery on the
Mount of Olives. However, she solved this problem. She got
in touch with the officers in command on both sides and asked
them if they would be good enough to stop the battle for two
hours. They did. She buried the aged member of the American
Colony on the Mount of Olives, and then the fighting began
again.

On another occasion, in 1947, some of the Arab forces took
up positions around Mrs. Vester's house and in the compound
of the American Colony. From there they were firing on a
Jewish convoy that apparently was on its way to Hadassah
Hospital. She told them that she would not allow it. They
could shoot her if they wished, but as far as it was within her
power she would not allow an attack to be made upon anyone
from the American Colony which for more than sixty years
had kept its doors open to Moslem, Christian, and Jew. She told
them: "To fire from the shelter of the American Colony is
the same as firing from a mosque or church."

I remember Field Marshal Lord Allenby's admiration for her,
of how highly she was regarded by T. E. Lawrence, of her
close friendship with John Finley when she helped him with

his Red Cross work in the Holy City. I have sat spellbound at her feet, in Jerusalem, listening to her tell of her adventures. And I have long admired her unselfish devotion to the inhabitants of the Holy City, to all of its many races and creeds. Hers is indeed one of the epic stories of our time.

CHAPTER ONE

A FEW months before the Great Chicago Fire, Father came to the conclusion that the law, while highly remunerative, was absorbing too much of his time.

He had no idea of giving up his practice. He was senior partner in the prominent and influential Chicago firm of Spafford, McDaid and Wilson, and was considered an authority on national as well as international law. "Horatio Spafford lives in jurisprudence," Mr. Luther Laflin Mills, one-time states attorney for Illinois, once told me. "We still say in Chicago, 'That's a Spafford case!' or, 'That belongs to the Spafford school of law.' "

But Father became convinced that dealing in real estate would give him opportunity to achieve honorable success without being wholly engrossed by it and also give him more time to devote his attention to philanthropic and Christian work, particularly that being started by his close friend the evangelist, Mr. Dwight L. Moody.

With this idea in mind, in the spring of 1871 Father, with several of his friends, invested in land in the direction of which the city of Chicago was expanding—land which is now part of Lincoln Park—and other extensive tracts north of the city, on the Lake Shore.

They put all their available money, and borrowed more to enlarge their holdings, into this project that seemed sound.

At this time he and Mother were living in the suburb of Lake View, on the north side of Chicago, in a vine-covered gabled cottage surrounded by twelve acres of lawn. They had four little daughters. I think of these children as my "little sisters" although this was before I was born. Anna, named for our mother, was nine. Margaret Lee, aged seven, was named after Father's favorite sister, whose husband, Colonel Arthur T. Lee, had been seriously wounded in the Battle of Gettysburg a few weeks before Maggie was born. Elizabeth, called Bessie, was five, and in July the fourth little girl was born and named Tanetta for our grandmother, who came from Norway and died when Mother was a little girl.

Lake View was some distance from the city limits, but the

family were sublimely happy in their isolation. Their nearest neighbors were Mr. and Mrs. Henry Waller, whose residence in rolling lawns, similar to their own, inspired Chicago's beloved poet Eugene Field to write "The Delectable Ballad of the Waller Lot."

Every day Father went to his law office in the city and was driven to and from the little station by Peter the houseman in a buggy drawn by old Billy the horse.

A narrow-gauge steam train, known as "The Dummy," carried commuters in and out of Chicago. There were no telephones, and when Father brought dinner guests home, as he often did, there was no way of letting Mother know beforehand. Since the last "Dummy" left early in the evening, a dinner guest usually meant one staying overnight.

Father and Mother drew devoted friends about them who shared the joys of their home life and who in the years to come gave them the love and devotion that sustained them in dreadful sorrow. Also, to the Lake View cottage came the weary of body and soul, for my parents were incapable of denying any share of their worldly goods or happiness to anyone who might be in need.

Martha Pirkens Halsey wrote in an article:

One of the most attractive places in the old township of Lake View in the seventies was a residence — ivy-hung and tree-embowered — that seemed in its surroundings the chosen abode of peace and happiness. The house, a picturesque. irregularly shaped cottage, not far from the Lake Shore, displayed in each nook and corner a rare taste and refinement. Grace, simplicity, and beauty everywhere prevailed. . . .

This was the home of my father and mother, Horatio Gates Spafford and Anna Lawson Spafford, who were to become the founders of the American Colony in Jerusalem.

The love and faith in that cottage were to cross the Atlantic and become incorporated in the American Colony. Also in the Colony was to go such strangely unrelated events as the Great Chicago Fire, the Moody and Sanky religious revival that was shortly to sweep two continents with unprecedented spiritual fervor, and the shipwreck of the *Ville du Havre* that is still one of the unexplained tragedies of the sea.

All that summer and fall of 1871 an unusual degree of heat prevailed in Chicago, and the rainfall was so slight as to give scientists cause for much speculation. Forest fires of extraordinary extent ravaged the Northwest, destroying the vegetation and even whole communities, especially around the southern border of the Great Lakes. Early in the fall high southwest winds began blowing and continued for weeks, parching the prairies near Chicago and every piece of timber within and around the city.

During the first weeks of October there was a continual succession of small fires in the city.

Father was in Indiana interviewing a prospective purchaser for some of the Lake Shore property. He was there on October 8, 1871, when the knell of desolation sounded across the American continent in gigantic headlines:

CHICAGO IN ASHES

THE GREAT CALAMITY OF THE AGE
THE SOUTH, THE NORTH, AND A PORTION OF THE WEST DIVISIONS OF THE CITY IN RUINS

There was no more thought of a sale. Father's only thought was to rush back to Chicago.

Mother, left in the Lake View cottage with four small children, three house servants, and Peter, the man of all work, was not alarmed for their own safety in the beginning. As she watched from the porch of the cottage she could see Chicago rising like a pillar of fire in the night. Lake View lay well outside the city, still the stretch of forest between was tinder-dry after the long, hot summer. The glare lighting lake and sky was terrifying, and adding to the terror were the explosions that continued to shake the burning city for days and that could be heard for many miles.

Chicago, roused from sleep, was trying to escape from itself.

Torrents of people were fleeing its blazing streets and struggling over flaming bridges to the country. Tragedy piled on tragedy in the stricken city.

As mile after mile of wooden buildings, homes, stores, and sidewalks caught fire, the glaring illumination showed a city gone mad with terror. Crowds of men, women, and children ran first in one direction, then in another, shouting and screaming, saving objects, no matter how worthless, carrying them, losing them again. Every explosion that shook the city added to their panic.

Drays, express wagons, handcarts, trucks, and every imaginable conveyance was being driven pell-mell through the crowded streets, laden with trunks, boxes, furniture, goods, and papers of every kind. Collisions happened every minute. Wagons broke

down and impeded traffic, causing frantic scenes. Hundreds were
trying to drag trunks along the sidewalks.

Truckmen were offered fabulous sums to carry people or goods.

Trucks drove along the streets with their loads blazing, and
goods dragged into the streets from homes and stores, and piled
there, caught fire. One man told of "delicate ladies standing
guard by their rescued pianos" while crowds swept around them
senselessly.

Many who were carrying bundles of prized possessions had
to abandon them, and the streets were strewn with valuables, oil
paintings, silver, books, musical instruments, toys, mirrors, and
every conceivable article.

One survivor told of an undertaker with an eye for business
who employed half-a-dozen boys, gave each a coffin, took a large
one himself, and rushed his mournful stock across the Chicago
River Bridge. The coffins bobbing along above the heads of the
crowd without apparently any means of motivation was such an
absurd spectacle, the observer said later, that in spite of their
ominous portent he could not help laughing.

Word spread that the bridges over the Chicago River were
burning and all escape to north and west was cut away. The
distracted crowds passed the rumor, adding to the pandemonium
in the streets. Women, half-dressed, carrying babies and with
other children clinging to them, screamed and ran until trapped
in the milling crowds. Passages and sidewalks jammed, and people clawed at one another in self-defense. Women and children
were flung down and trampled by men trying to save their goods
or their lives.

Invalids lay helpless on mattresses on the sidewalks, wailing
for help.

One woman knelt in the street with her skirt in flames, holding
a crucifix before her while she prayed, and a runaway truck dashed
her to the ground.

In the running crowds hundreds of lost children screamed for
their parents. Families were separated, and many never came together again, for unknown thousands lost their lives. Pet animals
whimpered their terror underfoot, hunting their masters.

In a city lawless with panic the brutality and horror of some of
the scenes were sickening.

Thieves and looters forced their way through the crowds to
satisfy avarice in streets lined with unclaimed treasure. Deserted
saloons and liquor stores were broken into, and shouting men

brandished bottles of whisky and champagne. Drunken boys reeled about carrying casks of whisky, offering drinks to crowds of excited men. A survivor told of seeing a little girl run screaming down a street with her long golden hair on fire. A drunken man threw a glass of liquor over her, and the child was covered with blue flame.

One man carried a blazing plank to a pile of costly furniture before a magnificent residence and ignited it. Then he mounted a packing box and screamed that this was the poor man's opportunity.

One ragamuffin lay dead under a fallen marble window ledge, with white kid gloves on his hands and his pockets bursting with plunder.

Large-scale disaster is bound to bring the worst in human nature to the surface. But also the noblest in man came to the fore. Many gave their lives to save others in those dreadful hours. Men and women perished trying to rescue invalids, children, and dumb animals. Strangers helped one another. Unknown heroes survived, and others died, in the Great Chicago Fire.

Mother, watching from the porch at Lake View, knew there would be refugees.

The first arrived that morning. She was a perfect stranger to Mother, and invalided, and she was to become Aunty Sims to the family. She was delivered at the door on a spring mattress laid across an express wagon, and she was to remain at Lake View for the rest of her days, to be alternately a tower of strength and a thorn in Mother's side.

Through that day and the second night and on through the next day Chicago continued to burn. Mother sent Peter astride old Billy, the horse, to hunt for provisions. After he left, a handsome but sooty carriage turned into the driveway filled with strange-looking people in curious costumes. Who were these colored people, Mother wondered, then she recognized her dear friends, the Miller-Morgan family, who were not colored but begrimed with soot and smoke and clad in whatever they had found first when the Great Fire drove them from their comfortable home.

Mary Miller had been one of Mother's schoolmates at Dearborn Seminary. Her husband, A. Halsey Miller, owned the large wholesale and retail jewelry store opposite the Chicago court-

house known as the "Tiffany of the West." With them were their
two little children and Mary's mother, Mrs. Morgan. Her father
had been separated from them in flight.

For two days and a night, without food or rest, they had battled
their way through smoke, wind, and flames to Lake View.

Mr. Miller's eyes had been badly seared with fire and he could
not see, so Mary had mounted the coachman's seat and driven
the horses ahead of the flames to Lake View. She was wearing a
dressing gown over her nightdress and its hem was scorched
and her bare feet blistered. Even when she reached Lake View
she would not rest, for the horses' feet were badly burned, and
Mary soaked their hoofs in hot water and poulticed them before
she would attend to her own scorched feet. Years later she told
me how Mother ordered food and beds prepared for them, and
put compresses of tea leaves on Mr. Miller's burned eyes, and
found a farmer's wife near by with a child of her own to nurse
Mary's four-month-old baby, for in the exodus her milk had dried
up.

Mrs. Morgan was wearing all the dresses she could wear, six
in all. "Fit for an asylum" was the way she described her appearance, but she had saved the dresses.

No sooner did Mother have them all comfortable than Mr.
Waller came hurrying over to say trees near by had caught fire
and he was moving his family to a safer place.

Aunty Sims and the others were in no condition to be moved,
and Peter had not returned, but there was nothing to do but join
the flight. Mother left a note for Peter, telling him she did not
know where they were going. She and Mary reharnessed the
Miller team and, since there was no horse for her own buggy,
she tied it to the back of the Miller carriage with a stout rope.
Into the buggy she hoisted Aunty Sims, with Annie and Maggie,
the two eldest little girls; Bessie and baby Tanetta went into the
carriage ahead with the Morgans and the Millers. The tired,
footsore horses had to pull the double load, but they seemed to
scent danger and were willing, even eager, to be off.

The little caravan plodded up Graceland Road through the
heavy sand. Aimlessly they drove west, not knowing where to
go. They were no longer alone. They were trapped in a river of
refugees dragging their way ahead of flames that still raged in
their wake, racing west from flaming Chicago.

The roads were crowded with every kind of vehicle. Men and
boys pulled heavy loads or carried their old and ill. Women bore

bundles and babies, and there were even dogs with baskets in their mouths, or drawing small wagons. And baby carriages! It seemed everyone had a baby. Little smudge-faced girls trudged through the ashen dust clutching their dolls.

Many survivors of the Great Fire dwelt upon the terrifying roar of the conflagration. Even more ominous, Mother said, was the silence of the fleeing population of a doomed city.

On Graceland Road they overtook a lumber wagon driven by a man Mother knew. She asked his advice as to where they should go.

"We live in Jefferson," he told her. "You are welcome to my home."

On their arrival at the man's house they found twenty other refugees there ahead of them, the majority total strangers to their host. But he and his kind wife did all they could to make them comfortable.

The next morning they drove back to Lake View and found it safe. Peter had proved the faithful servant, and, on returning to the house and finding Mother gone, had worked all night with the garden hoses keeping the roof of the cottage wet. The fire stopped at Fullerton Avenue just in time to save the house and grounds.

Mary Miller and her husband returned to Chicago to hunt her father. They found him safe. They also went to the Lake Shore, where they had first fled with thousands of other refugees, until the sands grew too hot to bear. They had buried several trunks containing jewelry, fine laces, furs, and wearing apparel, in the sand before leaving, and their coachman deserted them there. Later they heard that the faithless coachman was living with a woman who decked herself with their fine clothes, jewelry, laces, and furs.

All through the flight Mary had jealously guarded a heavy valise which she believed contained their choicest valuables but which, when she opened it at Lake View, was found to contain nothing but old shoes. Many in their excitement rescued heavy packages only to find what they had saved with so much effort was utterly worthless.

I do not think the Millers grieved too much over their losses. All their lives were safe, and possessions, contrasted with life, lose their value.

Father and Mother felt the same way.

Father had returned to a city of desolation. His friend General William Bross, who with Mr. Joseph Medill and Mr. Horace White published the Chicago *Tribune*, and who had fought to save the newspaper in the very heart of the holocaust, wrote of the fire:

> It was destruction of the entire business portion of one of the greatest cities in the world. Every bank, insurance office, law office, hotel, theater, railroad, most of the churches and many of the principal residences of the city—a charred mass—property almost beyond estimation gone!

His partner Mr. Medill, seeing the *Tribune* office doomed, sought and purchased a job printing office on the west side that had escaped damage, and collected type and printers. General Bross recounts with amusement how he who two days before might have offered a note for $100,000 anywhere and had it accepted, and whose fortune was now buried under ashes in a bank vault, could not even get four wood-burning stoves on credit, to heat the new plant. Eventually, by asking ten of his friends, he was able to borrow enough money to buy the stoves.

The next day the *Tribune* came out with a half sheet, containing the sad news of the disaster, and a notice that a lost persons' bureau had been opened.

Notices were printed:

Mrs. Bush is at 40 Arnold Street. She has lost her baby.

A little girl—she cannot speak her name—is at Des Plaines Hotel.

Mrs. Tinney's lost little girl, six years old, Katy, is at Harrison House.

Mr. Medill, when he died, left his large estate in equal shares to his two daughters and the *Tribune* stock in trust to their husbands, Mr. Robert W. Patterson and Mr. Robert Sanderson McCormick, a cousin of the Cyrus H. McCormick who brought the Theological Seminary to Chicago.

Colonel Robert Rutherford McCormick, son of Robert Mc-Cormick and grandson of Mr. Medill, later became editor in chief of the *Tribune* and a picturesque figure of world renown. When Lord Northcliffe, the English newspaper publisher, visited me in my home in Jerusalem, learning that I was born in Chicago, asked if I knew Colonel McCormick. "An extraordinary man," he described him. I am afraid my prestige was lowered when I had to admit I had not the pleasure of his personal acquaintance, although my parents had been friendly with his grandparents, Mr. and Mrs. Joseph Medill. During the Civil War Mrs. Medill and Mother had been active in the Sanitary Commission, which became the Red Cross, and later Mrs. Medill was identified with the soldiers' Home in which my parents took an active interest. After the Chicago Fire Mr. and Mrs. Medill worked on the same relief and aid societies with Father and Mother.

The Bross family have also kept up their interests in the *Tribune*. General Bross's daughter Jessie, one of Mother's former school-mates, married Dr. Henry D. Lloyd when he was a reporter on the *Tribune*. Their son, Dr. Henry Lloyd, Junior, still owns an interest in the *Tribune*, and owing to his mothers' lifelong friend-ship with Mother, has been a true friend to the American Colony in Jerusalem.

For a time there were sleepless nights for the survivors of stricken Chicago. With no street lamps, and "vagabonds and cutthroats flown like vultures from every point of the compass, attracted by the scent of plunder," only those with urgent business dared venture out of doors.

Evidently Chicago was again under fire from critics within a short time, for I find the draft of a resolution in Father's hand-writing which must have been prepared for a citizen's meeting soon after the Fire:

Resolved, that while we recognize that the temporary confusion and the unparalleled increase of population, and other results procceding from the fire, have produced an increase of crime in Chicago, that we altogether deny that any such state of things is here existing as controls New York under the Tammany Ring, or which led San Francisco to the appointment of a vigilance committee in our local and state judiciary and in the sufficiency of usual and strictly legal methods for the arrest, conviction, and punish-ment of all criminals and the suppression of crime....

The Great Fire was a crushing misfortune to nearly every inhabitant of Chicago. To Father and his associates in the real estate venture it was a calamity. Who at such a time could think of enlarging parks or expanding the city? But interest on the bor-rowed money had to be paid. Father's law library and adjoining law office in the city, built up with so much expense and pride, were in ashes. Only the contents of a fireproof safe were found and among them, charred and brittle from heat, was a little notebook that has revealed to me much of my parents' lives in these years before I was born.

Father rejoiced that his wife and children were with him and that the beloved Lake View cottage, although it would have to carry a small mortgage, was still their own.

CHAPTER TWO

WHEN my father was still a schoolboy he met with an experience that changed his entire life.

He was home on a holiday in the handsome and historic house in which he was born on October 20, 1828, and which still stands, hidden away in what has become an obscure section of North Troy, New York. His father, Horatio Gates Spafford, Senior, LL.D., was a historian and horticulturist, well-respected and well-to-do.

Father's family originated in Yorkshire, England, and is listed in *Domesday Book*, the world's first survey of lands. Succeeding generations were known as possessors of "yeomen, meadow and wood pastures"; many bore titles, and others occupied positions of influence in Church and State. The ruins of Spofforth Castle in Yorkshire are impressive and contain a large hall that must have been magnificent.

On Spofford Hill, near Georgetown, Massachusetts, a boulder of native granite bears this inscription:

ON THIS HILL IN 1669

JOHN SPOFFORD

DESCENDANT OF ORME AND OF CAMELBAR
OF SPOFFORD, ENGLAND, WITH HIS WIFE,

ELIZABETH SCOTT

FOUNDED THE RACE OF SPOFFORD IN
AMERICA. A RACE RESPECTED FOR
INTEGRITY, COURAGE, GENEROSITY
AND INTELLIGENCE

This first Spafford, Spofford, or Spofforth, to settle in the New World evidently arrived in 1639 with the Rev. Ezekial Rogers.

Father's early life was comfortable and secure. He attended the best schools and won many prizes. He was an avid writer of poetry, many of the poems dealing with the heavenly galaxies. In them he referred to the night sky as "always overcast."

One evening, with a school friend who was visiting him, he was standing on the porch of his home when his friend spoke of the brilliant stars.

Father challenged him at once. Here was his chance, Father said, to speak freely on a subject that was a sore point with him.

"Now, Charlie," he said, "be candid. Be honest. Do you really see enough beauty up there to warrant your outburst?"

His friend stared at Father.

"Horatio, I believe you are nearsighted!" Charlie exclaimed, and, taking off his own glasses, made Horatio put them on.

Father's joy at discovering the night sky in all its beauty is revealed in a poem published in *Wellman's Magazine* in April 1850:

NIGHT

Ye countless stars that tremble in the sky,
How bright and beautiful are you tonight!
I've known ye long, but never did my eye
So burn beneath the glory of your light
As it doth now; I kneel to ye—ye wear
The impress of the Deity that's there.

There is a spirit in the night that talks
To man, as man cannot. There seems to speak
A voice to him from out the depths. There walks
Amid its glowing halls a form that seeks
Communion with him—a pervading soul
That lives and breathes, and animates the whole.

How my whole being worships ye, ye skies!
How Godlike is illimitable space!
I see in every flashing ray that flies
Throbbing from forth your lights, the peaceful face
And aspect of divinity. Ye stand
As when first flung from the Creator's hand.

Ye are unchanged—the ceaseless lapse of years
Dims not your brightness—since the world began
And ye were summoned forth, the arch that rears
Proud and magnificent its giant span
Filling immensity—as now—has stood.
'Twill stand with time—eternity is God.

In later years, when Father became interested in the evangelistic career of Mr. Moody, he often spoke of this experience to illustrate the illumination of spiritual vision on becoming a Christian.

Before his vision was corrected Father had been a rather retiring boy. As a young man he was sociable and popular. He liked parties and had many friends, he had a healthy love for outdoor sports and games, and his love for music and literature grew with the years. His hair was thick and dark, his eyes dark and deep-set, and because bifocals had not yet been made, he had a way of focusing his attention upon those he met with more intensity than is usual with those of normal vision.

Much of his poetry dealt with the lure of the West, and westward he went, after admission to the bar. His West was not gold-bearing California, but the Midwestern frontier. In 1856 he settled in Chicago and began the practice of law.

He loved the freedom of the open and limitless prairies, the blue of the skies and the blue of Lake Michigan, limitless, to human eyes, as the prairies themselves. He felt the thrill of taking part in history and the building of the West.

His name first appears in the Chicago directory of that year as a boarder at Clifton House, at the corner of Madison Street and Wabash Avenue, where lived so many of Chicago's young bachelor set who were to become famous in the business, political, philanthropic, and scientific life of the budding young city.

There was even then a distinct line of demarcation between refined Chicago society, and the hordes who flocked there because of the opportunities the city offered. Despite the "high life" and levity which would give it such a strange reputation, there was, and still is, a serious and progressive element which dominates Chicago.

The year Father came to Chicago, when slavery was the burning issue, this item appears in the Chicago *Tribune* of September 3:

On last Saturday the Republicans of Laporte, Indiana, had a rousing meeting. Bonfires were lit and the greatest enthusiasm prevailed. The principal speaker was H. G. Spafford of Chicago, who made a telling and able address....

Three years later the name of H. G. Spafford, Esq., Professor of Medical Jurisprudence, was listed among the faculty names of the newly organized department of Lind University, subsequently known as the Chicago Medical College and the Medical Department of Northwestern University. Father retained his interest in public matters and found opportunities to step outside the limits of his profession to make himself heard through speeches and other forms of lecturing.

He also found time to teach a Snuday-school class, and it was in this capacity, toward the end of Father's first year in Chicago, that he met the beautiful Norwegian girl who was to become my mother.

When I was a little girl in Jerusalem Mother could hold me fascinated with stories of her girlhood.

Mother was born in Stavanger, Norway, on March 16, 1842, and baptized in the grand old Domkirke as Anna Tubena Larssen. I have been told she was a lovely child, with flaxen hair and blue eyes.

Her father, Lars Larssen, was a farmer and a skilled cabinet-maker, well-respected in the community. I do not know why he migrated to the United States with his family when Mother was four years old. Like so many other Scandinavians, he came to Chicago, and eventually Americanized his name to Lawson.

Chicago was not then a healthy city. Lying as it did on swamp-land, on the lower south shore of Lake Michigan, it was difficult to drain, and was infested with mosquitoes. No one connected the mosquitoes with the malaria, then called "ague fever," that swept the growing city at regular intervals.

When, because of these defects, an epidemic of cholera struck the city, it spread until the greatest part of the population was afflicted. Funerals were common in the streets, and Mother and the other children, always imitative of their elders, made burials their most popular game. She was the only member of the family who escaped cholera when the dreaded epidemic reached the Lawson home.

Her gay, capable young mother, Tanetta, and baby brother Hans, were most seriously stricken. My mother was sent to and from the drugstore for medicine and brandy. As she hurried through the deserted streets she heard on all sides the groans of Chicago's sick and dying. She was only seven years old, but she knew to the full the taste of human despair.

Her mother and baby brother died in the epidemic. Her father, it was discovered, was threatened with tuberculosis. With her halfbrother Edward, he moved to Goodhue County, Minnesota, in the hope that farming might benefit his health.

My mother was left in Chicago with a friend, Mrs. Ely. She loved this kind foster mother and was happy in her schoolwork and most of all in her music. But she could not remain in Chicago when she learned her father was ill and in need of her.

Mother, at fourteen, found herself keeping house for her father and brother in an unfinished log house in a wild, un-settled section of Minnesota. Wolves howled near by in the forest. Massacres and scalpings were not infrequent, and there were always rumors of prowling Indians. The nearest neighbor was seven miles away.

Pioneer living brought out latent qualities in the young girl. She worked every day until her strong young back ached, cooking, washing, milking the cow, tending the chickens, and nursing her father.

When he died, the two young people were alone in the cabin.

Settlers from miles around came and helped make a coffin of the new lumber Lawson had bought to finish his home. Edward stained it outside, to make it look as nice as possible, and my mother lined and padded it with straw covered with a white linen sheet. There were no flowers, but the children brought in fragrant branches of fir and laurel, and wove wreaths for their father's grave.

Mother thought it best to return to Chicago at the first opportunity. A few weeks later she heard that the pastor son of one of the Norwegian settlers was coming to visit his family. While there he arranged to hold a service to which the scattered settlers were invited. He planned to leave directly after this service, and he consented to take Mother with him across the country to the nearest railroad station, where she could entrain for Chicago.

Edward drove his sister to the farm where the pastor was staying, along with the trunk that contained all her wordly belongings. He left as soon as his horses were rested, for there were cows to be milked and chickens to be fed at home. Mother walked along the road beside the wagon until he advised her to turn back.

Edward lived on the farm to a ripe old age, surrounded by children and grandchildren.

But after my mother sadly watched him vanish around a turn in the road that day she never saw her brother again.

She turned back to the farm where the pastor was staying to find the barnyard filled with strange horses and oxen and vehicles of every make drawn up before the house. The settlers had been asked to a service conducted by a real pastor and were treating the occasion like a festival.

Scandinavians are innately religious, but living as these Norwegians did, miles from one another and on the outskirts of civilization, they could rarely attend congregational services, and the celebration of Holy Communion and baptism was possible only when a visiting pastor came their way. Their enthusiasm was great and sincere. Each family had brought food to contribute to the board, and the women were bustling about, arranging the long tables the men set up, and in excited Norwegian catching up with the news and gossip of the frontier.

My mother's troubled heart had no room for festivity. She was different even in speech, for she now spoke English far better than she did Norwegian.

Deeper than these differences was another, because of something that happened to her in Chicago when she was very young. This was an unfortunate experience with a so-called Christian, outwardly a church pillar, inwardly mean. She had seen this person behave cruelly to defenseless dependents who had no means of retaliation. She herself had been subjected to his petty tyranny.

As so many others have before her, she blamed Christianity instead of the individual.

Since that time she had not attended church or Sunday school. She had not prayed.

After the services she heard the pastor agreeing to remain one more week so that he could drive around the country and baptize the infants born since the last pastor had been there.

It was too late to return to Edward and the farm. No one was driving that way, and fear of wolves and Indians kept her from starting out on foot alone.

The pastor drove off with departing guests, and my mother was left with his family.

She found it consisted of a blind mother and a stepfather who leered at her in a sinister way. The pair cooked, ate, slept in the one enormous downstairs room, with a fireplace where the cooking was done on cranes. The only other room was a dark and dirty attic into which the blind woman led her.

In a corner Mother found a pile of straw. Worn out, she fell asleep.

She was wakened by something pawing her face and mumbling. She could see nothing. She wanted to scream but could not. Then she knew it was not an animal, for she caught incoherent mumbling in Norwegian. She lay motionless, holding her breath, until the creature shuffled away into another corner. She continued to lie on the straw, stiff with cold and fear, after she heard it snoring in sleep.

Then Mother prayed.

"O God," she cried in her misery, "deliver me, and I will never be discontented again."

Morning revealed a sleeping woman in the attic, looking more like an animal than a human being. Mother learned that this was a demented stepsister of the pastor's. After breakfast the crazy girl ran away into the woods, and there she remained until evening, when hunger drove her back to the house and the plate of food set out for her.

Mother felt that she could not endure another night in the attic. But the man in the downstairs room made gestured overtures to her under the blind eyes of his wife, and Mother was afraid. She returned to the attic and her demented roommate.

The girl, she found, was not dangerous. Mother spoke to her and showed her kindness, and the girl responded with pathetic gratitude.

The week, Mother said, was spent in a veritable gehenna, but out of it came the resolve to reject despair which was to uphold her in greater need.

Chicago, by contrast, was like a return to heaven. Mother's halfsister, Mrs. Rachel Frederickson, welcomed her, and she returned to her beloved music and voice training. She attended Dearborn Seminary and received tribute as a "brilliant scholar." She made friends who remained stanch all their lives. Among them was Mary Morgan, who married A. Halsey Miller, and Bertha Madison, who married Dr. Johnson and moved to Paris, and who was to be an angel of mercy to Mother after the tragedy that was to change my parents' lives. Jessie Bross, whose father was lieutenant governor of the state of Illinois, was also a Dearborn girl, and her friendship with Mother was very close.

Another school friend, Jenny Simpson, tried to persuade her to attend Sunday school.

"*Our* Sunday-school teacher is different," Jenny argued. "He does not talk down to us. He gives us a chance to express our opinions, and he loves an argument, Annie," she begged, "it will do you good to hear Mr. Spafford."

Mother was only fifteen, but she had lived through much, and in dignity and mentality was developed far beyond her years. One of her friends wrote this description of her as she was then.

Your mother had the bluest of eyes, and abundant fair hair, with beautifully molded mouth and chin, and very white and even teeth. Her ears were so pretty they were often compared to seashells. She had a merry, kind, and affectionate disposition that won the hearts of many poeple, but she could be mischievous, too, with a keen sense of humor. Her voice was lovely, and people predicted that when it was trained a great future lay before her.

This was the young Annie Lawson who, worn down by argu-

The Spafford's Cottage at Lake View, Chicago

The Palace Hotel burning in the Chicago Fire, 1871

Rescue of the survivors of the Ville de Havre

Manuscript of "It is Well with My Soul"

The Old House viewed from the North

Salon of the Old House

מִי שֶׁבֵּירַךְ אֲבוֹתֵינוּ אַבְרָהָם יִצְחָק וְיַעֲקֹב הוּא יְבָרֵךְ
וְיִשְׁמוֹר וְיִנְצוֹר וְיַעֲזוֹר אֶת הַשַּׂר **הָאַרְצִיא**
סְפָּאפָאַרְד וּבְנֵי בֵיתוֹ וְכֹל הַנִּלְוִים אֵלָיו
בַּעֲבוּר שֶׁהוּא מְרַחֵם עָלֵינוּ וְעַל עוֹלָלֵינוּ וְטַפֵּינוּ
יַאֲרִיךְ הַשֵּׁם יָמָיו בְּטוֹב וּבְנָעִים וִיהִי חַסְדוֹ חוֹפֵף
עֲלֵיהֶם בְּיָמָיו וּבְיָמֵינוּ תּוֹשַׁע יְהוּדָה וְיִשְׂרָאֵל
יִשְׁכֹּן לָבֶטַח וּבָא לְצִיּוֹן גּוֹאֵל וְכֵן יְהִי רָצוֹן
וְנֹאמַר אָמֵן

He who blessed our fathers
Abraham, Isaac & Jacob, - bless
& guard & keep & help Aaron's
Sapphard, & his household & all
that are joined with him; because
he has shown mercy to us, to our
children & little ones.
Therefore may the Lord make
his days long in righteousness &
peace joy, - & may the Lord mercy
[shelter] them - In his & in our days
may Judah be helped & Israel
rest peaceably, - & may the Redeemer
come to Zion -
                    Amen.

The Gadites' Prayer for the American Colony, 1883
(Written by the Yemenites, who were helped
by the American Colony)

Early days at the Old House

Bedouin from East of Jordan visiting the Colony

Haj Rashid Barakat of Abu Dis

Turkish Gendarmes

American Cemetery Inscription
in the Protestant Cemetery on Mount Zion

Wooden crate containing exhumed bones
from the Cemetery

The American Colony from the North
at the turn of the Century

The American Colony from the South West
at the turn of the Century

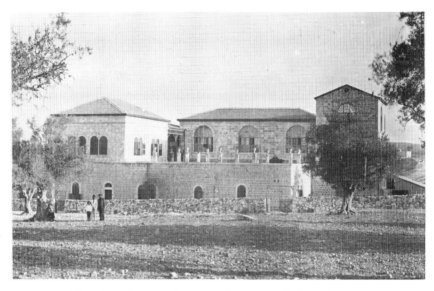

The American Colony at the turn of the Century

Horse and Carriage outside the American Colony

Sister Johana Brooke   Jacob Eliahu Spafford

The Larssen Family

American Colony members after the arrival of the Swedes

Children of the American Colony, 1900

Cows in the grounds of the American Colony

Reaping in the fields near the American Colony

The Milk Room

Sewing and spinning in the Sitting Room

The Kaiser's arrival at Haifa, 1898

The Kaiser's party passing the American Colony

The Kaiser's camp outside the Old City, 1898
(Present street of the Prophets)

ment, consented to visit Horatio Spafford's Sunday-school class "just once."

Father was attracted immediately to the lovely young Norwegian girl. After her visit to his Sunday-school class he could not get her out of his mind. He remembered how she looked one straight in the eye as she spoke, and how she had taken her part in his classroom arguments in a surprisingly intelligent manner.

He did not realize that Mother was only fifteen. He was fourteen years her senior, but the discrepancy was not apparent, for she seemed his equal in years.

"That is an unusual girl," he decided; "she must have had some unique experience to be able to make such deep and searching comments."

And he made up his mind to call on her sister, Mrs. Frederickson, where he had learned Mother was staying, and find out for himself who she was and what was the secret of her personality.

One year later he asked her to marry him.

Only then did he discover Mother's real age. He realized she was too young to marry, and it was arranged that she should leave her sister's home and for three years attend the Ferry Institute for Young Ladies in Lake Forest, about twenty-eight miles from Chicago. It is now known as Ferry Hall and a select school, as it was then.

Some years ago I visited Ferry Hall. I heard that the memory still lived of Mother and the three years she spent there, and of the Bible readings and discussion group she started while a student. I learned that she was considered one of the school's outstanding alumnae. I was privileged to address the scholars and tell them of Mother's life after leaving, and of her work in America and Jerusalem.

After the talk we visited a house near by that had been one of the dormitories in Mother's day. On a windowpane in one of the rooms was scratched a heart, and inside it the initials, HS-AL. No one remembered who had put them there, but the letters spoke volumes to me. "Horatio Spafford-Anna Lawson." Mother scratched them there with her engagement ring.

She wrote a letter from this school to Mrs. Ely. It is dated December 6, 1860, and reads in part:

I wish you were acquainted with Mr. Spafford. He is a true, noble man. I owe him a great deal, but still would not marry him merely from gratitude.

I have often wondered what he could see in me to like, for I am so simple and ignorant, while he is so strong and learned. I pray to God that I may be worthy of him.

Father was considered one of the most promising young lawyers in the city. He had family, social position, and money. Dowagers with marriageable daughters resented his "picking up with a young girl nobody knows, and foreign at that."

They were married on September 5, 1861, in the Second Presbyterian Church on the south side of Chicago. The young couple had decided on a very quiet wedding. War was on between the North and the South, and marriage in wartime must needs be simple. Announcements were sent to all their acquaintances, but only a few were asked to attend the ceremony.

Father invited only his closest friends to the church, and Mother her sister and several friends, one of them being Mrs. Lawson, who had been her confidant through many vicissitudes since her mother's death, and whose son, the late Victor Lawson, was editor and owner of the Chicago *Daily News*.

Mother's wedding dress was planned to be useful long after the wedding day. It was a dark blue taffeta with a hooped skirt, tight waist and overskirt, and with it she wore a small bonnet made of the same dark material trimmed with tiny pink roses. Its turned-up brim was lined with shirred pink chiffon, and Mother's friends who saw her coming down the aisle that day have told me she was lovely.

Much to the amazement of the bride and groom, they found the church filled with smiling people. It had been beautifully decorated with white flowers and ferns. This surprise meant much to the young couple.

From the church they had driven straight to the house at Lake View.

Chicago had grown since Father began his career there.

A fact not commonly realized is the tremendous momentum given the city by Cyrus H. McCormick, inventor of the reaper that bears his name, when he secured its patent and in 1845 built the first McCormick factory on the site of the Du Sable and Kinzie cabin, Chicago's first homestead.

The advent of railroads and mechanical farming implements put an end to Chicago's isolation. By the time Lincoln became President, Chicago was the crossroads of the continent and the exchange center for thousands of miles of prairie harvestings, and the McCormick factory was turning out more than 50,000 reapers a year.

Mr. McCormick, as more reapers sold and his wealth increased, used his influence to advance the religious, educational, and mercantile interests of expanding Chicago.

His offer in 1859 of one hundred thousand dollars to endow four professorships in the failing New Albany Theological Seminary of Indiana, on condition it was moved to Chicago, helped greatly in bringing the school to Chicago under the amended name of The Presbyterian Theological Seminary of the Northwest.

Father entered upon his duties with the seminary during its turbulent period, when feeling ran high over the matter of the McCormick chair.

He served as a director from 1867 to 1871 and from 1874 to 1876. He was a trustee from 1869 to 1870 and during that time served as secretary to the board of trustees.

He financed several scholarships which helped a number of students through the seminary. Conspicuous among these was George G. Stewart, class of 1879, who afterward became president of Auburn Theological Seminary in Auburn, New York, and whose son, George Stewart, was twice acting president of the American University of Beirut in Syria, otherwise, its treasurer.

Father had ardently supported Lincoln.

Mr. McCormick was Virginia born and his sympathies were Southern.

His proffered endowment was for four chairs, of which only one, that of theology, was to bear his name. Perhaps because of this there was more argument over its occupancy than over any of the others.

Any candidate of abolitionist tendencies was opposed by Mr. McCormick, who threatened to contest the board's demands for the final payments on his endowment fund.

The Chicago *Daily Tribune* of December 2, 1868, commented:

Mr. McCormick will not, if he can prevent it, permit any man, who contributed by word or deed to the abolition of human slavery, to educate preachers of the Gospel.

By the time the General Assembly of the Presbyterian Church met in Philadelphia in 1869 the division between the two factions was so clearly marked that two different reports were sent in.

Criticisms were written and circulated. "White papers" of defense were published and sent broadcast. Every religious paper of the period contained articles on the subject.

Father was sent to Philadelphia as one of the majority group of "new friends" of the seminary, to plead before the Assembly the special cause; that those who had given most to the seminary wanted to wield most authority in proportion to their gifts.

The opposing group of "old friends," or McCormick faction, let intimations go forth during the conclave that the properties Mr. McCormick had set aside to pay the promised endowment were not paying so well as heretofore, which would, they hinted, explain why his promised donations had been withheld.

As soon as Father heard this, he telegraphed his friend Mr. Kerfoot, a prominent real estate dealer in Chicago, to find out exactly what the property brought in. When Father rose to make his speech he held the answer in his hand—the property's income was undiminished. At one point he urged that Mr. McCormick be told either to cease using his money as a means of bringing the institution to terms, or to "cast it into the sea."

The decision was reached by the General Assembly, according to the *History of McCormick Seminary* by Halsey, by "releasing him (Mr. McCormick) from the bond which he refuses to regard as binding, established a vastly momentous principle. The civil courts have since, in defining and regulating trusts, acted upon the general principles of this ecclesiastical decision. A trust, like a promise, must in law and moral be interpreted as the maker understood it, and supposed the one to whom it was made understood it."

Terms were drawn up, recommending that "bygones be bygones, and no further controversy respecting past issues be indulged in, that Dr. Lord, opposed by Mr. McCormick, retain the chair, and that Mr. McCormick be released from the fourth installment of his bond." Signed, "this third day of November, 1869, by D. C. Marquis and H. G. Spafford."

So the feud ended, and years later the handsome seminary in the heart of Chicago took the McCormick name.

Through all the contentions and controversies Mr. McCormick and Father continued to be the best of friends.

Father was a man of independent character, thought, and action. He made up his mind about what was right and acted according to his conscience.

Cyrus McCormick was equally outspoken and independent.

The two men could radically differ in opinion, attack each other on disputed questions, but otherwise respect each other.

The year before the Great Chicago Fire the famous "Noon Prayer Meeting" was started in Chicago by Mr. Dwight L. Moody. Business and professional men met every noon for a few minutes of devotional inspiration and rest. Father was helpful in getting it started. He was a fervent believer in prayer. I have been told by Chicagoans that it was owing to him that it got started, but I know Father would be the last to accept such credit. It really was a spontaneous crying out in many persons as the result of spiritual hunger.

The remarkable part is that the noon prayer meeting is still functioning.

At this time Mr. Moody was in debt, selling shoes for his self-support and preaching when he could spare the time. Father was one of his supporters, and so was the head of the shoeshop. The manner in which they helped pay Mr. Moody's debts so that he could devote his full time to preaching is revealed in Father's notebook.

When my parents later took the decisive step and went to Jerusalem they left their home and all their possessions. Everything was lost. A few letters, papers, and notebooks of only sentimental value were all that were left of those early years in Chicago. It is from these, remembered conversations with Father and Mother and their friends, and pages in Father's irregularly kept diary saved from the Chicago Fire, that I have been able to present events and persons that influenced my parents then. In the notebook, in Father's handwriting, is a resolution, signed by himself and a number of his associates, which explains how Mr. Moody got some of the money which, as Mr. Moody says, "God made him steward of":

We, the undersigned, hereby agree to give during the year 1870 the sum set opposite our names respectively towards the salary of Mr. D. L. Moody. Such subscriptions to be paid in quarterly installments in advance, commencing Jan. 1st, 1870.

It is interesting to note that among the other contributors are the names of Mr. C. M. Henderson, Mr. E. W. Blatchford, and Mr. S. M. Moore.

Mr. Henderson was the proprietor of the wholesale boot and shoe house where Mr. Moody was working, and from which he was now being rescued.

Mr. Blatchford was the father of Mrs. Howard Bliss, whose husband was the second president of the American University of Beirut, Lebanon, and of Edward Blatchford, who came to Jerusalem as representative of the Near East Relief after World War I and was later attached to the Consulate General of the United States.

Mr. Moore was the father of Mrs. Gates, whose husband was for many years the president of Robert College at Istanbul, Turkey.

I also have a long letter in Mr. Moody's handwriting, written from Dundee, Scotland, to Major Whittle, who handed it on to Father, as part of it concerned him. Mr. Moody was expressing the hope that Father could help Major Whittle settle his debts as he had helped Mr. Moody settle his in 1870. The letter, written in Mr. Moody's fervid strain, and without a single mark of punctuation, reads in part:

Dundee January 30th 1874

MY DEAR WHITTLE

I am anxious to hear from you and to know your decision of the matter that Spafford was to see you about I sent $ 500 yesterday to Mr Holden and if you decide to give up business you can have that at once that will help you pay off some of your debts and if Spafford will take the other 2500 the latter part of the year all right and if he cannot do it without cramping him I will do so for five years My prayers have been that you might be a free man like myself but I never could see how you could do it until you got out of debt and how that was to be done I could not tell but now I see it all launch out my brother into the dark God has made me a steward at least of a little money and I can do as I please with it . . . Remember me to my friends and tell them I would like to see them especially Spafford and his dear wife I cannot tell you how I love them Much (remember?) me to Cole I am so thankful God is using him

Yours with a heart full of love
D. L. MOODY

This letter and the notebook agreement give an idea of the closeness of the ties of friendship between Father and Mr. Moody and the other evangelists who were associates at this time.

Father's life was profoundly influenced by this early association with Mr. Moody, and later Mr. Ira D. Sankey and Major Whittle, Major Cole, Dr. Pentecost, Mr. P. P. Bliss, Mr. George C. Stebbins, and others of that illustrious group who have gone down in history as the builders of American Christian evangelism.

The group of evangelists and musicians who gathered about Mr. Moody often met at our home in Lake View for conferences and discussions.

Another family friend was Miss Frances E. Willard of Evanston, Illinois, who was president of the National Women's Christian Temperance Union. Father had strong ideas on temperance. Once, in a discussion with her on the subject, Father said he fervently believed in it.

"Then why don't you join us?" she asked.

"Because," Father explained, "you advocate temperance and practice total abstinence."

Not long before the Great Chicago Fire, at one of the Moody Noon Prayer Meetings, Father prayed that God would "baptize us with the Holy Spirit and Fire." After the holocaust he received criticism. When I heard about it, many years later, I remarked that at least his critics gave Father credit that his prayers were answered.

My four "little sisters" loved Mr. Moody, and in later years the great evangelist told of the time Annie and Maggie expressed their wish to join the church. This was an unusual request for such young children, and Mr. Moody thought them too young to understand. So he took them aside and separately questioned them concerning the dogmas of the church and their obligations as members of the Christian community.

Then he led them to the minister. "These children know more than I do," Mr. Moody said. "They are quite prepared to join."

They were deeply religious little girls, but to them, as to my parents, religion was a matter of joy and not of gloom, as was too often the result of religious teachings in that day. They were happy children, and lived a normal childhood.

They had their hair cut short; this was one of Father's idiosyncrasies, which the girls hated, because it made them peculiar and unlike other children. I know from experience, for I, too, had short hair, like an Eton crop, until I was ten years old. There is nothing a child so hates as to be "different." But Father thought it was sanitary, cool, and less trouble, as modern people have come to realize. To satisfy their craving for long hair they contrived to make wigs of some material, tied with bright rags to represent the coveted hair-ribbons.

Their favorite game was acting bits of history, into which they drew the neighbor children and Cousin Rob, when he was home from boarding school during the holidays. In Father's gifts of history books, especially those of England and Scotland, they read about the executions of so many of their favorite characters, Annie prayed one night:

"Dear God, don't let Maggie or me ever be queens, but only princesses."

Cousin Rob, as we called him, was Robert Eugene Lawrence, Aunt Eureka's son.

Eureka, Father's sister, was born at the moment when my grandfather's spirit was exalted because of one of his discoveries. I always understood that it was the fact that tomatoes were edible. He may have tried the experiment on himself—it would have been like him—and his elation was the greater because he had survived.

Aunt Eureka died in our home in Lake View in 1870, I think. On her deathbed she implored Father and Mother to take Robert and bring him up as their own. He was a brilliant boy and as close to them as a son.

Also in this year 1870 Father made a four-months business trip to the British Isles.

In his notebook are notes about the Franco-Prussian War, still unsettled, and he ponders over "the striking incapacity of the French people to allow 500,000 Prussians to completely subjugate all France."

He was impressed by the fact that Saturday was a half-holiday in England, a custom which had not yet penetrated the United States, and by the outspoken sincerity of the British press. He ordered English newspapers and periodicals for his family and friends, and bought many books. He met and admired the great English non-conformist preacher, Dr. Spurgeon.

In Edinburgh he met Professor Piazza Smith, F.R.S.E., F.R.A.S., Astronomer Royal for Scotland, a meeting that changed the destinies of many people, including Father's.

The British-Israelite theory—that the Anglo-Saxon people are descendants of the lost tribes of Israel—was the topic of the hour in religious circles and Dr. Smith was a leading apostle.

Dr. Smith and his wife had recently returned from Egypt, where for four months they had resided on Pyramid Hill at Geza. With a variety of surveying and astronomical instruments Dr. Smith measured the Great Pyramid, using the inch. According to him each measurement of the passages, chambers, and galleries in-dicated a historical event or prophecy and elucidated many mysteries referred to cryptically in the Bible.

Dr. Smith believed that Isaiah was referring to the Great Pyramid when he said:

In that day shall there be an altar to the Lord in the midst of the land of Egypt, and a pillar at the border thereof to the Lord.
And it shall be for a sign and for a witness unto the Lord of Hosts . . .

Dr. Smith returned to Edinburgh convinced that the Great Pyramid of Geza was built by divine inspiration, and that the world possessed in it a "monument of inspiration," as it had long possessed a "book of inspiration," in the Bible. Academic archaeology, Dr. Smith went on to say, did not accept his theory.

Such a study could lead into a labyrinth that has no end, but it opened up a new vista to Father. This chance meeting with Dr. Smith instilled in him an interest in the prophecies of the Old Testament and the prophetic significance of the ancient pyramid. It was this, I think, that largely influenced Father and Mother, after the foundations of their lives had been shaken by tragedy, to turn to the Holy Land and a study of its prophecies.

Years later Dr. Smith and his wife returned to the Holy Land and visited Father and Mother.

A short time after Father's return Mr. Moody went to England and Scotland, where his genius as an evangelist was fully recognized. Nothing like the resultant revival wave had ever been known, and no one born in Chicago can fail to be proud that it started there, in a city too often made notorious.

In its wide sweep the revival caught up men as different as Henry Morehouse, Professor Henry Drummond, James Keir Hardie, Dr., later Sir, Wilfred Grenfell, and C. T. Studd.

In London Mr. Moody addressed an "acre of people" three times a day.

Leaders in all the churches showed sympathetic interest in the Moody work and many of them actively co-operated.

Moody and Sankey hymns were on every lip.

Sir George Adams Smith wrote of the Moody and Sankey revival:

The persent generation does not know how large it was and with what results upon the life of our nation.

George C. Stebbins wrote in his memoirs that in Dundee, Scotland, two clowns tried to make sport of the Moody and Sankey meetings then in process.

"I feel Moody tonight," one clown said, and the other retorted, "Well, I feel Sankeymonious."

The audience did not laugh. Instead, it rose to a man and burst into the hymn "Hold the fort for I am coming."

Mr. Moody's trumphant tour of England and Scotland won him a vaster appreciation in his own country.

He became the greatest exponent of Protestantism's leading tenets of that day, based on belief in a God given to swift and everlasting punishments meted out to all sinners, and all mankind, alas, as sinners born. Mr. Moody was converting uncounted thousands by what he called the process of "shaking people over hell to make them good."

But Father and Mother were slowly coming to believe that God's love was so great it took in every created thing, and that no one was so wicked but that he might eventually be saved. Father's legal mind reached the conclusion that if God were love, as the Bible said, then surely that love must extend to all.

This belief is accepted now, but it was controversial in the 1870s. It was not in accord with Mr. Moody's preaching. It was, in fact, dangerously close to heresy.

Mr. Moody's habit, according to one writer, was to "preach the wrath of God against sinners." But another evangelist wrote later: "Mr. Moody himself mellowed in his conception of 'shaking people over hell to make them good.' " He, too, would teach that "God is love."

But Father, as usual, was ahead of his time. As always he was frank in expressing his new convictions. As his belief in the goodness and forgiveness of God became more concrete and could be put into words, he discovered in his friends a growing opposition to his theory.

Still, it was only a cloud "as big as a man's hand" on his otherwise clear sky.

The winter following the Great Fire was one of poverty and suffering to many in Chicago. A huge organization was instituted for the distribution of relief. Money, food, and clothing were given by more fortunate citizens, and their donations were augmented by sympathizers from all over the United States, Canada, the British Isles, and the continent of Europe.

To distribute relief the city was divided into sections and a committee appointed for each quarter. Father and Mother worked on the Relief and Aid Committees and put into them all their resourcefulness and strength.

Years later, in 1917, when Jerusalem was delivered by the victorious British Army, and General Allenby, as the late Field Marshal Lord Allenby was then called, appointed me to the Relief Committee to alleviate suffering in the Holy City, it was Mother's experience and her advice that enabled me to organize a "setup" similar to that of the Great Fire, that made successful our work in Jerusalem. I divided Jerusalem into sections, had investigators report to me and relief administered, all according to the plan Father and Mother had followed in helping start relief work in the still-smouldering ruins of Chicago.

Father was a stanch supporter of the Y.M.C.A., and assisted materially in the erection of the new building in Chicago after the Fire.

In the minutes of the Board of Managers of the Chicago Y.M.C.A. there are many mentions of Father's active work for the Association up until 1881, when he left for Palestine. Often I have heard Father and Mother tell of incidents relating to the Marine Hospital that was situated very near our home in Lake View. Under the auspices of the Y.M.C.A. Father conducted religious meetings for the sailors, and Mother and my sisters did what they could to bring sunshine into their drab lives. The little girls carried fruit and flowers on their visits to the hospital.

Life continued pleasantly in the Lake View cottage despite somewhat straitened financial conditions and Mother's failure to regain complete health because of the fright and hardship she had endured during the Fire which came so soon after the birth of Tanetta.

Perhaps memories of the Fire wakened in Mother a dread of being separated from any or all of her family, even for a short time, although her health demanded rest and change.

One reason for this need was Aunty Sims. Since her arrival on the mattress the morning of the Great Fire, Aunty Sims had vowed never to leave Mother, and Mother never had the heart to send her away. Like the "simples in the Garden of Allah" Mother collected later in Jerusalem, Aunty Sims stayed on and on, and was part of the household, and utterly devoted to it and Mother, which made it more difficult to ask her to go. She was older than Mother, but was as dependent upon her as a child.

Aunty Sims had a husband somewhere, but he had treated her badly, and she was suing for divorce. Evidently Father was giving her advice, as I have notes he made on her case. Mr. Sims, however, was not to be found, and Aunty Sims had no means of support.

Aunty Sims used to say that if God forgave her husband and he went to heaven, then she did not want to go there.

Sometimes Mother would rebuke her for dwelling so much on her sorrow and being so unforgiving.

"Oh, it's all very well for you to talk," Aunty Sims would retort. "You have a splendid husband, lovely, healthy children, a beautiful home; it is easy to be grateful and good when you have everything you want. But look out," she would say, pointing a long finger at Mother, "that you are not a fair-weather friend to God!"

That warning returned to Mother all too soon.

Dear Aunty Sims, so dreaded and so loved. She made herself useful. She mended and sewed. The little girls were devoted to her, for she had a fund of stories with which she amused and entertained them. Once, when Aunty Sims finally did go away, and Mother was feeling gratified that she had managed the departure successfully without hurting Aunty Sims' feelings, the little girls all prayed that "Jesus would please let Aunty Sims come back," and Mother had an intuition, yea, even an apprehension, that their prayer would be answered.

It was not long before Aunty Sims was back, and installed at Lake View for good.

She was one of the reasons the family doctor advised a "change" for Mother. Dr. Hedges realized that going away without her family only aggravated Mother's condition, and she could not be happy without them, so he advised Father to take the entire family on a trip to Europe.

Since his own trip three years before Father had been looking forward to showing Mother the museums, art galleries, and all the haunts he had so enjoyed. It would be a costly journey, and the land investment he and his friends had made just before the Great Fire and the loss of his law office in the Fire had left Father rather heavily in debt. But he pursuaded himself that his wife's health was more important, and they planned for months, and finally all their plans were complete. They would go first to France, where they had many friends, and then on to Switzerland. Reservations were made for Maggie and Annie in a girls' school there, and Mlle. Nicolet, the French governess, would lodge near by with Bessie and baby Tanetta. Mlle. Nicolet was a charming woman, of a noble Huguenot family, and had become a companion to Mother as well as governess to the girls. After they were settled in Switzerland Father and Mother planned to go away by themselves for several months of European travel, a sort of second honeymoon.

Cousin Rob was doing well in boarding school and it was considered advisable to leave him there. Aunty Sims went to stay with Mother's sister, Aunt Rachel.

Reservations were made on the most luxurious ship then afloat—the French liner S.S. *Ville du Havre.*

Just before they left Chicago Father had an offer from a man who wanted to buy part of the land in which he had invested so disastrously before the Great Fire.

He could not afford to forego such an important offer. The sale would relieve the partners of almost all their indebtedness and enable Father to take his family to Europe without anxiety.

It was decided that their plans should not be entirely postponed. Mother, the children, and Mlle. Nicolet would sail on the *Ville du Havre* and Father would join them later in France.

Four French pastors who had been in the United States attending an evangelical alliance conference were returning to France on the *Ville du Havre.* One was the Rev. M. Lorriaux, whose sister had formerly been governess for my sisters at Lake View. Father asked Pastor Lorriaux if he would look after Mother and her brood, and it was finally decided they should stay in the quiet village of Bertry, near Paris, where the Lorriaux family lived, until Father came.

Then, to Mother's great joy, her dear friend and neighbor, Mrs. Goodwin, with her three children, Goertner, Julia, and Lulu, decided to go to Europe on the same ship. Also, Mother was asked to take "under her wing" Willie Culver, the son of other friends, who was being sent on a visit to his grandparents in Germany. Willie, Goertner, and Annie were about the same age, and the other little girls enjoyed playing together, so it was a merry and companionable group of twelve that left Chicago in November 1873.

Father went with the party as far as New York.

Aboard the *Ville du Havre,* just before sailing time, for no reason he could ever determine, Father went to the purser and asked to have the two cabins that Mother, Mlle. Nicolet, and the four children were to occupy changed to two others more toward the bow of the ship. He said afterward that he fought against the conviction that he must change them, not wishing to be troublesome, and also because he had no real complaint to make. He had chosen them himself, carefully, weeks before. But the feeling was so strong that he could not throw it off, and at almost the last minute he changed the rooms.

Just before he bade his family farewell a telegram was handed Father, stating that the man who had been about to buy the Chicago property had suddenly died of heart failure.

He put the telegram in his pocket. He could not depress Mother with this disconcerting news just as she was about to start out on her first voyage without him. Mother had been reluctant to go to Europe since she found Father could not accompany them, and Maggie evidently shared this feeling. Maggie adored her mother so much she dreaded being separated from her even for a night, but she had been willing to stay at home alone and in fact begged to be left behind.

She must have had a strange foreboding, for when my sorrowing parents returned to their silent home they found a little note written by Maggie and left in the children's play post office in one of the tall elm trees:

Goodbye, dear sweet Lake View. I will never see you again.

MAGGIE SPAFFORD

CHAPTER THREE

THE evening of November 21, 1873, found the *Ville du Havre*, according to Captain Surmount's report, prow east for France on a calm Atlantic, which was good news for everyone aboard. There had been a sharp squall off the coast of Newfoundland that gave most of the passengers a few seasick hours. But now there was no motion, and the calm was so complete that Mother said later she found it difficult to realize they were on the sea. The weather was clear and it was too early to fear icebergs.

The *Ville du Havre* was living up to its reputation as the foremost pleasure ship of the seas. The bouquets of flowers were still fresh in the large and sumptuous dining room, where Pastor Lorriaux, at dinner, was teaching Mother French from the menu in preparation for her stay in France.

The Rev. Emil Cook, another of the four French pastors, had organized a Sunday-school class among the many children aboard. The children themselves chose their first hymn: "I Want to Be an Angel."

After dinner Mother helped Mlle. Nicolet put the four little daughters to bed and rejoined her friends in the magnificent saloon. All the children had left for the night, but the young people returned from their after-dinner deck promenade and began organizing games. Another of the French pastors, Pastor Weiss, proposed a walk on deck, and Mother accepted.

Pastor Weiss was to write a small book, in French, a copy of which has come into my possession. It is his account of this last night on the *Ville du Havre*. He tells how Mother and he walked the deck, and of their conversation. The stars were unusually bright and the mantle of night diamond-studded, and although the moon did not shine, the air was transparent and clear. Mother remarked on the beauty of the night. Then she told him she had been very sad at the separation from her husband and home even for so short a time.

He reassured her. Only a few weeks, he said, and Father would be with her, and meantime she would be in France, where so many were waiting to welcome her.

"I know all this," she admitted, "and I have struggled against my feelings."

About two o'clock that morning, November 22, the *Ville du Havre* was carrying its sleeping passengers over a quiet sea when two terrific claps, like thunder, were followed by frightening screams. The engines stopped and the ship stood still. The passageways filled with terrified, half-dressed people shouting questions no one could answer. Mother and Mlle. Nicolet threw on dressing gowns, drew some clothing over the children, and ran on deck. Mother carried Tanetta, a big, healthy girl, more than two years old. They were among the first passengers to reach the deck. Pastor Lorriaux hurried across the dark deck to meet them.

"That must be the vessel that struck us," he exclaimed.

Several hundred yards away, to starboard of the *Ville du Havre*, towered the masted silhouette of a great iron sailing vessel. This ship that had rammed theirs and was itself badly damaged was the English *Lochearn*, Captain Robertson in command.

I have a copy of the famous Currier and Ives print that tried to portray the awfulness of this scene. Ships and sea were lighted only by the stars, but the *Ville du Havre* and *Lochearn* were like great wounded beasts caught in angry troughs of sea created by their struggles. Aboard the decks was indescribable confusion. Captain Surmount appeared on the bridge of the *Ville du Havre* and began shouting orders. Some of the officers and men were struggling on the afterdeck to loosen the lifeboats but they could not detach them, for it was only then discovered that everything aboard the beautiful pleasure ship was newly painted and stuck fast. By this time crowds of passengers, in nightdresses or scantily attired, were crowding about the boats or trying to extricate the life preservers suspended along the taffrail, but these, too, were stuck fast.

The sailors kept shouting that there was no danger, and all were to keep calm, but the passengers ran about frantically, fighting to reach the lifeboats. Curses, yells, and hysterical screaming made the deck a bedlam. Some people dropped to their knees and began praying.

Everything was happening so quickly, in such confusion, that it seemed impossible all this took place in a few seconds.

Tanetta was heavy, and Annie put her shoulder under Mother's elbow to help lift her weight. Maggie and Bessie stood pressed against Mother. Mlle. Nicolet and Willie Culver were there, and Pastor Lorriaux stood guard over the little group.

Then Maggie saw Pastor Weiss on deck and ran to him.
"You will stay with us, won't you?" she pleaded.

He promised he would. Then he noticed she was shivering with
cold. He said he would get some clothing, if Pastor Lorriaux
would keep the little group together and try to get them to a lifeboat. Pastor Weiss ran below and seized his own overcoat and
some shawls and wraps for the children. As he came back through
the passageway he saw Pastor Cook standing there in his night-
shirt, looking dazed.

"Why are you not dressed?" he demanded.

"Our stateroom was smashed in," Cook answered. "How I am
saved I cannot say. I helped a woman look for her children under
the rubbish and found the water rising fast."

By this they knew that the *Ville du Havre* had been struck on
the starboard athwart the mainmast. The staterooms Father had
insisted on changing were the first to catch the crushing blow of
the iron ship, and their unfortunate occupants were the first on
the *Ville du Havre* to die.

The hysteria mounted on deck. Hundreds were fighting and
crowding to reach the inadequate boats. Several clung to deck
settees which later saved their lives. Two or three succeeded in
wresting life preservers from the paint, donned them, and flung
themselves into the sea. Willie Culver was last seen trying to
loosen the ropes of a life belt with his penknife.

Mrs. Goodwin and her children did not reach the deck. They
were never seen again.

The ship's doctor, a kind and devoted man, ran below to care
for the wounded trapped in their staterooms, and died with
them.

Mother told me that in the space of a few seconds she was
forced through a spiritual struggle. She and the children, being
the first to reach the deck, were nearest a lifeboat being freed,
but others, scrambling, pushed her little group back. Was she
doing right, she wondered, to permit her children to be beaten
back by people whose frantic desire to save themselves left them
without mercy? Should she not fight for her children's lives, if
not for her own?

At that moment the ship shuddered, the screaming grew, the
confusion became more terrifying. Pastor Weiss thought there
were too many people on their side of the ship.

"Hurry to the other side!" he shouted, just as the mainmast
crashed down carrying with it the mizzen, and the two boats

over which there had been so much struggle were carried overboard together with all those struggling to free them and those who had fought their way in. Mother and Pastor Lorriaux were both hurt, but slightly, and Mother, hearing the heartrending death screams from the water, knew that if she had "stood for her rights" she would have perished with those who fought hardest to live.

The *Ville du Havre* was sinking rapidly. Mother knew this was the end; she knew, too, it was not hard to die. She thought of Father with anguish, then, "he would rather think of me with the children." That gave her courage.

The great ship careened to starboard. The water was very near. There was a moment of awful silence as the deck slid lower to meet the sea.

Little Maggie was holding Pastor Weiss's hand. She looked up into his face.

"Pray," she begged.

"God help us," he responded.

There was another loud crash as the bow broke from the ship and sank. Maggie, who until this moment had been terrified, dropped Mr. Weiss's hand and went to Mother. She was suddenly calm and unafraid. Tanetta, her arms around Mother's neck, was quiet. Annie was still helping Mother support her, and Bessie, silent and pale, clutched Mother's knees. Mlle. Nicolet, the two pastors, Mother, and her little girls stood quietly together.

As Maggie stepped beside Mother she lifted her dark eyes. "Mama, God will take care of us." Then little Annie said, "Don't be afraid. The sea is His and He made it."

The sea rushed over the afterdeck as a watery canyon opened to receive the vast ruin of the *Ville du Havre*. The little group went down together, with all on that crowded deck and all those trapped below into blackness whose depth stretched many miles, into a whirlpool created by suction of bodies, wreckage, and savage water. Only twelve minutes after the *Ville du Havre* was struck it sank with all on board.

As Mother was pulled down she felt her baby torn violently from her arms. She reached out through the water and caught Tanetta's little gown. For a moment she held her again, then the cloth wrenched from her hand. She reached out again and touched a man's leg in corduroy trousers.

Once in Jerusalem, when I was a child and we were very poor, someone gave me a little corduroy coat. Mother was pleased that I had a warm coat to wear, for winters are cold in Jerusalem, but I saw the agony on her face. She could never touch that material without reliving the moment of helpless anguish when she felt her baby drawn from her hands by the power of the Atlantic, and reached for her again and felt the corduroy.

The splash of an oar brought her to consciousness. She was lying in a boat, bruised from head to foot and sick with sea water, her long hair heavy with salt and her thick dressing gown in ribbons. She knew, with no need of being told, that her children were gone.

From a watch one of the passengers carried, that stopped when the ship sank, they estimated that Mother had been in the sea for an hour.

She had been rolled under and down, and as she rose unconscious to the surface a plank floated under her, saving her life.

The English sailors of the *Lochearn* were patrolling the littered waters in their smallboats, saving all they could of the survivors of the ship their own had sent to the bottom of the sea. Only drifting fragments were left of the once magnificent *Ville du Havre*.

A few minutes later the same boat that rescued Mother picked up Captain Surmount. He had been thrown from the bridge of his sinking ship. Aboard the *Lochearn* she found Pastor Weiss and Pastor Lorriaux. Mlle. Nicolet was among those lost.

Pastor Lorriaux could not swim, but he caught first a bit of wreckage and then a life preserver, and finally something like a raft which must have been a fragment of ship's flooring. While clinging to this he saw a log floating near by to which ten or fifteen people were clinging. A boat passed them but was too full to stop, and when it had hoisted its rescued to the *Lochearn* deck and hurried back, the log had gone down with all who had clung to it.

Pastor Lorriaux divided his time between Mother and his friend Pastor Blanc, who was picked up unconscious, covered with blood from many wounds, and nearly paralyzed. Some of Pastor Blanc's ribs were broken and he had great difficulty in breathing. Pastor Cook was picked up later.

No sooner was she aboard the *Lochearn* than Mother was told that two of her little girls, which ones she never knew, had come up in the sea near a man to whom they clung. He told them to hold to his coat, for he swam well and hoped to save them. First the smaller one relaxed and disappeared, and he had nearly reached a boat when the other child sank.

When Mother heard this, it was with difficulty that Pastor Lorriaux prevented her from throwing herself after them into the sea.

She knew her children were gone, but she could not forbear hoping. As each boatload was hoisted aboard the *Lochearn* she joined the others who ran to scan the newly rescued relatives or friends. There were parents who met their children and embraced silently and long. There were others who turned silently away. Poor Mother was one of these; still, as each boatload came she sought her four little girls.

The night stayed clear, and from the *Lochearn's* deck the rescued could scan every particle of floating debris. Under the direction of Captain Robertson of the *Lochearn* sailors continued to ply their boats over the scene of the disaster, without a thought of fatigue or even pausing to rest or eat. There were shouts of finds and of salvation, and over all, on the *Lochearn*, the tragic sound of lamentation.

Captain Surmount stood silent and apart on the deck, staring at the calm sea where his beautiful ship had been lost.

The sailors on deck were busy dressing wounds and helping restore the unconscious. They distributed warm drinks and whatever clothing they could scrape together. Some nearly stripped themselves trying to cover the rescued.

The cries for help that at first had come from every direction were growing fainter. The icy waters were crushing out the lives of the last survivors swept beyond range of the rescue crews.

One succeeded in holding his wife on the surface until a boat reached them, and just as he was helping her into it, his heart failed, and he died.

Another reached a boat just as a woman did. Fright crazed him, and when the sailors forced him to let the woman into the boat they found he had gone raving mad and was trying to bite.

A feeble cry was heard from a young girl struggling in the sea. A bloody gash across her face had been made by a man when she came close to a plank he was holding. From another direction came piercing, insistent cries from a little girl clinging to a piece of wood. "I don't want to be drowned," she was screaming. They were able to pick her up—the only child saved. As the last boat was returning with the last survivors the sailors saw a woman rise from the sea holding a child in her arms. They tried to reach her, but she did not reappear.

Again and again the *Lochearn's* boats went out, but no more survivors were found.

By this time it was nearly four in the morning.

The stars were still brilliant, and the skies clear, as they had been since the beautiful sunset the evening before. If the night had been stormy, not a soul could have been saved from the *Ville du Havre.*

Gradually the heart-rending sounds of affliction aboard the *Lochearn* gave way to the softer tones of mourning as the last hopes were replaced by sorrowful reality. Everybody had lost someone, and some families were totally wiped out.

Over the weeping was heard the tranquil murmur of the Atlantic, as if nothing had happened to disturb its calm. The sea looked so placid that it was difficult to realize that it had just annihilated one of the largest steamers afloat, and engulfed, as if in play, two hundred and twenty-six lives.

The *Ville du Havre* had been manned by Captain Surmount and a crew of one hundred and seventy-two officers and men. When Captain Robertson of the *Lochearn* completed the two-hours search after the collision, his men had picked up six officers and twenty-three of the crew, twenty-eight passengers, ten of them women, seventeen men, and the little girl, nine years old, making a total of fifty-seven saved.

The figures, so sadly eloquent, give no idea of the heartbreaking realization brought by this reckoning.

They extinguished Mother's last hope.

Among reports later spread about Mother was one that she claimed supernatural experiences while fighting to save her life under the sea. I found a scrap of paper on which she had written the following words:

> I had no vision during the struggle in the water at the time of the shipwreck, only the conviction that any earnest soul, brought face to face with its maker, must have; I realized that my Christianity must be real. There was no room here for self-pity, or for the practice of that Christianity that always favours and condones itself and its own, rendering innocuous the sharp two-edged sword of the Word which was intended to separate soul from spirit and the desires and thoughts and intents of the heart. This soft religion was as far removed from Christ's practice of Christianity as east from west. Nothing but a robust Christianity could save me then and now . . .

Mother told me, long after, that when she came back to consciousness in the boat and knew she had been recalled to life, that her first realization was complete despair. How could she face life without her children? Horrible as was her physical suffering, her mental anguish was worse. Her life had been bound up in her little girls. What was life worth now, and what could it ever be without them?

Then, she told me, it was as if a voice spoke to her. "You are spared for a purpose. You have work to do."

In that moment of returning consciousness she lifted her soul to God in an agony of despair and humbly dedicated her life to His service.

One of the first thoughts that came to her was a memory of Aunty Sims, pointing her finger and saying: "It's easy to be grateful and good when you have so much, but take care that you are not a fair-weather friend to God!" That phrase repeated itself in Mother's mind. She thought, "I won't be a fair-weather friend to God. I will trust Him, and someday I'll understand."

The shipwreck of the *Ville du Havre* would remain one of the unexplained tragedies of the sea and its greatest disaster up until the sinking of the *Titanic*. It was never determined what actually happened. There seemed no reason for the collision. Captain Robertson sighted the great steamer long in advance from the *Lochearn*, for it was, as has been said before, a clear night of starlight and calm. Sailing vessels were always given the right of way.

It will never be known whether the officer who had taken Captain Surmount's place on the bridge gave the order to stop, or if the order, once given, was badly executed, for he went down with the ship.

Captain Robertson did not realize at once that his ship had cut the *Ville du Havre* almost in two. Had he known six or seven minutes earlier how serious conditions were aboard the *Ville du Havre*, he said later, he could have rendered much more effective help. But he understood from Captain Surmount's shouted French that the steamer was not badly injured.

Captain Robertson said it was only twelve minutes from the time the ships rammed until the steamer sank, but the saving of the survivors took more than two hours.

He carried out the rescue work from a dangerously damaged ship. In fact, he expected the *Lochearn* to sink immediately after the collision and was astonished when it did not, for the bowsprit was demolished.

The fact that his damaged vessel was able to keep afloat encouraged Captain Robertson to think it was strong enough to resist
the pressure of the sea, and that by the use of pumps he might
bring her safely to harbor. Because she had no cargo, the *Lochearn*
sat high out of the water and the holes in her prow were above the
sea line, while the watertight bulkhead prevented the water from
forcing its way into the hold. But it was soon apparent the *Lochearn* was in danger.

The flag of distress was run up. This is generally the ship's
national flag—in this case the English—flown upside down.

For a second time the survivors of the *Ville du Havre* faced
death, this time with their rescuers.

In these days of radio and wireless it is hard to realize the
anxious watching these poor people had to endure with only a
flag to indicate their plight. But it was only a matter of hours
before a small ship was seen approaching under full sail.

Twenty times I have crossed the Atlantic, once by air, and I
know how rare the meeting with a ship can be and how seldom
one is sighted on that vast expanse of water. Yet here, within
the space of a few hours, three ships came together at a given point,
and the arrival of that stout little sailing vessel, the *Trimountain*,
commanded by Captain Urquhart, in time to rescue the survivors
of the shipwrecked *Ville du Havre* and the threatened *Lochearn*
was held to be then and must still be considered one of the mira-
cles of the sea.

Never shall I forget a day some years ago when my husband
and I called on Mrs. Urquhart, widow of the *Trimountain's*
captain, and her daughter in Brooklyn, New York, and were shown
a sterling tea service engraved with a testimonial of gratitude that
had been presented to the captain by the survivors of the *Ville
du Havre*. I looked at the service as if it were a holy relic. The
captain had died, and we were sad not to meet him, for he had
been so kind to those he took from the sinking *Lochearn*.

Captain Urquhart told a strange story to the heartbroken
people he saved.

An odd thought had occurred to him early on that voyage as
the *Trimountain*, carrying a cargo of canned meats, was taking a
northerly course from New York to Bristol, England. Through
a miscalculation made by the charterer a vacant space of about
seventy feet had been left in the upper betweendecks. Never
before had he had any space left by a charterer, and Captain

Urquhart thought how useful the space would be if he met a wrecked ship with passengers to be cared for.

Another thought persisted in the skipper's mind as they left the banks of Newfoundland and he took his observations by the Pole Star. A few nights before, at port in New York, several captains from other ships had dined aboard the *Trimountain.* Captains frequently meet on one another's ships when in port to exchange yarns over a bottle or two.

An argument started as to the actual existence of certain rocks of early maritime legend laid down in ancient charts as having been sighted between America and Europe. One of the party, Captain Robinson, insisted that he had seen with his own eyes the fabulous Rock Barenetha.

His ship passed the rock on a clear day, Captain Robinson declared, so close he was able to take two good observations and mark them on his chart, and in proof the chart was aboard his ship, the *Patrick Henry.*

The other captains hooted this story, and insisted that Captain Robinson had sighted the back of a sleeping whale. Only Captain Urquhart was enough impressed to go aboard the *Patrick Henry* and examine the chart. The Rock was plainly marked, and he thought it might do no harm to chart it, which he did, carefully noting the exact position and transferring it to his own chart when he returned to his ship.

On the night of November 21 he chanced to look at his general chart and saw to his surprise that if his reckoning was correct they were heading straight for the Rock, only a few miles away.

He tried to tell himself the Rock was mere legend and that he was a fool for having been impressed by Robinson's story. He went to his cabin and could not sleep, rose, and looked at the chart again. The dot in the circle seemed to grow. The Rock, according to legend, was large and dangerous.

By this time it was one o'clock in the morning. Since he could not rest, he went on deck.

His first mate was much older and had spent his life in the North Atlantic trade. He ridiculed Captain Urquhart's rather diffident hints about a fabulous rock dead ahead. Captain Urquhart returned to his rest, but the Rock continued to keep him awake. The sea moved under the ship suddenly, and the ship gave a curious lurch, and for a moment the captain was convinced that they had struck the Rock. He waited, but nothing else happened; at last he made up his mind, went on deck again, and

ordered the course of the *Trimountain* changed. Only then was
he able to fall asleep. He was still fully dressed, for his night had
been spent in apparently unreasonable apprehension.

He was not surprised when he was called on deck within the
hour and saw the *Lochearn* flying the distress flag, and knew at
once there had been a terrible collision.

Where was the other ship, he wondered? Only a few spars
drifted on the rising sea.

Captain Urquhart later calculated the time he had felt the
Trimountain lurch in the sea and thought they had struck the
Rock with the sinking of the *Ville du Havre*. His little vessel had
rocked to the ocean's surge caused by a great steamer going down
miles away.

Needless to say, no such rock ever existed.

Captain Urquhart remained convinced that a divine power
had linked the apparently trivial circumstances that drew his
small but adequate ship directly to the scene of disaster. As he
himself expressed it:

"I believe I was under some supernatural control that night."

It took more than three hours to transport the forty-seven
survivors and the *Lochearn's* crew through the rough sea to the
tiny *Trimountain*.

Pastor Blanc was too ill to be moved, so Pastor Cook volunteered to stay with him aboard the endangered *Lochearn* and share
whatever fate might overtake the ship. From its deck Pastor Cook
watched the others being carried in smallboats through the
mounting seas to the rescue ship. Captain Surmount attended to
the embarkation of his crew. He was obliged to leave a fireman
aboard who was even more seriously injured than Pastor Blanc.

These three men, left behind on a sinking vessel, were tossed
by every kind of weather, had to pump continuously to keep the
ship afloat, abandoned it finally, and were eventually picked
up by another vessel, the *British Queen*, and landed in England
only four days after those who had been rescued by the *Trimountain*.

Pastor Blanc recovered, but Pastor Cook did not long survive
the effects of exposure and the terrible fatigue of continually
manning the pumps. He lived long enough to see his family again
in Paris. Two months after the shipwreck he was dead.

The *Trimountain* was small, but the betweendecks space held
the rescued, and there were plenty of provisions. Captain Urqu-

hart broke into his canned-meat cargo and fed the survivors, but drinking water was very scarce.

He put everything the ship possessed at the disposal of the shipwrecked people. In his wardrobe there happened to be many articles of clothing belonging to his wife, who sometimes made the crossing with him, and these he distributed among the women. Thanks to the captain and the generosity of the sailors of both the *Trimountain* and *Lochearn*, everyone had something to wear, although the attire was often peculiar. One stout lady was wrapped in a woolen table cover.

That first night on the *Trimountain* was fearful. Captain Urquhart asked Pastor Lorriaux to conduct a simple service. Sleep came at last to the survivors only because of exhaustion.

Each day the realization of loss seemed more acute. The companions in grief, living under crowded, almost intolerable conditions, showed calmness and courage. They organized themselves for their mutual benefit and each had some duty to perform that drew forth their spirit of ingenuity and helped make life bearable on the tiny ship.

Pastor Weiss, in his report on the journey, states that as the days went by Mother became quieter and outwarldly more reconciled. He quotes her as saying:

"God gave me four little daughters. Now they have been taken from me. Someday I will understand why."

Nine days after the shipwreck, on December 1, 1873, the *Trimountain* reached Cardiff, Wales.

Captain Urquhart was not expected to touch Wales, and by cutting the journey short for his sad passengers he ran the risk of forfeiting the insurance, and I believe he was censured for it.

As soon as the survivors of the *Ville du Havre* were landed they were able to send dispatches. Mother's cable to Father consisted of two words: "Saved Alone."

On the other side of the Atlantic, Father was waiting for news of his family. A curtain of silence descended upon the *Ville du Havre* after she left American waters. Father quieted his anxiety with the hope that "no news was good news."

On the night the ship went down there was a brilliant wedding in Lake View. Father was present, and to the many inquiries about his family he smilingly replied that they must be nearing the other side and he hoped to receive word soon.

He wrote Mother a gay account of the wedding three nights

after the shipwreck:

Lake View, Tuesday evening
November 25, 1873

Day after tomorrow will be Thanksgiving Day. I will not say how I shall miss you and the dear children. But I will not think too much about that. Let us instead strive to profit by the separation. I think this separation has touched me more deeply than anything else which has ever occurred in my life. . . .

I feel more and more that the absorbing pursuit of anything earthly is not well for one's spiritual life. I scarcely know what to do about the Park matters. If I should withdraw altogether from taking an interest in things, it is very possible that great injury might be the result, not only to my own, but other interests, and yet I feel half inclined to do so, so harassing, so vexatious, so even dangerous to one's spiritual peace do I esteem these selfish contests about money, money, money.

Oh, but it is a long distance across the ocean! But, never mind, my heart. If the Lord keeps us, we hope before many months to be all together again, better understanding than ever before the greatness of His mercy in the many years of the past.

When you write, tell me all about the children. How thankful I am to God for them! May He make us faithful parents, having an eye single to His glory. Annie and Maggie and Bessie and Tanetta—it is a sweet consolation even to write their names. May the dear Lord keep and sustain and strengthen you. . . .

It was weeks before Mother received that letter in France. When Father wrote the names of his children, he had no idea that they were no longer on earth.

Then the blow fell; the cable arrived, not from France, from Wales. All that night, with Major Whittle and another devoted friend beside him, Father walked the floor in anguish.

Major Whittle said that toward morning Father turned to him.

"I am glad to trust the Lord when it will cost me something," he said.

He cabled Mother that she should proceed to Paris with Pastor Lorriaux, where she had friends, and where he would join her as soon as he could cross the Atlantic.

The steamship company of the ill-fated *Ville du Havre* conducted the survivors to London and provided clothes for them. They were taken to the best shops specializing in mourning. As Mother stood before their somber wares, black dresses, black bonnets and hats, black veiling, black everywhere, she felt her little daughters' reproof. She had taught them to believe in heaven. She could almost hear their voices, "Heaven is lovely; it is a happy place." The familiar quotations rushed through her thoughts, "We shall see Him face to face." "We shall know as we are known." "Pearly gates ... golden streets ... no sorrow ... no tears ... no night there. ..."

She thought: "I have not lost my children. We are only separated for a little time." So she invested in a simple black-and-white costume, in keeping with her thoughts, but not what her companions in sorrow thought suitable for a mother who had lost all her children. She saw their glances and sensed their disapproval but she did not explain.

She felt closer to her little girls after she had made this choice. It helped her to bear her sorrow inconspicuously and alone.

CHAPTER   FOUR

RECENTLY I read a novel that interested me greatly, *All This and Heaven Too* by Rachel Field. When the heroine, accused of murder in France, is finally acquitted, she goes to the home of the Rev. and Mrs. Fréderic Monod, and their ten-year-old son Theodore comes to her room and talks with her.

This same lad, Theodore Monod, grown and taking his father's place, was among the first to reach Mother with comforting words when she arrived lonely and bereaved in France.

He had met Father and Mother on a trip to the United States and visited them at Lake View. At this time he was pastor of the Eglise Reformée Evangélique de Paris, which made him, I understand, the most famous Protestant clergyman in France. He wrote:

Paris, 114 Place Lafayette
December 6, 1873

MY DEAR MRS. SPAFFORD,

On my return from Havre, where the fearful news reached me, I find a letter from Mrs. Sims enclosing one for you. It seems cold and hard to forward it without a line, but oh! what words can express what is in my heart, as a friend, as a father; and what voice, except the voice of Jesus himself, can bring the least degree of comfort to your desolate heart.

I will not, dare not, cannot speak of you nor them nor of your husband. I had tried to hope the name did not, could not, mean *you*, until one item of information after another left no room for doubt. We cry to God on your behalf.

Mother was waiting for Father's arrival in the village of Bertry near Paris, where she had gone with Pastor Lorriaux. Mme. Lorriaux, practical and kind, did not overlook Mother's heartbreak in the joy of having her husband safe. She nursed Mother for two weeks until she was strong enough to go to Paris and to her friend Mrs. Bertha Johnson.

I have a scrap of paper with a sentence in Mother's handwriting, dated December 6, 1873:

Oh, how sad my heart is without my birds. How little I thought when I left my happy home that I should set my foot first upon foreign soil alone!

She was overwhelmed by kindness. Letters came from friends all over the continent, offering money, a home, help of every kind. Friends surrounded her: Mme. Demougeot, Mme. Ribot, Pastor Monod, and many others. Letters began pouring in from America.

Margaret Morse has written me that her mother, Mrs. Ely, "described vividly to me the darling and beautiful children, so gifted and wonderfully trained in love of God and knowledge of the Bible, and in obedience. The news of the disaster was overwhelming to all who loved your mother."

In Chicago, Father searched his life for explanation. Until now it had flowed gently as a river. Spiritual peace and worldly security had sustained his early years, his family life, and his home. Then had come one terrible event upon another. The Chicago Fire with its losses, the failure of his real estate venture, now the loss of all his children, all had come within the space of two years.

The important thing was not to lose faith. He must wrestle until he could say all was well.

Added to his grief was spiritual conflict.

The Puritan foundation of the Protestant churches had carried into the United States many of the harsh Old Testament tenets. It was universally accepted by all Christians then that sickness or sorrow was the result of sin. One was the just retribution of the other.

What had Father done, what had his young wife done, that they should be so afflicted? He felt that eyes were looking askance at him, wondering.

All around him people were asking the unvoiced question, What guilt had brought this sweeping tragedy to Anna and Horatio Spafford?

Father wrestled with the question on the sad train trip to New York with Mr. Goodwin, whose wife and children had also been lost in the shipwreck.

Search the Bible teachings as he might, Father could not reconcile this harsh Puritan tenet with his concept of Christian teachings. He had to have a deeper faith in the goodness of God. Father remembered Christ's answer to the disciples when they asked whose sin it was, the parents' or the man's, that caused him to be born blind; Jesus answered it was neither the man's nor his parents' sin that had caused the blindness, but that the works of God should be made manifest in him.

Father became convinced that God was kind, and that he would see his children again in heaven.

This thought calmed his heart, but it was to bring Father into open conflict with what was then the Christian world.

On the train he wrote Aunt Maggie of this conviction, and in a letter to Aunt Rachel he asked that she go to the Lake View home and see that all the children's things were put carefully away.

On the way across the Atlantic the captain called Mr. Goodwin and Father into his private cabin.

"A careful reckoning has been made," he told them, "and I believe we are now passing the place where the *Ville du Havre* was wrecked."

Father wrote to Aunt Rachel:

On Thursday last we passed over the spot where she went down, in mid-ocean, the water three miles deep. But I do not think of our dear ones there. They are safe, folded, the dear lambs, and there, before very long, shall we be too. In the meantime, thanks to God, we have an opportunity to serve and praise Him for His love and mercy to us and ours. "I will praise Him while I have my being." May we each one arise, leave all, and follow Him.

To Father this was a passing through the "valley of the shadow of death," but his faith came through triumphant and strong. On the high seas, near the place where his children perished, he wrote the hymn that was to give comfort to so many:

> When peace like a river attendeth my way,
>   When sorrows like sea-billows roll,
> Whatever my lot, Thou hast taught me to say;
>   "It is well, it is well with my soul."
>
> Tho' Satan should buffet, tho' trials should come,
>   Let this blest assurance control,
> That Christ hath regarded my helpless estate,
>   And hath shed His own blood for my soul.
>
> My sin—oh, the bliss of this glorious thought!
>   My sin—not in part but the whole,
> Is nailed to His cross and I bear it no more;
>   Praise the Lord, praise the Lord, oh, my soul!
>
> And, Lord, haste the day when the faith shall be sight,
>   The clouds be rolled back as a scroll,
> The trump shall resound, and the Lord shall descend—
>   "Even so—it is well with my soul."

For me, be it Christ, be it Christ hence to live
If Jordan above me shall roll,
No pang shall be mine, for in death as in life
Thou wilt whisper Thy peace to my soul.

That he could write such words at such a time was made possible by the fierceness of his struggle and the completeness of the victory.

P. P. Bliss, the predecessor of Sankey with Mr. Moody, wrote the music for this hymn. "It Is Well with My Soul" became famous and appeared in many hymnbooks; it is still sung in many Protestant churches.

Hymns that are the fruit of anguish victoriously overcome are bound to bring blessing. I have sat by the bedside of a woman dying of cancer and, holding her limp and clammy hand, have quietly sung this hymn over and over again. I have sung it by other bedsides as war after war came to Jerusalem; once, by the bed of a private from the Argyle and Sutherland Regiment, taken prisoner by the Turks before Jerusalem was delivered by Allenby's army in 1917. Blood poisoning was in an advanced stage, and we had very little medicine and no narcotics to alleviate his suffering. He was doomed, and his agony was great. I sat by him hour upon hour and sang softly, "It is well with my soul." Just before the end he looked up into my face. "Sister, you have fought half this battle."

Innumerable letters have told me the same story in different ways, as the hymn affected and helped the despondent and despairing. I turned on the radio once at random and heard a faint voice coming from a remote station telling the story of the writing of the hymn. Another time I was standing in a snowstorm on Riverside Drive, in New York, waiting for a bus, when I heard the carillon in the tower of Riverside Church send forth its lovely message in music, "It is well with my soul." I stood transfixed with joy and wonder; tears rolled down my cheeks. I let one bus after another pass, and was late for my luncheon engagement, but I could not tear myself away from the spot until the hymn was finished.

On Christmas Eve Father and Mother were in Paris. Of their meeting Mother never spoke. Some things are too sacred to mention.

This had always been their happiest season, with candles and tinsel on the tree, and evergreen, holly, and mistletoe decorating

the cottage "joyous with the merriment of children," as one friend
wrote. In Paris, where they had planned so much of happiness,
memories of other years must have crushed them. What did they
do at this time of almost unbearable depression?

A letter from the Rev. Theodore Monod holds the answer:

Christmas Eve, 1873

MY DEAR FRIENDS,

Our Christmas tree is over; the hymns are sung, the addresses are among the
things of the past; the many brilliant lights have burned themselves away or
have been extinguished, as all earthly joys must be.

Mr. Weiss was with us and spoke, as you might expect him to do, of his
recent experience, alluding also to the dear children who, on the Sunday November 17th sang, "I want to be an angel," and before the week was over were
singing in heaven. I was not at all surprised that you, my dear friends, should
have both kept away and spent the evening quietly, prayerfully, tearfully, hope-
fully, one with another, but I *was* surprised when I got home and found that
parcel. At first we could not tell where it had come from; then the handwriting
(I once received a letter from you), the remembrance of your taking down those
five names on Saturday, and—I shall add, the sweet sad words "from the
children," told us from what hand, no, from what heart came the pretty presents, so thoughtfully chosen, so well adapted to each. But ah! with such tender
memories clinging to them, such brotherly affection, such truly Christian
fellowship of your sorrows with our joys, as made us look upon those play-
things with tears in our eyes. Oh, may "the Father of mercies and the God of all
comfort" continue to uphold you, to pour into your stricken hearts the fullness
of his love, and to make that love and power visible to others through you.

Thursday evening—Christmas Day

The children are in possession of their treasures, highly delighted and thankful. Marcel, who never yet had a plaything given him, smiled at the bright little
doll. I fear I shall not be able to go and shake hands with you today, but we are
with you in spirit, nor do we forget your friend Major Goodwin.

THEO MONOD.

On Christmas Eve Mother wrote her friend Mary Miller in
Chicago who had taken refuge with her during the Great Fire:

Paris, December 24, 1873

MY DEAR MARY,

I received your letter this morning. It was very sweet of you to remember me
in this time of sadness for me—but joy to my dear children.

Yes, Mary—all are gone Home—so early. How thankful I am that their
little lives were so early dedicated to their Master. Now He has called them to
Himself. I thought I was going, too, but my work is not yet finished. May the
dear Lord give me strength to do His will. The dear children were so brave.

They died praying. Annie said to Maggie and me just before we were swept off
the steamer, "Don't be frightened Maggie, God will take care of us, we can
trust Him; and you know, Mama, 'The sea is His and He made it.' " These
were her last words. Maggie and Bessie prayed very sweetly. I have much to
comfort me, Mary; they are not lost, only separated for a season. I will go to
them—only a few years at the longest.

Dear little Tanetta sang all the day before we were wrecked "The sweet bye
and bye" . . . If I never believed in religion before, I have had strong proof of
it now. We have been so sustained, so comforted. God has sent peace in our
hearts. He has answered our prayers. His will be done. I would not have my
children back again in this wicked world. . . .

Shortly after this my parents left for England on their way
home. Before leaving Paris a telegram came from Mr. Moody
saying he would meet them in London. He and Mr. Sankey were
conducting the revival meetings in Edinburgh that were making
them world-famous.

Mother told me that when Mr. Moody met them, in the hotel
in London, his sorrow was so great over the loss of the children
that she had to comfort him.

I can well imagine this meeting, for I remember Mr. Moody's
coming to the American Colony in Jerusalem after Father's
death. He was a thickset, short, and highly emotional man, who
always wore long frock coats. With my sister Grace on his knee,
he wept unashamed for the loss of his friend until two pools of
water were formed on the floor by his tears. I met Mr. Sankey,
too, in Jerusalem, the same year the Kaiser visited the Holy City.
I was eighteen and had been to Jericho and had "Jericho boils"
on my face and a swollen nose, caused, we now know, by the bite
of an insect. Mr. Sankey had called on Mother, and Mother insisted that I go to see him. So I did, and Mr. Sankey seemed
astonished by my appearance, but he did not say anything. He
was not so demonstrative as Mr. Moody.

With an understanding few could give, Mr. Moody divined
my parents' struggle against their natural inclinations to indulge
in sorrow. He also realized that a disastrous reaction might follow
this high resolve when they reached their empty house, unless
a power stronger than their grief upheld them. He knew their
present state of trust and faith must be sustained. He begged
Mother not to stay at home, where every room, silenced by the
absence of her children, would remind her of what had been.

"Annie, you must go into my work," Mr. Moody told my
mother. "You must be so busy helping those who have gone into
the depths of despair that you will overcome your own affliction

by bringing comfort and salvation to others."

Mother promised to follow his advice.

The anguish of their homecoming cannot be visualized. Aunty Sims was first to greet them, convulsed in tears on the doorstep. Well-meaning friends, in the custom of the period, had had the latest photographs of the four little girls enlarged, and they were on easels in the living room, the sweet faces surrounded by festoons of smilax. Upstairs four little beds stood empty and four dressers filled with garments that would never be worn by them again. Toys, books, lesson papers were reminders of all that had been.

Saddest of all was the attic, where four rows of little rubber boots and all the paraphernalia of winter sports bespoke the merriment that once had filled this house and grounds. Last of all, the childishly scrawled letters were found in the play post office in the elm tree.

Only Rob, Father's nephew, was left, and he was away at school.

Mother followed Mr. Moody's advice and plunged into his relief work.

She had not taken much active part in charitable or philanthropic work before. "Charity began at home," and she believed her duty lay in making an agreeable home for Father and bringing up four small children in Christian ideals. Only a brief period spent on the board of the Home of the Friendless and the months of relief activity following the Chicago Fire had prepared her for the extensive and important work she now took on. Mr. Moody put her in charge of all women's activities for Chicago. Mother realized she was handicapped by inexperience, and remonstrated with Mr. Moody, but he would not take no.

Mother did not like serving as the impersonal executive of an evergrowing organization. She preferred coming in actual contact with the women and doing the real work. She appointed her friend Miss Emma Dryer, one of Mr. Moody's workers, to act as her advisor. It proved a happy choice, for Miss Dryer served first as a shadow executive and later took over and held the official position.

Mother's approach to the women's work and her theories in aiding them were original and her experiences many and varied. She saw a seamy side of Chicago life far removed from the placid existence at Lake View.

A friend wrote of this period in Mother's life:

... she devoted almost her entire time to Christian and philanthropic work.
She was the first woman, I believe, who in Chicago encouraged mother's meetings. They met once a week in the church parlors, and there she taught many a
mother to pray. In the meantime your father led the noon prayer meeting at
Farwell Hall.

Mother told me that the women who attended her mothers'
meetings were of many nationalities and some were especially
vocal in complaining about their lot. Frequently their complaints
were about their husbands who used most of their earnings for
drink. In a state of intoxication the husband would return home
with little or no money left, to find hungry children crying, a
harried wife infuriated by his conduct, and no supper. Unpleasant
words would end in a voilent quarrel; more often than not the
wife got a beating. The poor woman would then complain to
Mother about her husband, and black-and-blue marks would be
proof of her story.

Mother, incensed, would get Father to prosecute the guilty
man. But when the time came to take evidence against her husband the wife would invariably take her husband's part, and the
case would be dropped. Mother learned by experience that the
best way was to let them "worry it through" and settle their
quarrels themselves.

But she was a sympathetic listener and gave sensible advice.
Because she put her life and soul into the work, she was successful.

I remember Mother telling of a predicament she found herself
in when in following Mr. Moody's work she was put in charge of
the rescue work for fallen women. One meeting affected a girl
so much that she wanted to leave her degraded life. Mother knew
she should be taken out of it at once, but where could the girl go?
Mother applied to one home and institution after another, none
of which was prepared to accept a girl straight from a "house of
ill fame." Mother was like the little girl who went to the prayer
meeting for rain carrying an umbrella—she expected results.

She felt with keen indignation this defect in the rescue work,
that there was no new environment ready in which these poor
derelicts could be fitted once they were saved.

There was nothing to do but take on the girl's support for a
period of years. She married happily at last and raised a family
of healthy children.

In this pioneer welfare work I do not think Mother was so
much shocked by what she saw as by the complacency of the rich
who permitted such things to be.

The years following the shipwreck were anxious ones, but also rich in spiritual experience to my parents. In Father's letter to Mother, written before he knew of the loss of his children, he spoke of his growing distaste for giving so much of his life to the struggle after money. The struggle even seemed dangerous to his spiritual peace; and this feeling must have increased as the months passed into years. Possessions seemed unimportant in the light of his recent experience, which gave him a feeling that everything was transient.

His letters and notes at this time are revealing, as are the poems and hymns he composed. Studying both sides in legal fashion, he pondered the question of future punishment. "I was . . . surprised to find how many devout and learned men, in every age, had believed in the final universal triumph of God's love." "Who is there who would not wish to believe if the Word will permit it, in the eventual restoration of all?" A hymn, inspired by one of the Psalms, begins:

> There's darkness all round in my earthly affairs,
> Wave following wave, tribulation and cares;
> My way is shut up on the left and the right;
> And yet, I've a mind for a song in the night,
> A song in the night—a song in the night,
> My heart, canst thou give Him a song in the night?

A little book of his poetry, *Waiting for the Morning*, was printed privately for distribution among his friends, and met with so much more appreciation than had been expected that it was reprinted for public sale.

When, in 1876, Mr. Moody rebuilt his tabernacle on the north side of Chicago, Father found means to help him financially, and wrote the dedication hymn beginning:

> Our Father, God, Eternal one!
> And Thou, the living cornerstone!
> And Holy Spirit—one and three—
> We dedicate this house to Thee!
>
> Take for Thine own, and write in power,
> Thy name on wall and shaft and tower;
> And make it, by Thy blessing given,
> A house of God—a gate of heaven.

I find it difficult to interpret to this modern generation Father's and Mother's attitude toward life at this time and throughout

the following years without making them seem impractical, fanatical, narrow, and visionary. They were none of these things. The
world has so changed in its outlook, its conceptions, its manners,
and its vocabulary in the last threescore years that the problems
which were important to them then seem almost unintelligible
and meaningless now. Therefore it is hard to do them justice.

This period must have been difficult for my parents in every
way. Their religious life was undergoing a transition—nothing
was quite clear.

On November 16, 1876, a little boy came to the childless home
at Lake View.

He was my parents' first and only son, and was named Horatio,
after Father and Grandfather. Also he was named Goertner, for
Goertner Goodwin, my sisters' playmate who had gone down with
them on the *Ville du Havre.*

Little Horatio was a healthy baby, and his birth must have
seemed like a renewal of life to Father and Mother.

In a letter written by a friend in 1876, Father is described as
"walking up and down in the living room at Lake View, holding
his baby son and talking about his Heavenly Father and heaven
in the most intimate and homelike fashion. . . ."

In another letter written by Miss Dryer from Mr. Moody's
home in Northfield:

Mr. and Mrs. Moody talk of you affectionately. He, I think, has a deep interest in your financial troubles. In talking about them one evening he said that
he thought Mr. Spafford would do well to resume his practice of law until this
hard time is passed. He spoke of Mr. S's success in the past and that he was in
a fair position to succeed again. . . .

I get no comfort except from *the promises.* How glad I am to know that they
cannot fail.

I think these last words expressed Father's sentiments as well.
He had found the things people strove after in this world as sinking sand under his feet, and he longed now only to build "on
the rock," where the rain could descend, the floods beat, and the
winds blow, but his house would stand.

In this rather difficult period, on March 24, 1878, I was born,
and named for Mrs. Bertha Johnson, who had been so kind to
Mother in Paris. It proves how near and dear our family doctor
had become, for I was also given his family name, and became
Bertha Hedges Spafford.

In February of 1880 Mother was taking little Horatio and me away for a visit. I am not sure where we were going, but it must have been some distance from Chicago, for we were on a train when she noticed we both had fever. Before we reached our destination she left the train and caught the next train back to Chicago. Her one idea was to be near Dr. Hedges. She had to wait in a stuffy waiting room with two sick babies, then came the long journey back, when she could see we were growing more ill with every passing mile; then the scramble to catch "The Dummy" to Lake View.

Peter, who had been telegraphed to, met us with the horse and buggy. Father was away on business. It was snowing, and the flakes swirled in the driving wind and settled on us in the open buggy. The air was bitterly cold, and cold, too, was the house, for the furnace had been allowed to go out with the family away.

Dr. Hedges diagnosed our malady as scarlet fever. Horatio had also taken a bad cold and was dropping off into a coma. Father was telegraphed to, but reached home only in time to witness the death of his little son on February 11, 1880.

CHAPTER FIVE

MOTHER never spoke of little Horatio's death. It was a blow that time never softened.

She could not go to the cemetery. She had to take care of me. Also, she had a horror of the grave. She wanted to think of her little boy with her four daughters in heaven.

Our house was in quarantine and only a few learned of this new sorrow and came unsummoned to the funeral. The tiny white coffin was taken to the family plot in Graceland Cemetery and Father read the funeral service.

Many wondered at his doing this. Gossip filled in gaps and distorted facts.

Among my treasures is a little cardboard box found in Father's desk after his death in Jerusalem. In it are some faded flowers bound with white ribbon and the words: "Flowers from little Horatio's funeral." He brought this with him to Jerusalem when so little was taken. No one knew how deep was the grief he and Mother shared in losing their four-year-old son.

Mother's letters to friends after my brother died show perfect faith and trust. They would shock some people, who would have understood her mourning better with a touch of self-pity. People love to pity others, but pity was the last thing my parents wanted.

After Horatio's death Father wrote the hymn, "A Song in the Night," which, set to music by Mr. George C. Stebbins, was sung by our choir when the American Colony celebrated its jubilee in 1931, commemorating the fiftieth anniversary of the arrival of my parents and their group of friends in Jerusalem.

> Long time I dared not say to Thee
> O Lord, work Thou Thy will with me,
> But now so plain Thy love I see
> I shrink no more from sorrow.

Refrain:

> So true, true and faithful is He,
> Kind is my Savior;
> Alike in gladness and in woe,
> I thank Him who hath loved me so. . . .

My parents were trying to practice what they had come to believe since the shipwreck through heart-searching wrestling with doubt and fear. It was not easy to see wisdom in affliction, or reconcile God's dealing with God's love. Since the church held sorrow to be retribution for sin, the tone of conversations with friends and acquaintances after Horatio's death stressed again the question raised when the four little girls died:

"What have the Spaffords done to be so afflicted?"

The Spaffords had long asked themselves the same question. Now they could only pray for endurance and strength. Father wrote to a friend: "There is just one thing in these days that has become magnificently clear—I must not lose faith."

The most eloquent proof of their struggle was in Mother's saying "I will say God is love until I believe it!"

The first shock of total misunderstanding came when one of the leaders of the evangelist group that had met so often in our home in Lake View, and a friend they had trusted to understand their motives, came to Father and Mother to ask if they would like him to adopt me.

Why this offer was made I do not know. I was two years old and the only child left to my parents out of a family of six.

The request opened a wound that only by the grace of God could Father and Mother forgive. It was the first crushing blow of many that culminated in their decision to leave Chicago, for a time at least. The hitherto vague idea that someday they would go to Jerusalem to watch the fulfillment of prophecy on the spot, and perhaps find refreshment of the body, soul, and spirit there, became resolute.

From the day of that offer they began to make definite plans for the journey.

A year after Horatio's death there is an entry in Father's notebook: "Little Grace was born this morning at 6:30, Jan. 18th, 1881."

Mother was very ill when Grace was born. She lay in her bed exhausted and weak, wondering what to name this baby who had come as a godsend after her little son's death. She went over in her mind the names of the four little girls who romped no more through the house—no, they were not lost, she could not name this baby after one of them.

Her eyes rested on an illuminated text hanging on the wall. "My grace is sufficient for thee."

So my sister became Grace Spafford, without any addition of a middle name.

She was born while Father and Mother were completing their plans to go to Jerusalem.

I did not realize until I was reading letters written at this time that the move was suppsed to be temporary.

When the time came my parents walked out of their lovely home, leaving everything—valuable furniture, paintings, silver, linen, a library of several thousand books—the accumulation of more than twenty years of married life, and a friend and his family came in and took possession.

Only a single trunk went with us to Jerusalem.

If Father had lived, I think he would have returned to Chicago. He was seeking peace and solace for mind and soul. He was leaving the center of a controversy he was tired of, and hoped to be able to see things plainly and more in perspective. In a letter to a friend he explained:

Jerusalem is where my Lord lived, suffered, and conquered, and I wish to learn how to live, suffer, and especially to conquer.

He and Mother had no grandiose plans or expectations of what their going to Jerusalem would mean to anyone but themselves.

But that was far too simple a reason to satisfy the curious, and human nature is credulous of spectacular rumors that make a good story.

Father and Mother had battled with doubt; they had come to believe in the truth of God's love; they were winning.

They had come to believe that the blows that had been dealt them were not in punishment for their sins.

They could not believe that their innocent babies, or any other babies, were in hell. Father probed further—he could no longer believe in a tangible hell or a personal devil.

Naturally this doctrine exploded the idea of eternal punishment, and this was contrary to what was then the tenets of the Orthodox Presbyterian Church.

Father was not one to keep his discovery to himself. He wanted to share his comprehension of God's all-embracing love. Father expressed himself freely, perhaps too freely. He made a prodigious effort to express the state of his soul, and it was misunderstood. It shocked the complacent; it brought to a head a controversy that stirred Chicago. The newspapers took it up, and in their misunderstanding of the vital core of his belief and their misrepresentation of the facts it took on the ridiculous.

Father and Mother were asked to leave the Fullerton Avenue Presbyterian Church, the church Father had helped to build, the church of which he was an elder, the church where my sisters and brother had been baptized, the church they loved.

This arbitrary act caused a rift in the church. A number of their friends, among them Mr. and Mrs. John E. Whiting, church members who admired Father and Mother for their courage in adversity and sorrow, walked out of the church at the same time, in protest.

This rift was the last thing Father and Mother wanted. The unpleasant publicity it caused was obnoxious and distressing to them. Now they longed to get away. A complete break was necessary to brace them to take up life anew.

Perhaps the sojourn to Jerusalem and the Holy Land would help! Perhaps there, where the "Man of Sorrows," acquainted with grief yet triumphant, had walked the shores of Galilee and the hills of Judea, His life and passion would be revealed in such a way that life would again bring consolation.

They set a definite date for departure.

The Church suffers from its symbolism: presenting an immortal truth in the terms of the time and generation. Years pass, and a whole new set of mental pictures and cosmic conceptions take the place of the old, which lose their value and become meaningless.

Less than a decade after this, in 1890, when the New York Presbytery discussed the revision of the Westminster Confession, the revered minister Dr. Henry van Dyke declared: "I intend to teach that there are no infants in hell and that there is no limit to God's love, and that no man is punished save for his own sin."

By this time no one thought this teaching strange. Dr. van Dyke's announcement had the full approval of the church. Even ten years had wrought a tremendous change in religious outlook. Father, for coming to the same conclusion, was turned out of the church.

Father lived ahead of his day. His belief had been too liberal too early.

One after another, friends learned of my parents' final plans
to visit Jerusalem and asked if they might join them on their
pilgrimage. Many of those who had left the church with them
wished to go. Then others wanted to join the party, and there
was much coming and going and meetings and conferences as
to what should be planned and what taken, for travel was not
the easy matter it became later and Jerusalem seemed at the
other end of the world.

By this time the Chicago press had become aware that a group
of people were meeting at Lake View for closer religious fellowship and were planning a pilgrimage to the Holy Land. Father
and Mother and their friends were subjected to a campaign
of ridicule. The cottage was invaded by reporters who left to
write stinging banter. A great deal was said in the meetings
about "overcomers," and accused them of thinking they were
the only people capable of defeating evil.

One newspaper article stated:

> A singular sect of Christians which has recently arisen in one of the northern
> suburbs of Chicago is known as the "Overcomers." They believe in personal
> inspiration, in direct communication with God, and in the literal rendering of
> the Scriptures as applied to mundane affairs, and in the final salvation of all the
> universe, including the devil. A party under the leadership of Mr. Spafford is
> about to go to Jerusalem to build up the ruined places.

Mother wrote to a friend:

> A reporter came to see me this week. He asked what was the foundation of
> our religion, and I told him "to love the Lord God with all our hearts and one's
> neighbor as one's self." He read me what had been given him by an "influential
> Christian," and it was that I went into trances, etc., and wore spiritualistic
> emblems (which was my poor little pin of ivory with a cherub's head—you know
> it). Although I denied his statements I am afraid his article will appear in the
> paper.

I have mentioned that a number of people who left the church
when my parents were asked to leave, accompanied them to
Jerusalem. But there were others who remained behind. Their
connection with the church had been severed, and they were
left unattached and without leadership. Father warned them
to be wary of dissension, but his warnings were ignored.

Before our group reached Palestine there was dispute among
the Lake View remainder.

When the baby of one of the members died, and another
member refused to allow it to be buried, claiming she would

raise it from the dead, an end came to the little group. The scandalous episode came out, with much unpleasant publicity, and some of the group, instead of placing the blame on their own gullibility, blamed Father and Mother as having originally founded the Lake View Group. The fact that Father had warned them against this happening seemed to make them more resentful. Some were to go so far as to send violent letters denouncing us to the English Mission and to the Consul of the United States in Jerusalem. Garbled rumors flew ahead of the pilgrims.

Not all those left in Lake View became our enemies. Some remained loyal. Others relented later and wrote asking forgiveness, and some even joined us in Jerusalem.

But abuse always travels faster than praise, and a religious persecution had been started.

For many years the stories continued to grow wilder on either side of the Atlantic. Any bit of fact was magnified, to spread eight thousand miles. Among the many absurd claims Father was accused of thinking himself the second Messiah.

Subtlest of all accusations, because it wore a sham mantle of magnanimity, was that "poor Mr. and Mrs. Spafford have suffered so much they are unbalanced."

Some reports were vicious, others harmful, all untrue.

A story which appeared in the Chicago papers soon after our arrival in Jerusalem was that we went every afternoon to the Mount of Olives to wait for the Lord's arrival, and made a cup of tea so we would be the first to give Him refreshment.

As always, there is a sliver of truth in this tall tale.

One of our favorite walks was to the Mount of Olives. We took simple picnic spreads on these expeditions, and, since we quickly met many English people in Jerusalem, Mother soon learned to take along the proverbial tea basket without which no outing was complete for our British friends.

However, the story persisted through the years, and only a short time ago I met a lady in New York who, when she heard I had lived many years in Jerusalem, said: "You don't belong to that group of people, do you, who went every day to the Mount of Olives and prepared tea for Christ's second coming?"

I told her that as far as I knew no such group ever existed. She retorted: "Oh, don't spoil a good story; I have often told it."

On August 17, 1881, the band of pilgrims left Chicago. Father wrote in his tiny pocket diary:

"Started for Europe at 9:10 P.M. (for Jerusalem via Quebec)."

They chose the shorter though colder route to England in preference to the longer one to France, which would have carried them over the scene of the sinking of the *Ville du Havre*.

With my parents was my sister Grace, seven months old, myself, aged three years and five months, Cousin Rob, grown to a tall, good-looking, brilliant boy of nineteen who teased me a great deal and was the love of my life, Aunt Maggie Lee, whose husband had recently died, Mrs. William Gould, Mr. and Mrs. John C. Whiting and their baby Ruth, eleven months old, Mr. William H. Rudy, Mrs. Caroline Merriman, Mr. and Mrs. Otis S. Page and their daughter Flora, about ten years old, and Nora, the daughter of Mother's washwoman at Lake View, who came along as nurse to Grace and me. Aunty Sims had died.

Mrs. Gould and Mother had worked together on the committee of the "Home for the Friendless," and formed a friendship that was perhaps the most cherished of Mother's life. Mrs. Gould's husband, with his brother John, had a large wholesale grocery business in Chicago. Mr. Gould had fallen ill, come with his wife to our home in Lake View, and remained there until he died. Mrs. Gould was intelligent and aristocratic, with gracious manners. The Gould family played an important role in the life of my parents and the history of the American Colony.

Mr. Page had been a salesman for Mr. Gould.

Mr. Rudy was an Easterner who had been the proprietor of flour mills, and after a serious illness retired from business. Mrs. Merriman was his foster mother.

Mr. and Mrs. Whiting were among those who had left the Fullerton Presbyterian Church when Father and Mother were asked to leave. Mr. Whiting came originally from Massachusetts and was related to the famous paper manufacturers although he had no share in the business. Mrs. Whiting, his mother, was still living, a dear old lady, wholly in sympathy with her son's desire to go to Jerusalem. Mrs. Whiting's mother was also living, but she was not in sympathy, and later played an important though unhappy part in the history of the American Colony.

In London the group was joined by Captain and Mrs. W. C. Sylvester.

Some years before Captain Sylvester had been the youngest captain in the British Army. He had broken first one kneecap, then the other, each time by slipping on icy pavements, and was forced to retire from active service. He came with his wife to Chicago, where once more, on an icy winter morning, he slipped and smashed the first kneecap which had been sown with silver wire. This time it had to be entirely removed, and the captain was told he would never walk again.

During this period of his invalidism Father met him, and the two men and their wives became friends.

Captain Sylvester had returned to England, determined that his broken knees should not prevent his living a useful life. He turned evangelist, and in a specially constructed van equipped with many conveniences he and his wife toured England and Scotland preaching the Gospel.

If their labor and this pilgrimage had resulted in only one conversion which was to mean so much to the country of Palestine, it was ample reward. For Dr. Herbert Torrence once told me it was Captain Sylvester's preaching and his brave fight against his physical impediment that helped him make his own choice and become a medical missionary. Dr. Torrence started the Scottish Seaman's Medical Mission on the lake shore at Tiberias which for more than fifty years gave the only medical help the native people had for miles around. His son, Dr. Herbert Torrence, Junior, followed in his father's footsteps and continued the work of healing in the name of the Master. In the summer of 1946, despite the troubles in the Holy Land, Dr. Torrence celebrated twenty-five years of work, and Arabs, Jews, and British and American Christians joined in honoring this great but unassuming man.

The Sylvesters loved children and had lost their only son. Once, I remember, the captain asked me to kiss him, and I said, "I will if you'll lift up your fringes." He laughed—that contagious laugh that drew everyone to him—and drew up his mustache for the kiss.

This and a ride on the old elephant Jumbo, who gave his name to all succeeding elephants, comprise practically all my memories of our stay in London.

Our arrival in England did not go unnoticed. The following

paragraph appeared in an English newspaper, dated September 8, 1881:

H. C. Spafford, of Lake View, leader of the new sect of "Overcomers," arrived in London with a band of these peculiar believers, including several children, en route to Palestine. They will proceed to the Mount of Olives, where they expect to receive a new and direct revelation from the Lord.

CHAPTER   SIX

And then I saw Jerusalem. . . .
A city from the skies let down
To be henceforth the whole earth's Crown
Set mid the Holy Land.

JOHN FINLEY

IT WAS a warm September day in 1881, and Father, Mother, and the rest of our group were bumping over the rough cobblestone road leaving Jaffa for Jerusalem in several high, uncomfortable spring wagons.

Around us, though I did not know it then, lay the Holy Land. I was to become familiar with the utter desolation of the country arid from the long, dry months of summer and the choking reddish dust coating the road and hills. Such aridity, Cousin Rob wrote in a letter home, would bring famine to another land, and the Chicago pilgrims found it difficult to believe that the rains would soon come, making the hills green and filling the plains with fruits, vegetables, and brilliant flowers.

I had a vague remembrance of our home in Lake View, but the journey across the Atlantic I do not remember at all. I do not recall our short stay in Jaffa, which we were leaving behind us, hidden in the dust of our small caravan. Jaffa had been the principal port of the Israelites, the portion given by tribal division to Dan. At Jaffa Jonah had taken ship to escape being sent to Nineveh. Hiram's Phoenician workmen brought there the floats of cedar for Solomon's temple. On a reef of low rocks running parallel to Jaffa's shore, according to Greek legend, Andromeda was chained while threatened by the sea monster or dragon, until her rescue by Perseus. Saint George, whose birthplace was at Lydda near Jaffa, had his opposition to paganism symbolized in local legend by Perseus's dragon.

At Jaffa, where the lighthouse now overlooks the Mediterranean, stood the house of Simon the Tanner, where the Apostle Peter sat on the housetop, waiting the preparation of the evening meal, and saw the vision of the sheet let down from heaven which prepared him for his mission to Cornelius, the Centurion at Caesarea.

There was no actual port in Jaffa then. Passengers were brought ashore in small boats, weather permitting, and not even mail could be dropped when the rocky coast was lashed by tempest. How longingly we were to await the mail held at Jaffa by storm or quarantine so that it was late in arriving. Normal delivery from America took three or four weeks. For imaginary or real cholera scares the Turkish and Egyptian governments indulged in reciprocally imposing quarantine on each other's passengers and mail, and letters were received punched full of holes and smelling of sulphur.

We were to spend many pleasant holidays in Jaffa, where evergreen orange groves formed an ever-increasing circle around the town. The world-famous Jaffa orange was developed and exported by Arabs many years before. Up to World War II the orange industry accounted for almost the whole of Palestine's income from export.

The American-made spring wagons that were carrying us to Jerusalem had been brought to Palestine by a group of "Latter-Day Saints" who had come from Maine, I believe, about twenty years before, bringing prefabricated farmhouses in sections that they set up near Jaffa, where some are still standing. They introduced modern—for that time—farming implements, including wagons, to the Holy Land.

Among remaining members of this colony at Jaffa, occupying their original houses, were Mr. and Mrs. Rolla Floyd, who proved such wonderful friends, and Mr. Herbert Clark, representative of Thomas Cook and Son, and who was in charge of our transportation, as we were traveling on Cook's tickets. Because the high wagon seat terrified me, Mr. Clark held me on his knee all the way to Jerusalem.

I do not remember my first glimpse of Jerusalem. To me, it has always been home. But I know how it appeared to the others, climbing 2,700 feet over the dusty plain to the hills surrounding Jerusalem on the Judean watershed about thirty miles from the Mediterranean and twenty miles from the Dead Sea. The old city stands on four hills, surrounded by historic walls, and set with mosques and minarets, Herodean towers, and crowded ancient houses, their flat roofs set with domes.

We stopped first at the Mediterranean Hotel, situated just inside the Jaffa Gate. It was the only European hotel, and was kept by Mr. and Mrs. Moses Hornstein, who, with their daughters, did all they could to make the newcomers comfortable and initiate them into the strange new ways of this strange and difficult land.

I remember the hotel very well, for I was put to bed early one night and was wakened by the moon rising, an immense globe of molten silver, over the Mount of Olives. I had never seen the moon rise, and I dashed downstairs in my little nightgown and into the dinning room where the hotel guests were assembled at dinner to announce: "The Lord has come!"

The amusement that met this puzzled me.

We stayed six weeks at the hotel, while the Group went sight-seeing, to the Holy Sepulcher and the Jews' Wailing Place, and, often and repeatedly, to the Mount of Olives, usually in the late afternoons to watch the lovely sunsets. Father's diary held many notes of "walks about Jerusalem." I think he felt very much as Dr. Henry van Dyke did later when he wrote *Out-of-Doors in the Holy Land*. Father loved walking about the curious narrow streets, and, most of all, in the country around Jerusalem; this, he wrote, "is the land that makes one feel Christ's presence."

On October 4 he notes:

"We are looking at Jerusalem houses."

The Group had arrived without plans, and it seemed feasible that all should live together. Some had money, other had none, but this made no difference, nor would it ever do so.

They were shown many houses, but one appealed to them most because it "stood on a hill with its nose in the air," as it were, a point to be considered in an oriental city without sufficient water, drains, or the rudiments of sanitation and hygiene. The house was on the tip of the hill Bezetha, the highest spot in the walled city, between the Damascus Gate and Herod's Gate, and over-looked both the old and the new sections of Jerusalem.

It was not quite finished, and belonged to an officer in the Turkish gendarmerie, or mounted police. At this time Palestine was under Turkish rule and had been for four hundred years. This officer, Yousef Aga Dusdar, was an Albanian by birth. Later he became a colonel of the Turkish gendarmerie and was known as Yousef Bey; still later he performed the pilgrimage to Mecca and became a haj. Father paid our landlord forty napoleons, French gold pieces, in advance. The first payment was made on the first of Muharram, the Moslem New Year. The Moslem calendar, being lunar, is shorter than ours by thirteen days, so that in thirty-three years one pays an extra year's rent.

Before our Group bought the house, we had lived in it long enough to pay Yousef Bey for that extra year.

Father noted improvements to be made, and we stayed in the hotel until the house was finished. A railing around the roof he considered important as a safety provision, for roofs are much used in Palestine. Downstairs there were no windows at all, so Father had windows cut, and barred, as all windows, upstairs and down, are in Jerusalem.

Next to this house was a smaller and older house and garden which the Group also rented, paying twenty-two napoleons. There was still another in which Father had his study and sometimes it was used for extra lodgings. We called it the "down-to-the-other house."

The houses were ready by October 9, and we were glad to escape from the hotel. Our combined luggage consisted of twelve or fourteen large trunks and "no end of parcels." According to Rob, the entire lot was carried from the hotel and up the hill to the new house, a quarter of a mile, on Arab backs for $1.60. Wages were extremely low, Rob comments in a letter. A man worked hard to earn £5.00 a month and would carry two hundred pounds on his back—as much as a camel would carry—to any part of the city for eight or ten cents.

Rob was nineteen, and his notebook and copies of his letters form a sort of diary which gives a vivid though juvenile picture of the conditions under which the Group labored in those early days.

Customs and practices have changed since then, and Rob's descriptions do not represent life in present-day Jerusalem.

"It is a beautiful house," Rob wrote, "although a little damp because of its newness. Dampness is common because of the thickness of the walls, which are from three to five feet thick and of white stone." Little wood was used in Jerusalem's houses, as it was scarce and expensive. All the roofs were flat with domes, so the walls had to be substantial, and, Rob added: "The city looks at a distance like a village of prairie dogs."

Rob gave a good description of it:

Our house is on the highest point of the city and so we have delightful air and are not troubled by the terrible filth of the low portions of the city....

Read in your Bible the curses against Jerusalem and this land and you will get an exact description of it today. The center of the city lies in the Tyropean Valley. It rises in the east toward the Mount of Olives on two hills, Moriah and Bezetha, and on the west toward the Jaffa Gate to Mount Zion and Acra. Mount Zion is the Armenian Christian quarter and many of the English live there. S. west is the Jewish quarter and the east and n. east is the Mohammedan, while the south east is the Temple site. On Mount Bezetha, is the Moslem quarter. We are up so high that no one disturbs us. The Church of the Holy Sepulcher is in the center of the city and quite unlikely to be the authentic spot.

Around us were Moslem, Jewish, and Mohammedan slums, so closely set that we could not trace the narrow streets.

Jerusalem lay at our feet. It seemed beautiful then. It will be beautiful again.

By night the city was dark and mysterious-looking. Only kerosene lamps lighted the streets and houses. Those who ventured into the dark carried kerosene lanterns. These cast only feeble flutters of light.

The house itself was large and comfortable. It was the first home I really remember, and it was to be my home for many years. It is now the Anna Spafford Baby Nursing Home, named in honor of my mother.

Our group lived together as one large and happy family. Only those I have mentioned, who came from Chicago with Father and Mother, were members then, but others joined, and many years later the Colony grew to contain as many as one hundred and fifty.

How strange and primitive the new life must have seemed to the Group. The house hunting and furnishing, employing of servants, and the many problems connected with the new life were confusing and perplexing at times.

Rob wrote:

We get along amazingly well, considering that we came to Jerusalem with scarcely one housekeeping article....

We are having bedding made and other articles. I have had several Arab women to watch from sunrise to sunset. They are a curious but interesting set of people, and I have had a good deal of amusement with them. I am learning Arabic gradually and hope soon to "carry on" at least a limited conversation. Here everyone speaks two or three languages, and many can use parts of eight or ten, for it is absolutely necessary in order to be tolerably conversant. In Jerusalem you can find every nationality under the sun represented, so you can see how many tongues can be used.

The Arab women are good workers when you stand over them and shout "Yellah (Get going)!"

Rob spent much time watching the native carpenters at work, and felt he could do as well as men who did not even know the use of a square. No sooner were we moved in than Rob purchased a fine set of German and English tools and set up a bench in an empty room, where, he wrote:

> ... I carry on a trade of all kinds indiscriminately, blacksmith, mason, carpenter, and literally astonish the natives with a slight exhibition of American go-ahead-ness. This keeps me busy all the time, although you wouldn't think so—but among half a dozen women there is always something that is wanted to be done, especially in a new house.

Among other things, Rob made a finely polished desk with pigeon-holes for Father for Father's first Christmas in Jerusalem; and Father used it for the rest of his life, and I ever since, and much of this book has been written on it. He made a bureau for Mother which is still in use in the American Colony, and child-size furniture for our nurseries.

Mother had tender feet, and when her American shoes wore out, Rob took them to pieces for a pattern and cut a new pair from the softest of kid leather; Mother wore the shoes Rob made for five years.

We had no rugs at first, but local matting made of rushes was cheap and decorative.

There was little choice in materials to furnish the new house, but Mother used Turkey-red material which was gay against the white walls. Other curtains were made of white or cream muslin banded with the Turkey red, so our windows gave a cheerful appearance.

In the living room—we learned to call it the salon—Mother used bunches of wild grass and palm branches for decoration, and for pictures mounted the cards we received for Christmas.

Aunt Maggie wrote in a letter:

> It is a large room, and Annie with her natural ingenuity has made it lovely with Turkey-red curtains and divan covers . . . on the south the salon has large double windows with broad window sills, one made into a lounge, and the others hold pots with maidenhair and other ferns. . . .

A garden on the east and south had seven almond trees that were a great attraction in the beginning, but they died and were replaced by mulberry trees. There were pine and cypress, and soon we had a beautiful garden. In time the central open court was enhanced by pink ivy geraniums and white roses climbing all the way to the second story.

There was a great deal of work to be done getting the house

in order and Mother, Aunt Maggie, Mrs. Gould, and Mrs. Whiting were kept busy. I enjoyed the excitement of housekeeping and never had the feeling of being pushed back, as we children were always part of everything.

In his diary Father noted that one day "we" made quince jelly. I am sure it was the first time Father had put his hand to domestic service. Mother had in him a willing but clumsy helper, and she always tried to get him out of the house and off on one of his sightseeing expeditions when there was any special work to be done.

Evidently we moved into the snug new home just in time for the first rain, for Rob wrote this in October:

This afternoon we received the first wetting of the rainy season and are rejoicing exceedingly in the fact. You would understand the reason for rejoicing if you were to stay here one hour. Imagine a city crowded with people, without rain for six months, and you have Jerusalem.

Everything is utterly barren—not a green thing to be seen except the olive and fig trees and they are literally covered with dust. They say that now the hills will become beautifully green and everything will be lovely.

Three months later:

The fields are just turning from a reddish brown to a bright green. The wild flowers and the new grass cover the slopes and everything has the appearance of spring. It is a most bewitching climate and nothing could ever persuade me to leave Jerusalem. . . . I am taking drawing lessons, in self-defense.

Rob was out in his spare time sketching the ruins, the scraggling olive trees, and the people in their strange costumes. His work was interrupted by youngsters beggings for baksheesh (a present or alms). He made a lovely drawing of the Damascus Gate, near our house, which I treasure, and drew little landscapes on olivewood with India ink, which, when polished over, made nice souvenirs for his friends back home.

We were surprised to find winter could be cold in Jerusalem. Soon the wind blew loudly around our stone walls as if threatening to sweep even the stout building away, and sounded, Rob said, "exactly as it did at Lake View when the snow came down by the yard." We even learned that it occasionally snowed. One night the gale blew the "whirligig" off our salon chimney. Rob went up to repair it and if it were not for the railing Father had insisted upon our landlord's putting around the edge, Rob would have been blown off the roof.

I find a letter written by Mother on January 6, 1882, in which she said:

Our Christmas was a very quiet one and did not seem a bit like those at home, as there was nothing to remind us of it.

Three Christmases later Mother wrote:

Christmas! Glorious rain all night. Fifty-two outsiders here during the afternoon and evening. The tree beautifully trimmed, supper served to young and old. Thirty-two outside our "family" received gifts from the tree. The most wonderful peace and order combined with joy filled the house.

Christmas was always a joyous celebration, as all our holidays and birthdays were. Even the ordinary days combined joyous well-being with hard work. In one of Mother's letters she tells of the large numbers of people, both Jews and Arabs, who came every day to the American Colony to visit and attend the daily meetings and listen to the singing. Among others they became acquainted with Mr. Steinhart, a Jew who had traveled widely and was very interesting. He was employed by a private banker to buy land, which was sold to the immigrant Jews.

His sister made and sold small cakes, and every Friday we ordered enough for Sunday afternoon tea, and larger ones for birthdays or other days we wished to celebrate. We called them "Steinhart cakes" and thought them delicious.

I find a typical birthday description in a letter from Mrs. Gould to Aunt Rachel in Chicago in which she describes one of Mr. Rudy's, soon after we moved into the new house. Mr. Rudy was business manager for the Colony and, Mrs. Gould wrote:

. . . so kind and thoughtful for us all, it was a pleasure to have a celebration for him.

Mrs. Whiting and Annie made a large cake and sent it out to be baked, and we frosted it at home. Rob put Mr. Rudy's name and the date and good wishes on with the chocolate frosting. We had nuts and raisins and coffee with it that evening in the parlor and Flora and Bertha were allowed to sit up until ten o'clock.

I remember that evening and the many fancy little parcels wrapped with funny inscriptions. Not all the gifts were funny, many were lovely, and among them was a silk scarf worn by certain Arabs and Bedouins, a headdress appropriate to this country where the sun is very hot.

Our daily fare was simple but healthy. Our kitchen, Aunt Maggie wrote, was "different from any you've ever seen." We had no oven at first, and all the cooking was done on charcoal, in a row of small grated ovens set into the kitchen wall. We had little sheet-iron stoves to heat the rooms in winter which burned olivewood although, looking out over the barren country, one wondered where the wood could possibly come from.

There were copper utensils in the kitchen and lovely copper dishes, the finest of which came from Damascus.

Our native cooks were taught to make American dishes, but we had only the local foodstuffs and soon learned to like the native cooking. We had no potatoes, but rice and cracked wheat, cone sugar—solid and very pure—and plenty of vegetables. We never ate anything raw that was not peeled, or lettuce unless it was grown in our own garden. But we had radishes, and a squash called *cusa*, like vegetable marrow. Cusa was cooked with tomato sauce and mutton, or prepared as *cusa mashy*, when it is stuffed with meat and rice, a dish we loved. Mutton and fowl were our only meats.

Mo'a lubi, meaning "upside down," was another native dish we liked. It was made by putting a layer of chopped mutton roasted in butter in the saucepan, then a layer of sliced and fried eggplant. The right amount of rice was added and seasoned with salt, pepper, a bit of cinnamon and allspice, with saffron to color the rice. This was boiled until dry, then the whole thing was turned upside down on a large copper dish and over it was poured melted semin in which snobar (pine-cone nuts) had been roasted.

Semin was goat's butter boiled until concentrated.

Joseph the milkman kept the goats, and his shepherd herded them in and out of the city. We had to boil all the milk, of course. Later we had our own flock of goats, and, still later, cattle.

Sundays we frequently had pancakes with *dibbis*, a molasses made of boiled-down grape juice.

We made American coffee for breakfast and tea in the afternoon. To Arab guests we served coffee in tiny cups, very strong, made in the Arab way. Once we offered one of our large cups of coffee to our Arab friend, Abu Nassib, and he was astonished. "What is this you are giving me—a cistern full?"

We had no servant problem in Jerusalem in those days.

Our cook was a Christian peasant woman from Ramallah. We had five servants, Miriam and her daughter Hannieh, and three young men who did the marketing, waiting on table, and other work. There was no electricity in Jerusalem, and cleaning and filling the kerosene lamps was a task that in itself took much time.

We had an ironing woman named Katrina. She used irons that were like little stoves. The charcoal was put inside the iron and lighted and by the time the fumes were gone, the iron was hot.

Rob wrote that our cook, Miriam, looked like a queen, and presided with as much grace and dignity over her fireplace as any lady in her drawing room. She wore the costume of the northern villages, a straight-cut gown of cream-colored hand-woven linen, heavily embroidered in cross-stitch in red with a touch of blue and green on the side seams, the back of the skirt, and breast. The square "breastplate" was heavily embroidered and very beautiful. A silken or woolen girdle around the waist and red leather heelless slippers completed the costume.

Most beautiful of all was the headdress of the married woman. Bits of cloth plaited into the hair made a firm foundation for the headdress, which consisted of a small, close-fitting cap quite unlike the tall headdress worn by the married Bethlehemite and southern peasants. On the cap was the dowry, of silver coins sewn closely together in such a way that they stood up. Some authorities say that this headdress may have been the inspiration for the halo to early artists. From it an elaborate silver chain or chains, with silver coins attached, hung down to the breast, culminating in one large silver coin, or, if the woman were of a wealthy family, a gold coin. Over this went the heavily embroidered veil or shawl, the "veil" Ruth wore when Boaz said: "Bring the veil that thou hast upon thee and hold it;" and when she held it he measured six measures of barley.

When Miriam and her daughter Hannieh were dressed in their Sunday best they were like pictures of beautiful women in Bible days.

We thought it a pity, when, around the turn of the century, the Palestine women began discarding their picturesque costumes in favor of European. The bright colors they loved, so becoming in native costumes, looked cheap and dowdy when used in European clothing.

Hannieh was a sort of under nurse and often took Flora and me walking. We loved going with her; we met other nurses and children in the Russian Compound and had delightful adventures.

One afternoon Father took me to the Holy Sepulcher. Near the entrance, at the Stone of Unction, I asked my astonished

father to wait, while I knelt, kissed the stone, and crossed myself.
"Roman Catholics do it that way," I explained.

Hannieh was Greek Orthodox.

Another time Father asked me where I should like to walk,
and I answered promptly, "To the Russian Cathedral, where
they serve refreshments."

He learned that we had been in the habit of going with Hannieh
to the Cathedral where hundreds of Russian pilgrims received
the sacrament from a large bowl of wine with bits of sacred bread
floating in it. I remember the priest would carry the bowl and
with a spoon he would shove a piece of the soaked bread into every
waiting mouth. Everyone was devout and exceedingly religious
during this ceremony, but Flora and I, not understanding, only
knew we liked eating the soaked bread.

This put an end to our strolls with Hannieh to the Holy Sepulcher and the Russian Cathedral.

In the narrow, exciting streets there were little cookshops that
sold *kebab* (*shish kebab* is the Turkish form), bits of meat, tomato,
and onion broiled on spikes. In the early spring bunches of
green chickpeas, roasted in the bread ovens, were sold. These
foods were sold to the peasants who came into the city to work,
and our nurses liked them, and we liked them too.

Father put a stop to all this.

That we did not contract some serious disease remains a
mystery. But we were healthy and robust children and as fascinated by our strange new surroundings as were our elders.

Of the three young men who were our original houseboys in
the American Colony, one is still with us after sixty-eight years,
and a loved and highly respected member of the Colony. Elias
must be nearly ninety by now.

One was dismissed after several years, and the front door still
bears the dents he made pounding with the iron knocker, hoping
he might wear us down and make us change our minds.

The next time we saw him, he was wearing the reversed collar
of a preacher. He had been to England, joined a small religious
sect, and was conducting a group of Bible students through the
Holy Land. He brought his party to visit the American Colony,
and on entering the front hall knelt and said, "Let us bray,"
and of course we children giggled.

The Arabic alphabet has no equivalent for the letter *p*, which
is often pronounced *b*. A cook we had used to say, "I can say *p*

but I don't know where to but it."

Maarouf, the third young man, was a Moslem, about eighteen years old. All our "help" came to morning prayers, and Maarouf's interest grew from day to day, until in 1884 he announced his wish to become a Christian.

Father knew the consequences that would follow—persecution and perhaps even death, but Maarouf seemed steadfast, and eventually he was prepared in the Christian faith and baptized by Father. All his family, except his mother, turned against Maarouf.

His stepfather was a muezzin who called the Faithful to prayer five times a day from a minaret near the Dome of the Rock. He felt that Maarouf's apostasy was an insult to the family and to himself in particular. The simplest and most effectual way to remove Maarouf from the scene was to request the Turkish Government to draft him into the army for five years of service.

We were helpless. We had no idea of surreptitiously hiding him, but evidently Maarouf's family thought we might have, and they appealed through Raouf Pasha, governor of Palestine, to our American Consul, Selah Merrill, who wrote Father a not unfriendly letter pointing out that the governor was requesting the delivery of a Turkish subject named Maarouf, and under existing treaties and regulations the United States could not prevent the delivery of Maarouf when he was called for. Father answered that we would certainly not detain Maarouf; in fact that his summons was expected. But it was a surprise to find that when the Turkish soldier came to arrest Maarouf he was accompanied by the American Consul's dragoman.

Maarouf was held in the Turkish barracks inside the Jaffa Gate. On April 1, 1884, as we were at supper, a man came with a scrap of paper on which was written a little note beginning "Dear sisters and brethren." It was from Maarouf, and I found it many years later in Father's desk. Maarouf and other prisoners were about to be taken to Damascus and at that moment were standing outside the Damascus Gate. Everyone hurried out to say good-by to Maarouf.

Mother wrote, "We found ourselves silently surrounding the dear boy."

All the recruits had their hands tied behind them, only Maarouf's were not tied at the wrists like the others, but by his thumbs. Later we heard this caused great suffering, for his thumbs became infected.

In this fashion Maarouf walked approximately three hundred miles to Damascus, where he was kept in solitary confinement, and beaten, to make him recant. Then tactics changed. He was taken to Beirut, treated with flattering consideration, and offered a government position and an advantageous marriage if he would give up his Christian faith.

Maarouf stood by his convictions. He managed to send several letters to Father. One read in part:

> . . . The Lord is teaching me many lessons and bringing me close to Him. They said to us that they are going to send us away to the place where the war was. But I am not attending to what they say. I am waiting to the dear Lord for deliverance. Anyway He want it only may I glorify His name in this thing. Salute the dear ones at home and my earthly mother comfort her for me. Salute the children.
>
> Your son, MAAROUF.

Then we learned that Maarouf was sent to Yemen, where the Arabs were continually rising against the Turkish rule, where the climate was unhealthy, and he could not be expected to survive the five years of hard military service. It must have seemed the easiest way to get rid of him.

The Turks were having difficulty. In 1881 Abdul-Hamid lost Tunisia to France, and the following year England occupied Egypt. The whole of North Africa was lost to Turkish domination with the exception of Libya. Arabia was a continual source of trouble.

Maarouf survived his five years in Arabia.

I remember being awakened in the dead of night by a great banging on the front door. Everyone in the Colony wakened, and when the door was opened, there stood a dirty, weary, and forlorn Turkish soldier, who said simply, "I am Maarouf."

When he was rested and fed and his beard shaved off, we could recognize the lad, now about twenty-two, who had been led away from the Damascus Gate with his thumbs tied at his back.

We children were much excited and made a great ado over our hero.

The respite was short. His stepfather heard Maarouf was back and began his old intrigues. Six months later Maarouf was again taken from us, this time as a reserve to quell the troubles in Crete. Across his *taskara*, or military paper, was written that he was never to be released because he was a 'kafir"—an unbeliever.

Maarouf was in the mountains of Candia for two years, but when the Greeks conquered the Turks, Maarouf took advantage of a midnight retreat. By slow degrees he got to Jaffa, to Jerusalem, and to the American Colony.

The stepfather heard Maarouf was home again. He was dumfounded, for he believed he had secured his permanent banishment and probably his death. He came to the American Colony, bringing Maarouf's mother and all his brothers and sisters.

"I see now," he said humbly to Maarouf, "that you have not changed your outer garment (religion) but it is a change of heart. If I work against you, now that I am convinced of this fact, I will be fighting against God. It is written—kismet. I have become your friend, and I respect you."

All our Moslem friends treated Maarouf in the same manner. He was received by his Moslem superiors as an equal. In the American Colony he was no longer regarded as a servant.

Another who was to live with us for the rest of her life was Wardy, a Greek Orthodox Arab woman who was John Whiting's nurse. John grew from babyhood to manhood and went away to the United States and returned again and Wardy was still part of the family. When she was taken ill, we nursed her, and when she died, and was prepared for burial, a ragged cap John had worn as a boy was found inside her clothing, next to her heart. "Tat-toot-mat-toot" was her absurd pet name for him; it was the last word on her lips.

These early days were stirring and eager for the Group from Chicago. The tempest brewing in Lake View had not yet burst over our innocent heads, and we were making new friends, both nativeborn and otherwise, for, as Father noted in his diary, "at one time or another the world and his wife come to Jerusalem. . . . Let no one think of the Holy City as out of the world. One has opportunities of meeting people one would never meet at home under normal circumstances."

The very day we were climbing the hill to our new home Father and Mother were stopped by one of the neighbors, who shook their hands. His name was Abu Ali, and he was the kavass, or guard, to the Russian Archimandrite. He welcomed them to this portion of the walled city and promised he would always be their friend. This promise was kept, and today the third and fourth generations of his family are just as loyal in friendship to the American Colony as was their great-grandfather, Abu Ali.

Father noted in his diary that on their first Sunday in Jerusalem he and Mother attended Christ Church, seat of the Anglican bishop, and met several of the leading men in the "Society for the Propagation of the Gospel Among the Jews." He wrote that on June 26, 1882, Raouf Pasha, the governor of Jerusalem, called at the American Colony, and that the next week he and Mr. Rudy, with Mr. Gargour as interpreter, returned the Pasha's call.

One of the first things Father did was to pay his respects to our American Consul in Jerusalem, the Rev. Selah Merrill, former Congregational minister of Andover, Massachusetts, who served from 1882 to 1886, and then, after four years of respite, returned to complete a tenure of office which, with one more break, covered eighteen years. Father's call was not returned, and as long as he remained in Jerusalem Mr. Merrill never set foot inside the American Colony Compound. In all those years his acrimony against the American Colony never abated, and his official position lent weight to his disapproval and increased his ability to do us harm.

Consuls in the East, before the Capitulations were abrogated, and especially for Americans who had extraterritorial rights, had enormous powers for good and evil. This was before the United States had a consular service as a career for trained men. Consuls were political appointees.

Mr. Merrill had definite ideas as a Congregational minister about how philanthropic work should be done, so he would have nothing to do with our Group. His resentment was hidden at first and did not disturb our serenity for several years.

But we were on friendly terms with all the other consular groups and especially the British Consul.

Father's notebook continues to hold accounts of walks of exploration within and outside Jerusalem's walls. He wrote of going to the "Valley of Hinnom . . . returning by the village of Siloam and back through the Zion Gate." He tells of a trip on horseback to Bethlehem, with Mother tumbling from her horse several times on the way, until she learned the poor beast had "the staggers." They enjoyed many interesting journeys in these early years, and Father never tired of his rambling trips of discovery.

CHAPTER SEVEN

JERUSALEM in those days was a medieval city, snugly crowded within its walls and only beginning to spread its suburbs beyond.

It is generally believed that Salem, to whose king, Melchizedek, Abraham gave tithes (Genesis 14), was Jerusalem. Apart from this, the earliest records referring to this city are the cuneiform Tell el-Amarna tablets, written about 1400 B.C. to the King of Egypt.

Later the King of Jerusalem is named as one of the five who undertook to punish the Gibeonites for making their truce with Joshua. To help the Gibeonites Joshua came and defeated the confederation (Joshua 10). Later, in Samuel, we read: "David took the stronghold of Zion, the same is the city of David."

This first small Jebuzite settlement was situated near the Virgin's Fount, the only living water near Jerusalem.

According to some scholars, but not universally accepted, David, learning that the Jebuzites had a tunnel by which they drew up the water from the Virgin's Fount, boldly conceived the plan to surprise them that way, and succeeded. What is believed to be that tunnel has been discovered. The Jebuzite village then became the national capital and in time Jerusalem was the religious center.

Titus destroyed Jerusalem in A.D. 70 so thoroughly that it was plowed with salt so that nothing would grow. It even lost its name at one time under Hadrian and for several centuries was called Eelya Capitulina.

The city has had one of the most checkered careers in history, having suffered something like fifty sieges. Some of these made only slight changes; others resulted in partial and even total destruction, filling up the valleys and greatly altering the city's aspect.

The miracle is that Jerusalem has survived.

The Valley of Kedron separates the city from the Mount of Olives to the east, while the Valley of Hinnom, which starts on the west side, protects the city there and then swings eastward

to join the Kedron, so furnishing sufficient defense on the south
side. The vulnerable point has always been the north, where
no valley guards the city, and where at two different periods
suburbs grew up which needed defense. Hence in Roman times
the north side had three walls. It is noteworthy that almost
every attempt against Jerusalem except Allenby's has been
directed from the north side, from which point alone it has
been successfully taken.

The Tyropean Valley runs north to south through the city
and is filled up near the southern end to a depth of ninety feet.
It was across this valley that Josephus tells of two viaducts
spanning the valley which enabled those in the Upper City
to get to the Lower City and Temple.

The present city walls are Saracen and date from 1542 and
are the work of Suleiman the Magnificent. They vary in height
from thirty to seventy-five feet, and follow in part the line
of wall of Christ's day, especially on the east side. A goodly
section on the south, which now lies outside the walls including
the Pool of Siloam, was within the walls in Solomon's day.
The present south wall probably follows the line of the Crusader's south wall limit.

Few cities can claim rampart walls of such perfect preserva-
tion. These picturesque battlements narrowly escaped demoli-
tion by Djemal Pasha, who was Turkish Generalissimo of the
campaign against the British in 1914—17. *Demolire* was one
of his favorite words. I heard him say that he intended to give
Jerusalem fresh air by demolishing the city walls and make
it more modern by hacking a boulevard, which would of course
bear his name, from the Jaffa Gate to the Temple area. Such
"hacking" might have uncovered much of antiquity that would
have been of inestimable archaeological value, but at a time
when no one was there to record it scientifically, and it would
have been immediately and irretrievably lost.

The last fifty years have done much to obscure the western
and northwestern sections of the wall by the erection of huge
buildings hard against it, but this has been stopped, and recently
some of the unsightly modern buildings near the Jaffa Gate
have been pulled down, exposing the old ramparts. During
the recent civil war many of these buildings belonging to Arabs
and Armenians were demolished by the Israeli army.

January 17, 1883, a letter by Aunt Maggie told of the new
buildings going up in and around Jerusalem:

The activity of rebuilding is by no means confined to the Jews. Catholics, Greeks, Mohammedans, and Protestants are all taking part in it. There are at the present time more than one hundred buildings going up, all of stone, and most of them of carefully cut stone. The new method is to use iron girders to support the ceiling. This is then covered with French tiles instead of the older and more picturesque dome roof.

Each house had its cistern, Jerusalem's only water supply. Aunt Maggie said she believed the new tile roofs became so popular because they afforded an increased area for collecting water.

She tells of the Grand New Hotel, then being built, just inside the Jaffa Gate opposite the Tower of David, with an arcade and shops below. All were being built by the Greek Orthodox father who was the treasurer of the Holy Sepulcher.

Still deeper inside the old city he built massive blocks of shops with chambers overhead, covering the site of the Crusader inns, hospitals, and churches, especially those of the Knights of Saint John of Jerusalem. Inside the Jaffa Gate the Franciscans were finishing their church, with a clock tower adjoining which "will contain chimes of bells." I remember Father took me up on the scaffolding of the church tower before the tower was finished, and I was frightened but would not acknowledge it because I was thrilled at being treated like a big girl.

Near this church the Franciscans were also erecting large buildings to accommodate priests and pilgrims, and workshops for the employment of men of the community. The French hospital building was outside the morth city wall—its first story barely finished when we came. Adjoining it the French Catholics were building a large, expensive stone structure called the Notre Dame de France to accommodate six hundred pilgrims.

One hotel was building an addition to be used as a restaurant, for there was not a restaurant in Jerusalem except the "cook-shops," where people bought native food.

Aunt Maggie wrote again in 1883 that on the Jaffa-Jerusalem Road, more than thirty miles long because of its winding course up the hills, about four thousand men, women, and children were employed making a new road. In places they followed the old cobblestone road, which in turn followed the still older Roman road. Near the little village of Kulonia they built a beautiful arched stone bridge over the watercourse, which is dry in summer but in winter swells to a dangerous torrent.

From this watercourse, but lower down where it reaches

the plain, David picked the five stones that killed Goliath.

Nearing Jerusalem the Jaffa Road becomes "main street." It was treeless, with long lines of ugly houses put up cheaply for the incoming Jews, over which a good deal of speculation was practiced as their demand increased.

The British Consulate, where our friends the Moore family lived, was the last house west on the Jaffa Road. Two stucco lions stood before the gate. It became a police station during the British Mandate.

Opposite the British Consulate—on the Jaffa Road—a half-built house stood. Years later it was completed and used as the Municipal Hospital, and still later, after the British occupation, it became the headquarters of the Public Health Department. The reason it remained unfinished so long is another of Jerusalem's tales.

It was being built, about the time we arrived, as the future home of a couple about to be married. The young man was the only son of an Arab Roman-Catholic family who lived near our home in Haret-es-Sa'ad-ieh. Before the wedding took place he died. Mother attended the funeral services, where the actions of the heart-broken parents can be attributed only to wild and uncontrolled hysteria.

The mourners gathered in the room where the dead man was propped up in a chair and his lovely young bride was brought up to him, gorgeously decorated with jewels and flowers and wearing an elaborate brocade dress and the customary wedding veil. The "joy shout" was raised by the mourners, or guests, and his mother danced before the couple with a lighted candle in each hand, the traditional dance the mother and relatives perform before a bridal pair.

"It is my duty to dance," she repeated, and the guests joined in, "Yes, it is your duty."

As she finished her dance she tore her clothes, gave the terrible death cry, and snatched the veil from the bride's face.

Then the corpse was laid in the coffin and the funeral ceremony held.

Mother came home shaken by the spectacle. The violent demonstration of grief evidently killed the mother, for she died soon after. So one more house stood unfinished for many years in Jerusalem.

On what is now the Street of the Prophets but was then called the "back road" was the house where Holman Hunt, the pre-Raphaelite artist, had lived with his family while painting some of his most famous pictures, including the "Shadow of Death," or "The Shadow of the Cross," a robed figure standing in the sunset with arms lifted, casting a shadow of a cross. Many of Hunt's pictures, painted in and around Jerusalem, were reproduced in two large volumes, *Pre-Raphaelism and the Pre-Raphaelite Brotherhood*. He was gone when we came, but we heard many anecdotes about the famous artist and met many of his models; I remember particularly a converted Jewish girl whose waving golden hair he had copied for the Christ in one of his paintings.

The "back road" was muddy or dusty according to the season of the year.

The London Jews' Society had a small house on the "back road" in a large compound which was used as a camping ground in summer by the English missionairies. Later the English Mission Hospital and girls' school were built there. As I write this it is being used by the Hadassah Hospital as their buildings on Mount Scopus are in the Arab zone. The Mission House and the home of the clergyman, Mr. Kelk, stood conspicuously in a large garden.

The Arabic Church, belonging to the Church Missionary Society, stood apart, not surrounded by houses as it is now.

There was then no *Mea Shearim*, in Hebrew, "One Hundred Gates", which became such a blight on the landscape and where so much of the fighting took place in 1947—48 between Jews and Arabs. There is a tragic story connected with the construction of these hundred houses. They were not built by Jews, as might be supposed, since they became a one-hundred-per-cent Jewish quarter, but by a Swiss banker who thought the return of the Jews to Jerusalem was imminent but was not too pious to make a little money out of it, so he bought up all the property on the measuring line supposedly laid down in Jeremiah 31:38—40 and put up rows of rooms, each room with a small kitchen attached and intended to hold a family. These dwellings were sold to the newcomers who flocked to Palestine in consequence of the Russian persecutions, which became almost a hegira about 1882.

This banker built a magnificent residence for his large family where we enjoyed playing with his children in their nursery and garden, which was filled with many toys and other equipment for play and where one of the boys who used to tease me was

Frederick Vester, whom I later married.

I remember Father remonstrating with the banker for speculating with the prophecies and before long he did come to grief.

Every once in a while Sultan Abdul-Hamid of Turkey would become alarmed at the great influx of Jews into Palestine and issue an order that the immigration must stop. I remember how distressed Mother and Father would be whenever they heard this, knowing of the hardships the immigrants must endure. The Jewish people would leave their ships at Jaffa in rowboats to be taken to shore, as there was no harbor, only to find the Turkish authorities would not let them land. They would be rowed back to the ship, where the captain would not accept them. Between boat and shore they were taken back and forth, and eventually landed when the bribe, under these trying conditions, had grown as large as could be extracted. Then pressure would be brought to bear on Constantinople by a great power, and the doors of Palestine would open again, until again, suddenly, and without warning, another order would clamp down on whatever unlucky group arrived at that inopportune moment, and they, in turn, would be caught between the upper and nether millstones.

It was during one of these periods, when Palestine was closed to the Jews, that the Swiss banker found he had bought property too lavishly. The poor man was forced into bankruptcy. The mansion he once occupied is now the Evelina de Rothschild School for Girls.

Some distance to the south of Jerusalem was a cluster of houses known as the German Templar Colony. Few buildings were between it and the Jaffa Gate, so it stood conspicuous and alone. These people were Unitarians who had left Germany to obtain religious freedom, drifted to Palestine, and founded colonies.

In 1881 the hills around Jerusalem, so thickly populated now, were open fields where we picked wild flowers in the spring.

Ras Abu Tor, or the "Hill of Evil Council," was marked by a large dark green mace or hackberry tree on which Judas was supposed to have hanged himself. I remember being afraid of that tree and thinking how wicked it looked. It vanished, and Ras Abu Tor became covered with modern buildings. The hill has seen much fighting in recent years and little is left of the buildings now.

Two windmills were conspicuous in the Jerusalem landscape,

one built by Sir Moses Montefiore, who also built near by the row of houses used for the accommodation of poor Jews rent free, still called the Montefiore Quarter.

After the Montefiore mill was built no one knew how to set the sails and Cousin Rob was called in. He made a study of windmills and did his best, but the mill was only partially successful. The other, the property of the Greek Orthodox Convent, is now part of Rehavia, the large new Jewish settlement.

No buildings existed in those days between this windmill and the Convent of the Cross, the fortresslike monastery on the traditional spot where the tree grew from which was made the Cross of Calvary. Now the solid mass of buildings there is Rehavia.

The Convent of the Cross was used as a seminary for Greek Orthodox students, who, after graduating, were eligible to become members of the Brotherhood of the Holy Sepulcher. From this Brotherhood the Orthodox Patriarch was chosen when he had risen to the proper ecclesiastical rank. An Arab could never become a Patriarch of the Orthodox Church because Arabs were not permitted to attend the seminary. This was and still is the burning controversy between clergy and Arab laity.

The olive grove surrounding the Convent of the Cross, *Musalaby*, as the convent is called in Arabic, was one of our favorite resorts for picnics and we children loved to go there. In one of the upstairs rooms there was a sort of museum. One of the exhibits was a rather moth-eaten stuffed lion with staring glass eyes, said to have been killed in one of the nearby valleys. I often begged to be taken to the convent, and the lion was the attraction. I would hold tightly to Father's hand and keep my eyes shut until we came before the lion, then I would open them quickly and stand transfixed by that menacing glassy stare. In my mind I was convinced that this was the actual lion that had not eaten Daniel, but I was scared because I wasn't sure he wouldn't eat me. I was no saint like Daniel, of that I was sure.

The Russian Compound outside the walls northwest of the city was much as it is now, only the glaring new white stone has mellowed with age and the saplings of cypress and pine are grown to large trees, and there are fewer of them. A strong wall surrounds the cathedral, hospital, consular residence, and hospices for pilgrims.

Enormous crowds of Russian pilgrims trekked through Palestine in those days and up until World War I. They began to gather in Jerusalem at Christmastime—we saw them that first Christmas in 1881—and by Easter there would be between fifteen and twenty thousand. They came on foot in large caravans, always escorted by a kavass on horseback, heading the procession, while another brought up the rear. These were generally in Cossack or Montenegrin costume and looked fierce but very grand, and as a child I imagined them to be generals at the very least. Many of these pilgrims had beautiful voices and sang and chanted as they walked along.

After the Holy Fire, which takes place on the Saturday before the Greek Easter, there would be a great scramble among them to get away by carriage and, in later years, on the narrow-gauge railroad to Jaffa, the port of embarkation.

The Russian State Church was Greek Orthodox and encouraged these pilgrimages by building hospices as accommodations in many of the Palestine cities and in remote spots which marked holy sites. In these the pilgrims could be housed and served hot water in samovars and leave a few kopeks when they departed. The Imperial Russian Government also subsidized the steamers that brought the pilgrims from Odessa on the Black Sea to Jaffa and back again to Russia.

The pilgrims had little money individually, but because of their vast numbers they contributed the major part of the support of the Greek Orthodox Convent and Holy Sepulcher in Jerusalem and the hospices. They created a demand for all kinds of trinkets, and many kinds of industries in the manufacture of souvenirs gave occupation to the inhabitants of Jerusalem and Bethlehem. Candle-dippers worked the year round to have a supply equal to the demands of the thousands of Russian, Greek, Armenian, Coptic, and Macedonian pilgrims who attended the annual celebration of the Holy Fire. Then there were the makers of ikons and mother-of-pearl and olivewood trinkets. Shroud makers made a good living stenciling black skulls and crossbones on white muslin to be worn by the Russian pilgrims when they were dipped in the Jordan River at the Feast of Epiphany, and eventually to be used when they were buried, and they would carry back dipped shrouds to their relatives and friends. They believed by symbolic washing they would obtain a blessing because it was there the Lord was baptized.

The Russian pilgrimages that were part of life in Palestine and supported so many families ceased with World War I and the Russian Revolution.

In a letter dated 1885 Aunty wrote:

. . . on the very summit of Olivet the Russians have begun to build a tower.
It is said it will be one hundred and sixty-two feet high when completed,
and from its top they hope to see the Mediterranean and the Dead Sea.
A 12,000-pound bell, cast in Russia, was brought for the tower. It was
drawn from Jaffa to the top of the Mount of Olives last winter by Russian
pilgrims, mostly women. It took them three weeks to get it to its destination.
These Russian peasants have beautiful voices and they chanted the whole
way. They changed places every few minutes, the rested taking the places
of the tired.

I remember the day the bell passed below our house on its
way to Gethsemane. We all went up on the roof and watched and
listened. The singing reached us and was very sweet. Before the
faithful workers was still the great pull up Olivet, but they were
cheerful, waved to us on the roof, and proceeded with their
precious load.

A slaughterhouse stood where the Dominican Monastery and
Church of Saint Stephan now stand in their lovely tree-shaded
grounds, the supposed site of the stoning of Saint Stephan. As
the prevailing wind in summer is northwest, we in our home on
the city wall at times got the full discomfort of the dreadful
stench. It was a happy relief when the property was bought by
the Dominican Fathers and the slaughterhouse was moved to the
Valley of the Kedron. The Fathers soon began their excavations
and unearthed a number of tombs. I remember they had a narrow-
gauge and hand-propelled railway to carry the debris away, and
I often stole a ride on it, for it was the nearest thing to a railroad
I could remember.

Mamilla Road, now one of the principal business streets of
Jerusalem, was then an insignificant lane. It improved near the
corner, where the present Saint Julian's Way crosses it. A large
house on the corner was used by Thomas Cook and Son for their
tent-equipment depot. Everyone traveled on horseback in those
days and needed tents. It was expensive to travel in comfort,
but you were not whisked from Dan to Beersheba in a day, so
that you were likely to forget, as did one tourist I recently met,
whether you saw the Church of the Nativity in Bethany or Bethlehem.

Farther west on Mamilla Road the only residence belonged to
the Vester family, where lived the twelve-year-old boy I would
eventually marry. Mr. Ferdinand Vester, Senior, his father,
came to Palestine in 1853 as a Lutheran missionary, and lived

first, like all Europeans then, inside the city walls. In 1868 he
had considered the country safe enough to settle outside. Bishop
Gobat had built his school outside the walls on Mount Zion,
and others were taking the risk of building out where the air was
fresher and the houses less crowded together. My future husband
was born in the new house in 1869. It is now the Consulate
General of the United States.

A conspicuous landmark on Mamilla Road near what is now
King George Avenue was a huge mysterious building, unfinished
then, and still unfinished after nearly three quarters of a century.
It was known as the "Home of the Hundred and Forty-four
Thousand." Of excellent masonry, the large stones well cut, it
bespoke large sums sunk in a visionary but frustrated enterprise.

It was built by a rich Dutch lady, a countess, who had come
to Jerusalem in the late seventies and bought the land through
an agent and in his name, since it was against Turkish law for
a foreigner to own property in Palestine.

She evidently possessed an *idee fixe*, as do so many who come
to the Holy Land, for she felt an exaggerated responsibility for
housing the ransomed souls spoken of in Revelation 7:4. The
massive and expensive foundations testify as to the enormous size
of the planned structure. The venture was interrupted by the
Serbian War, and the countess returned to Holland to equip and
command a company of soldiers to help fight the "Infidel Turk,"
doubtless expecting to see the Turkish Government's removal as
custodian of the Holy Land.

I do not know what became of her plans for a personal army,
but after the Serbian War ended she returned to Jerusalem and
stayed for a time as a guest of the American Colony. I remember
her quite well indeed; one could not easily forget such a person.
She was tall and masculine-looking, with a few hairs growing on
each side of her mouth that increased her masculinity, but she
had a very real feminine love for pretty clothes. She wore her
long hair piled fashionably on the top of her head and dresses
with long, enveloping skirts under which were heavy boots that
made such a loud clopclopping when she walked that I wondered
if they were not topboots.

One afternoon some Turkish officers called on Father. Tea
was announced, and the countess came, as usual, into our drawing room. Father rose to introduce her to his guests, but at sight
of them the countess stood rigid. Her dark eyes snapped fire and
the atmosphere in the room was electrified. This was the field of

battle, where enemy met enemy.

Father, having no idea as to the cause of this, tried to say something to ease the situation.

The countess finally spoke. "This is a house of peace and I offer my old enemy my hand."

Soon after this the countess left Jerusalem.

Her martial undertakings had taken most of her money and she was unable to complete the house on Mamilla Road. For years there was litigation over the monstrous pile, with the agent claiming possession, and finally winning, after her death. The ruin stands, a monument to another of the strange dreams in Jerusalem.

The year after our arrival, in 1882, the Turkish Government began to repair the streets and improve the sewers. By 1883 they had made an important beginning and were digging the foundations for some shops just outside the Jaffa Gate, on the new Jaffa Road.

I remember quite well being taken by Father to watch these improvements. At the Damascus Gate near our house we could see where Roman pavement was exposed about fifteen feet below the present level of the street. "Look down, Bertha," I can still hear Father saying; "that is the very pavement our Lord and Saint Paul walked upon." The Roman cobblestones were still there, unbroken.

The mayor who made these improvements was Salem Effendi al Husseini, who held the post for eighteen years, and both of whose sons, Musa Kazim Pasha and Hussein Effendi, also in time became mayors of Jerusalem. It was Hussein Effendi who capitulated to the British on December 9, 1917 and delivered the letter of surrender to General Sir John Shea on that memorable day, at which I was privileged to be present.

Before Cook's on Mamilla Road was a beautiful old terebinth tree. This spot had been used for public executions by decapitation, but by the time we arrived the Turks had abolished capital punishment and fifteen years' imprisonment was the sentence for murder. There was a legend that when the tree died it would signal the end of Turkish rule in Palestine. Every care was taken to preserve it: iron bands were fastened around its trunk and props placed under its branches.

By strange coincidence, in 1917, the year Allenby's victorious entry marked the end of the Turkish rule in Palestine, this tree did die.

The valley outside the wall under our house we called "Our Valley." About halfway up the hill between our door and the Damascus Gate the ruin of a Crusader clinic was now used as a pottery. The potter was an Orthodox Jew who wore the little skullcap, beard, and side curls. He was very good to us. His son Chaim was about my age and one of our playmates.

The potter taught us how to shape pottery and turn the wheel, and we made and baked our own dishes and ate from them when we gave "play parties." We children often picnicked over an open fire in "Our Valley." One of the elders lowered our tea in a basket on a rope over the wall, which was about sixty or seventy feet high at this point and twelve feet wide. Our Arab nurses taught us to cook over the open fire.

We invited Father to our outdoor teas, but when he accepted Mother insisted upon our having baked potatoes. She drew the line at letting him eat our messes. The Arabs, like the French, eat snails, and once we were going to be very clever and cook some. We did, and I hated to eat them, but I forced myself to and was terribly ill.

The old moats surrounding the city wall were filled in with rubbish, especially near the Jaffa Gate and the Damascus Gate, where they were still being used as dumps. Carcasses of dead animals were brought there to be devoured by pariah dogs, but, even worse, living animals, worn-out or disabled, were left there to suffer until slow death brought relief.

Several times Father and Rob went out and put poor dying beasts out of their misery. Each time the owners promptly put in an appearance, clamoring for compensation. They demanded, and received, the price of a healthy animal.

Directly below our house was Solomon's Quarries.

The entrance was an opening in the ground about three feet high. Cousin Rob set out alone one day to explore the excavations made by King Solomon. It is supposed that the stone to build the Temple came from these quarries. It is very white, and Josephus describes the Temple as "a mountain of snow."

Rob wrote of his adventure:

I took a lantern and a ball of string and started in. The bats flew past my face by the hundred, but I kept on, tied my string fast, and went through blackness, room after room, from which stone had been cut.

He saw marks of ancient iron picks on the walls, and wandered

on and on, even after his string ran out. But he knew this subterranean roving was dangerous, so he finally retraced his steps.
He had entered the quarry in daylight and when he came out
it was night. The quarries ran underground from the north end
almost to the Dome of the Rock.

Another time Rob wrote:

> The other day we were visiting a vineyard outside the city, on the north
> side. In the vineyard was a rock-hewn tomb. (Rob is not describing the so-
> called Garden Tomb but another tomb of earlier date).
> You go down a hill to the entrance, enter a large room hewn from solid
> rock where a cistern opens, then another doorway you stoop to enter, as in
> the Bible "stooping down" you descend three steps into another room. In
> this, niches were cut to hold bodies, and in the center was a shallow place
> cut about ten inches deep. . . .
> On such a place the Lord was laid. I tell you, this sight made me feel the
> nearness of God. . . .

North of the Damascus Gate on the Nablus Road is the
"Tombs of the Kings." The name is misleading; it is not, as
one would think, the tombs of the kings of Judah, but the tomb
of Queen Helena of Adiabene in Asia Minor, who became a
convert to Judaism and whose philanthropic distribution of help
in time of the famine spoken of in The Acts won the respect of
the Jews. Here she was buried, with her sons and grandsons,
in this masterpiece of man's workmanship. The tomb has enormous courts and steps leading down and reservoirs with the rock-
cut gutters to conduct the rain water to them—which was used
for the washing of the dead—all hewn out of solid rock. Beautiful
carvings adorn the outside of the tomb. Here was an example
of the "rolling stone" in perfect condition.

Rob wrote of his first visit to the Church of the Holy Sepulcher,
"rather hodgepodge from being destroyed and repaired so many
times":

> Thousands come to worship here from all parts of the world. This alone
> makes it sacred. But on entering you see Turkish custodians sitting cross-
> legged on an elevated platform. Just think of its being necessary, in the most
> sacred church of Christendom, to place a lot of these men there to keep
> Christians from fighting.

This church, so familiar to us as children, had a large courtyard and Rob describes the way it was "always crowded with
vendors of rosaries, relics, pictures, and the endless little knick-
knacks of olivewood made for the tourists and pilgrims, and the

miserable-looking beggars raised the cry of 'baksheesh' with redoubled vigor there."

Rob wrote that "it was impossible to imagine the wealth represented in the Church of the Holy Sepulcher, with its costly images, jeweled halos, and altars covered with precious articles of gemmed silver and gold."

So little of Jerusalem lay outside the walls in 1881 that I remember Mother saying that she could look out from our roof over the Damascus Gate and count the buildings outside the walls on the fingers of her two hands. Looking from our roof now it seems unbelievable that such a change could have taken place in sixty-eight years. Jerusalem is at least ten times larger.

Beyond the walls were a few scattered buildings, with fields and olive groves between and unpaved roads that were dusty in summer and rivers of mud in winter.

As a child I picked flowers outside the walls, first the big anemones with long stems—one must go far to find them now—then the red ranunculus with its tinge of yellow; later the scarlet poppy with its black cross. These carpeted the fields, and we came to believe the "lilies of the field that toil not" were meant to mean Palestine's flowers in the aggregate and not one individual flower. The flowers begin in March and reach their peak of color in April and May. Then the drought comes, and there are few flowers in summer.

We longed for green as we longed for rain. The principal trees were olives, their silvery green too often veiled in dust. Palms and citrus were along the coast, but it was too cold for these in Jerusalem. A few palms survived ancient planting. Later, when we moved our residence outside the walls, we planted palms in the garden.

Sometimes summer started early and other years we would have a late spring. Mother's first letters home speak of "brazen skies without a cloud," and in our first May, she wrote with delight that we had rain, "an almost unheard-of thing here."

About half a mile north of the Damascus Gate is the Sheik Jarah Mosque, supposed to be named for the surgeon of Saladin's army. Jarah means surgeon in Arabic, and he may have been the identical Jarah sent to King Richard by Saladin, made immortal in Lord Beaconfield's *Tancred*.

Between the mosque and the Damascus Gate in those days there was a still smaller mosque or *weli* dedicated to two lovers,

Sa'ad and Se'ed. During Whitsuntide the olive groves surrounding this shrine would be filled with Christian, Moslem, and
Jewish picnickers. They brought out their tom-toms and other
musical instruments, pitched tents, and spent a happy and carefree week in a way that has quite disappeared.

Close to the Sheik Jarah Mosque was a cluster of houses
surrounded by large vineyards where grape clusters grew, as
they will in Palestine, some three and four and a half feet long.
Several of these houses, since enlarged, are now the American
Colony. The largest was bought from the Husseini family. This
is one of the oldest Moslem families in Palestine. They claim
descent from Hussein, one of the two sons of Fatima, the Prophet
Mohammed's only daughter.

In one of these houses lived Rabbah Effendi, who was, I suppose, the richest and therefore the most powerful member of
this large family. He was an old man when we knew him; he
was still head of his clan. One story his family loved to tell about
him was that many years before he gave a picnic in one of the
vineyards. It must have been about May, for it was the season
of ripe *mish-mish*, as apricots are called in Arabic.

In those days the summit of the Mount of the Olives, reaching
as far as Bethany, was covered with mish-mish trees. The trees
were later demolished by a scourge of locusts which visited
Palestine in 1864, and they were never replanted, because of the
severity of the Turkish law taxing fruit-bearing or any trees from
the date of planting.

One of the guests at the picnic was the "Father of Wind," as
the sheik of the village on the summit of Olivet was appropriately
named. He brought a large basket of the ripe mish-mish as a
present to his host, Rabbah Effendi, who said to his guests:

"Shall I divide this fruit among you with the justice of God or
the justice of man?"

"With the justice of God!" the guests shouted in unison.

So Rabbah Effendi gave to one man a single apricot, to others
two, to another twenty, or five, and so on in a seemingly hap-
hazard manner. If a guest tried to protest, Rabbah Effendi put
up his hand for silence until he had finished his work of division.
Then a burst of protest came from his guests. "We asked for
the justice of God!"

Their host stopped them with dignity. "Is this not the way
God divides His bounty?"

CHAPTER EIGHT

JACOB ELIAHU was two years younger than my cousin Rob and his closest friend. His parents were Sephardic of Spanish Jews who had come to Palestine from Turkey, and were among the first converts made by the London Mission to Jews, i.e., London Jews' Society, in Jerusalem. Jacob was born in Ramallah, a village about twelve miles north of Jerusalem, where his mother had gone to escape a cholera epidemic then raging in the Holy City.

He was seventeen years old and a pupil-teacher in the Boys' School conducted by the London Mission when he left the mission and came to live with us in the American Colony. Father continued his education, and a year later I found a note of Father's: "During family prayers on July 9, 1883, Rob and Jacob were formally adopted to be our children."

Later he took our name and assumed great responsibilities in the American Colony as Jacob Spafford.

Jacob was above the average in intellect, with the oriental aptitude for languages. He spoke five fluently, with a partial knowledge of several others. He was interested in archaeology, and the year before we came to Jerusalem he discovered the Siloam Inscription.

The year before our arrival, when Jacob was sixteen and a scholar in the Boys' School of the London Mission to the Jews, his imagination was fired by learning about the subterranean tunnel in the Ophal Hill that had been excavated by King Hezekiah to bring water inside the threatened city. King Hezekiah lived in what is called the Middle Iron Age, or early Iron Age II, and when threatened with siege by the King of Assyria.

Hezekiah took council with his princes and his mighty men to stop the waters of the fountain which were without the city, and they did help him. (II Chronicles XXXII:3.) And the rest of the acts of Hezekiah and all his might, and how he made a pool and a conduit and brought water into the city. . . . Are they not written in the book of Chronicles of the Kings of Judah? (II Kings XX:20.)

On the approach of Sennacherib, Hezekiah diverted the spring through the tunnel that pierces the hill sinuously and empties its waters into the Pool of Siloam; by covering up the spring the water was thus insured for the city but made inaccessible to the enemies. (II Chronicles 32:2-4.) From the overflow of these waters the King's gardens were sustained.

The tunnel therefore ran from what was now called the Virgin's Fount or Well to the Pool of Siloam.

The Virgin's Fount was the small living spring where, it is quite certain, the first small Jebuzite settlement stood that became Jerusalem, and the women of the city drew water and did their washing there.

It is supposed to be haunted by a dragon or genie. Even in Biblical times Nehemiah referred to it as "the Dragon Well."

Nevertheless, Jacob determined to explore the tunnel.

Because of its reputation for being haunted he had some trouble persuading his friend Sampson, a boy about his own age, to explore it with him, but at last he was persuaded. The boys kept their plan a profound secret.

They had no idea of the height or width or length of the tunnel, nor how deep the water. They prepared floats with candle and matches attached, and tied these around their necks with strings. Jacob started from the Pool of Siloam side while Sampson entered from the Virgin's Fount. Their plan was to meet in the middle.

Jacob found himself in total darkness and muddy water up to his chin. It was cold and drafty in the tunnel, his candle blew out, his float with the matches submerged in the water, and he could not relight the candle. But he kept on, guiding his way by keeping his hand on the damp stone wall and feeling under his fingertips the marks of ancient chisels going forward, from right to left.

The tunnel he followed forms an enormous and irregular *S*, a fact that has puzzled archaeologists. Why did the King's engineers follow this crooked course and not a straight line? Père Vincent wrote of this "wonderful installation" in his book *Underground Jerusalem:* "Its curious form arouses curiosity. Why this long, winding circuit? Being almost a semicircle, instead of a straight line direct from the spring?" M. Clermont-Ganneau, the French archaeologist, suggested that the great sweep of curve might be to avoid the rock-hewn tombs of the Kings of Judah.

Jacob, feeling his way, suddenly was conscious that the chisel marks had changed and were now going from left to right. He realized he must be in the exact place where the King's workmen had met under the city. Carefully he felt all around the walls, and was certain that his fingers detected an inscription chiseled in the stone.

He hurried through the watery tunnel to tell Sampson. A point of light shone ahead and he knew that he must have reached the other end and was coming out at the Virgin's Fount where he was certain Sampson would be waiting. He did not know Sampson had long since abandoned his friend and gone back to school.

Jacob rose out of the pool dripping muddy water and half blind from the dark tunnel, and dimly perceived many figures about. Among them was a lad about Sampson's size. Jacob clutched him, crying: "Sampson, I have succeeded!"

It was not Sampson but a peasant boy, who thought the genie of the tunnel had captured him, and collapsed into the water in a dead faint.

The women about the pool, filling their jars with water and doing their washing, nearly tore Jacob to pieces. He ran for his life, followed by their screamed curses.

When he reached school, he confessed the escapade to the head master. He expected punishment. Instead, his report of an inscription in the Siloam tunnel caused a sensation in the school and throughout Jerusalem. Plans were soon afoot to investigate, but before they were completed a Greek with an eye to financial gain entered the tunnel by night and blasted the inscription out of the solid rock, breaking it in the process. Before he was able to spirit it away the Turkish authorities captured him. He paid for the theft, and the inscription is now in the museum at Istanbul, with the crack plainly across it.

The inscription is not on a separate piece of stone but crudely cut in the wall, very likely by one of the workmen. Its translation was published by the *Palestine Exploration Fund Quarterly Statement* for July 1881:

Behold the excavation. Now this has been the history of the excavation. While the workmen were still lifting up the pick, each toward his neighbor, and while three cubits still remained to be cut through, each heard the voice of the other who called to his neighbor since there was an excess of rock on the right hand and on the left. And on the day of the excavation the workmen struck each to meet his neighbor pick against pick and there flowed the waters from the spring to the pool for a thousand two hundred cubits and a hundred cubits was the height of the rock over the head of the workmen.

Professor Sayce, the great archaeological authority, described the Siloam Inscription as the oldest record of Biblical Hebrew yet discovered. Subsequent discoveries, the Samaria Ostraka, for example, are older.

My foster brother often told the thrilling story of the Siloam Inscription. But Jacob spoke of the discovery as made by "a schoolboy." He seldom mentioned the fact, well known to archaelogists, that he was that boy.

Jacob was one of my teachers.

I always say I was educated in spots, but I found many who enjoyed a regulated curriculum who feel the same way.

When the late Dr. Mary E. Wooley, president of Holyoke College where my daughter Tanetta graduated, asked me to address her students, I was warned I might find the girls inattentive or blasé. I made up my mind to shock them into listening, and opened my talk with the assertion that I had never been to school a day in my life.

I had no trouble holding their attention after that.

On another occasion an association of university women in Jerusalem asked me to join. I was pleased that the kind ladies should consider me eligible, and startled them, I think, by confessing that I had not only never attended a university, I had never attended any school, only a kindergarten.

This was the kindergarten of Miss Clara Johanna Brooke, the English missionary who was headmistress of the London Jew's Society. Miss Mary Hornstein was my teacher, later my dear friend, and I have two memories of this short session with formal education, a note of Father's of a birthday present I made him of a "pussy's head framed with straw," and of coming to Miss Mary and asking her to wash my cheeks, and when she asked me why, answering: "Because the boys have been kissing me."

In a letter to Aunt Rachel in February 1882 Father mentions that I was attending Miss Brooke's kindergarten and that I was given to writing my aunt letters "which I fear Mr. Rudy, with lacking respect, never mails." I can understand Mr. Rudy intercepting these missives, for I have a specimen:

DEAR ANTY,

How I wod like to see you i am a big gril now I am five now. ther are no florss now or I wad send you some.

My papa has skul (school) with us every day too or thee ars. after skul

Flora gose to sister Carline and has sowing too or tree ars then she plase or
woks her sum She is 12 now. She has got nu doll I havnt got any doll.

from Bertha
to Anty.

I soon stopped going to the London Jew's Society. Miss
Brooke became interested in the Bible-study classes Father was
conducting and was thinking of joining when one of the mission
heads who disapproved of the Group, ordered her not to visit
the American Colony. This arbitrary order helped her decide
which course to take.

That summer of 1882 the Whiting children, Ruth and John
David, were "dedicated to the Lord." Miss Brooke and six other
guests were invited, and our servants were also present. Father
baptized the children.

I have heard I disgraced myself at the baptism. A beautifully
decorated cake stood in readiness for tea on a low table, with
silvered candies and roses made of frosting in the decoration.
We seldom had a large cake, and while everyone else had their
eyes shut in reverent prayer my naughty little fingers were
picking off the candies. I suppose I was punished, but as I never
seem to remember my punishments I must have felt that I
deserved what I got and held no resentment. That I was sometimes spanked by Mother is certain, for once when Father tried,
I turned around over his knee and told him he should hit harder,
for Mother's spanking hurt more.

After the baptism Miss Brooke turned to Mrs. Gould.

"The Lord is very near to you all here," she said. "I want
the Lord to take the same tender care of me."

Mrs. Gould said she might have that care as she chose, that
we did not claim any special or singular treatment, we only
desired to live "very close to God, and that God came very
close to us."

Miss Brooke then spoke to Father and Mother, and as a result
she left the English Mission School and came to live at the
American Colony. She took charge of our education, and Aunt
Maggie implies in a letter that the Colony was educating Miss
Brooke. She had been the type of Christian, Auntie writes,
"who has been very strict in keeping the exact letter. She is
learning now that 'the letter killeth but the spirit makes alive.' "

The British Consul, Mr. Moore, had a large family, and his
three younger children, two sons and a daughter, came over
every day on donkeyback to share our splendid teacher.

As I have mentioned, I was educated at home, and my teachers were excellent, first Father and Aunt Maggie, then Miss Brooke, and Mr. Drake—the young Church of England chaplain who came to Palestine with General Gordon—and my foster brother Jacob.

I can understand my parents, who had lost five children, not wanting to put eight thousand miles between themselves and Grace and me. But when I became a mother, my husband agreed with me, and we sent our six children to school and college in the United States.

The salvation of the British colonists has always been in their sending their children back to English schools. It is all too easy to lapse in an alien land. All around us in Jerusalem we saw families who had lost their standards of living.

We children were never allowed to wear the attractive native costumes, as this might be construed as a letting down of standards. But we did wear at home, and loved, the little red native slippers.

Most of all, I missed school companionship in my schooling. Mother's stanchest friends were those who had been her schoolmates, and I missed contacts made early, when one is more trustful and less critical and friendships made then often remain firm through life.

Still, there were enough colony children for pleasant times. There were the Whitings, Flora Page, my sister Grace and I, and often Arabic children came in to play with us so that we learned to speak Arabic as well as we did English. Only a few who learn Arabic as adults speak it correctly.

As we brought no belongings, we had very few books and fewer toys. There were no native toys; the children of Jerusalem did not know how to play, but the Floyds sent us some from Jaffa and Father and Mr. Whiting made us pinewood blocks, and with a fret saw they made us jigsaw puzzles, pasting pictures on thin board and cutting them into pieces. Rob also made toys for us, little chairs and tables and cradles, and a wonderful doll carriage of spools and a little peasant basket.

Books were more difficult to get. The Turkish censors held books for months in Jaffa and then they would "get lost." Some arrived censored without reason. For example, Dr. van Dyke's *Out-of-doors in the Holy Land*, the most innocent and even reverent sort of book, arrived with entire sentences cut out.

But we had Shakespeare and other classics, and *Plutarch's Lives*, and an old encyclopedia which we wore to ribbons, and, best of all, Father and Mother told us stories. We knew all the children's fairy tales, and, better still, the Bible stories, for all we saw around us was straight from the Bible and we saw them being lived.

The Bible stories were familiar to me before I could write. I can remember carrying my big Bible, which I could not read, to Sunday school, which was held in the large living room or in the sewing room.

Living in the Holy Land we almost spoke in Biblical speech, and I still find myself saying, "I verily believe . . ."

We became archaeologists as children, and all we experienced we tried to translate in Biblical terms.

In our garden was a cemetery we kept for years, where all our pets were buried. Twice we had pet gazelles that we had to keep tied up for fear of "pye-dogs," the scavenger dogs of mixed origin that would set on a helpless animal left alone. One tangled and choked itself and we had a splendid funeral.

Then there was our pet sheep, that, grazing in a pleasant meadow, toppled over and died before our eyes without apparent reason, until we found on its nose the mark of a sand viper, one of the few poisonous snakes in the Holy Land. His enemy, of course, we children reasoned! From that time on we were convinced that the Twenty-Third Psalm was entirely a pastoral song: "The Lord is my Shepherd . . . Thou preparest a table before me in the presence of mine enemies . . ."

When in the hot summers, in the far pastures, we saw the shepherds anoint their heads with olive oil, we remembered: "Thou anointest my head with oil."

The Arabs believe that running water is pure, but there were few running streams around Jerusalem, and cisterns and troughs held the never-adequate supply of water. So the Arabs let water pour: "My cup runneth over."

I remember the summer I was five, standing on a stool in the nursery wearing crisp white muslin while Nora, the nurse, tied my sash in preparation for a children's party. My greedy eyes were on a level with the broad stone window ledge where Grace's can of condensed milk was kept for coolness, as there was no ice. Nora had to leave the room for some reason and on her way out turned to me and said, "Now don't touch the condensed milk while I'm gone."

I loved condensed milk and still do, and of course her warning gave me an irresistible urge, and Nora returned to find the evidence of guilt smearing my face and party dress.

Soon after this I was in Sunday school. It was our custom to learn a verse each Sunday. I was too young to read, but I opened my Bible, laid my finger on a verse, and said, "Teacher, may I learn this one?"

She read the verse: "Touch not, taste not, handle not."

"Does that mean condensed milk?" I demand.

Evidently she knew of my misdeed in the nursery, for she smiled and agreed that it must.

Some years later I insisted to Father that it was expressly forbidden in the Bible to touch condensed milk. After some discussion I turned to Colossians 2:21 to prove my point, and it was a shock when I could not find the words "condensed milk," I had been so certain they were there.

Five is not too young for hero worship, and my hero was a frequent visitor to our house, General Charles George "Chinese" Gordon, "the fabulous hero of the Sudan." He was fulfilling a lifelong dream with a year's furlough in Palestine, studying Biblical history and the antiquities of Jerusalem.

This was the only peaceful time the general had known in many years, and it was to be his last. He was the hero of the siege of Sebastopol and the occupation of Peking. As head of the "Ever-Victorious Army" in China he had taken Suchow. He had been awarded the Yellow Jacket, the highest Chinese honor, and was a Companion of the Bath. As Governor General of the Sudan he had traveled eighty-five hundred miles in three years, on camel- and muleback, always trying to eradicate the evils of slave trading and to improve the living conditions of the people. His genius lay not only in generalship, but also in diplomacy. He had the ability to make peace between great nations and the power of making friends with and befriending the common man. He once rode alone into an enemy camp to discuss terms.

The general lived in a rented house in the village of Ein Karim in "hill country of Judea," which is one of the sites shown as being the birthplace of John the Baptist. No road led from Ein Karim in those days, only a bridle path wound over the hills, and General Gordon came often from his village home to Jerusalem riding a white donkey. He had a servant, a man of all work and cook, named Joseph, and as he was a native of Ramleh, the traditional Aramathea, General Gordon called him "Joseph of Aramathea."

Whenever General Gordon came to our house a chair was put out for him on our flat roof and he spent hours there, studying his Bible, meditating, planning.

It was there that he conceived the idea that the hill opposite the north wall was in reality Golgotha, the "Place of the Skull," mentioned in Matthew, 27:33, Mark 15:22, and John 19:17.

He gave Father a map and a sketch that he made, showing the hill as a man's figure, with the skull as the cornerstone. Part of the scarp of the rock of what is known as Jeremiah's Grotto made a perfect death's-head, complete with eyesockets, crushed nose, and gaping mouth.

Ever since then this hill has been known as "Gordon's Calvary," although archaeologists are skeptical on the subject, and some prefer the site of the Holy Sepulcher. Until excavations place the correct location of the second wall there will always be a controversy over Calvary.

Father did not agree with all the general's visionary ideas, but he liked to talk about these and many other subjects with him, and they were good friends.

Mother wanted General Gordon to have peace when he was meditating on the roof, and cautioned me not to disturb him, but I would creep up the roof stairs and crouch behind a chimney; there I would wait. I watched him reading his Bible and lifting his eyes to study the hill, and my vigil was always rewarded, for at last he would call me and take me on his knee and tell me stories. He was not very tall, and had fair, curly hair, and I remember how blue his eyes were, and the blue double-breasted suit he wore.

He told one special story about a brave knight who lived and died in Palestine and who killed a dragon. Not until I was much older did I realize that he was telling me about Saint George and the Dragon, and of the town of Lydda, about twenty miles from Jerusalem, where Saint George was born, and buried after his death by torture at Nicomedia. The Mohammedans identify Saint George with the Prophet Elijah.

I did not know General Gordon was famous, only that he was my friend, and I loved him.

I always say the general taught me to swear. This has shocked those who made a saint of him, but to me it makes him more lovable, less the myth and more the man, and besides, I did not retain the habit.

He often stayed for meals, and once Mother asked him to stay to lunch, and he accepted, adding, "I hope you are not having chicken."

Then he told us how Joseph asked every morning: "General, sir, what shall we have for dinner?" "Well, Joseph, what have you got?" "I have chicken, Sir General." "Then have chicken, Joseph." This was repeated daily, until one morning the general saw Joseph approaching and anticipated him by saying, "Damn it, have chicken for dinner."

The general gave one of his hearty laughs and said: "And now you see, Mrs. Spafford, why I do not want chicken."

I was taking all this in, and soon after, when asked about my supper, which was invariably bread and milk, I said, "Damn it, have bread and milk."

To my utter consternation J was punished. For many years I puzzled why, when General Gordon said "damn," Mother had smiled, but when I said it, I was spanked.

Before his year of furlough was over General Gordon was called away from Palestine. He left in 1883; there was revolt in the Sudan. Then we heard of the dreadful siege of Khartoum in 1884 - 85, and of General Gordon holding it, with only one white officer and native troups, long after it seemed any human power could hold it. I heard Father and Mother discussing the siege. The general thought his uncanny power over the dervishes would keep him inviolate, and I heard Father and Mother speaking of this. The world knows what followed, how Kitchener sent his army into the Sudan to his rescue, but it was too late. Khartoum had fallen, and the revolutionists, knowing of the approach of the British across the desert, made haste to kill General Gordon.

He left his communion service and a few trinkets in Father's care. Father gave them to his friend Mr. Henry Gilman when he was the American Consul in Jerusalem.

The Rev. Herbert Drake, the young chaplain who had come to Palestine with General Gordon, whether in an official capacity or not I do not know, stayed on after the general left and joined the American Colony. He gave me lessons, especially in English literature.

Besides taking charge of the education of the children of our Group, Father and Mr. Drake and Miss Brooke taught English in several schools and to Christian and Arab individuals as well.

Father was never able to master Arabic, but Cousin Rob in about nine months learned the language sufficiently to serve as Father's interpreter and accompanied him on a horseback trip through Samaria and Galilee.

Father wrote this hymn while riding along the beautiful Galilean Lake shore:

Blessed Land of Galilee

O Blessed land of Galilee!
Rare was the lot that fell to thee—
Familiar to His gaze so long:
So oft thy paths His feet among—

Chorus:

O Galilee, dear Galilee,
Knit with His life and ministry!
What shall thy heights and vales yet see?
Thrice-blessed land of Galilee?

Ye heard the cries, ye saw the tears.
The suffering of those waiting years,
Ye saw Him stand in glittering white;
Ye saw Him clothed in risen might.

To toilers on thy hill-bound sea,
First came His word, "Come, follow me!"
And men from out thy coasts were those
His lips last blessed, that day He rose.

O Galilee that lieth now,
A stranger's brand upon thy brow,
By strangers' feet thy shrine downtrod,
Yet standeth sure the word of God!

The longer Father remained in Palestine the more he found of interest. Bible history, of which he had long been a student and an authority, was unfolded to him in a new light, illuminated by living in the country and seeing the people and becoming acquainted with their customs at firsthand. Archaeology at this time was emerging from amateur to scientific handling and in consequence was increasingly important. The pursuit of botany, stimulated by the large number of wild flowers in the spring, was a continual source of pleasure to him. He regretted the denuding of the hills and mountains of trees by wanton cutting down with no reforestation through centuries of Turkish misrule. He deplored the consequent erosion of the soil, exposing rock, and making the country look barren and arid. He spoke much about the necessity of planting trees. He tried to stimulate tree planting, but as the Turkish policy was to tax a tree from the date of planting there was no incentive.

I found an entry in Father's diary in January 1883 saying that he had received from his friend John B. Cotton of Tasmania a packet of blue gum tree seeds that he had sent for. Through his friend Mr. Nissim Behar this packet of seeds was given to Mr. Netter, then headmaster of Mikveh Israel Agricultural School near Jaffa. At that time Mikveh Israel was conducted by the Alliance Israelite.

Father adds, "May a mighty blessing come through these seeds to Palestine."

In 1940 I told the late Dr. Arthur Rupin about this discovery in Father's diary. Dr. Rupin searched the school records and found that the group of eucalyptus trees in the grounds near the schoolhouse had been planted in the spring of 1883 by Mr. Netter. My husband and I, with Dr. and Mrs. Arthur Rupin, visited the school soon after this. We made the acquaintance of Mr. Klause, the present headmaster of Mikveh Israel Agricultural School and his talented daughter. We visited the different departments and saw a few Jewish and Arab lads learning to become farmers, using modern methods and machinery; we saw cows that the school had crossed and recrossed with different European breeds making a species that are good milkers, able to stand the Palestine climate, and, most of all, could subsist and produce milk on the minimum of green fodder. We were gratified to find a few Arabs who were broadminded enough to allow politics to take a back seat and to avail themselves of what they could learn at the school.

We were interested to see youths who had been rescued from Nazi tyranny trying to forget the horrors of their experience in wholesome outdoor occupation. But to me the high spot of the afternoon was to stand under the mammoth trees while their branches met overhead like a Gothic cathedral. I felt that the moment was sacred as I thought what one person's vision had done for Palestine. A simple act: just a few seeds planted in a fertile soil! These trees, as far as we can know, are grandfathers and great-grandfathers of all the eucalyptus trees in Palestine. Dr. Rupin said that this group of trees should be called the "Spafford forest."

What greater memorial could Father have? Now there are eucalyptus trees everywhere in Palestine. They are quick-growing, they supply firewood and useful lumber, and they are planted in swamps to help absorb the superfluous water, thus turning malaria-ridden places into healthy localities. "A mighty blessing... to Palestine."

As I stood under those magnificent trees I thought how truly Father's prayer had been answered.

CHAPTER NINE

I AM often asked how the "work" of the American Colony started.

Soon after we were settled in our house on the city wall we went on a picnic to Wad ez Joz, which means "the valley of walnut trees," although only a few were left standing in the valley that was once filled with beautiful trees. One comes to realize, in a treeless land like Palestine, the meaning of "the shadow of a rock in a weary land." There are many more rocks than trees in the Holy Land.

Above, on the hill, were some Mohammedan residences, and a young man, hearing our merry voices, came down to investigate. We had not known we were trespassing on his land. Through an interpreter he asked who we were and what we were doing. He was very friendly and Father invited him to share our picnic lunch. Mother was feeding Grace her bottle, and he was interested. "My mother has twin baby girls she cannot nurse," he said, and added that she was trying, without much success, to feed them artificially. Mother went at once to his house and was given a friendly reception. She told the mother, through an interpreter, how ill baby Grace had been and how, through experience, she had learned what foods agreed with her. The twins were put on Nestle's Condensed Milk, the only tinned milk we could buy in the market, and a friendship began that lasted to the present day and which was to start child welfare and nursing in the Holy City. The grapevine method of transmitting information soon spread the news.

The young man who joined our picnic was Mehedean Effendi Husseini and one of his baby sisters whose life Mother saved was Sitt Zakieh, who became the wife of Musa Kazmi Pasha, at one time the great nationalist leader of the Arabs who is buried in the Dome of the Rock compound—the Arab Westminster.

Immediately after the picnic in Wad ez Joz the Group was asked to give private lessons and instruction in schools.

Soon Mother's letters home were filled with accounts of the work that needed to be done—far more than the Group had the strength or ability for. She, Mrs. Gould, and Mrs. Whiting were nursing many sick people and teaching Arab and Jewish mothers how to care for their children, and Father and other men of the Group were teaching English and nursing.

They were beginning to find the consolation and healing of their spirits that they had hoped to find in Jerusalem.

Before long our house was a gathering place. Father's Bible-study classes were popular. The mothers' meetings conducted by Mother and Mrs. Gould were well attended. More people, Arabs and Jews, flocked to the daily meetings and to hear the singing.

The days were not long enough to accomplish all they were asked to do. They had not anticipated this need, and were happy in the openings for usefulness they found.

Before long our Group was conducting a sort of Y.M.C.A. or settlement work. Settlement work, as we know it now in Hull House Settlement in Chicago, Henry Street Settlement in New York, and Bethnel Green Settlement in London, had not yet started. Our work pre-dated any settlement work, although it resembled it more than any other.

Mother wrote to her sister, Aunt Rachel:

Last Saturday two hundred and twenty Jews came and among them were three learned Rabbis. About twenty of them surrounded Horatio, with the three Rabbis, for discussion. Horatio would not enter into any argument with them. He said that only love would conquer the world, and before they left they seemed melted. Their questions made us realize so clearly how Christ had to answer them. They talk in the same manner now. "Do you keep the law?" That is their great question. They are exceedingly polite to us, which they are not to everyone. They have invited us to their synagogues and to their Feast of Tabernacles. . . . One Sunday we had two Mohammedan Effendis, rich and learned men who came to inquire about our religion. They took dinner with us. At the same time we had two Greeks. They sat down together as happy as could be. Sheik Racheed Arakat and Abou Nasib came too. Miss Brooke can speak to the Jews in French or German, and Jacob can speak to them in Spanish, Rob can speak Arabic, so we get on beautifully.

A description of the Colony was written by our friend the late Rev. T. F. Wright after a visit to Palestine:

There is in Jerusalem at the present time a remarkable American Colony which it was my privilege carefully to examine. The house of these Americans is daily visited by persons coming from all parts of the land to inquire into this wonderful phenomenon. The Bedouins of the desert lean their tall spears against the wall and are cordially welcomed. The fellaheen, or peasant class of the country, find always here a cordial welcome. No evening passes without seeing its company of poor and rich, of peasants and Turkish effendis gathered in the salon, to listen to the hymns, which the Americans sweetly sing, and everyone on leaving the room expresses his gratitude for what he has come to regard as the greatest comfort of his life. Mohammedans and all classes in Jerusalem are reached for good, and a lesson is taught us in regard to the spirit in which Christian missions should be carried on.

I was never afraid of the tall Bedouins and their spears. But then I was never very much afraid of anything until I met up with the New York subways.

One of the first friends Father made in Jerusalem was Mr. Nissim Behar, headmaster of a boys' school conducted by the Alliance Israelite, attended by both Arabs and Jews. Father volunteered to give English lessons to the boys. Mr. Behar was a highly educated French Jew, a public-spirited man of culture, and his friendship was a source of much pleasure to Father. Through these classes Father came in contact with and taught English to many who are now among Jerusalem's prominent citizens, both Arabs and Jews.

Some of Father's pupils were not so apt at learning English as others. Ali supplied us with many amusing anecdotes. "One devil! One devil!" he exclaimed when the sunsets from our windows were particularly beautiful, convinced he was saying: "Wonderful!"

Once, when he was incapable of pronouncing a difficult word, he challenged Father, "Can you say this in Arabic?" and rattled off a catchy limerick. Father could not twist his tongue or use his throat to pronounce the Arabic guttural sounds, so he turned the tables on Ali by saying, "You try to pronounce, 'It is a suspicious hypothesis,' and 'I guarantee the authenticity,' and it will be my turn to laugh." Ali mastered these sentences after much practice. One day when he was on the "Green Hill" (Gordon's Calvary) he met a tourist, an American clergyman. Ali was a dealer in antiquities and had a quick eye to business. He saw in this gentleman a potential purchaser of his antiques, so he approached him with an old coin in his hand. "Is it genuine?" asked the American. "I guarantee the authenticity," answered Ali. The gentleman was impressed. "Seeing your English is so excellent and your intelligence so good, please tell me," he said, "whether this is actually the place of the crucifixion of Jesus Christ?" Ali looked at the man and repeated the only other English sentence he knew perfectly. "It is a suspicious hypothesis," he said. The clergyman was dumfounded. "Where did you learn your English?"

Ali's education and culture, given him by the American Colony, sent his family far up in the social scale. We are dealing now with his descendants. Every day, through the Arab-Jewish troubles, Ali's great-grandson called at the American Colony to see if all went well with us.

The Arab's sense of humor is different from ours. They are touchy but humorous, and love to play practical jokes, and even the children play them. They like to laugh, and are highly amused by funny words. Our Arab friends would try to get Father to repeat odd-sounding words and double up in glee at his atrocious Arabic.

Another friend, Abou Yousef, dealt in charcoal, and when we could afford it, we bought from him. The open fireplaces in which we burned it were the only means we had for cooking in those days. When money got scarce, we told Abou Yousef not to bring charcoal at regular intervals as had been his wont, but to wait until we ordered it, and naturally we would order it only when we had money to pay for it. Abou Yousef took no notice of our admonition, but kept our charcoal room full all through our lean years. Mr. Rudy kept strict account of what he brought. However, Abou Yousef trusted us. He was devoted to Father. He said once that Abou Horatio had the head of a king or sultan and he was going to pray to God to make him one.

Abou Yousef could not understand a word of English but he came regularly every day to the Colony and sat through the morning family prayers. He wore a white turban and robe and looked venerable. When he became old and deaf, and could hear nothing of what was taking place, it made no difference, he still came and remained silent, sometimes fingering his prayer beads, until our Christian prayers were over, and then he would go away. He said he could feel the spirit of the prayers. This continued until he died. Some of our Group nursed him through his last illness, which happened while I was in America, about 1895. But before he died we were able to pay him in full.

Another Moslem who came frequently to our home wore a green turban and was the custodian of a mosque on the western boundary of the city limits. In a note Mrs. Gould wrote: "The Dervish came and said he wanted to spend the three hours in prayer here, rather than in the Haram es Shareef."

I reproduce these notes because they show the friendly feeling between the community and the Colony.

Cousin Rob commented in a letter:

We have been greatly favored in our relationship with the Arabs. While other Europeans and Americans complain of the Turks and Arabs and warn us against them, we go right into their gardens and find people ready to do any favor for us. We have met the greatest kindness, bankers and merchants give us credit without asking for security, and not only give us this, but offer it of their own free will.

As the work grew, the American Colony grew. After Miss Brooke and Mr. Drake joined, others, from the Church Mission to the Jews, the House of Industry and Inquirers Home, were attracted to the American Colony.

There was Mr. Nathanial Piazza, Mr. Pincus—we called him Noah—and Joseph Vinietsky. Mr. Klinger, a consumptive, who was very ill, we took in and nursed. There were Yoffe and Maurice, and the Hermaline family with all their children.

Some Father baptized. Some had quarreled with groups they had left and Mother wrote that under these circumstances resolutions were taken not to listen or allow gossip or faultfinding against the organizations or places they had left. "How often unkind gossip is mistaken for valuable criticism," she wrote.

There was Jacob Rosenzweig, a Rumanian Jew, who spoke Yiddish and was very poor. He was called "Kleine Yacob" because he was so diminutive. He was a dapper little person with quaint and courtly ways and excessively proud of his stiffly starched shirt and bowler hat, remnants of the past affluence, I suppose, in which he appeared resplendent on Sundays.

It was the custom since the Colony group had increased in numbers to sing grace before meals. Generally we chanted,

> *"God is great and God is good,*
> *And we thank Him for this food.*
> *By His hand must all be fed,*
> *Give us Lord our daily bread."*

But sometimes one or another at the table would call instead for a favorite hymn.

I remember a Sunday when Kleine Yacob appeared at dinner with a harried air and took his usual place next to Mrs. Gould. One of Mrs. Gould's duties was to distribute the Colony laundry. Just as grace was about to be said, Kleine Yacob leaned over and whispered to her in his broken English, "Him steal away my shirt," meaning his beloved Sunday shirt had not returned with the wash.

Mrs. Gould misunderstood, and told Mother, "Kleine Yacob is asking us to sing the hymn, 'Steal Away.' "

Mother was rather surprised, although one was seldom surprised at anything Kleine Yacob might do, but she closed her eyes and started the old Negro spiritual, "Steal Away to Jesus." Around the table the choir joined in, their voices clear and rich. The choir was noted for its harmony, especially when singing the Negro spirituals. Those who did not sing were absorbed in listening to the beautifully rendered hymn, all except Kleine Yacob, who was convulsed in noiseless laughter.

Like so many others who came to us, Kleine Yacob remained with us until he died many years later.

When Miss Brooke came to live with us at the American Colony, she brought a number of things that helped make our lives more interesting, notably books and pictures, for she was a student and artist. To us children, conspicuous among the innovations was "Waterloo."

Waterloo was a large black donkey. In those days donkeys were the usual means of transport in Jerusalem, and people rode donkeyback on their business rounds and even when paying social calls.

Waterloo was well named; he was a fighter. Being well fed, with little work, his donkey stubbornness and assertiveness were well developed. Other donkeys, poor little underfed beasts of burden, Waterloo passed with his nozzle in the air and braying lustily.

Mother told me her first experience in the Near East was of awakening to a sound so dreadful that she was positive some monster, at least as large as an elephant, was loose in the street. Father showed her a tiny gray donkey tethered below the window.

"You don't mean to say that small animal made all that noise?" Mother demanded.

She had never heard a donkey bray, but she became accustomed to the sound as people at home are to the purring of a cat.

Our Arab nurses told us the story of how the donkey got his bray when we were little, solemnly assuring us it was true. When Noah was collecting the animals for the ark, Mr. and Mrs. Donkey came early, but lingered a few minutes on the green turf for a last nibble of grass. They did not notice the gathering clouds nor the first huge drops of rain. Then Mr. Donkey looked up to see that the door of the ark was closed!

He was terribly frightened. What if he and his mate were left behind? So he lifted up a loud voice and called, "No-ah! No-ah!"

The rain beat and the lightning flashed and thunder tore, and suddenly Noah opened the door of the ark to them.

Mr. Donkey was so relieved to see Noah that his shouting subsided into "Ah! ah! ah!" and that is how the donkey got his bray, and the reason why it is so loud, for he had to raise his voice above the downpouring of the Flood.

The story is much better told in Arabic, where the cries of Noah sound exactly like the donkey's bray.

We children had glorious times riding Waterloo. He was big and strong and could carry several of us at one time. An ingenious contrivance of panniers made of two upholstered kerosene boxes was slung on either side an Arabic saddle, on which was fastened, thronelike, a coffeeshop stool upside down with one rung cut out to make a chair. Plump and cheerful John Whiting sat in this, his sister Ruth and my sister Grace in the kerosene boxes, and we older children walked or ran alongside. Mr. Drake or Captain Sylvester led Waterloo, who held strong notions as to actual leadership and would nip the arm of anyone urging him in a direction he did not care to take, so the captain invented a broom-handle lead covered with tin which was fastened to Waterloo's bridle, and the frisky donkey could be managed at "arm's length."

We often went donkeyback to Ein Farrah, and in my parents' letters are many mentions of picnics in this wildly picturesque and rocky gorge near Anathoth, the birthplace of Jeremiah. It holds the most capious living spring in the vicinity of Jerusalem, flowing even through the dry season, therefore many shepherds from Jerusalem and the adjacent villages gathered there with their flocks in summer. The herds pasturing on the slopes made it a perfect Biblical setting, and some authorities consider Ein Farrah the place the Shepherd King had in mind in the Twenty-Third Psalm.

We liked going to Ein Farrah early, to avoid traveling in the summer heat, and generally arrived by sunrise at a certain plain which we children dubbed "The Plain of the Rising Sun," for we loved giving names to places. On this plain was a Moslem shrine or "weli," and we noticed that all the donkeys lifted up their voices in a tremendous bray as they faced the first rays of

the rising sun, which was usually just as we were approaching
the weli. Because of the Arabic tale of the donkey and his bray,
we called the shrine "Noah's Tomb."

A few years ago I gave a tea party to a group of Biblical students
visiting Jerusalem. They were late, and in their apology mentioned that they had been taken to see Noah's Tomb. I questioned
them, for I knew there was no tomb in Palestine that could
possibly be attributed to Noah.

To my amusement I found they had been taken by one of
our old "donkeyboys," now graduated into a dragoman, or guide,
to our shrine on our "Plain of the Rising Sun," both named by
us when we were children. So does fantasy get handed down
to become tradition.

One of our favorite excursions with Waterloo was to the Garden
of Gethsemane. We children became good friends with the
Franciscan father who was custodian of the Garden. On the
slope above, where the Church of Saint Mary Magdalene now
stands, was open ground with numerous olive, mulberry, and
charub trees, where we often picnicked. All this property belonged
to our friend Abu Nassib.

Later he sold it to the Russians, and we children watched the
entire process of building the church beside his house, from its
foundation to its golden domes. We called it "The Church of
the Golden Domes," because the onion-shaped cupolas were
coated with real gold leaf, and Abu Nassib's daughter picked
up enough tiny specks after the workmen left to make herself
a ring.

Abu Nassib was tall and quite dark, with flashing black eyes,
and he was very kind. Like all Arabs, he was also very hospitable,
and during one of our first visits to his towerlike house on the
slope of Olivet he urged us to enter. We found ourselves, when
our eyes got accustomed to the subdued light after the glaring
sun, in a large room. We also perceived sick people lying about
the room on mattresses.

Abu Nassib, without the slightest suspicion that anything was
amiss, informed us cheerfully that his family had smallpox.

We left with haste, but the mischief was done. Poor little
Grace had the worst case, and I escaped most lightly of all.

This was the first of many experiences with Abu Nassib.

He came to my rescue soon after this. I had gone with Father
and Mother and some guests from America and Hannieh to
watch the Nebi Musa (Prophet Moses) procession, which was

one of our yearly excitements. This feast and procession are to the reputed tomb of Moses on the west side of the Jordan, although the Bible tells us he never crossed the river. The custom was instituted by the Turks some hundred years ago as a political measure to attract Moslem pilgrims and offset the large number of Christian pilgrims who gather in the Holy City for the Easter festivities, or it was feared that at such a time the Christians might rise and take possession of the Holy Sepulcher.

The shrine of the Prophet Moses, a huge rectangular building of about one hundred rooms, is richly endowed, and during the feast days the pilgrims are housed and fed in the building. The cenotaph, covered with green cloth, is in the mosque on the ground floor. Pilgrims occupied the rooms surrounding the court and overflowed into tents stretching out over the surrounding hills. The shrine is in the foothills of the Judean mountains with a magnificent view of the Dead Sea and the Jordan Valley. Since the feast at Nebi Musa always coincides with Greek Holy Week, the rolling foothills at this time are covered with short spring grass and beautiful wild flowers—yellow and white mustard so tall that "the birds of the air find shelter" in it, wild stock scenting the evening breeze, yellow daisies or wild chrysanthemums that give the scene a golden aura. The beauty is shortlived.

The celebration always starts with a procession from Jerusalem, where the Holy Flag is kept. Days before Hebron, Nablus, and the other cities and the surrounding villages send their own flags and bands, consisting of drums and cymbals, into the Holy City to take part in the procession. Bandsmen and banner bearers gather in the compound of the Dome of the Rock or the Mosque of Omar.

The Husseini family are custodians of the shrine and the hosts at Nebi Musa. The Grand Mufti, a member of the Husseini family, always rode on horseback in the procession immediately behind the Jerusalem Holy Flag made of rich green and black satin embroidered in gold. Crowds of spectators milled around, and the road was lined with Turkish soldiers to keep a passage open for the procession.

As the Jerusalem flag reached Saint Stephen's Gate or the east gate a salute of cannon thundered and the women in the crowd gave the joy cry described by Cousin Rob. Then the procession, led by the Turkish band playing Turkish music in a minor key

slightly off pitch, slowly wound out of the city and past Gethsemane. At the point where the Bethany road turns east, a large marquee was pitched, where the mayor of Jerusalem received the
Mufti and other notables in the procession. Coffee was served,
and a short prayer offered by the Mufti while the guests stood
with their hands out, palms upward, then wiped their faces to
receive the blessing. Another salute of seven cannon shots sent
the procession on its way to the shrine in the hills. Carriages
were used from this point, but many who could not afford carriages rode on donkeys, horses, mules, and camels. Later, when
automobiles were introduced, the picturesqueness faded, and halts
at the tent became a great social event. I was in the marquee
during World War I when Djemal Pasha received the Mufti, and
I have been there with each successive British High Commissioner. In 1947, because of the unrest and political tension between the Arabs and the Jews, the procession of the Nebi Musa
did not take place for the first time in several hundred years.

Nor do we now have the many kinds of dervishes who lent so
much color to the celebration when I was a child. They came
to Jerusalem especially for the Prophet's feast and procession.
Some ate live coals, others forced spikes through their cheeks.
Snake charmers came from Upper Egypt.

During this particular procession, when I was five or six, I was
walking along unconscious of fear when I realized I was alone.
Father and Mother were busy with their guests and Hannieh
had stopped to chat with some Arab friends.

It is one thing to watch such a scene from a safe distance and
another to be in the midst of it. Suddenly I found myself walking
in the procession surrounded by one of the village bands. Over
me towered fierce-looking men carrying banners, and others were
pounding on large and small drums, while others were making
a terrific clashing with their cymbals. Amidst these were dervishes
twirling round and round in religious frenzy, their bushy hair
sticking out all over their heads, their eyes rolling, and spikes
sticking through their cheeks.

I did not cry—for once I was too frightened to cry. I just stood
petrified, and suddenly, pushing through the hysterical crowd to
my rescue, came my tall, dark, kindly friend, Abu Nassib. Oh,
how glad I was to see him.

As well as the land on Olivet, Abu Nassib owned a plot of
ground outside Saint Stephen's Gate which he kept planted

with tomatoes.

In those days potatoes were a luxury, they were imported I believe from France, and when we could get any they were a great treat. Father succeeded in getting some potatoes for seed and prevailed upon Abu Nassib to plant half his field with them, leaving the other half for the tomatoes.

Some time later he came to call, and Father asked Abu Nassib about his potato crop.

"Oh! No good! No good!" said Abu Nassib, and emphasized his disgust with freely gesticulating arms and hands. "Tomato plant here, good. Batata (the Arab pronunciation of potato) plant here, good. Tomato grow, batata grow, good. Tomato much fruit, good! Batata not one fruit—no good!"

And Abu Nassib struck his hands together in the Arabic gesture of finality.

Father took a shovel and went with Abu Nassib to the field, where he dug the first crop of potatoes ever grown in Jerusalem. Abu Nassib had no idea "fruit" grew underground. After this he was known as Abu Batata—Father of the Potato.

Once, excavating for a new cistern in his property on the slope of Olivet, Abu Nassib uncovered a pottery cruse filled with silver shekels. He was very secretive about his discovery, but he must have uncovered other valuable antiquities as well, for after this food was more plentiful in the tower house and the family better clad. He built a handsome new home in the old city.

An old Arabic saying describes the perverse nature of Beni Adam (son of Adam, meaning man), "when his wealth increases, he commits folly, precipitating his fall." This proved true of Abu Nassib. His bonanza left him restless, and although he was married and the father of two daughters and two sons, he began looking about for a bride. A girl cousin secretly let him know by a professional "go-between" that she would not be adverse to a proposal of marriage.

Abu Nassib confided his secret to Father.

This was Father's first encounter with the custom of plural marriage. He argued with Abu Nassib, but as Moslems are allowed four wives by the Sharia, or religious law, there was not much he could say about it.

One would think that as the Arab's religion allows plural marriage and Moslem women are brought up to consider it right, they would not mind, but this is not so. The wife lives in fear all her married life that this may happen to her, and if it does, it is a real tragedy and causes suffering, as it would to any family.

After Father's talk with Abu Nassib the matter seemed to drop for a time. Then came the three days' feast at the end of Ramadan, which is the month of fasting.

In those days it was the custom to picnic in the open fields outside Herod's Gate, where the American School of Oriental Research now stands. No buildings were there then, only level fields and a few sparse olive trees.

Merry-go-rounds and swings were erected for this celebration, and there were peep shows—many exhibiting obscene pictures—and hawkers who made a roaring business selling Damascus sweetmeats and *Sha'r el Banat* (maiden's hair), candy shredded so fine it resembled hair, and *Rahit el Halkum* (Turkish delight), and salted and roasted watermelon and pumpkin seeds, and, in season, green and roasted chick-peas tied in bunches. There was *sus* (licorice water) and pink lemonade in brightly decorated receptacles, served in shallow brass cups the vendors used almost like cymbals in a dexterous rhythm to attract customers. Gypsies, notorious fortunetellers, in their gay costumes gathered there from neighboring countries.

The scene resembled an old-time country fair. These quaint customs with an atmosphere of conviviability have all disappeared.

The people wore their best clothes and spent lavishly the savings stored up for the occasion. Crowds of women were kaleidoscopic in their brightly colored *izzars*, or outer street costumes, and the bright parasols they loved added color to the already gay picture.

Horse racing was the chief attraction. Arabs do not have our idea of competitive racing. The gaily-bedecked horses rushed madly around the field, while their excited riders dug in their spurs. Some of the horses' trappings were really beautiful, with silver-mounted bridles and gaudy tassels, and some even had ostrich feathers fastened to their heads. The wilder the horse and rider became, the more the spectators enjoyed the race. There were no cups or prizes, and the only award was a handkerchief tied to the horse's bridle. The winner, generally the most reckless rider, carried off the greatest number of handkerchiefs. Especially imported cheap but highly colored handkerchiefs or veils were sold in the crowd to award the riders.

Abu Nassib was racing his mare wildly in the contest when he saw the professional go-between among the watchers on the field. A secret signal, which he understood, led him to ride toward a group of women. He knew the closely veiled charmer who tied her kerchief to his horse's bridle must be his "fair one," and, inflamed with desire and excitement, he whirled his steed, dashed madly into the center of the field, and was thrown.

He was carried to his towerlike house near Gethsemane, and the same messenger sent to fetch a doctor also came for Father, who went at once to our friend. For three weeks Abu Nassib was nursed back to health by the men of the American Colony, and he told Father the accident which nearly cost him his life had brought him to his senses, and that he gave up his idea of a second marriage.

For a time Abu Nassib remained aloof although the cousin began her overtures again. He and his wife had another child, a much-wanted som. Then one day we heard that Abu Nassib had succumbed—he had married the cousin. We also heard that his little son, now almost a year old, died on the evening of his marriage.

After a long interval we saw Abu Nassib again. He was a sad man. "Abu Nassib naughty boy," he said, and seemed to mean it. His two families lived separately—the new wife in the home he had built inside the city—and at odds with each other, and serious troubles had come to both. The second wife had lost her first baby and was to have another, and wanted to make her peace with the American Colony. All Father's warnings about a dis-united household had come true and, being superstitious, she was convinced she was under a spell or curse. She was assured of our blessing and friendship, and Mother and Mrs. Gould nursed her when her second baby arrived, a beautiful boy.

He grew to be a fine man, and only a short time ago called on me, with his wife and children, and recalled this story. I was surprised at how much he had been told. He concluded by say-ing, "So you see I am an American, for I was their (the Colony's) son and I have their blessing on my head." He had made peace between the two families and brought about the first happiness they had known in many years.

We all cared a lot for Abu Nassib. He lived to be an old man, handsome still. I remember him best at our table, when he drank with a great noise and ate with loud smackings, which is Arab courtesy, to show how much you enjoy your host's food. "You mustn't eat like Abu Nassib," I warned my children, and once Anna Grace, in her high chair at the table, watched, fascinated, as he drank his coffee, and piped, "See, he's drinking like Abu

Nassib!"

He recognized his name and became quite excited. "You must tell me what she said. Wallah! you must tell me."

I steered through a touchy situation. "Anna Grace said, 'I'm drinking coffee like Abu Nassib.' "

Abu Nassib took it as a great compliment.

During the bombing in 1948, Abu Nassib's great-grandson's widow made her way through the blitz to ask me for aid. His children and grandchildren still live in the towerlike house above the Garden of Gethsemane.

CHAPTER TEN

WHEN the teaching and nursing of the Group won a reputation, it became apparent that the American Colony was being regarded as a nuisance by certain staid and static missionaries working in Jerusalem.

It is a fact and perhaps unknown to Father and the others of the Group that in the 1870s a controversy had arisen in Jerusalem between the American and English missionary societies. An understanding had developed of dividing the spheres of influence. Syria was to be the American sphere and Palestine that of the British, a decision, alas, that carried the American University to Beirut.

While our Group knew nothing of this agreement, I doubt if it would have made any difference in the chioce of domicile.

As far as my parents were concerned, our residence in Jerusalem was still temporary. They were more concerned with what the country was doing for their souls than what they were doing for the people of the country. It was only as the work grew, because of the need for it, that the Colony took on a more permanent aspect.

The local people first called us the Americans, later they added the American Colony. We had not taken that name. We were as yet unique in our approach to the people and perhaps on that account we were misunderstood in certain circles. The very success of the venture was in part the cause of misunderstanding.

Our Group, as devout Christians, felt there was nothing highe under heaven to teach than the Christian ethics and way of life, but did not believe in coercion, or, as sometimes happened, turning a good Jew into a bad Christian.

Some of the missionaries regarded this new work with the narrow regard of the conformists for the non-conforming.

One article in a mission publication made these charges against the American Colony: "One of their beliefs is that none of them will die before the Lord's coming." . . . "Nobody seems to know what their religious beliefs are, for their members never reveal them." "They do not believe in missions and so they never make any missionary efforts among the Jews and Moslems."

By this time the hysterical attacks by members of the Lake View group had arrived in Jerusalem. The garbled facts were seized upon and enlarged, and everything we did was distorted by the missionaries who resented the American Colony.

These were trivial clouds on our horizon, but they were to grow.

Among the most virulent of the attackers was one of the heads of the English Mission, who resented Miss Brooke's leaving it to join our group, and spread the report that the American Colony had exerted undue influence to cause her to do so. Father's notebook contains an account of a visit he and Miss Brooke paid this man, in which they tried to explain the Colony's position and its work "so that he, a school head and minister of the gospel, could no longer make such charges through ignorance."

"But he declared," Father wrote, "he would say this house was a house of devils as long as he had breath and strength."

Not all Jerusalem's missionaries resented the American Colony. We had many friends among other groups, and mission leaders from every part of the world were to visit the American Colony and study our work as it grew. Among Father's and Mother's papers are hundreds of letters from ministers and missionaries bearing friendly testimony and appreciation for work quietly done. Some, after their visits, sent back gifts of money to further the work of the American Colony and others sent their appreciative acknowledgment and prayers.

I am not running down mission work. I know how much good missionaries can do and have done in many countries, and I do not underestimate the heroic sacrifices of many. I only state that in Jerusalem, at the time about which I am writing, some of the missionary workers used formalized and antiquated methods and resented any innovation.

Their unfriendly attitude toward us embittered my early years with a feeling that we were different, marked and strange. That is an unpleasant experience for a child. One of our games, I remember, was to dress up and call ourselves missionaries, and, looking down our noses at the smaller children we made represent the American Colony, we would say: "Oh, those are the crazy Americans!"

From notes and letters I get the impression that the Colony turned neither to right nor left on account of the misrepresentations, persecutions, or whatever one chooses to call them.

Sometimes it seemed to me, in my younger days, that a complete circle of opposition had surrounded us, starting with the Lake View group as originators, followed by the antagonistic missionaries, and completed by the Mr. Selah Merrill whose resentment of Father and the American Colony tormented us for eighteen years.

What faith did the American colonists hold to make them the victims of a religious persecution that would last nearly two decades? I find it best expressed in a letter Mother wrote to Father in January 1884. She was worn out by much nursing, and had gone with Rob for a few days of rest with the Floyd family, in Jaffa. She writes first of a visit to a mission hospital where all around lay sick and wounded and dying men, women, and children, some in bloody rags, others shaking with fever, while over them a nurse stood, in immaculate white uniform, and in classical Arabic read the Bible.

Mother wrote:

An hour of it—the price the patients had to pay for receiving medical attention. In a corner a sheik lay in dirty rags stuck fast with dried blood, with many severe wounds from a village fight; his leg seemed fractured. . . . All around sick people were waiting for the scripture to end.

Christ would have relieved the suffering with gentle fingers and tender words and allowed the spirit to do the preaching.

The long Bible reading, she said, was in the Arabic of educated people, far above these simple people's understanding, and after it came prayers, and then a hymn. . . .

One evening in Jaffa a group met in the Floyd's living room. They represented several faiths, including Episcopalian, Methodist, and Friend. Mother joined in the conversation, and she wrote Father:

I spoke concerning our faith and belief that someday God would unite the whole Christian world. I cannot describe to you the strange feeling that I had. Here we were, all professing Christians and yet separated and divided as far as possible. It was so evident that each one was worshiping God from behind the little fence that he had made to enclose himself. . . . How I would like to see all these man-made "walls of partition" broken down. I asked if they could explain to me these separations between Christians, each claiming that the Holy Spirit has taught them, but they could not attempt an answer. Someday the Episcopalians and Methodists, and even the man from Ramallah and Plymouth Brethren, will all join in a great world power for unity. We must press forward and pray that such a power will unite all Christians.

In the notes and letters written during these early years there are many allusions to nursing English and European patients as well as Jews and Arabs. There were no trained nurses in Jerusalem, and Mother, Mrs. Gould, and Mrs. Whiting were considered the best to be had and were in great demand. There are numerous mentions of nursing different members of the Bergheim family.

The Bergheim family was a rich English-Hebrew-Christian family who conducted a private bank in Jerusalem, and were kind and generous to us.

We made no specific charge for teaching and nursing. People paid what they could, and this might be little or nothing. Most of our patients were poor. Sometimes they paid us in food, so that often we would be surfeited with one kind of food while lacking in others. The Bergheims were among the few who gave more, but then they had more to give. Their splendid residence was surrounded by a large quantity of land, and among their large properties they owned the historical village of Gezer, called in Arabic Abu Shuche.

In revenge for wrongs, imaginary or real, one of the Bergheim sons was murdered by the fellaheen (peasants) while riding in his carriage near Gezer. The motive was not robbery, for his money, watch, and other valuables were found untouched on the body. His English wife was pregnant and the shock endangered her life and the unborn babe's. Mother and Mrs. Gould nursed her through trying weeks, and both mother and child survived.

When the Bergheim bank failed, the Bergheim holdings passed into other hands. Why the Marquis of Bute had invested money in Bergheim's bank I cannot tell, but after the bank failed he was given the Bergheim residence in lieu of part of his money. Under the British Mandate the house was enlarged to become Government Hospital including the British section.

The vacant property facing the Bergheim residence was given to the Jerusalem municipality to be made into a much-needed park. From one part of this gift a large modern building was erected. The southern half was Barclay's Bank (D. C. and O.) and the northern half was municipal offices.

On May 15, 1948, when the British Mandate ended, it was taken over by Israel.

Gezer continued to hold its place in history. The site was first identified by Dr. Clermont-Ganneau, who had excavated the so-called Tomb of the Kings and detected the forgery of the

Temanite scroll.

Extensive excavations have been carried on at Gezer by the Palestine Exploration Fund under the able supervision of Professor R. A. S. Maclister, LL.D., Litt. D. F.S.A. Remains that were found covered all periods from the Neolithic to the time of the Maccabees. There was much evidence of Egyptian influence.

In I Kings 9:16 we find that Pharaoh, King of Egypt, went up and took Gezer and burned it, killing its inhabitants, and then gave it as a present to his daughter when she became Solomon's wife.

In 1924, Palestine's first High Commissioner, Sir Herbert Samuel, cut the first sod at Gezer in land which had been acquired for an English-Jewish settlement.

One of the Bergheim sisters married the German Consul, who was the son of Dr. Von Tischendorf who discovered the famous Sinai manuscript and in whose home I spent many pleasant afternoons as a small girl. Frau Von Tischendorf was anxious to improve her painting, and our Miss Brooke was an art teacher, so we started a painting club. We met each week at the different houses of the members.

Miss Brooke must have been teaching me to enlarge, for she allowed me to copy on a large scale a small picture of Axel Strasse in Geneva, in the William Tell country, and I presented this atrocious painting to Father's friend, Hadj Racheed Nashashebie.

Many, many years later my husband and I were invited to an Arabic luncheon in a palatial house in Wady Ehnain on the Plain of Esdralon near Rehoveth. As we sat in the drawing room I whispered to my husband, "I believe that painting over there is mine!"

I went over to investigate, and sure enough, there was my maiden name, Bertha Spafford. My host, seeing my interest, followed me.

"I see you are admiring that painting, Mrs. Vester," he said. "I also admire it very much. I got it as a present from my good friend Hadj Racheed Nashashebie. It is the work of a famous artist."

What could I say?

As the demand for such services as the Group could render increased, with it increased the personal animosity of Mr. Merrill. It seemed a waste of time to deny his ridiculous accusations, but they were refuted eventually, and in an astonishing way.

His campaign of antagonism began when the American Colony gave shelter and support to the Bentons, a family of the type we came to classify as "Simples in the Garden of Allah."

CHAPTER ELEVEN

JERUSALEM attracts all kinds of people. Religious fanatics and cranks of different degrees of mental derangement seemed drawn as by a magnet to the Holy City. Some of those who particularly came into our lives were men and women who thought themselves the reincarnations of saints, prophets, priests, messiahs, and kings.

Among the first Americans we met in Jerusalem was a family I shall call Benton. Old Mr. Benton thought he had invented perpetual motion. Why he came to Jerusalem on that account is hard to tell, except that people less cranky than he believe Jerusalem to be the center of the universe and he may have thought his discovery would get a better start from this point. He was sure his theory was plausible, yet it was quite evident Mr. Benton was not right in his mind.

He bought a small bit of property in the open fields beyond the city limits, near the spot where Jerusalem many years later, in 1917, was surrendered to the British, and built a small house consisting, I believe, of two rooms, one upstairs and one downstairs. In it he lived isolated and alone. In those days it was considered dangerous to live so far outside the city limits, but because Mr. Benton was noticeably simple even the peasants of the village of Lifta, the notorious thieves of that time, would not molest him. The Arabic conviction that "God has touched his head" established Mr. Benton as a "holy man" or dervish, and assured him safety.

He had been occupying his lonely abode for some time when his wife and son Frank arrived. They had hunted for him everywhere and at last traced him to Jerusalem. They bought a small bit of property adjoining his, put up a slightly larger replica of his house, and moved in. Their intention was to look after Mr. Benton, but he thought differently. Soon after his wife and son settled in their small house Mr. Benton vanished, and as far as I know was never heard from again.

Mother and son were taken ill with malaria, the so-called Assyrian fever, and Mother and Mrs. Gould, Rob and Mr. Rudy took turns nursing Frank, two by two, for he was dangerous in delirium.

Mother wrote to Aunt Rachel while sitting up during the long night vigil beside young Frank Benton as he raved with fever, on the verge of death, while an Arab sang outside in the dark field:

"He has been singing for an hour, I should think, on two notes. To me it is a most distressing sound and they call it music."

The mother and son got well. Later, very early one morning, Mrs. Benton arrived at our home in a state of collapse. A number of men armed with knives had burst the door open at night and fought with Frank while she hid in the upstairs room. They gashed her son's throat several times and left him apparently dead while they ransacked the house.

Father and Rob took a doctor who sewed up Frank's cuts, which had missed the jugular vein. He was taken to a hospital until he was strong enough to be brought to our home. Mrs. Benton stayed with us.

Father asked Mr. Merrill to request the Turkish governor for a guard to be stationed at the empty Benton house to prevent the furniture, doors, and windows from being stolen while Frank and his mother were being nursed back to health at the American Colony.

Mr. Merrill had little if any knowledge of law. Because Father was an attorney, people in need of advice naturally came to him. Mr. Merrill would have found a willing assistant in Father had he wanted one, instead, he seemed jealous and resentful of the fact that Father was giving legal advice. Wanting, perhaps, to put Father "in his place," Mr. Merrill refused what was the legitimate and obvious thing to do under the circumstances.

"Go and watch the house yourself if you like," he answered.

Father answered that it was not his place to stand guard and that the Turkish governor would be glad to grant such a request. The Consul stubbornly refused to ask for a guard.

Father did not want the poor Bentons to lose the little they had left. There was nothing he could do but ask Raouf Pasha to protect their property. The governor promptly set a guard over the Benton house.

Mr. Merrill was very angry and accused Father of meddling.

As far as I know, this was the first open clash between Father and the American Consul.

In 1885 an excitable, moody lad by the name of Joseph Vinetsky came to the Colony with a sad story. He had been brought to the London Jews' Society Boys' School by a stepmother when he was about four years old, and that was the last seen of her. Since then he had drifted. The Colony took him in and cared for him for several years. Joseph was a big-hearted, demonstrative lad who was a sore trial to everyone. Father placed him as a day scholar in the Alliance Israelite School for Boys, where Father taught English. It was an industrial school, and Joseph chose to learn blacksmithing. He would return home in the evening with black hands and face and before cleaning up would give an affectionate greeting to Mother and Mrs. Gould, who were his favorites, ruining their spotless white dresses or blouses. We children were terrified by his fierce temper. When anything crossed him Joseph would say warningly, "Look out, I have the beast," and we would scatter for safety.

Joseph was eager to be a sailor, and when the United States flagship *Pensacola* came to Jaffa and the chaplain visited the American Colony, Father took Joseph to Jaffa and delivered him to the chaplain.

In 1908 we heard from Joseph again. A letter signed Joseph Spafford came to the American Consul in Jerusalem inquiring about Mother and the Colony, and enclosing fifty dollars for Mother. Mother said she knew no one by that name and refused to accept the money until she discovered who had sent it and for what purpose.

Back came a fifteen-page letter giving Joseph's history from the day he left us. He apologized for assuming our name without permission.

"I took it from the time I came to the States," he wrote, "and I have kept it good and true. . . ."

He asked for everyone, remembering something about each of us, and of Father: "I remember how gentle he was with me. I often think of the time he took me to Jaffa, and I can hear him now as he said to the chaplain, 'take care of my Joseph.' "

He had retained his faith in the Christian religion and reminded Mother that he was born of Jewish parentage. He wrote: "From you I learned a great deal. All the goodness I have in me I can thank your household for."

In 1922, when my husband and I with our three children returned to the United States, we got in touch with Joseph. He was the same Joseph I remembered, warm-hearted and generous, and just as touchy in temper. He visited us often in our home in Lynn, Massachusetts, and was the same trial to our children as he had been to us.

In the American Colony we still say in cross-tempered moments: "Look out! I've got the beast!"

Elijah, as he called himself, was a naturalized American and converted Jew. His education was scanty enough to make him certain he knew all there was to know, and he brought his family to Jerusalem evidently expecting to be the only Americans in the Holy City and perhaps in the Holy Land. He thought of himself as unique. He was not pleased to find an American colony in Jerusalem, and was even more disappointed when he learned one of our members was of Jewish origin. He had very little money and failed to find employment. Mother learned the family was suffering and invited Elijah to come to our house with his wife and four-year-old son until he could find work.

Elijah did not come down to meals for two days. On the third day he was so weak he had to keep to his bed. Mother, thinking he was ill, went to his room to inquire.

"I'm all right," he insisted, then began to question Mother as to what she thought about Christ's second coming.

Mother told him she was certainly looking for it, but instead of setting dates she thought the important thing was to get ready. Then he asked what she thought about the Elijah "who must come first and prepare the way of the Lord."

From his talk Mother suspected that he was convinced he was the prophet. She answered that she did not believe any one person was the Elijah, that it was a principle or dispensation in which to get ready.

He became terribly excited. "You've got to take that back!" he shouted over and over.

Mother understood and pitied his poor, unbalanced mind. By this time we knew several like him, who thought they were John the Baptist or Elijah, or another of the prophets. There were several Messiahs, too, wandering about Jerusalem. She saw how physically weak the man was, so she prevailed on him to take a little milk.

He rose early next morning and left the house, and, as we learned later, went to the top of the Mount of Olives. He had fasted three days and expected the hill to "cleave in two" before him. I'm afraid he had his prophecies slightly mixed, but as no two people agree on them, that part was not important. He had been so positive, that when the prophecy was not fulfilled, his disappointment was terrific.

The poor man could believe only that his failure was owing to breaking his three-day fast, and that Mother was the evil spirit who had tempted him.

He came back from his unsuccessful pilgrimage in an excited state, shouting, gesticulating, and condemning everyone in the Colony, especially Mother, to outer darkness. We did not have to ask him to leave, he had already arranged for that. It was Sunday, and during our afternoon service the Arab porters came to remove Elijah's trunks and other belongings. Since Arab porters can do nothing, however small, without making a great deal of noise, there was considerable disturbance.

We knew Elijah intended to disturb the meeting, so we took no notice of him or of the noise.

We were sorry for his wife and little boy, who were the victims of a maniac. Later we heard they were living in a pitiable state of poverty in a small room in a Jaffa Road tenement, that he had no work, and they were really starving. After that we carried provisions to them every day. I remember going to the tenement house with Father, and how frightened I was for fear we would meet Elijah, but we never did. We always found the empty basket of the day before outside the door with a scrap of paper in it, with a note from the man's wife, "Thank you," or "God bless you."

From Father's notes, on September 21, 1883, the Group was leaving the dining room and passing into the open court when they caught sight of a man who had crossed the court and darted up the stairs. Elijah stood above us on the balcony, his face flushed and wild and his hand raised, holding a large stone. For once I was scared. I rushed into Mother's room and crawled under the bed and stayed there. Father was beside Mother, and he was the first to realize Elijah was dangerous. He made a rush for the steps, and Elijah, seeing him coming, aimed the stone at Father's head. Mr. Drake threw himself on Father as a shield, and Elijah, seeing he could not hit Father, screamed: "I'll kill that Jew, anyway."

"That Jew" was my foster brother Jacob, who had stepped beside Mother to protect her. Elijah hurled the stone but instead of hitting Jacob it grazed Elias, hurting him slightly, and by this time Father and Mr. Drake were at the top of the stairs and had him pinioned. He smelled strongly of arak—the strong native liquor—and was shaking violently. He struggled to reach his penknife, evidently to cut his throat, so Mr. Drake tied his hands behind him with his handkerchief.

Food and strong coffee gave Elijah a different frame of mind and rendered him quite harmless.

Then he confessed that he thought he was "the Elijah" and had expected great things to happen when he got to Jerusalem. His first disappointment was finding other Americans already in Jerusalem, then one disillusionment had followed another.

We brought his wife and son from the old tenement and cared for them all at the American Colony until a collection was taken up and they were sent back to the United States.

One of our first callers when we visited Chicago twelve years later was Elijah. I got a shock when his name was given, but Mother welcomed him cordially. He invited us to his home on the outskirts of North West Chicago, bordering on the prairies, where he and his wife were raising poultry.

Their four-year-old son had grown to be a splendid young man, and there were other sons, all wage earners. They seemed to be in comfortable circumstances. His wife was very pleased to see Mother and pressed her to her heart and kissed her warmly, and I remember we had stuffed turkey and cranberry sauce for midday dinner.

Elijah came to Jerusalem again. This time he was selling vacuum cleaners, a type that was pumped by hand. He sold only one, to our family, and so it happened that a second time we had to help pay Elijah's passage back to the United States, for he had settled down on the American Colony with every apparent intention of remaining with us for the rest of his life.

Miss Poole, a dear, queer little English gentlewoman, lived in one large room in a big tenement house near the Russian Compound. Flora, the eldest of the Colony children, went to Miss Poole for English lessons, and came home with such wonderful stories of her remarkable room that I was crazy to see its wonders for myself.

Miss Poole had lived many years in Jerusalem and in that room, and accumulated so many objects that one could hardly move about in it. She could not bear to throw anything away. "Waste not, want not," she would say, and her red-apple cheeks would shake with a winning laugh. However, when she wanted anything she could never find it and still the accumulation grew.

When General Gordon was in Palestine he called on Miss Poole several times. The matches he used in lighting his cigarettes were never thrown away, but treasured in a box and shown to visitors.

Miss Poole was even more remarkable than her room. She was like a character in a Victorian novel. She still wore hoopskirts and lace caps, under which her tiny curls bobbed up and down in the most charming manner.

She was an astronomer and an astrologer. She studied the skies and read your horoscope if you would let her. She was highly educated, and Father enjoyed her conversation, but there were drawbacks, for she never stopped talking. When Miss Poole came to call no one knew how long she would stay, but she always got a welcome at the American Colony. She would arrive with the condescension of a gueen. Very soon after her arrival she would explain that she must go home shortly, as she had some important writing to do. Teatime would come and go. Dinner would be served. Miss Poole would still be with us. Then, of course, it was too late for her to go home, so she must stay the night.

These apologies would be repeated before each meal for several days. What made her finally leave we never knew, but she did not become a burden, for everyone went about their affairs as though she was not present.

With all Miss Poole's eccentricities, she graced any drawing room. Her conversations were amusing and often interesting. She was kind and generous, and gave away what she needed herself. She visited the poor in the worst parts of the old city, and I am sure she never went empty-handed.

By a strange coincidence a meteor dropped one night. It tore down out of the skies like a bomb and lodged before the door of Miss Poole, the astrologer and astronomer of Jerusalem! Poor Miss Poole could not leave her room, for the large stone was wedged against her door. She called through the window to her neighbors and made them understand they must get help from the American Colony.

Mr. Drake went to Miss Poole's rescue. It took several strong porters to shove the meteor away and set her free.

As we were finishing family prayers one morning there was a loud summons at the front door, and when it was opened ten Germans entered with an air of rightful assurance. The leader was a stocky, dark man and by contrast his fragile wife looked

downtrodden and dispirited. There were three old women, looking more like witches than humans. A young couple with three
children seemed to be the only normal members of this strange
group.

They stalked into the living room without invitation and seated
themselves without being asked.

Father questioned them through Miss Brooke, who knew
German.

The leader's answer was in the form of a proclamation. He had
a spiritualistic mission in Jerusalem, he announced, and had been
led by the Spirit from Germany to Palestine, to Jerusalem, and
to this house, to take possession.

How soon could we vacate? he wanted to know.

He added that we would be allowed to stay if we joined him
in his undertaking.

It was quite in vain that Father tried to convince him we had no
intention of leaving our home or aiding his mission. Hours went
by, and the Germans were still "in possession." During the long-
drawn-out discussion food was brought, and they devoured it
ravenously. Father realized that a higher authority would have to
intervene. He went to the German Consul, who sent his kavass,
who persuaded the strange company that they must go.

The leader marched out neither crestfallen nor dejected. Our
residence, he said in parting, was his by right of supernatural
revelation and would soon be his. We felt very sorry for the old
women and children. They had seemed so hungry, and almost
as if hypnotized with fear of their leader.

Not long after they left the young man came back, bringing
his family. They had at last seen through the leader. He went into
trances, they said, in which he had promised them great riches
spiritual and material, but his "revelations" were chiefly about
his own greatness. They begged our protection.

We rented a flat for them near the Damascus Gate, and until
they could manage for themselves allowed them to have their
meals at the American Colony. The young man was a tailor by
trade and our Mr. Rudy got employment for him as assistant to
Mr. Eppinger, a German merchant tailor in Jerusalem. It was
not long before they were on their feet again.

The rest of the group were still dominated by their leader.
He was enraged by our refusal to vacate our home, so he took
up his abode below us, under the city wall in Solomon's Quarries,
to wait until the spirits moved us out. The immense cavernlike

quarries under the old city, from which Solomon is supposed to have hewn the soft white limestone out of which he built the temple, were dark, damp, and unsanitary.

We were astonished when an Arab reported that "some Europeans" were living in Solomon's Quarries. After investigating and finding the rumor true, Father notified the German Consulate. The spiritualists were brought out and given medical care, but the women had endured hardships too difficult to imagine, and the leader's wife and two of the old women died in the German hospital. The mad leader was sent back to Germany by his government.

In 1886 a man asked if he could get board and lodging at the American Colony. He had a name, but he called himself "Titus." He was a tall, heavy-set German-American from Texas, with small, piercing dark eyes, black hair and beard, and a rather uncouth appearance.

After some discussion Titus was taken in as a paying guest.

Like so many others, Titus was in Jerusalem in answer to what he considered a special call from God. He interpreted a remarkable dream he had had in Texas to mean that he was destined to be a conqueror and ruler of men. He felt convinced that he was signally chosen by God for this unusual destiny, which was to be carried out in Jerusalem.

At first he seemed harmless. He was illiterate, and at his request Father taught him to read and write. He attended family prayers and came to the meetings for Bible study. He seemed to have money, and once he offered to pay in advance for his board and we accepted, for this was after we had spent considerable sums on the Gadites, or Yemenite Jews, and were in need of money.

After making this advance, Titus began behaving strangely. He was away from home for long periods, and returned smelling of liquor. Mother went on a visit to the Friends' Mission in Ramallah and wrote back that the head of the mission there had warned her against Titus, as he was considered to be a dangerous character.

Not long after this Titus began making unseemly advances, first to our maids, then to the ladies of the group. Father asked him to leave. Titus refused, saying that if we insisted he would bring the "American Consul down on us!" The Colony was in a predicament, for we did not have enough money to pay back what Titus had advanced for his board.

Finally, when his behavior had deteriorated below the confines of decent hospitality, we persuaded him to move into a room in the detached "down-to-the-other house." Here we promised to keep Titus housed and fed, with the understanding that he was never to come near the main building for a period of time that would more than compensate for his advance payment, including interest.

Titus was drinking heavily now of the powerful local arak and looking crazier than ever. When in his room he spent his time writing reams of interpretations of his dreams. He did a great deal of shouting and muttering, and when we passed the window, he was often there looking out, as though watching for us, and he would shake his great fist in a terrifying way.

The neighbors began to complain that his shouting and pacing his room all night kept them awake. Once he developed delirium tremens and screamed of goblins and devils in his room; that cats were sitting on his chest and choking him. The men of the Colony had to go down and quiet him.

No matter how much disturbance Titus might make, he did not approve of noise made by others. I remember an incident during the Mohammedan fast of Ramadan. As we lived in a Moslem quarter, we heard the man come round every night to wake the "faithful" for their last meal before dawn, when the fast began. He carried a small drum and pounded it to the chant, "Let the faithful arise and take refreshment. Your prophet is passing and will bless you."

Titus shouted down to the man to keep quiet.

Of course the summoner went right on calling the faithful, so Titus came out on his balcony cursing, and emptied onto the poor fellow's head the contents of the receptacle he kept under the bed.

What excitement followed! What recriminations and explanations! I shall never forget Father, summoned from his bed in the middle of the night, tall and majestic in the Turkey-red dressing gown Mother had made him out of a blanket, and surrounded by a great crowd of the neighbors who had risen for the last meal. Father and Mother met such crises with calm, but Father knew no Arabic, and it was difficult to explain that the man living on our premises did not belong to us and that we were not responsible for his actions.

Maarouf was there, and Elias, and they translated and explained, and once the Arabs understood they forgave all. Ill feeling vanished the instant they realized Titus was simple.

"Allah has touched him," they said, as they do in such cases, only they simply say, "Touched," and pat their heads. Many of the dervishes were "touched."

It was a day of rejoicing for the American Colony when the debt to Titus was finally paid. For years we used to see him roaming about Jerusalem, living where or how we did not know, but looking wilder and more unkempt as time went on.

Then there was the "Prophet Daniel," so called, who had been "summoned" from the United States to the Holy Land, where he believed his identity would be publicly proclaimed by supernatural means. We first learned of him when word came that an American couple and their five children were lying ill in the Jewish quarter of Jerusalem. The Prophet and his family had been stricken with smallpox and the baby had died. A kind missionary lady had bravely gone to nurse them, but she was worn out with tending them all, as well as doing all the cooking and housework.

Two of our Group volunteered, and went into a month of trying exile. During their quarantine all the food for both invalids and nurses was sent from the American Colony. When our nurses left, the house was clean and the patients well.

Gratitude is not always returned for unselfish and devoted care. One day when on the road the Prophet's wife met one of our ladies who had nursed her family back to health she turned her head away. We did not share, she had learned, some of the pet theological beliefs of her husband, the living reincarnation of the great prophet saved from the lions' den.

Mother heard that another American, "looking like one of the prophets, with a flowing white beard," was ill in the home of an Arab in the poorest quarter of the city. She found him and brought him home. His malady proved to be smallpox.

In those days smallpox was thought to be one of the illnesses that children must go through, and instead of shunning an infected house some mothers took their children there to "get it over." The nature of the old man's sickness made no difference to the American Colony, except that proper precautions were taken so it would not spread.

The old man was Mr. George A. Fuller from Lynn, Massachusetts, U.S.A., which information he gave to everyone, never omitting the U.S.A., which he pronounced with emphasis on each letter.

He was a carpenter by trade, and had read glowing articles in the *Age to Come Herald* that led him impulsively to pack his tools and sell all his possessions, which brought him just enough money to take him to Jerusalem.

He drifted about the city with his carpentry tools, doing odd jobs. Because of his advanced age and ignorance of Arabic, he could barely earn enough to keep body and soul together.

He was nursed back to health and his devotion was touching. He lived with us for the rest of his life. He made himself useful in the carpenter shop, and we loved dear old "Brother George A."

He studied his Bible assiduously and was troubled by the many sins he might commit without being aware of sinfulness. Before he knew Father, he would lie awake at night begging God to forgive him. His sins seemed all in his own imagination, for I never knew a more simple and guileless individual. Father's theory of God's complete forgiveness was a comfort to Brother George A., and he became a different man, cheerful and contented.

We children haunted his carpenter shop and liked to handle his tools. He taught us to use them correctly, and this knowledge has stood me in good stead all my life. We must have bothered the dear old man, but he never grew impatient. Our questions never ceased: "Brother George A., what are you making? How is this done? Are you going to do this? What is that? Why?"

One time he had enough of this, so taking us gently by our hands he led us to the door. As it closed behind us I heard him say, "My dears, it is a fact: I know it is true now that children and fools should never see unfinished work."

Another day, when one of the small boys was put to work sand papering the back of a bureau Brother George A. was making, the boy asked why he had to clean the back of the bureau, since it would never be seen. Brother George A. answered, "Your behind is never seen and yet you keep it clean"—a lesson the small boy never forgot.

Brother George A. mended old furniture and made new. His work was neat but graceless. Mother was given a large plush photograph album Brother George A. considered beautiful, so he made a box of common pine shellacked a bright yellow with black trimmings to hold it. It took up half the center table and was a dreadful eyesore to Mother. We children nicknamed it "The Coffin."

One day the milkman arrived with a large bill. We were hard

up for funds, and as Mother stood wondering how to pay, he pointed to the box and offered a substantial reduction of the bill for it. His offer was gratefully accepted.

Brother George A. saw the milkman leave the house with "The Coffin" under his arm. We heard him groan. "My conscience, there goes the box!" But he never mentioned it to Mother.

There was an old American couple living in Jerusalem named Black. Mr. Black thought he had discovered the North Pole. He would talk endlessly, if one had time to listen, about his imaginary experiences in the land of the Midnight Sun.

They had some money which they deposited wisely, as they thought, in the two private banks in Jerusalem, not to have "all their eggs in one basket." First Bergheim's banks, then Frutigar's, failed. The Blacks were old, simple, and now penniless. Mother and other members of the Group visited them regularly and sent provisions, but when they both got sick, and their room rent.came due, there seemed no other way but to make room for them in the American Colony.

After several years Mr. Black died, but Mrs. Black lived on with us for many years. In conversation one day she disclosed that her first husband was killed in the Civil War. We took the matter to the American Consul, and he succeeded in getting her a small pension.

Her whole outlook changed with her first installment. She felt independent, and became critical and hard to please. She accused us of stealing some handkerchiefs we had given her on Christmas and which she had mislaid. When we denied this, she said she must leave us, delivering this declaration like an ultimatum.

She had gone only a few days when she asked to come back. This time, however, the Colony was firm. A group of Mormons lately come to Jerusalem as missionaries had taken her in, and it developed that the Blacks had been Mormons all along. We were glad and relieved to know she had found some of her own people and had friends who were willing to look after her.

The Garners had no special or grandiose ideas about themselves but they had drifted from New England, I believe, to Palestine among the "simples." I was a child when I first met Mrs. Garner, who was housekeeper for a strange Englishwoman who certainly had a mental twist. This lady was doing what she considered missionary work by showing the natives how to dress.

She used great economy in her materials, and her skirts were so narrow she could hardly walk. I remember imitating her walk, and the other children would be convulsed with laughter. Another of her idiosyncrasies was exaggerated modesty. She draped the legs of her chairs and tables with material so as not to have the legs uncovered. She was so economical with her food that Mr. Garner had to leave her, and when she was found dead in her room, it was believed she had died of starvation.

The next we heard of the Garners, they were in Jaffa. We were paying Mr. and Mrs. Rolla Floyd one of our annual visits when Mrs. Garner, looking very old and exhausted with worry and hard work, came to ask the Church Missionary Society Hospital in Jaffa if they would take in her husband, who had had a stroke of paralysis. The verdict of the Society was that they could not accept a chronic case.

Of course Mother put her shoulder under poor Mrs. Garner's burden. Mr. and Mrs. Garner were brought to the American Colony and Mr. Garner, a large, heavy man and completely helpless, was nursed there for five years, until he died.

He had been a soldier in the Civil War and the Colony tried to get a pension for Mrs. Garner, appealing through a friend to Mr. Merrill, who in turn appealed to Washington. Nothing came of his attempt, and the American Consul wrote to the friend:

I fully expected to succeed, but at last his claim was rejected on what seemed to me a most flimsy excuse. I was thoroughly disgusted and ashamed that our government should treat in such a way a faithful soldier who had been in over fifty battles.

The house where she (Mrs. Garner) is in Jerusalem does not bear a very good reputation and she ought to be got away from there. If she had a pension and it were put into her hands the people in that house would get it away from her I am almost certain.

Yours sincerely,
SELAH MERRILL

That Mrs. Garner had contributed nothing to her support made no difference to the American Colony and evidently less to Mr. Merrill. She lived on with us through many years. The children of the Colony serenaded her on the morning of her eightieth birthday. One verse had this line: "May you in wisdom grow," and in memory I can still hear her protests, for she thought it was an insinuation against her mentality.

I remember one exaggerated case that shocked us all. I have forgotten the sect that called the meeting, but a zealous leader preached an impassioned sermon on the text in Matthew 5:29, "If thy right eye offend thee, pluck it out, and cast it from thee; for it is profitable for thee that one of thy members should perish, and not that thy whole body should be cast into hell."

This was taken literally by a young girl in the audience. That evening, in her room, she tried to cut off her right hand. She was taken to the German Hospital in a mutilated and bleeding condition, but the hand was saved. Next morning, when the doctor entered her room, he found one of her eyes on the floor, and she was digging out the other with her fingers, so that it had to be surgically removed.

Later, when she was in a sane and sorrowful frame of mind, we were asked to give her shelter. We kept her for some time and taught her Braille.

After leaving the American Colony she went to the Syrian Orphanage Blind School and found consolation in service.

During our lives in Jerusalem we witnessed many tragedies caused by religious frenzies and fanaticisms, and followed the courses of numerous unbalanced cranks. There is a thread of similarity in all their stories of the same sad, exaggerated egotism. Something in the brain suggests the idea of their uniqueness as chosen by God, or reincarnated to fulfill some tremendous purpose. I could continue indefinitely, for the simples in Allah's Garden were many, seeming to gravitate to the Holy Land to enter our lives for long or short periods of time, sometimes with direful consequences. The few I have told about are typical.

CHAPTER TWELVE

THE Gadites entered our lives a few months after our arrival in Jerusalem, and until civil war divided Jerusalem into Arab and Jewish zones, with no intercourse between except bullets and bombs, they continued to get help from the American Colony.

One afternoon in May 1882 several of the Group, including my parents, went for a walk, and were attracted by a strange-looking company of people camping in the fields. The weather was hot, and they had made shelters from the sun out of odds and ends of cloth, sacking, and bits of matting.

Father made inquiries through the help of an interpreter and found that they were Yemenite Jews recently arrived from Arabia.

They told Father about their immigration from Yemen and their arrival in Palestine. Suddenly, they said, without warning, a spirit seemed to fall on them and they began to speak about returning to the land of Israel. They were so convinced that this was the right and appointed time to return to Palestine that they sold their property and turned other convertible belongings into cash and started for the Promised Land. They said about five hundred had left Yena in Yemen. Most of them were uneducated in any way except the knowledge of their ancient Hebrew writings, and those, very likely, they recited by rote. As appears, they were simple folk, with little knowledge of the ways of the world outside of Yemen, and that is the same as saying "the days of Abraham."

When they landed in Hedida on the coast of the Red Sea, they were cautioned by Jews not to continue their trip to Jerusalem and that if they did so it would be at peril of their lives. Some of the party were discouraged and returned to Yena. Others were misdirected and were taken to India. The rest went to Aden, where they embarked on a steamer for Jaffa, and came to Jerusalem before the Feast of Passover.

They told about the opposition and unfriendliness they had encountered from the Jerusalem Jews, who, they said, accused them of not being Jews but Arabs.

One reason, they said, for their rejection by the Jerusalem Jews was because they feared that these poor immigrants would swell the number of recipients of halukkah, or prayer money. Early in the seventeenth century, as a result of earthquakes, famine, and persecution, the economic position of the Jews in Palestine became critical, and the Jews of Venice came to their aid. They established a fund "to support the inhabitants of the Holy Land." Later on the Jews of Poland, Bohemia, and Germany offered similar aid. This was the origin of the halukkah. The money was sent not so much for the purpose of charity as to enable Jewish scholars and students to study and interpret the Scriptures and Jewish holy books and to pray for the Jews in the Diaspora (Dispersion), at the Wailing Wall in Jerusalem, and in other holy cities of Palestine. The halukkah, as one could imagine, was soon abused. It only stopped, however, when World War I began in 1914 and no more money came to Palestine for that purpose.

In 1882, when the Yemenites arrived, those who had benefited from the generosity of others were unwilling to pass it on.

Father was interested in the Gadites at once. Their story about their unprovoked conviction that this was the time to return to Palestine coincided with what he felt sure was coming to pass—the fulfillment of the prophecy of the return of the Jews to Palestine. Also, Father was attracted by the classical purity of Semitic features of these Yemenite immigrants, so unlike the Jews he was accustomed to see in Jerusalem or in the United States. These people were distinctive: they had dark skin with dark hair and dark eyes. They wore side curls, according to the Mosaic law: "Ye shalt not round the corners of your heads, neither shalt thou mar the corners of thy beard." Otherwise their dress was Arabic. They had poise, and their movements were graceful, like those of the Bedouins. They were slender and somewhat under-sized. Many of the women were beautiful, and the men, even the young men, looked venerable with their long beards. They regarded as true the tradition that they belonged to the tribe of Gad. They believed that they had not gone into captivity in Babylon, and that they had not returned at the time of Ezra and Nehemiah to rebuild the temple. For thousands of years they had remained in Yemen, hence their purity of race and feature.

The thirty-second chapter of Numbers tells how the children of Gad and the children of Reuben asked Moses to allow them to remain on the east side of Jordan, which country had "found favor in their sight." It goes on to tell how Moses rebuked them, saying, "Shall your brethren go to war, and shall ye sit here?" Then Moses promised them that if they would go armed and help subdue the country, then "this land shall be your possession before the Lord."

In the thirteenth chapter of Joshua, "when Joshua was stricken in years," he gives instructions that the Gadites and the Reubenites and half the tribe of Menasseh should receive their inheritance "beyond the Jordan eastward even as Moses the servant of the Lord gave them."

In the *Apology of al Kindy*, written at the court of al Mamun, A.D. 830, the author speaks of Medina as being a poor town, mostly inhabited by Jews. He also speaks of other tribes of Jews, one of which was deported to Syria.

Would it be too remote to conjecture that the remnants of these tribes should have wandered to and remained in Yemen? I know there are other theories about how Jews got there, and about their origin, but Father believed that "Blessed be he that enlargeth Gad," and the Group did everything in their power to help these immigrants. We called them Gadites from that time.

They were in dreadful need when we found them.

Some of them had died of exposure and starvation during their long and uncomfortable trip; now malaria, typhoid, and dysentery were doing their work. They had to be helped, and quickly. No time was lost in getting relief started. The Group rented rooms, and the Gadites were installed in cooler and more sanitary quarters. Medical help was immediately brought. Mr. Steinhart's sister, an Orthodox Jewish woman, was engaged to purchase kosher meat, which, with vegetables and rice or cracked burghal (wheat) she made into a nutritious soup. Bread and soup were distributed once a day to all, with the addition of milk for the children and invalids. One of the American Colony members was always present at distribution time, to see that it was done equitably and well. The Gadites had a scribe among them who was a cripple. He could not use his arms and wrote the most beautiful Hebrew, holding a reed pen between his toes. He wrote a prayer for Father and his associates, which was brought one day and presented to Father as a thanksgiving offering. They said that they repeated the prayer daily. I have it in my possession; it is written on a piece of parchment. The transation was made by Mr. Steinhart.

This amicable state of affairs continued for some time. Then the elders, who were the heads of the families, came as a delegation to Father. They filed upstairs to the large upper living room, looking solemn and sad, and smelling strongly of garlic. They told Father that certain Orthodox Jews, the very ones who had turned blind eyes and deaf ears to their entreaties for help when they arrived in such a pitiable state, were now persecuting them under the claim that they were violating the law by eating Christian food. Some of the older men and women had stopped eating, and in consequence were weak and ill. They made Father understand how vital this accusation, even if false, was to them, and they begged him to divide the money spent among them, instead of giving them the food.

Everyone knows how much more economical it is to make a large quantity of soup in one caldron than in many individual pots; however, their request was granted. A bit more money was added to the original sum, and every Friday morning the heads of the Gadite families would appear at the American Colony and be given coins in proportion to the number of individuals to be fed.

They explained to Father that they were trying to learn the trades of the new country and hoped very soon not to need assistance. They had been goldsmiths and silversmiths of a crude sort in Yemen, but Jerusalem at that time had no appreciation or demand for that sort of handicraft.

One by one the elders came to tell us they had found work, to thank us for what we had done, and to say they needed no further help. Father was impressed with the unspoiled integrity of these people.

The Colony continued giving help to the original group of Gadites in decreasing amounts until only a few old people and widows remained. But these came regularly once a week. Their number was swelled by newcomers and we still shared what we could with them: portions of dry rice, lentils, tea, coffee, and sugar, or other dry articles. After the British occupation of Palestine and the advent of the Zionist organization, with its resources and vast machinery to meet pressing necessities, after forty years our list of dependent Gadites was taken over by them.

Even then, individuals continued to come to the doors of the American Colony to ask our help.

One night in June 1948 the American Colony had been under fire all night between the Jews west of us and the Arab legionaries east of us. In the morning a Yemenite Jew lay dead in the road before our gates. I recognized Hyam, a Yemenite from the "box colony" near the American Colony. He was one of those who had been receiving help from us for years.

For all this relief work the American Colony was using the money of its members. In the meantime Mr. Merrill had succeeded in adversely influencing our friends at home in the United States, and our checks in this mission of mercy were not valid. This was the origin of our getting into debt.

In 1884, two years after their arrival, the Gadite elders were again at our door urgently asking to see Father. They were excited and agitated, for in Jerusalem, they said, they had caught sight of a "rabbi" who had won their confidence back in Yemen, Arabia, and forcibly abducted their most ancient and precious manuscript, the Temanite Scroll.

The "rabbi" turned out to be a man whom I shall call Mr. Moses. He was a converted Jew. His wife, before their marriage, had been a Lutheran deaconess. They had two daughters, and at this time they were living in one of the villas in a garden outside the walls of Jerusalem. I remember on one of our walks standing with my nurse and watching the peacocks in their garden. Mr. Moses and his family attended Christ Church and Father remarked that, when he began to pray, "one might just as well try and make oneself comfortable," for he would go on and on ever so long.

Mr. Moses was an antiquarian and trafficked in antiques. He had enough knowledge coupled with ability and coggery to deceive the archaeological students for a long time. To relate this story in full I must go back a number of years.

When Emperor Frederick II of Germany came to Jerusalem as Crown Prince in 1869, the Turkish Government presented him with a valuable bit of property inside the old city, near the Holy Sepulcher, known as the Muristan. It is the site of the hospitals, caravansary, and church of the Knights of Saint John. It was in ruins at the time, but the stones lying about showed what the buildings had been. The church was reconstructed later, and Kaiser William II came to Jerusalem in 1898 for the dedication of the Church of the Redeemer. While Crown Prince Frederick of Prussia was in Jerusalem, Mr. Moses presented him with a number of Canaanite pottery idols, which he claimed he had found in a cave in the mountains of Moab, east of the Jordan.

These idols, according to one description, "were the teraphim or household gods of the Edomites and were all of them revoltingly coarse presentments of erotic passions." They had been on exhibition in the lecture room of the London Jews' Society before the presentation was made, so that the public could have a preview of them, and my foster brother, who was then a boarder in the London Jews' Society Boys' School, was given the privilege of seeing them with the other scholars, and he was frightened to death by the sight.

He knew the Israelites were always getting into trouble because they worshiped idols. He thought they must have been impelled by supernatural power to do so, for no one would willingly worship such ugly things. Poor Jacob tried to keep his eyes fastened on the toes of his shoes, but in spite of himself he would look up and get a glimpse of the hideous objects. However, the Crown Prince seemed highly pleased with the gift, for Mr. Moses was decorated, and the idols were carefully packed and dispatched to Germany.

Mr. Moses frequently disappeared from Jerusalem for long periods, and it was understood that he made journeys into dangerous and remote places in search of antiquities. Archaeology in those days was not the science it is today, and research time was carried on more or less by amateurs. From one of these trips Mr. Moses returned and remained only a short time in Jerusalem before proceeding to England. No one knew where he had been and great secrecy was maintained about his actions and movements. Soon it was rumored that he had offered to sell a very old Hebrew manuscript to the British Museum. This manuscript is now in the British Museum, and is called the "Temanite Scroll." It is the oldest Hebrew manuscript in the museum, and Mr. Moses got a large sum of money for it.

After selling the Temanite Scroll to the British Museum, Mr. Moses returned to Jerusalem and for some time was lost to the outside world.

His shadow occupation in Jerusalem was being the proprietor of a shop. On his signboard were these words, "Bookseller and Antiquarian," and underneath this was painted, "Correspondent to the British Museum."

However, he spent most of his time in his home, at some mysterious occupation, and it was during this time that our Gadite elders recognized him and came to Father for advice.

They told Father that he had come to them in Yemen purpotr-

ing to be a rabbi, which he may have been, before his so-called
conversion, and it was in that capacity that he lived among them
when he was in Yemen, joining them in prayers in their synagogue
until he had won their confidence. When he succeeded, he asked
if they had any very old manuscripts. They told him that they
had, but that they never brought them out except on a certain
feast day. As that special feast was not far distant, "Rabbi" Moses
remained in Yemen, ingratiating himself in the good graces of
these simple folk. When the Temanite Scroll was uncovered he
saw, with his experienced and practiced eye, how old and valuable it was. He offered to buy it, but they said they would rather
part with their eyes or their lives than with their beloved manuscript. When Mr. Moses saw that entreaties were no good,
he went to the Turkish governor. One can only imagine what
transaction took place there, for a sufficient escort of soldiers
was given to him and he went to the synagogue and forcibly
took the Temanite Scroll, leaving a nominal sum of money.

Before their talk with Father could be translated into terms
of action, Mr. Moses left Jerusalem, and the next surprise came
when we learned he was in London, offering the British Museum
a much older manuscript than the one he had already sold to
them two years before. This one, he claimed, had been written
by Eliazar, grandson of Aaron. He said he had found it in a cave
in the mountains of Moab, east of the Jordan. For a number of
weeks the archaeological students of Europe were agog with
eager expectations and the desire to know if this remarkable
manuscript was authentic. Many of the scientific periodicals of
the day had articles about this baffling manuscript. Students
from Germany and France went to London to study it. The
parchment was supple and very old, no one could gainsay that.
The characters were of the oldest Hebrew, like those of the
Moabite stone. Here was a problem: how could parchment,
buried for thousands of years in a cave in Moab, remain so supple
and soft? Yet it was old, very old, there was no doubt about that.
Sentiment swayed this way and that, and more articles were
written.

In the meantime Mr. Moses was waiting in London to be paid
the £1,000,000 he was asking for the manuscript, and the British
Museum was zealously guarding the treasure. The controversy
had been going on for about six weeks, gaining publicity with
time, when a certain M. Clermont-Ganneau, who had been
French Consul in Jerusalem and had excavated the so-called

Tombs of the Kings, appeared in London. It was during his residence in Jerusalem that the presentation of the idols to Crown Prince Frederick had taken place, and he had suspected their authenticity even then. His suspicion had been confirmed by Mr. Moses's servant, Saleem, who always accompanied him on his expeditions to Moab. Saleem had quarreled with his master, and in revenge had gone to M. Clermont-Ganneau and confessed his complicity in the forgery of the idols. M. Clermont-Ganneau had exposed Mr. Moses through a pamphlet, but by the time he was negotiating for the sale of this precious manuscript the pamphlet had been forgotten.

However, the appearance of M. Clermont-Ganneau in London caused Mr. Moses to quake in his shoes. M. Clermont-Ganneau asked to see the manuscript in question, and with the knowledge he had tucked away in his memory, he looked at it with a more than ordinarily critical eye. He asked to examine the Temanite Scroll as well. He noticed the tiniest black dot at certain intervals along the second scroll. He put the two scrolls together and found what he suspected to be the case, that the parchment of the second had been cut off the first. It was the wide margin which Mr. Moses had carefully cut off, and the minute black speck at equal intervals along the edge, which M. Clermont-Ganneau had discovered, was the continuation of the marginal line of the original scroll. The parchment was truly old, but the writing was very cleverly done by Mr. Moses himself, and not by Eliazar, the grandson of Aaron.

Mr. Moses wasted no time when the fraud was exposed. He crossed the Channel to Rotterdam and committed suicide.

He had been busily writing the second scroll in Jerusalem when our Gadites recognized him as the "rabbi" who had abducted their manuscript.

Father wrote to the authorities of the British Museum, telling them the real story and asking for some remuneration for the Yemenite Jews, but the Museum authorities had paid heavily for the first scroll and had been harassed by the fraud which followed, and evidently wanted to hear nothing more about the matter.

CHAPTER THIRTEEN

IN THOSE early days, before the Group became acclimated, it was necessary for the older people to take some rest from their strenuous work. There are many accounts in Father's diary of picnics in the fields, especially in the spring when wild flowers cover the hills and valleys. There were also pilgrimages to farther places.

Horse, camel, and donkeyback were the only means of transportation. The only carriage road was between Jerusalem and Jaffa; the carriage roads to Jericho and Hebron were not built until 1890.

We rode many times to nearby Bethlehem, the "little town" hallowed by the Church of the Nativity. Bethany, on the Mount of Olives, was another of our favorite villages; the traditional tomb of Lazarus was shown there, and the place where Martha met the Lord.

There were trips to Ramallah, and farther away, to Jericho and Moab.

Ramallah was particularly pleasant because of our amicable relationship with members of the Friends' Mission station there.

There were annual visits to Mr. and Mrs. Floyd in Jaffa. Their cottage was small, but Mr. Floyd was a contractor for tourists, and had the equipment to make us comfortable. Tents were pitched in the garden with camp beds set within, and thus a most enjoyable week could be spent. The reputation for good singing by the Colony quartet, which consisted of Mother, soprano; Mrs. Gould, alto; Jacob, tenor; and Elias, bass, had gone before us, and crowds gathered in the evening around the fence to listen to the singing. Soon the audience learned which of the hymns and Negro spirituals they liked best, and they would call for "Go Down, Moses," "Swing Low, Sweet Chariot," "In the Secret of His Presence," and many others, keeping the American Colony choir singing for hours.

The native people were very kind and appreciative. One of our Moslem friends rented a house in an orchard in the village of Ein Karim and invited a few of our Group at a time, until he had given us all a turn. Another time we rented the vineyard belonging to our cook in Ramallah, and the guest room or "madiafieh" of the village was put at our disposal. Those were happy days, when, in the early mornings, we would step out of doors to pluck and eat delicious grapes and purple figs, sweet and fresh with the dew still glistening on them.

Early in 1884 our Moslem grocer asked if he might bring some Bedouin sheiks from east of the Jordan to call on us. He traded in grain with them. Father was especially pleased to make their acquaintance and the first visit by Sheik Ali Diab, the paramount sheik of the large and powerful Adwan tribe, was the beginning of a friendship which has continued through several generations of sheiks to the present day.

The invitation for us to return the visit came through Ali Diab's son, Sheik Fiaz. And so in November 1884 a party went to Hesban or Heshbon, high up on the mountains of Moab. Heshbon was the capital of King Sihon of the Amorites. It is only a bare site now, but it was an important Levitical city of Reuban and Gad. It came again into the possession of the Amorites before the captivity.

I remember well the visit to Heshbon, although I was only six years old. In July I had been ill with what was considered to be rheumatic fever. It left me weak and pale. I begged to be taken on the exciting expedition to the Bedouin country, and as my parents thought a change might be beneficial to me, I was allowed to go. I rode sometimes behind Father and Rob on their horses, but nearly all the time I was perched high on top of the load of the pack horse.

Mother told about the trip in a letter to a friend:

We started early in the morning, on horseback, without any protection except our Bedouin friends who were armed to the teeth with swords, pistols, knives, etc. I wish you could have seen us start out with these wild Ishmaelites.

The ride to Jericho took the entire day. For this trip we followed the road with which we were most familiar, from the Damascus Gate below our house, along the city wall to the northeast corner—a picturesque bit of masonry, although, as considered in this part of the world, of recent date. It was built about the time America was discovered by Columbus, which we Americans think is ancient history, but it is not considered so in the Holy Land.

We now faced the Mount of Olives, lighted—as we started

such expeditions early—by the morning glow that gives everything that mystic charm which is so particularly beautiful in
Palestine, and descended into the Valley of Jehoshaphat across
the small bridge where the Kedron Brook flows after a hard rain.

To our right, as we turned to go over the bridge, is a building
marking the spot where the Greek Orthodox Church claim that
Stephen was stoned. The Dominican monastery and church on
the Nablus Road, already mentioned, is the more authentic site.
We are accustomed to these dual sites in Palestine, for nearly
every saint has two birthplaces and more than one burial place.
These discrepancies shock the tourists. Some people visit Jerusalem and the Holy Land in the hope that doubt will be eliminated
and faith fortified in religious belief. When they come in such a
spirit, the churches guarded by Mohammedan soldiers, to keep
so-called Christians from fighting, the foul-smelling shrines
pointed out by some greasy, repulsive-looking man, or the numerous sites shown for the same occurrence, repel them. The hot
trip to Jericho and the "muddy creek" which is the River Jordan
could be disillusioning.

But there is much beauty and great interest everywhere.
Greasy and repulsive looking many may be on the outside, but
earnest souls can dwell in dirty garments. The hills and valleys
and the costumes of the people are those He saw, and one finds
Jesus wherever one may go in the Holy Land.

It was with such thoughts in our minds that we passed Gethsemane at the foot of the Mount of Olives. That small garden,
walled in and kept in such immaculate condition by Franciscan
monks, with old-fashioned flowers of every kind and hue bloom-
ing the year round in the shadow of the old olive trees with their
curiously gnarled trunks, known to be nine hundred years old,
may or may not be the real spot where heaven and earth met on
the wonderful Thursday night two thousand years ago. But we
do know Gethsemane was on the side of Olivet across the Kedron.

To those who have a deeper understanding of what these experiences mean, the actual spot does not matter much.

We rode over the brow of Olivet between high walls surrounding Jewish cemeteries, where the graves have crept until they
reach the top, for the Jews consider themselves fortunate to die
in Jerusalem and be buried on the slope of the Mount of Olives,
near the Valley of Jehoshaphat, in the hope that they will be the
first on hand in the Day of Judgment where all will meet, according to the verse in Joel.

We always turned back from the Mount of Olives for a last view of Jerusalem. The Mosque el Aksa and the Dome of the Rock (Mosque of Omar) stand in grandeur above the parapets of the city wall, and below the deep descent of the Valley of Jehoshaphat—all rich in sacred memories and impressively beautiful.

This is nearly the same view which Christ and His disciples looked upon when the latter were impressed with the benevolence of the Jews and drew Christ's attention to the wonderful buildings. "Is it possible that all these edifices which are built from unselfish offerings are not acceptable to God?"

We passed through quiet and dusty Bethany. A steep, winding descent took us down the deep valley separating the hills around Jerusalem to the Apostle's Fountain, En-Shemesh (Spring of the Sun) of the Old Testament, marking the boundary between Judah and Benjamin.

This spring lies in a hollow, the hills forming a small amphitheater, and the road makes a horseshoe around it. I remember picnics there in the warm hollow with the sun glaring down, and a *sharki* (east) wind blowing.

This was sometimes an exciting place to be, for caravans of Bedouins rest there on their way to and from the "medenie" (city) where they bring their grain for sale. There are terrible blood feuds among the Bedouins, and if persons from the respective parties meet here, and want to water their animals at the trickling spring at the same time, a terrific battle ensues that may end in bloodshed. We witnessed such a battle once, as children, when we were picnicking at the Apostle's Fountain, and the pastoral scene suddenly changed to a bloody feud with bullets flying.

Riding on, we came to Jericho, situated on the plain a short distance from the Judean hills.

Jericho was not an attractive city then.

It contained several hotels and a Russian hospice. Here thousands of pilgrims were accommodated, especially at Epiphany, when a service was held on the banks of the Jordan and the pilgrims, men and women together, immersed themselves in the river, wearing their shrouds.

Besides the above-mentioned buildings, with the exception of a small Greek church, Jericho contained nothing but dirty hovels where the inhabitants eked out an existence. They were even less fortunate than the roving tribes who leave a place when it becomes thoroughly dirty and pitch their tents on some clean spot, and when spring-cleaning time comes, move again.

Not far from Jericho is Elisha's Fountain, which was cured by Elisha with a cruse of salt.

But Jericho was blessed with a tropical climate, which we often came to enjoy in cold winters for several weeks at a time. Before many years passed rich Arabs began building winter residences and hotels there, and in 1948 the city filled with Arab refugees. These unfortunate persons, driven from their homes, flocked to Jericho because of its warmth during that unusually cold winter.

On this visit with our Bedouin friends we arrived in Jericho in late afternoon after, as Mother wrote in her letter, "going down-hill all the way."

She continued:

We have a friend in Jericho, who visited our home several times and asked us to visit him in Jericho. We had a warm welcome and were ushered into an orange and lemon grove. There were also bananas and other tropical fruit trees.

It was a refreshing sight after our long ride. We remained in Jericho for the night and started early in the morning on our journey. We rode an hour and a half and then arrived at the Jordan. There was no bridge, and as the water was too high for us to ford the stream, we all crossed in a ferry, horses and all. The ferry was a most quaint, primitive affair.

The scenery about the Jordan was beautiful. The weather was hot although late in November. We remounted on the other side and rode for another hour and a half across the plain, then the son of the sheik rode on before us to announce our arrival to an encampment of Bedouins belonging to this tribe, but who were shepherds. The tent we entered was prepared with rich rugs on the ground for us to sit upon. The encampment was an interesting sight; men, women, and children flocked about to greet us. Some of them had never seen a white or European lady before. I assure you it was refreshing to be able to lie down and rest under this tent for it was still hot. Very soon after our arrival they killed the "fatted lamb" and "baked the cake" for us, just like in the days of Abraham. The "savory dish" was put before us with the "cakes" of bread and we surrounded the dish. We ate with our fingers. Our hosts picked out choice bits with their hands and offered them to us to eat. In the evening a wood fire was built before the tent and all gathered round it in a reclining attitude, facing the fire. It would be hard to describe the wild scene. The dark faces of the men, some of them almost entirely covered by their "kaffiyeh" or headdress arrangement, with only their bright eyes showing, and all of them armed with pistols and knives. It was a strange sight, and, I must confess, it was a little frightening—one I had read about but never witnessed before. I have no doubt that we were as strange to them as they were to us. After supper they wanted to entertain us to the best of their ability, so they arranged one of their war dances. It was the wildest scene one could imagine. About a dozen men stood shoulder to shoulder swaying back and forth with rhythmic movement and singing a war song, which was weird enough. Before them a woman danced with a drawn sword in her hand, which she brandished with dexterous skill. Her dress was very long and also her sleeves. Both her dress and sleeves flew back and forth with her rapid movements. The faster she danced the more excited the men got, until it all finished in a grand finale of noise and dust.

We remained in this encampment until early the next morning, when we resumed our journey. We were now in the country of Moab. The mountains of Moab, seen so often from Jerusalem looking like iridescent silk, were before us to climb, but in reality they were rocks and stone with no made roads, only steep bridle paths. We had a long, hard ride until about three in the afternoon when we reached our destination. The tent we were ushered into was 150 feet long, woven out of goats' hair and quite waterproof. Nora, Bertha, and I were taken into the women's compartment and the men were taken into the sheik's compartment. A beautiful Kalim carpet hung and divided the tent.

The wife of the great sheik met us with the gracious dignity of a queen. She stood at the door of the tent welcoming us in a dress of dark blue material ten feet long and sleeves eleven feet long (we measured them). The dress in the same length all around, and it takes an experienced person to walk inside this bag, with the dress trailing behind her. It is let down on state occasions, otherwise it is tucked up around her waist in several folds. She stood there commanding her servants and handmaidens who in response brought out mattresses covered with rich red satin. Our shoes were taken off and we were given water so that we might wash. Then the handmaidens hurried to bring us lemonade, sweets, and coffee. Directly the whole encampment was astir. The fatted lamb or kid had to be prepared, the bread baked. Butter and "laban" (clabbered milk) were brought with the cooked meal and set in huge trays and bowls on the ground. Rich Persian rugs were laid round for us to sit upon. After we had partaken of the evening meal, all the retainers were served according to their rank. Even the casual passer-by, no matter how ragged, was fed. After the remnants of the meal and the dishes were removed, the evening fire was rekindled. The sheik and the male part of his family and retainers surrounded it. Then the court joker and singer came forward and sang the praises of the great sheik—telling about the numerous battles he had fought and won, and recounting the many enemies he had killed. He threw up the dust with his hand and said "so many more than could be counted." The women sang in companies, one side answering the other like the women who sang in I Samuel 18:7: "And the women answered one another as they played. Saul hath slain his thousands and David his ten thousands."

These people live just as Abraham did. Their customs have not changed. They have two or more wives and each wife has her handmaidens and servants. It is interesting to see actually with one's own eyes how Abraham, Isaac, and Jacob lived. They had the "cake of raisins" and all such terms used by the ancient fathers are everyday expressions. The Bible becomes a living book.

The Bedouins are feared by all, especially by travelers. The Turks have not been able to subdue them. No one dares to travel in their country and here we were being entertained by them.

The sheik with a number of his sons and retainers followed us to Jerusalem and spent a few days with us at the American Colony.

They sat in our sitting room or salon, as they call it here, which was decorated with their pistols, knives, and swords hung upon the wall.

While these wild visitors were our guests, we were as fearless of danger as though they were the meekest of men. We have become very warm friends now, for if one has ever eaten salt with them, they will never turn from that friend.

In copying Mother's letter, I realize how customs have changed since then. The grandchildren of these Bedouin friends still visit us, but they arrive in automobiles, and when I visited them recently in Amman, Trans-Jordan, it was to a European and modernly furnished house that I was taken, although the stuffed sheep and the laban were still "served in a lordly dish."

Lately I have had the great-grandchild of Sheik Ali Diab Adwan in the Anna Spafford Baby Nursing Home.

Some time ago a group of Bedouins came to visit the American Colony, and one, looking across the room at me, said, "Is that not Murtha?" This is the nearest they can get to pronouncing my name, Bertha. He had been one of the younger, lesser sheiks who escorted us on the ride to the shepherds' encampment at Shunet Nimrin, where King Abdullah of Trans-Jordan now has his summer camp, and he had shot a beautiful little bird and brought it to me as a present.

"I expected you to be pleased," he said. "Instead of being happy, as our children would have been, and roasted it on hot coals and eaten it, you cried, and put it into a beautiful handkerchief, and buried it!"

It was a reaction that had puzzled him for nearly half a century.

Mother tells in her letter that the Bedouins were interested in seeing the first white woman and child. As a compliment to Father, they initiated me into the tribe and ever since have called me "Murtha Adwan."

In all Mother's letters written at this time there are many affectionate references to "our son Rob." I remember so well how greatly Rob enjoyed this trip into Moab and other journeys we were able to make in those days, and how greatly Rob loved Palestine.

I did not know that before leaving Chicago our family doctor had warned Father and Mother of a loss sure to come, and that my parents, knowing this, had taken Rob out of school and brought him with us to share the wonderful experience of life in the Holy Land.

When Mother took her four little daughters to Europe, Rob had been left behind in "prep school." He was skating one day near the school when the ice broke, and when found he had been in the water a long time. After that there was always a heart murmur, and I could hear it when I sat on his knee. He was very tall, with proportionately broad shoulders, although he was thin. He had a winning manner and made friends quickly—everyone loved him.

In September, 1885 Rob went to help some friends near Media, a village on the plain of Sharon, mark out and prepare for planting trees when the rains came. It was very hot, and Rob, interested in horticulture as he was in anything new, ignored the sun mounting to its zenith.

His friends brought him home in a spring wagon, and he was unconscious and burning with fever by the time they reached the Damascus Gate. He was carried up the hill in a stretcher made from a blanket. Loving hands could not bring back a ray of consciousness. His death on September 10, 1885, was the first in our Group.

The young men of the German Templar Colony, in whose cemetery for some reason he was buried, were all Rob's friends, and offered to be his pallbearers. Wearing dark suits with broad white bands over the shoulders, they carried his coffin down the hill to the Damascus Gate where a lumber wagon waited, for there was no hearse in Jerusalem then, nor in all Palestine, nor was there one until the late 1930s. The cemetery was about two miles from the Gate and we walked along the dusty road following the wagon.

As we came through the Templar Colony, on the only tree-lined road at that time in Jerusalem, other young German Colony men who comprised the brass band played from the upper balcony of one of the houses the "Dead March" from *Saul* by Handel. They played it beautifully, and although I was only seven, whenever I hear that music I remember how I stood in the road, my heart aching with sorrow, holding tightly to Aunt Maggie's hand, and in memory I feel again the utter loneliness that came over me. Handsome, brilliant Rob, the cousin who had been like a brother, my dear friend, my greatest tormentor, was gone.

I was grieving, too, because Father and Mother were so sad. They, who had borne so much sorrow, knew how to meet this blow.

That night when I went to bed I wept bitterly, and Mother came and talked to me. I remember some of her words. "What a wonderful awakening!" "Now he sees Him face to face." Her face rediated such sublime joy that it removed the sting of death for me from that moment, and the fear of it as well. Something happened to me then, for Mother made heaven near and real to me, and I was comforted, and went to sleep.

One week after Rob's death Mrs. Merriman had a stroke and quietly passed away. The dear old lady was laid to rest beside Rob, whom she had dearly loved. So Death came to the American Colony.

CHAPTER FOURTEEN

IN 1886 A shifting in American politics changed the Consul in Jerusalem. Grover Cleveland was now President of the United States. His term of office proved a blessing to the American Colony, for Mr. Selah Merrill left Jerusalem and a new Consul arrived, giving us a few years of respite.

New Year's Day, Mother wrote:

A quiet day. The house is trimmed with mistletoe and evergreens, and presents a festive appearance. (Mistletoe in Palestine is a parasite which grows on olive trees and has red berries.) In the evening Mr. Arbeely, the new American Consul, came to tea and spent the evening. All our Mohammedan friends came and were so glad to see him. They gave him a hearty welcome.

Mr. Arbeely was a Syrian by birth, but an American by adoption. The Turkish Government did not recognize the loss of a subject through mere naturalization by another government. As Syria and the Lebanon were then under Turkish rule, they considered him a Turk and not an American. As it happened, Mr. Arbeely was soon recalled from Washington and Mr. Henry Gilman of Detroit, Michigan, came to take his place.

Mr. Gilman and Father had met as young men in connection with the Detroit Public Library which they assisted in founding. It afforded Father much pleasure to have his old friend in the American Consulate. Mr. Gilman took keen interest in the people of the country and made many friends. He was a student, and associated himself with archaeology and social welfare. His son, Dr. Robert Gilman, now a prominent ophthalmologist in Detroit, was then a medical student. On a visit to his father, he associated himself with the Ophthalmic Hospital of Saint John of Jerusalem, where he was allowed to assist.

Henry Gilman wrote a novel called *Hassan: A Fellah—A Romance of Palestine.*

Other old friends came from Chicago in this pleasant year.

In the spring of 1886 Mrs. Buckingham and her younger daughter, Rose (who later married Mr. Gordon Selfridge,

proprietor of the large department store in London), with an
elder sister and her husband, Mr. and Mrs. Chandler, visited
Palestine.

The party was personally conducted by our Jaffa friend Mr.
Rolla Floyd, the tourist agent. There was no good hotel in Jerusalem, so they camped on the Mount of Olives. Such camps
were magnificent, the equipment sumptuous, and the service
excellent. They were constantly used by tourists. The tents were
and still are made in Egypt. Strong sailcloth is used on the outside
and this is lined with indigo blue every inch of which is covered
with bright patchwork in arabesque patterns. The camp consisted of a bedroom tent for each person or couple, and every
morning a tin bathtub would be dragged into the tent by the
attendant. Hot and cold water stood beside the tub in big con-
tainers, usually Standard Oil tins. A large tent with double
poles was used for dining and sitting room with comfortable
camp chairs.

The kitchen tent contained a stove consisting of an iron
frame on legs with places for a charcoal fire. The camp cooks
were excellent, and the waiters, well trained. In those days of
leisurely travel, the camp provided the ideal way, and they were
used by Thomas Cook and Son and all tourist contractors. These
equipments were commandeered by the Turkish Army in 1914
and that ended camp life on the grand style. When travel started
up again after the war good hotels had been built. Automobiles
took the place of carriages and horses and changed the tempo
of travel.

I went with my parents several times to meals in the beautiful
camp of the Buckinghams and Chandlers, and we saw them
often during their visit to Jerusalem. They went on to Jericho,
the River of Jordan, and the Dead Sea. As Mother intimates
in her letter about her visit to the Bedouins, the country was
unsafe and the Turkish Government conceived a clever device
to guard travelers. One of the villages was considered the "robbers'
home" of eastern Palestine. The family of the paramount sheik
was officially made responsible for the safety of the Jericho
Road. All travelers paid a fee to this family, and a member
would then accompany the party. This made the village with
the sheik and his family responsible for safety and insured no
molestation. Woe betide the party that had not paid its fee.
"Racketeering" is not an American invention!

As the Buckingham party was important and also rich (such

information travels fast), Sheik Mustifa himself accompanied
them on this trip. He rode a beautiful Arab mare with the usual
oriental trappings on saddle and bridle. All the party were on
horseback. Sheik Mustifa soon observed that Rose was a good
horsewoman and resolved to play a practical joke. He secretly
took Rose into his confidence and told her to remove her feet
from her stirrup. In those days all ladies rode sidesaddle and
wore flowing riding habits. Rose was quite thrilled with the
idea and acquiesced in this escapade. Sheik Mustifa lagged
behind for a bit and when they came to a level stretch of road
appropriate for his demonstration of Arabic horsemanship, he
came forward at full gallop. As he passed Rose, he grabbed her
around her waist and, placing her before him on his horse,
continued his wild race, his bright-colored kaffiyeh and abayah
waving behind in the wind as though in farewell to the rest of
the party. Mrs. Buckingham and the Chandlers imagined Rose had
been kidnaped, and they followed in pursuit. When Sheik Mustifa
felt he had continued the joke long enough, he retraced his
tracks with a radiant Rose.

It is the kind of humor an Arab delights in.

Among the many tourists whom Mr. Floyd conducted through
the Holy Land was Mark Twain. The famous author rode a
horse he named Baalbek, because he was such a "magnificent
ruin." *Innocents Abroad* was written after this trip. Mr. Floyd
used to amuse us by telling us anecdotes about Mark Twain.
I remember one special story which, as far as I know, has never
been published. The party was camping in Galilee, where in
the spring of the year the wild flowers are plentiful and very
beautiful. Herbs and plants grow to abnormal size but retain
their luscious and tender qualities. The cook had gathered some
wild greens and made a salad which was served with roast lamb
for dinner. A member of the party asked the author why he
was like Nebuchadnezzar, and expected the answer to be because
he was eating the "grass of the field." Mark Twain promptly
replied "because I am eating with the brutes."

In spite of Father's busy life he carried on an extensive correspondence. He kept in touch with the homeland and his friends
in this way. Also, he kept them in touch with Jerusalem.

Miss Frances Willard in a letter to Father, dated August 2,
1888, wrote:

It was kind of you to write me, and let me have a little insight into your
remarkable life. I pressed the flowers, and have put them in an album, in

memory of you and your society. I am sending you some documents, that
you may know a little of what we are trying to do here, and I shall take the
liberty to mention you to Mrs.———when I write to her. She will very likely
be in Jerusalem within the year.

Believe me, I have at heart the same outcome that engages you so earnestly, and though we may have different ways of looking at it, I like to think the
spirit is the same.

Ever yours, with high esteem,
(*signed*) FRANCES E. WILLARD

Another friend who had visited the American Colony in Jerusalem wrote to Father: "Please take some pains to see Americans
who visit Jerusalem. There is great interest associated with your
work. I have advised all my friends to visit your Colony." We
met many Americans every tourist season, who came in the
spring or early summer, because tourist agencies combine the
trip to Egypt with that to Palestine.

Mr. Henry Waller, who had been our neighbor in Lake View
and partner with Father in certain undertakings, wrote to him:

The picture you so vividly draw of the peerless, springlike sky of Palestine
resting upon the Mount of Olives, the mountains of Moab, and the heights
where Titus camped, in full view of your windows, was very stimulating to
an old man, although hard at work in the midst of books and papers, but who
often meditates upon that wondrous land of balm and blessing for both body
and soul.

I would indeed love to enjoy one long, soul-inspiring look of that land
which our blessed Lord's eyes rested upon whilst in the flesh, and upon which
his precious feet have trodden. . . . Quite a stir took place in Chicago when
Reverend———in a recent sermon in Unity Church avowed his disbelief in
a God and Immortality. . . . His congregation has asked him to resign.

It was this letter, I believe, which called forth Father's hymn.
"Thou Man Divine," which we often sang in the American
Colony:

O Jesus Christ, Thou Man Divine,
'Tis sweet to follow paths of Thine
Where Thou by faith pursuing still
Discerned the Living Father's will.

Round Thee, as now a world's demands
Pressed for some tribute at Thy hands;
Some words, so bare conforming nod,
Unswerving Thou didst follow God.

Faith to Thy heart the time made known,
To lay this world's employments down,
And there at Jordan meet the word
That sealed Thee Son-of-God and Lord....

This hymn of Father's proves how false Mr. Merrill's accusation was that we did not believe in the divinity of Christ.

Our life in Palestine was busy and pleasant except for the anxiety about funds.

Father realized that he could not look after his financial obligations from a distance of seven or eight thousand miles. From his letters I am convinced that had he not been taken ill, he would have returned to the United States, at least temporarily. He speaks longingly of his last years in America, but he loved his work in Jerusalem. He writes: "We came to Jerusalem to learn, and it has been a wonderful experience."

Father was taken ill the summer of 1888 and a change was considered beneficial to his health. There were few resorts to go to in those days, and our finances were so low that friends who owned a vineyard on the outskirts of Jerusalem allowed us to pitch tents there. Although Father was not well, he enjoyed the outing. He wrote in September to Mrs. Piazza Smith:

I am writing you under a tent in the midst of a vineyard and fig orchard out on the top of the Hill Gareb, just outside Jerusalem. Here some of us have been camping for a week or two. I wish you and your husband were here to enjoy it with us. Six years ago I was walking on this same hilltop with a friend. The hilltop was perfectly bare, not a house upon it. Now there are more than five hundred houses, all solidly built of stone.

I like to think that the last months of Father's life were so happy. But his fever grew worse and developed into malignant malaria, which is akin to the dreaded blackwater fever. Father came back to our home at the Damascus Gate from the camp on Gareb, and he never left it alive. In writing about his death I cannot do better than copy what I wrote about it a few years ago:

My husband and I went to Saint George's Cathedral (in Jerusalem) today, October 16, 1938. The old city is shut, almost besieged, perhaps for the first time in two thousand years. The gates have been shut by Arab rebels who are protesting against the increase of Zionist immigration. There is great tension in the air. The Anna Spafford Baby Nursing Home is still doing its work. Electric-light wires are cut by the rebels. So far the Anna Spafford Nursing Home telephone is intact. These are the conditions under which I write.

The sermon was on John II, verse 25.

"And Jesus said (to Martha): 'I am the resurrection and the life; he that believeth in me, though he were dead yet shall he live.' "

The chaplain spoke about how some lives attain their ideal, but with the inequality of life on this earth some people had opportunities, riches, talents, while others had none; other people were "world-weary" and looked forward to nothing but to be blotted out. They had struggled to get on, to provide for their families, to be honest, to succeed in business. They felt how far from ideal was their relation to their families, their friends, their superiors, their subordinates, and as they grew older their shortcomings overbalanced their accomplishments; they were only too glad to be "snuffed out," to become part of the ground. Yet a future life was part of the belief, creed, or religion of people from earliest times, varying in conception with different dates and civilizations. But the glories of the Christian conception of a future life were a realization of all that had been impossible here, in this life, and should be inbred in us from the earliest moment when our life of comprehension began. "We shall see Him face to face!"

When the preacher got so far, I thought back over my own life. I thought how marvelously Mother had been able to instill just this view of the future life into us as children.

When Father lay unconscious and apparently dying, I was ten years old. Father and Mother had given up their "all" truly to come to Jerusalem. Father was the strong and compelling spirit. On his shoulders rested the responsibility of life. Mother was the follower; Mother felt "he knew." He was her counsellor and best friend. Together they had passed through many vicissitudes, dangers, sorrow, death, and calamity. Together they could face anything. Their love could rise above sorrow. As long as they had each other they were masters of every situation— they had proved this. Now Mother, as she looked down on Father's unconscious and emaciated face, realized that she must face the work, future sorrows, and whatever was ahead of her alone. I stood beside her; I was conscious of her struggle. As she listened to the measured breathing that became more labored as time went on, and felt the declining strength of a pulse that was beating ever more irregularly, I could see she was being overwhelmed with anguish. But she must be worthy of this brave man—her life's partner. Her stand, though alone now, must be so close to heaven that she must still feel him near her.

She left the room and stood in the arbor, watching a waning moon rise red over the Mount of Olives. All was quiet, all was still—not a leaf moved in that second spell of sirocco that sometimes comes in October. She lifted her breaking heart to God; she quoted Scripture, not knowing chapter or verse: "I will dance before the Lord," she said, from the Psalms, meaning she would do that which was the most difficult to do. In that phrase she expressed her determination not to give in to overwhelming sorrow. It lifted her above her natural inclination. It was the expression of her determination really to believe—"I am the resurrection and the life."

Nora was the only other person present. After a short absence, comforted and strengthened, Mother returned. Just at that moment Father opened his eyes, looked at Mother, and said; "Annie, I have experienced a great joy; I have seen wonderful things," and he tried to tell her, but weakness and unconsciousness overcame him, and he could speak no more. The end was very near. She turned to me and the nurse. "Bertha," she said, "stay with Father to the end. I must go away." It was only a short time, and I went to tell Mother. My sister Grace was with her. "He knows it all now," she said. "He has seen Him face to face. We must not sorrow like those who have not hope." She made me feel the truth of this, for she did not outwardly sorrow; she did not lament. I felt it was unworthy of her courage to cry. My heart was breaking, so I crept away from sight on the rampart well, into one of the niches behind the house, and there I cried until my poor little heart broke. My sobs shook me; my sense of loss was almost too much for me. Father had been such a companion; we were such good friends, but my admiration for my mother was greater than all else at that moment. I felt that I must stand by her, so I dried my tears.

The superhuman effort Mother had made was too much for her; she had been ailing for a long time, and only Father's illness had kept her from giving way. But as the need of her ministration for him ceased, the strength she had long overtaxed snapped, and she went to bed with a high fever. Nor was she able to go with us to the grave in the little American Cemetery on Mount Zion.

Young as I was, I remember what a comfort it was to me to see the flag of the United States of America flying half-mast as we passed the Consulate. Our American Consul, Mr. Henry Gilman, was walking by my side and was holding my hand.

In those days Jerusalem offered little that would be accounted as essential to a Western funeral. There was no flower shop; not a flower could be bought anywhere. So all wreaths were woven by friends, of flowers grown in private gardens. There was no hearse. It was a long way from the Damascus Gate to Mount Zion. The roads were unpaved and dusty. A long lumber wagon carried the casket made of rough pine planks and covered with black cloth. Mother had tried to cover up the ugly black sides with branches of the pepper tree, and I never smell its pungent fragrance without its carrying me back to that day. We were covered with dust as we walked behind the cart, and we entered the cemetery with the beautiful promise over the door: "Jesus Christ is the resurrection and the life."

The nurse met me as I returned. I wanted to rush to Mother's arms, but Mother was too ill to see Grace and me. A desolation came over me that seemed unbearable.

For many long weeks after this Mother lay at death's door. I remember sitting quite unnoticed, looking at the faces of those entering and leaving the room and trying to discern a ray of hope in their expressions. After several weeks Mother felt she was not making the progress she hoped, and a bed was made in a large carriage and she was taken to Jaffa. Mr. and Mrs. Rolla Floyd made her a welcome guest. Mrs. Gould went with her and faithfully nursed her. Later she was invited to stay at the home of Baron and Baroness Ustinov in Jaffa, where she could sit in their beautiful garden and regain her strength.

Never shall I forget the ecstasy of joy when Mother returned to us, weak but recovered.

CHAPTER FIFTEEN

AFTER Father's death life became more difficult, more beset with anxiety. Mother's long and severe illness cast a gloom over the household. It was many months before she was able to take an active part in the work.

Another blow hit the Colony, and so soon after Father's death and Mother's illness that it was staggering. Captain Sylvester, who had suffered for years from angina pectoris, had an attack which proved fatal. He realized his serious condition, and as he was dying, asked his wife to lay him to rest beside the best friend he had ever had. That was next to Father in the American Cemetery. How little we knew then what complying with that request would mean to the American Colony later on.

Two years later, in 1890, Mr. Drake died during an epidemic of the dreaded and then little-known influenza.

Although cramped in finances and experiencing sickness and death, these were years free from external persecution. Our friend Mr. Gilman was still American Consul.

It was soon after Father's death that Mr. Dwight L. Moody came to Jerusalem to visit. He came to call on Mother. He held me with one arm as he sat on the divan with my sister Grace on his knee. He was disappointed not to have seen Father, and I remember that he was not ashamed to let the tears run down his cheeks.

He held an open-air service on the top of Gordon's Calvary. Someone should have informed him, for he would never willingly have offended anyone if he had realized what he was doing. The top of the hill (Gordon's Calvary) is a Moslem cemetery. There were not many graves there at that time, and those that existed were in a rather neglected condition. In his enthusiasm and his utter abandon of thoughts other than on his sermon, he stood on an old grave that he might see his audience better. That incident so infuriated the Moslems that they forbade any Christian to enter the cemetery without a permit, and as rapidly as funds were available they built the high wall all around the top of the hill.

In 1889 Mr. W. E. Blackstone, who was Father's friend and associate in Chicago in the days when he and Mother were active in Mr. Moody's work, came to visit us with his daughter Flora. They were our guests at the American Colony, and Mother was very pleased to see them.

Mr. Floyd conducted their party. They left February 4, going through the country on horseback, with a full camp equipment, to Damascus.

When Mr. Blackstone got back to his home in Oak Park, Illinois, he was interviewed by a Chicago reporter. He was asked about his visit to Jerusalem and about the Group who had started from Chicago eight years before. The interviewer asked:

Q.   "By what name are they known in Jerusalem?"
A.   "Simply as the Americans."
Q.   "How do they employ themselves?"
A.   "In works of charity and devotion. They are constantly engaged in feeding the hungry and nursing the sick. Their house is a sort of free hotel for everyone who needs shelter. Bedouins, Arabs, Jews, and all sorts of people drop in there and are kindly entertained. They hold gospel meetings. The singing at these meetings is the nearest to the Music of Heaven as any I ever heard."
Q.   "Who attends these meetings?"
A.   "All sorts of people, including a great many Jews and Mohammedans, and they join in the singing and evince a deep respect for the service."

In that year, 1889, Benjamin Harrison, a Republican, defeated Grover Cleveland in the presidential elections and became President of the United States.

With abated breath we read the news, and wondered if that would mean a change of consuls. We had had five years' respite with Mr. Henry Gilman. We wondered whether Mr. Merrill would come back to Jerusalem. He did. In 1891 Mr. Merrill returned as Consul and renewed his attacks against us with greater determination.

Letters and notes tell about the remarkable manner in which we were provided for during those years. One entry says, "No money, no bread, but sixty loaves of beautiful white bread arrived unexpectedly this P.M." Later we learned that a friend from Chicago who was in Jerusalem had sent the bread. About a week later is another entry: "Mr. Floyd sent us twenty loaves of bread and a large quarter of mutton." Again, "Butter came from Safid" (from the Eliahus very likely). "Monday will be Grace's birthday and we have no money to buy any cake or sweets. Later in the afternoon the grocer sent dibbis without being asked."

Salman, "the egg man," as we called him, who left eggs without being asked, became blind through trachoma, and the American Colony were able to help him for years until he died.

Mr. Merrill was a D.D. and I notice that during his second term of office he was generally called Dr. Merrill. Dr. Merrill accused us of contracting debts under false representations. He stated that "we had not a dollar to pay them with." The origin of our indebtedness was feeding and housing the Gadites (Yemenites), and our money was stopped from coming to pay these debts through Dr. Merrill's intervention. That no suit for debt was ever instigated against us alone shows that no creditor ever seriously invoked the Consul's services.

I am compelled to expatiate on this subject as an introduction to the chapters that follow.

Dr. Merrill was interested in archaeology. He considered himself an authority, and wrote books and articles on the subject.

He started excavations inside the wall of the American Cemetery and found ancient remains. To follow an ancient wall he disturbed the graves.

We knew nothing of this until Aunt Maggie's death.

On August 12, 1891, my aunt and Mrs. Sylvester went to call on a friend and were leisurely walking home along the "Back Road," now the Street of the Prophets, when Aunt Maggie said, "I'm not feeling well," and fell to the ground. Friends carried her to the nearby Kamanitz Hotel.

The doctor's verdict was that Aunt Maggie had died instantly.

In this hot country interment must follow death by a few hours. The funeral started from the Kamanitz Hotel the next day.

Dr. Merrill had no warning of any illness among the members of the American Colony to prepare him for the news of a burial. When we took Aunt Maggie to the American Cemetery, I was horrified to see my father's coffin exposed and huge holes and trenches cutting across the cemetery. I gave one shriek at the horrible sight and fainted.

CHAPTER SIXTEEN

DR. MERRILL'S unrelenting attacks soon plunged us into another chapter in the Colony's history, "the strange episode of the Whiting estate."

I have never been able to relax over a detective story. I cannot read of villainy with amusement or interest, because, as a child, I knew what it was to fear the enmity of another human being. The American Consul in Jerusalem wrought seemingly endless harm against my father and mother and the American Colony, and although my parents tried to keep this from us, I felt it keenly, and lived through many years of dread of this man who hated us, for a reason I could not understand.

John C. Whiting and his family had come with us to Jerusalem with the consent and approbation of his mother, Mrs. Mary C. Whiting of Springfield, Massachusetts. Her two brothers had since died, leaving a considerable estate to Mrs. Whiting, Sr., which was managed for her by a businessman who knew the intrinsic value of dollars and cents. From his point of view, John Whiting was an impractical visionary.

John Whiting died on Sunday, December 5, 1886. What a sad day that was! As I write these lines the depression I felt then comes back to me. We children loved dear "Brother John." He was so gentle and kind. He never refused to make kites for us in the summer kite season, and taught us many useful things. Bookbinding was one, but I have sadly forgotten all he taught me about it. One thing remains, however, how to take care of books.

Shortly after Mr. Whiting's death his mother died in America, leaving the business manager full and absolute discretion about investments and reinvestments of her estate, "In trust for the two children of her son now deceased." Until John, the younger, reached the age of twenty-one, he was to use his discretion about the payment of the interest, or part of it, for the maintenance and education of John and Ruth, while Mrs. Whiting was not to receive anything unless she returned to the United States to live.

Mrs. Whiting chose to remain in Jerusalem. The manager saw

fit to send no money at all. Not a ripple of change occurred in their manner of living. Ruth and John were educated with the rest of us and shared everything.

This was contrary to the plans of Mrs. Whiting's mother, Mrs. Regina Lingle, who was determined to bring her daughter and the children back to the United States.

An unhappy incident gave Mrs. Lingle the opening she needed. It was provided by Nora, the girl Mother had brought from Chicago as nurse to Grace and me.

Nora had long since ceased to be treated as other than a member of the household. She seemed sincere and devoted, and took her place with the others in nursing and teaching and in all the other activities of the Colony. Her letters to Mother when she happened to be away and to Aunt Rachel in Chicago are full of enthusiasm about the work and the happiness of her life. She called herself "Miss Spafford," and although she had never been adopted, as Rob and Jacob had, Mother let it slip by.

Nora had been one of the most vocal in refuting Dr. Merrill's accusations.

Now, instead of confiding in Mother, she left a note:

Dear Mother, I must go, so say Good Bye to one and all—I cannot look at you nor speak nor see Grace, so go now. I am going to Kamanitz Hotel to see if they will let me stay there for the present—I cannot hear or say any more. It is between me and God.

Mother went at once to the Kamanitz Hotel. She had no idea of the reason for Nora's leaving. The moment she arrived Nora made a confession that deeply disturbed Mother.

Nora was in love with a Moslem.

In these modern days one often finds in Jerusalem a Moslem man married to a Christian girl or a Jewess and leading a normal and happy life, but it was unheard of then. Mother felt it was her duty to Nora to know how matters stood, so she sent for the young man, who came at once to the hotel.

"Nora says she loves you," Mother told him, "and I want to know what your feelings and intentions are toward her."

He answered, looking straight at Mother, "Nora knows that I am of noble birth and cannot marry her. She also is aware that I am an engaged man."

He left after emphasizing that all his dealings with Nora had been honorable.

Mother begged Nora to return to the Colony until we could

raise enough money to send her back to her mother in Chicago. But Nora was deeply humiliated by having her carefully laid plans frustrated, and she refused to return.

From that hour Nora's attitude toward Mother and the Colony changed. She felt certain that if Mother had not "meddled," she would eventually have maneuvered the young man into marrying her.

She did not tell people she had fallen in love with a Moslem. She explained her departure from the Colony by saying she had wanted to go to her mother in America. Presently she was saying Mother had prevented her going, by force. Then she hit on another means of revenge—she went to Dr. Merrill and said that all his vile and numerous reports against the American Colony were true.

Friends of the American Colony went to see Nora, and among others Mr. and Mrs. Rolla Floyd made a sworn statement, dated May 21, 1893, to certify that Nora had sent for them to say she regretted her outburst and wished to retract, that she had never seen any immorality of the kind Dr. Merrill described in the Colony, that she had, in fact, seen no immorality and had always been treated with extreme kindness.

Several months later Nora left for the United States.

She had not completed her vengeful attacks against us; she went to Mrs. Lingle and told her that Mrs. Whiting, her daughter, was being held at the American Colony against her will.

Mrs. Lingle, on her visit to us in Jerusalem, had known Nora as a trusted daughter of the household. Nora's change in attitude confirmed in her mind the worst of Dr. Merrill's tales.

The result was a series of incidents that baffle comprehension. They could not have been possible, of course, had the American Consul not been unfriendly to the Colony, and possessed, under Turkish rule, with extraterritorial rights and capitulations to enforce almost unlimited power.

One afternoon we were in the "sewing room" when Mrs. Whiting came in, quite excited, and said, "Just listen to this note that I received from Dr. Merrill."

She read aloud:

"July 18, 1895

DEAR MRS. WHITING:

There is a gentleman from America here who knows you and your friends in Chicago, and who would very much like to see you and your children. He cannot very well call upon you. This note will be given to you by one of my kavasses, who will wait and return with you from the Damascus Gate.

Yours sincerely,

(*signed*) SELAH MERRILL."

Mrs. Whiting finished reading, then she said, "It sounds like kidnaping."

My sister Grace had never heard the word "kidnaping," and wanted it explained, which impressed the word and the incident on my memory. I also remember that the older people rather smiled over Mrs. Whiting's letter and could not believe it was so serious as she thought. She wrote a short answer, stating that if any person knew and wanted to see her, her home was the proper place for him to come.

It seemed only a few moments until a man appeared at our door. Her note had not gone to the Consulate but to him, where he was waiting below at the Damascus Gate, with a carriage and horses ready to drive her with her children straight to Jaffa. He acknowledged frankly that this had been his plan. The man proved to be her own brother.

He said he had been in the city seven days with Consul Merrill, contriving the best way to spirit her away from the American Colony, and that the sole purpose of his trip was to take her back to the United States.

Mrs. Whiting's presentiment of kidnaping had not been wrong.

She told him that she would follow the dictates of her conscience and remain in Jerusalem.

The man stressed that a large estate was involved and that she and her children were the heirs, but the condition was that she must live in the United States.

When he was convinced that he could not change her mind, he became so vehement in his abuse of the Colony that she could stand it no longer and asked her friends not to leave her alone with him.

About six days after this the dragoman of the Consulate of the United States came with a kavass to the Colony and served a summons on Mrs. Whiting. The summons read:

U.S. Consulate, Jerusalem

August 5, 1893

Summons:

To Mary E. Whiting, residing in the Community known as the Spafford American Colony in Jerusalem. You, Mary E. Whiting, are hereby summoned to appear in this Consulate at 3:00 'clock this afternoon to attend to some important business. Your children Ruth and John must accompany you.

Gabriel Farwagy and the guard, Assad Kassas, will convey to you this summons as they are officers appointed to accompany you hither. Refusal on your part renders you liable to the penalties of the law.

(signed) SELAH MERRILL
U.S. Consul

Whom could she consult? The Austrian consul general in Jerusalem was a friend of the Colony. From him she found out that the summons was illegal. She was advised to write an explanatory note. Before she returned, the dragoman came back with several men—including a Turkish policeman—to arrest her.

We told him that Mrs. Whiting was not at home; we asked for his warrant. He had none, but said he had been instructed to search the house. We mentioned the fact that there were English subjects as well as Turkish in the house. He took no notice but searched.

Seeing this utter disregard for law and decency, we sent a warning to Mrs. Whiting to stay at a friend's house that night.

We had heard that several of the American staff from the Beirut College—it was not then a university—were in camp on the Mount of Olives. The college was then part of the mission, and as a little girl in Chicago my mother once went without butter, which she loved, for an entire year to save a contribution for the Presbyterian Board of Foreign Missions which was founding this particular mission.

Five days later the same dragoman of the United States Consulate and the kavass reappeared and with them a stranger, who, we learned, was one of the teachers from Beirut. The dragoman had a warrant of arrest for Mrs. Whiting. This time he did not give it to her. Instantly half-a-dozen other men appeared. Four were from the American staff of the College of Beirut, sworn in as constables by the Consul.

Mother tried to reason with them.

One of them said, "Don't listen to her; she is the next one to be hauled out."

Mrs. Whiting and her two children were taken under the escort of the American missionaries to the Grand New Hotel, where Dr. Merrill and the man from the United States were stopping, and were locked in a bedroom. Some of the men of the Colony went along and heard the Consul sentence Mrs. Whiting and her children to twenty-four hours' imprisonment for contempt of court, making the visitor her jailor and one of the Beirut missionaries her guard. Mrs. Whiting appointed Mr.

Rudy her counsel.

The next day when he went to the hotel to bring her home, the twenty-four hours having expired, Mr. Rudy was told that she had been delivered over to the emissary for an "indefinite period" until he was convinced that she was not being kept in the Colony by compulsion. Mr. Rudy asked for a copy of the charges, but Dr. Merrill refused to give them.

Where could we look for redress? I suppose if we had had money, the most natural act would have been to employ a lawyer. Even that would have been of little use. In Turkish times Americans had consular courts. Dr. Merrill would have been our judge. But we had no money. What were we to do now? We wanted to telegraph to the American Embassy in Constantinople and cable to Washington. I learned later that the cost of the two telegrams was obtained from the sale of Brother Jacob's watch.

I have good reason to remember the Whiting affair, for I was helping to nurse a Moslem and her child through a bad attack of conjunctivitis. I began helping to nurse early. I wished to be part of the work, and the need was always great. I loved nursing, and look back on my youth with happiness, although it might seem strange compared with girlhood in America. We were congenial in the Colony, and one felt safe there and secure, and we were always busy. No matter how money difficulties might loom, we spoke very little of such things. We were happy together and in the work we were doing.

On this occasion I had sat up all night, frequently applying compresses to the eyes of the child and the mother. Conjunctivitis is very painful. When morning came I was to be relieved, but no one arrived from the Colony to take my place. I was sure something serious had happened at the Colony, because it was so unusual not to be relieved at the proper time when nursing. About noon I could bear it no longer and left my patients to learn what had happened. I found everyone in the Colony absorbed in the problem of how to help Mrs. Whiting.

Mrs. Whiting, Ruth, and John were still being held in the Grand New Hotel.

Dr. Merrill threatened to send out his kavass with a horsewhip to be used on Mr. Rudy or any other member of the Colony who came anywhere near the hotel.

All the American citizens in the Colony signed a petition requesting Dr. Merrill to issue a writ of habeas corpus in behalf of Mrs. Whiting and her children.

Dr. Merrill refused to receive the application.

We knew that an answer to our telegrams to Consul General Hess in Constantinople arrived, as well as one form Washington, because we received the following telegram:

INSTRUCTIONS SENT MERRILL (SIGNED) HESS.

Mrs. Whiting, Ruth, and John were released the same afternoon. What rejoicings there were that day at the American Colony! We all went down to the Damascus Gate to meet them, and they made a triumphal entry.

Mrs. Whiting said that when the man from America, who had been their jailor, knew his mission had failed, he told her that she had not heard the end: that he would go to the length of stigmatizing her with living an immoral life or accuse her of being demented, but he would still get her children away from her. Those were his farewell words upon leaving Jerusalem.

We filed a complaint against the treatment received at Dr. Merrill's hands, addressing it to the Secretary of State, Walter Q. Gresham. We accused Dr. Merrill of conducting a long-continued religious persecution against us, maligning the Group, and circulating derogatory insinuations that could be interpreted as damaging character. We accused him of advising those in America who had our money in their hands to withhold it from us, and when he succeeded, because our rightful funds were withheld, and we got into debt, he incited our creditors to proceed against us by legal actions at his consulate.

We further accused him of illegally summoning one of our number with her minor children, and finally imprisoning her without charge and refusing those imprisoned a legal hearing or interview with their counsel or legal advisers, or the right to habeas corpus or the right to communicate with the Consul General at Constantinople to appeal for his decision, and refusing to allow any of us to see the consular record and papers of the case, although allowing others to see them.

We demanded an investigation.

On December 11, 1893, Mrs. Whiting received through Dr. Merrill a citation from the Probate Court of Hampden County, Massachusetts, to appear at Springfield on the "first Wednesday of February next to show cause why some other suitable person should not be appointed guardian to the minor children Ruth and John Whiting, and the guardian be decreed the custody of the persons of the minors, for that she, their mother, was unfit to have such custody." This time the children were not summoned.

Mrs. Whiting requested that the proceedings be held in Jerusalem, where she was widely respected and loved. This was refused. She knew by the visitor's last words what her antagonists were going to try to prove against her. Mrs. Whiting decided to go alone.

Dr. Merrill was furious when he learned that she was going to America without the children. He wrote to Mrs. Whiting, "Tell Mrs. Spafford in as stormy language as you please that if anything happens to those children of yours she may be held responsible, as they are in her house."

Mrs. Gould decided to go to America with Mrs. Whiting and release her own money. Jacob went with them. He had never been to the United States before. Much responsibility had fallen on his shoulders since the death of Father, Captain Sylvester, and Mr. Drake. It was considered advisable by the Group that he should accompany them.

We knew that Consul Merrill was holding money for Mrs. Gould and Mrs. Whiting in case they wanted to return to America.

I have in my possession a curious assemblage of notes, all written on the same day, that indicate the petty activities of Dr. Merrill. He was treating Mrs. Gould and Mrs. Whiting like idiots. "Certainly I shall not give you a check for outfits," he wrote in one note. "People do not get outfits in Jerusalem when they go directly to England and America!"

These slips of paper, signed Selah Merrill, are all dated January 15, 1894. They are addressed to Mrs. Gould and Mrs. Whiting, who were sitting in his outer office at the Consulate. They, in turn, wrote their requests and sent them into his inner office. He refused to see or speak to them.

As I remember it, they finally borrowed money for their passage to the United States.

Just as they were about to leave we heard the amazing news that Dr. Merrill was recalled. He, too, prepared to leave for the United States.

It was soon apparent that the investigation we had so long hoped for was not to be granted, at least not then. Evidently the authorities in Washington considered the fact that the Consul being changed was sufficient reason to stop the Colony's demand for an investigation.

A letter was addressed to President Grover Cleveland, appealing against the apparent decision that as a successor had been
appointed to Dr. Merrill there was no need for an investigation
of his conduct. The Group was still pressing for an investigation.
Our hopes that the change in consuls would bring about an
improvement were also dashed, for Dr. Merrill's successor, Mr.
Edwin Wallace, arrived in Jerusalem to assume his office as
American Consul before Mrs. Whiting and Mrs. Gould left for
the United States. Mr. Wallace did not enter upon his duties
of office for several weeks, and in the meantime Dr. Merrill
remained in office.

During this interval Mrs. Whiting was preparing testimony
and replies to the citation from the Probate Court in Springfield,
Massachusetts. She appealed to Dr. Merrill, since he was still
in office, to take a number of depositions as to her normal character and for himself to nominate physicians to give testimony
as to sanity.

He refused to do either.

She then appealed to Mr. Wallace, and he readily agreed to
nominate physicians and write a letter stating the facts leading
up to her case. He also promised to confirm his nomination of
physicians as soon as he took office.

When she went back, as soon as he became Consul, to have
this done, his reception of her indicated that in the meantime
he had been prejudiced against her and against the American
Colony.

The whole of Jerusalem, with a few possible exceptions,
would gladly have testified for Mrs. Whiting.

Many prominent people volunteered to bear witness for her
and the Colony from among Christians, Jews, and Mohammedans of Jerusalem, including high government officials, high
military officers, physicians, directors of schools, and others, but
neither of the Consuls would accept any of them.

On January 18, 1894, Mrs. Whiting, Mrs. Gould, and Jacob
sailed from Jaffa, where they had gone, from Jerusalem, on the
new railroad.

For years there had been talk about building a railroad between
Jerusalem and the seaport of Jaffa. A Greek civil engineer by
the name of Mr. Frangia was employed by the Turkish Government to work out the plans. It was Mr. Frangia who laid out all
the carriage roads in Palestine at the time, the roads to Jaffa,
Hebron, and Jericho. The road to Haifa was started but not

completed until many years later. These roads were built by forced labor. In 1892 the narrow-gauge railroad between Jerusalem and Jaffa was completed. It was the only railroad in Palestine and about thirty-eight miles in length.

Its opening was a gala affair in Jerusalem. The European-styled stations were beflagged, and Turkish officials, foreign consuls, church dignitaries, and Arab notables were invited to see the first train arrive from Jaffa. The guests were entertained at luncheon in a huge Egyptian tent with the usual gorgeous arabesque patchwork lining, which in itself is decoration enough for any occasion. The ever-present military band blared oriental discords and almost unrecognizable European tunes. It was all very gay and the populace was duly impressed. After this there was a daily train each way, which took between four and five hours to travel the thirty-odd miles.

About a month after this Mother, Grace, and myself with Flora and Gertie, older children from the Colony, were visiting the Floyds in Jaffa. Most of the ships that stopped at Jaffa were tramp steamers, but while we were there a large steamer called, and Mrs. Floyd thought we young folks might like to go aboard. Grace and I had not traveled by sea since we came from America and did not remember much about it, so we were delighted. One of Mr. Floyd's dragomans, who had an errand on the ship, took us aboard.

Embarking at Jaffa was an exciting experience. There was still no port there. Steamers anchored two or three miles from shore, and large rowboats took passengers to and fro. Jaffa boatmen were renowned for their bravery and skill in controlling the large boats. Rowing, they sang in unison, and when our boat reached the opening in the forbidding circle of rocks, to which, according to legend, Andromeda had been chained, they waited with eyes fixed on their captain, watching for his signal to put all their strength into the exact second that shot the heavy boat through the narrow rock channel and into the open sea.

When we reached the steamer the dragoman went off to perform his errand, and we were left on deck to amuse ourselves. There on deck was Dr. Merrill. He was on his way home, recalled from Jerusalem, and the fact that he blamed the American Colony for his dismissal was sufficient proof to us that our charges had been heard. He saw us, just as we recognized him, and came to us at once.

"Where are you going? To America?"

Flora answered that we had only come out to see the steamer. Dr. Merrill said, "That wicked Mrs. Spafford hates and curses me. Don't you believe that they will ever get their money! They will not. Mrs. Gould will not get a cent of it. That wicked Jew Eliahu (he meant Jacob), what is he going to America for? He is nothing but a Turk. Who would listen to such a wicked fool?"

He raved on, slandering Mother, the Colony, the life we lived, accusing us all of immorality.

"Mrs. Spafford is a liar, she is a bad, wicked woman, but who is this?" He had turned to me. "Is this a Spaf-Spaf-Spafford?" He could scarcely speak, and he spat the name at me.

I spoke then. "Dr. Merrill, I ask you to stop talking. If you were a gentleman you would not talk like that."

We all got up and moved away, but he followed us over the deck.

"I can come here and talk just as well as there!" he shouted. "You think you will last, but I tell you, you have only a month, or five at most, to continue. Mrs. Spafford has got me out of Palestine, but I am coming back! I am coming back! Look at the beautiful weather and calm sea. Doesn't that show God is with me? When your people left for the United States the sea was raging and the wind howling."

Dr. Merrill was raving like a madman. We could not bear it. Grace began to cry, and we all followed suit.

Mother wrote in a letter from Jaffa, dated February 21,1894:

The girls returned from their excursion to the steamer with red eyes. I asked them what the matter was and they explained that Dr. Merrill had given them a farewell salute. What the poor girls went through was simply shocking.

Dr. Merrill kept his promise to return. Four years later the Republicans were in again and Dr. Merrill was back in his post at Jerusalem, more venomous against us than before.

It was during these trying days of anxiety that I first met the young man who was to become my husband. Rather, we had met as children, but did not remember each other. It was August, during the Greek Orthodox Feast of Our Lady Mary. In those days the Greek and Arab Orthodox Christian Community camped for a week prior to the feast on the slopes of Olivet, near the church over the Tomb of the Virgin, and it was a pretty sight to watch the campfires in the evening as they prepared their evening meal. Those were the carefree days in Palestine, when people had little money but could buy things with it. The eight days of picnic and pleasure culminated in the service in the church to which the Orthodox Patriarch and his clergy went in great pomp.

In the afternoon the Greek Patriarch held a reception, with music. To the unaccustomed ear the sound was uncanny. First one brass instrument then another would screech discords, while the whole band was droning in monotonous minor strains something that they called "mosika." The drum gave its full share to the noise. When the different consuls or their representatives appeared to pay their respects to the Patriarch, the attempt at playing the respective national anthems was quite fantastic. The "Star-Spangled Banner" baffled the bandmaster, so he resorted to playing "Yankee Doodle" or "Old Black Joe." Turkish coffee and sweetmeats were served to the guests.

We were returning from the reception when we were overtaken by our friends the Vesters. Frederick Vester had just returned from Switzerland, having completed his education there as well as his compulsory military service to Germany. His parents were German-Swiss missionaries in Jerusalem, and they and their daughters were good friends of ours. We walked home together, and that sealed our fate. For about a year we met frequently at each other's homes, and then Mother began to get anxious about this friendship. She felt that I should see men of my own country and get acquainted with my father's family and friends before I should think seriously of marriage.

The following August Mother found means to take Grace and me to America.

I was only sixteen, and Mother did the right thing in taking me away. But my country had no temptations for me in a romantic sense. Money, position, and family held no allurement.

Mrs. Whiting, Mrs. Gould, and Jacob were already in the United States. Mrs. Gould's money was released. The case against Mrs. Whiting was dropped, since the children were not with her.

When Mother decided to visit America, Mrs. Whiting asked her to bring Ruth and John along. She thought the danger of having the children removed from her custody was past. Mr. Rudy went with us as the children's guardian.

In Chicago we rented a house on the west side. It was one of those semi-detached, two-story-and-basement, inconvenient houses so popular in those days. There was a bit of back yard, where the washing was hung to dry and nothing grew. The view from the windows was a long line of front doors and stoops looking just alike, with the same architectural line of houses on the other side of the street. This we had exchanged for the magnificent view from our housetop, the highest point in the old city of Jerusalem, where we looked down on historic buildings so close together that one could not pick out the streets; then, looking the other way, to the hills around Jerusalem and the mountains of Moab.

We children hated 1084 West Monroe Street. The noise of the trolley cars distracted and annoyed us. Nothing came up to our expectations. I was homesick for Frederick and Jerusalem.

In May 1895 Mrs. Lingle and her representative renewed their suit to try to appoint a guardian and deprive Mrs. Whiting of the custody of her children. Where and to whom should we turn for advice? Mr. Rudy thought of Mr. Luther Laflin Mills, once State's Attorney for Illinois. They had been friends in the old days. Mrs. Whiting, Mother, Mrs. Gould, and Mr. Rudy went to see Mr. Mills and told him the whole story. They did not dare to hope that he would defend Mrs. Whiting, they simply went to him for advice and to ask him to suggest someone who could. Mr. Mills listened to the long tale of woe. He had been an admirer of Father and knew a great deal about his work in the legal field. Then he said, "It is a religious persecution in this land of religious freedom, and I will fight the case free of charge."

The case, presumably against Mrs. Whiting, was virtually against the American Colony.

The Chicago papers during the days of the trial had many articles about the case. Most of them ridiculed the Colony; some were abusive, and a few got facts more or less correct. Such headlines as "Mrs. Lingle Drags Spafford Colonists into Court"; "Mrs. Regina Lingle petitions to have a guardian appointed for her grandchildren Ruth and John Whiting"; "Hearing in the Probate Court This Afternoon," et cetera.

Mrs. Lingle's chief witness was Nora. She was brought to testify as to the immoral character of the Colony, but failed. In her cross-examination she said that people of the Colony were good and had done many good works in Jerusalem.

We all had to testify. Poor Mother was kept on the witness stand for hours. An attorney for the prosecution cross-questioned her about her religious belief. Her answers were so straightforward, so simple, that he thought he could get her to admit some of the accusations brought against her by her accusers.

Yes, she believed in the divinity of Christ.

"Do you receive direct communications from God?"

This question was asked in a hundred different ways. Mother never veered from her point; she said, "As a Christian who believes in prayer, I believe God can lead and direct, but I claim no special or unique power."

"You were not with your husband when he died," the attorney flung at her. Mother said she had been with Father until a few minutes before.

"And," the lawyer pursued, "I believe you danced when you heard he was dead."

I remember this moment well, because I noticed the anguish that passed over Mother's face. She looked straight at Nora as she answered, "Not in the manner you imply." I remember, too, that at this point Mr. Mills, our advocate, intervened.

Dr. Merrill declined to appear on the witness stand, but sent a deposition which was read. He charged that "Mrs. Spafford had hypnotic influence over the Colonists, and that we obtained goods under false pretenses, claiming that we were to receive money from America." Dr. Merrill said the Colonists all lived together in several large houses in a manner which could arouse suspicion. He said our manner of living without actual work was "disgraceful and criminal." At the end of his affidavit he admitted that he had never been inside the premises of the "so-called American Colony"; that what he wrote he had heard people say.

Another affidavit was from Mr. Henry Gilman, who had followed Dr. Merrill as Consul after his first term. He said that he had been a constant visitor to the American Colony; he had studied the Colony and knew that the life of its members was above reproach. This affidavit mysteriously disappeared from its place among the court records and could not be found; it was never returned, but the fact that it was lost by the opposition was evidence in our favor. Other laudatory testimony was given in our behalf.

Judge Kohlsaat heard the case in the Probate Court room. Much interest was aroused; it was something new in law and ethics, because it involved the point as to whether or not two children could be taken away from their mother because of the mother's religious belief. The accusers failed, however, to prove anything peculiar in her theology. Another matter in which the court was called upon to deliver an opinion was embodied in the petition of Mrs. Regina Lingle to have the guardianship of her daughter's two children removed from their mother, Mrs. Mary E. Whiting, on the ground that they were being brought up in the American Colony in Jerusalem, where the moral atmosphere was not of the right sort for children to live in. This also they failed to prove.

Dr. Merrill had said in his deposition that we did not have enough to eat, that "the children had only cracked wheat, bread, and oranges." I remember the ripple of laughter that went round the courtroom when Ruth, John, and I were called to the witness stand to testify. Both Ruth and John were robust children and I weighed a hundred and fifty pounds at seventeen, the most I have ever weighed in all my life.

Judge Kohlsaat dismissed the petition filed by Mrs. Lingle before Mr. Mills had time to sum up his case.

Ruth and John got no money at the time, but that was not what the fight was over as far as Mrs. Whiting was concerned. She had the custody of her children; she had won!

The Chicago papers announced: "Colony a Winner."

CHAPTER SEVENTEEN

WHILE the case was being conducted in Chicago the newspapers wrote such sensational articles attributing fantastic beliefs and practices to the American Colony that a great deal of attention was turned upon us.

A small group of Swedish people were living on the south side of Chicago. They had no peculiar religious belief; they were simple, pious fundamentalists. They owned some property on which they built a chapel where they held their gospel meetings. There were about thirty members in the group, including seven children. The majority were women. To support themselves these women went out in domestic service. They brought their earnings to their leader. His home was considered their home, and whenever they were out of a job or had a day off, or during their holidays, they came to his house and family as they would to their own.

A strong character among them was Miss Matilda Holmstrum. "Sister Tilly," as we soon learned to call her, read the derogatory articles about the Colony in the Chicago papers, but she had discerned that the truth lay between the lines. She hoped she had found what she and her associates had been looking for.

They were simple Swedish folk, most of them peasants. A few had taken out American citizenship, but the majority were still Swedish subjects. Mother and I had met a number of them serving as cooks, waitresses, and housemaids in the homes of our friends, where they were loved and respected by their employers for their honesty and integrity. During the two years of our sojourn in the United States a number of people had joined us. There was a family of farmers from Kansas, a Polish-American couple, and others. Two sisters and the daughter of one who had been affiliated to the first group before they left Chicago in 1881 now wanted to go to Jerusalem with us. They could barely pay their fare; but to Mother, with her big heart, this made no difference.

When at last there was no valid reason for our remaining in the United States any longer, all these people expressed their

desire, nay, determination, to return with us. This news came
as a shock. It was a severe test of faith. The Group felt they had
no right to refuse any who wanted to devote their life to the work
we were doing in Jerusalem. However, Mr. Rudy, upon whose
shoulders rested the financial responsibility, advised delay until
they had well counted the cost. Our life in Jerusalem was one of
self-denial. We were often without things to which the members
of the Swedish community were accustomed. But we found, to
our amazement, that they had already put their property up for
sale and were making all arrangements to go with us to Jerusalem.

When, finally, our party was made up it consisted of seventy-
seven souls. Twenty-five were children, among whom were
several babies in arms. Mr. Rudy consulted Henry Gaza and
Son, Ltd., Universal Tourist agents, and a small freight steamer
was chartered to take us across the Atlantic to Liverpool. There
the company was trans-shipped to another freighter, which
brought us to Jaffa.

The cordial welcome the enlarged group got from those left
behind in Jerusalem was a gratification and surprise to the new
members. Arabs and Jews came to the house in crowds to welcome us back and to welcome the newcomers. I was in seventh
heaven to be near Frederick again. While I was in America,
Frederick had become a member of the American Colony.

We realized that it would be quite impossible for us to be married under present conditions. We were for the good of the
Colony as a whole. Before arranging for ourselves, all the new
members would have to be settled into the home and new ways
of employment found to support them. The new group had not
added substantially to the finances of the Colony. The greatest
economy would have to be practiced. Frederick's training in
banking and business proved useful.

The most urgent need was more living space. Our house in
the old city, although enlarged by renting additional space in the
vicinity, was still too small to hold the newcomers. The present
American Colony happened to be untenanted. It needed much
repair. Since Rabbah Effendi's death his palace had been roughly used. It was large, and on this account difficult to lease, but it
was exactly what we needed. We rented it at once. Nearly all
the rooms were enormous and surrounded a beautiful open
court. Rabbah Effendi had lived a patriarchal life there surrounded
by his four wives and other relatives, retainers, and servants.

From Hadj Raghib and his son, therefore, we rented the present

American Colony building in Sheik Jarah Quarter near the
Kedron Valley, sometimes called the Valley of Jehoshaphat.
Renting property in Palestine is not such an easy matter as it
sounds. Innumerable heirs who have inherited bits and pieces
all have to receive their share of the rent and sign the lease.
Later, when we finally bought the property, we went through
the same procedure. Every bit purchased increased the nuisance
value of the unbought. The last two shares, from the Mufti of
Jerusalem and his brother, whose mother had been Rabbah Effendi's fourth wife before she married the Mufti's father, were
acquired at an exorbitant price. In Turkish times all property
was divided into twenty-four shares or "carats." From the Arabic
we get the expression "twenty-four carats," denoting pure gold.

We also retained the old house.

Our enlarged group had just got settled in the new home when
a number of Swedish farmers from Nos in the county of Dalana,
Sweden, who were affiliated to the Chicago Swedish group,
wrote, saying that they had decided to sell their farms and join
their coreligionists in Jerusalem. If those joining us in Chicago
had been a test of faith, this was a far greater test. It was decided
that their former leader and Jacob should go at once to Sweden
and advise them to remain where they were. These dear people
were so enthusiastic about the idea of going to the Holy Land,
however, that they would accept no advice to the contrary. Some
of them were old, a few were ill. These were the most enthusiastic
of all to come to Palestine. No advice, no warning deterred them
from their resolute determination. Lest something should interfere with their cherished plan, they sold their farms with such
haste that they did not get the best price.

There were thirty-eight in all, counting seventeen children,
one a babe in arms.

Their friends and neighbors thought them crazy to undertake
such a journey into what was to them "the unknown." They
were sure they would be left stranded after their money was
used up. When no persuasion to the contrary availed, Jacob went
to Goteborg to arrange for their passage. These simple country
people brought their hand looms, knitting machines, and many
farm implements with them. They sailed July 23, 1896, singing
"We're Marching to Zion," and arrived in Jaffa in August at
the height of a Palestinian summer. The sunlight was dazzling,
the dust choking, the heat exceptional, but here was abundant
fruit, which was scarce in their land. Jacob kindly but not wisely

ordered every fruit then in season for their first lunch at the Jaffa Hotel, and they ate abundantly. They learned that they had to eat fruit with discretion.

The courage of these people was remarkable. They came to a strange country of strange customs. There was nothing to remind them of home. They must often have been lonely and homesick, but they never made us conscious of it. They lived in stone houses with stone floors. I don't suppose they had ever seen such structures.

Few of them could speak a word of English. Our morning Bible readings were translated into Swedish. Jacob, with his oriental aptitude for learning languages, soon picked up enough Swedish to converse freely with them.

They were accustomed to bake bread once a year, the hard, thin cakes of rye bread with a hole in the middle through which ropes were strung and then suspended from the ceiling. From this store they had helped themselves as the need arose. In the Colony we baked wheat bread every day. We thought our bread was delicious, but to them it was distasteful. They loathed the smell of it. Did they complain? Not a bit. I only heard this fact and realized what they must have gone through years later, when they had learned to like our bread as much as we did, and could talk and laugh about their past experiences. The old people among this group studied English diligently, the young went to the Colony school, and soon we were able to stumble along together in broken English and broken Swedish. We learned to sing many of their lovely Swedish hymns, and we bacame a bilingual association.

There were several acres of vineyard north of the house running down to the Kedron Valley. Our Swedish farmers started on this to create a farm.

The looms and knitting machine were set up, and cloth woven for tablecloths. Weaving in all sorts of cotton and linen thread was tried, and the patterns were lovely. For many years we never bought table linen. It was all woven at the Colony. They wove material for furniture coverings that was beautiful. They even wove tweed for suits for our men out of native white-and-black lambs' wool. The mayor of Jerusalem, Hassain Effendi el Husseini, wore a suit made from this material for many years. Its durability was everlasting. My sister Grace carded, spun, and wove herself enough material for a suit.

Other industries were started, and little by little, with diligence, the Colony emerged from poverty.

There were a few drones. There always are in such a community. It would be strange indeed if all the people who joined the Colony in this impulsive and non-selective manner had turned out to be what they represented themselves as being. One old Chicago couple were particularly troublesome.

In about a year they decided to leave the Colony. They complained to the Consul that they had contributed considerable funds. In fact the amount received from them after six months amounted to only one hundred and eighty dollars.

There were several other cases of misfits and malcontents, but these are typical.

The addition of so many new members without a corresponding addition to the financial situation was serious. Mother wrote:

Our family is very large. Many times larger than it ever was before, and consequently my cares are much greater. We number about one hundred and thirty, and forty of this number are children.

The Mohammedans and Jews are most kind to us. When we arrived back from the United States one of them gave us a horse, another killed a cow and sent us the whole of it. Others sent us bags of rice and charcoal. Another gave us olives from twenty-seven trees. These olives we have pickled and put up for the winter. Where we can, we return their kindness. We nurse their sick and teach their children. There are many ways in which we can help them.

It might seem that the life in the Colony was dour, overburdened by problems, and blighted by persecution. But that was not so. The incidents I have chronicled happened—many of them were tragic—but the atmosphere of the Colony was happy, the aura reverential and devout. Need was the incentive that put every bit of accumulated knowledge to work and every talent to use. To carding, spinning, and weaving we added a knitting machine, which made woolen and cotton underwear, socks, stockings, sweaters, and jerseys.

The flock of goats, which was our first venture, was dispensed with, and cows were installed.

In the early days, when we got our own flock of goats, our milkman's old shepherd Hassain took our flock to pasture. Hassain came from the village of Mukhmas, north of Jerusalem, the scene of one of the thrilling episodes in Old Testament history. Its strategical position commanded the north side of the Pass of Mukhmas which was the headquarters of the Philistines and center of their raids against the Israelites in their attempts to subdue the rising under Saul. Jonathan and his armor-bearer held the pass alone, took the Philistines by surprise, and won a decisive victory.

Hassain claimed to remember the invasion of Palestine by Ibrahim Pasha of Egypt. If that was true, and there was no way of checking the validity of his statement, he must have been very near his centenary. From years of leading sheep and goats to pasture he had acquired a robust physique. From playing the shepherd's pipe his fingers were bent and rigid in a flute-player's position.

Now we exchanged the flock for a herd, and Hassain had no more work, so he was cared for by the Colony for more than fifteen years, until his death.

We started a bakery and supplied Jerusalem with pies and cakes. Jams and preserves were another branch. The American Colony confectionery became famous. The shoemaking, tailoring, and dressmaking departments were kept busy. The school, which was greatly enlarged by the children of the new members and swelled by the children of Jerusalem residents, was under the able management of Mr. John E. Dinsmore, who was principal of a seminary in Maine before he came to Jerusalem.

The old vineyard to the north of the Colony buildings became a productive farm.

Mrs. Gould in a letter gave some "home news":

About the farm the olive trees have been pruned. What with Ismain's and Hussain's ground, which we have rented, we shall probably have sufficient olives, not only to eat but to make oil, which will help us greatly with our expenses, as well as the barley and wheat crops and potatoes, all of which are doing well.

Our Swedish and American farmers had tilled these bits of ground so well that there was evidence of excellent crops. Some Orthodox Jews came to inspect the wheat and offered us a higher than usual price for it to make matzoth (unleavened bread) for their Feast of the Passover on condition that we harvested it under their supervision. We agreed.

We had no machinery; it was harvested by hand. One stipulation they made was that we should not begin work until the sun had risen and dried any moisture from dew fallen during the night. After breakfast we all went out to work in the field, our Jewish overseers keeping watch. As our custom was when working, washing dishes, or over the washtub, or at any other task, we sang hymns. So now we started in the harvest field. Singing helped the work, which went with a swing. But we were not allowed to sing by these Orthodox Jews. Peradventure a bit of moisture might fall from our mouths and cause fermentation. It would no longer be unleavened.

So we gathered the sheaves silently.

We were accustomed to rising early and working hard. The rising bell rang at 6:30 A.M. in the American Colony, and breakfast was served at seven. All who could manage it helped with the dishes, and we sang as we worked. Dishwashing time offered the place and opportunity to practice new hymns and songs. At eight another bell rang, and we gathered in the large upper living room for morning prayers.

By nine or a little after we were all dispersed to our different departments and work.

We had a healthy social life as well. All the consular corps in Jerusalem, with the exception of our own, were our friends, as well as the Arab and Jewish communities. We attended teas and receptions and gave them in return. Mother wrote:

This afternoon Bertha and the young people are giving a party on the housetop, or rather the roof of our dining rooms. About thirty ladies and gentlemen are invited. They will have music and drills for the entertainment. People like to come to our house.

The young people of the Colony had a literary club, an art club, choir, and band. People outside the Colony joined all our activities. Sunday afternoon there was a service at 3 P.M. followed by a social hour. The choir sang, the band played, tea and coffee and coffee bread were served. As many as thirty or forty people would visit the Colony on Sunday afternoon. In the tourist season whole parties would come to visit the Colony. The hymn singing, which followed as daylight waned and the lamps were lighted, was popular. Often a number of guests remained for supper. There were not many attractions in Jerusalem in those days before World War I. The American Colony filled the place of a Y.M.C.A.

In another letter Mrs. Gould told of Christmas and "the usual beautiful gifts from our Mohammedan friends."

Many of these gifts were payments in kind for the education of their children and for nursing their sick; others were simply Christmas presents.

Ahmed Effendi sent a sheep; Sheik Mohammed a basket of rice, the same came from the Mayor of Jerusalem, two turkeys from Hussain, two ducks and two geese and four baskets of oranges from Faidi Effendi al Alami. From others (I can't remember the names) we got four trays of "buklaway" (Arabic sweetmeat), one tray of geribi (like Scotch shortbread), one tray of "mamoul" and another of "Karabidj Halab" (whips of Aleppo—a delicious sweetmeat). Suliman sent a large tray of candy for the tree. A beautiful large tree came from Mr. Baldensperger, and many other gifts which I cannot remember. Many of the effendis came on Christmas Eve, also the Floyds, the Lyons, and many other guests. The tree was lighted. The children went through several new drills and exercises, greatly to the delight of all. They had learned a new fan drill, the instructions for which Miss Laishley had sent out from England. It was very pretty, and the children did well. Christmas morning the children who had all hung their stockings on the backs of their chairs before going to bed found them full of gifts. The old folks found theirs at their plates. Miss Laishley remembered all the old and many of the younger members, and was in turn remembered by many of us, more than she thought she ought to be, but not more than was our pleasure to do; and so passed a happy and pleasant day.

In March 1897 Ismail Bey Husseini, the newly appointed Director of Public Instruction, came to Mother with the request that the American Colony take charge of the only Moslem girls' school in Jerusalem. It was rare for an Arab to be appointed to a senior position under the Turkish regime. Ismail Bey had been one of Father's pupils and wanted to do something to improve the education of the Moslem girls. I was anxious to undertake the work, but as I had only just passed my nineteenth birthday, Mother considered me too young and inexperienced to shoulder so great a responsibility. Miss Brooke, who had been head of a girls' school before joining the Colony, was getting on in years and too old to cope with the difficulties of organizing a school. So it was decided that we should take it jointly. In Miss Brooke, wisdom, knowledge, and discretion were represented; in my youth there was courage, enthusiasm, and complete lack of comprehension of the difficulties which such a position involved.

Ismail Bey took Miss Brooke and me to inspect the schoolhouse. It was an ancient building forming part of the northern boundary of the large compound surrounding the Dome of the Rock. The walls were four to five feet thick on the ground floor. The building was supposed to date from Saladin's time. It was an old madraseh for Moslem theological students. After extensive repairs were completed, Miss Brooke and I remained in charge of the school for one year, after which I continued as principal for six more years, until I married Frederick Vester.

One day during this period I returned from the Moslem Girls' School to our old home on the city wall, which was being used as a school for the children of the Colony. I was asked to show a gentleman the view of the old city from the roof. It was considered the best view to be had from any place inside the walls. We talked for a while about the view and history. When he left, he said his name was Rider Haggard.

Also while I was directress of the Moslem Girls' School I first met Miss Gertrude Bell, traveler, alpine climber, archaeologist, author, and diplomat. She spoke correct and classical Arabic. After attending an Arab luncheon at which Miss Bell and I were the only women present, she asked to see the ladies of the house. So different is the classical Arabic from the colloquial that these women could not understand what she said. It fell to me to translate from classical to the Arabic of the ordinary folk.

Miss Bell played an important part in placing King Feisal, son of King Husein of Arabia, on the throne in Damascus and later in Iraq. It was she, I believe, who drew the attention of the War Office to the young archaeologist, T. E. Lawrence, who later became the famous "Lawrence of Arabia." Miss Bell and I remained friends until her death in Baghdad in 1926. A pleasant coincidence is that my eldest son, Horatio, married Miss Gertrude Bell's niece, Valentine, daughter of the late Admiral Sir Herbert and Lady Richmond.

And still the American Colony, no matter what it accomplished or tried to do, remained anathema with the American Consulate. Derogatory articles continued to appear in American newspapers, and others, equally strong in opinion, praising the Colony, were printed.

Any disgruntled or dissatisfied person with a complaint against the American Colony found willing listeners at the American Consulate during the tenure of office of the two Consuls, Messrs. Merrill and Wallace.

In September 1897 a pamphlet which became known as "The Alley Paper" was printed for distribution in Jerusalem. Its title was *Spaffordism. A Conclusive Exposé of the Spaffordite Fraud in Jerusalem*. The pamphlet went on at great length to accuse the community of every vile practice in the category of sin.

It was signed by sixteen American citizens. An edition adapted for non-Americans was signed by eleven people of other nationalities. We were puzzled. A number of the signers of this shocking pamphlet were, we believed, our friends. When they were faced by us with their contradictory behavior, they convinced us that they had never seen the original of the manuscript.

Then an abusive article appeared in the Chicago *Journal* of December 20, 1897. It was signed by Mr. Edwin Wallace.

The tradition of the Colony to take whatever came, good or bad, as a steppingstone to mount higher, was attempted if not always attained. Mr. Wallace's article made us realize finally that there was no redress, no possible adjustment to our relationship with the American Consulate.

We prepared to fight for vindication.

CHAPTER EIGHTEEN

In OCTOBER 1898 Kaiser Wilhelm II of Germany, who had for many years flirted with Sultan Abdul-Hamid over the Bagh-dad Railway and the *Drang nach Osten*, used the opening of the reconstructed Crusader Church on the property known as the Muristan, given by the Turks to his grandfather, as an excuse to visit both Turkey and Palestine.

The Lutheran Church of the Redeemer, which stands almost in the shadow of the Holy Sepulcher, was reconstructed as far as possible from the old stones lying in the ruins. On this spot was the Palestine headquarters of the Order of Saint John of Jerusalem, and here the Knights Hospitalers had their hospice for pilgrims, hospitals, and "madhouse" clinics.

Strangely enough the imperial party traveled on Cook's tickets, and Mr. Bernard Heilpern, a converted Jew, who was the manager of Thomas Cook and Son's office in Palestine, was in charge. *Punch*, with its usual humour, dubbed the imperial visitors "Cook's Crusaders."

The imperial visit was a great occasion for Palestine. The American Colony had bought an old camera, and in this small way started the Photographic Department which later became famous for its large selection of photographs and stereopticon slides. Frederick, with Elijah Meyers—Brother Elijah, a con-verted Jewish-Indian who had a partial knowledge of photo-graphy—followed the Kaiser and his entourage on the entire Palestine trip.

The landing was made at a jetty newly constructed for the occasion at the foot of Mount Carmel and adjoining the Templar German Colony in Haifa.

The entire route of the imperial party was decorated, beflagged, and illuminated at night. In Jerusalem they encamped in the grounds where later the German Propstei and school were built, on the Street of the Prophets. There were no buildings there at that time. The Sultan sent magnificent tents to be used for receptions. Pre-fabricated asbestos sleeping quarters were sent from Germany and erected in the grounds.

I was asked by the Turkish authorities in charge of the arrangements to select from any house belonging to a Turkish subject in Jerusalem furniture and carpets which would be appropriate to furnish the royal tents.

A few weeks before the imperial visitors were due to arrive, the Ministry of Education in Constantinople had sent an order that the Moslem Girl's School in Jerusalem (of which I was principal) should present some of their handiwork to the Kaiserin. The only possibility at such short notice was the Turkish coat of arms in tapestry, which had been ordered and was under construction by the girls of the school. This was appropriately framed and enclosed in a beautiful olivewood box. One of the schoolgirls was to present it, and the Kaiserin graciously appointed the day and hour.

I had not anticipated the difficulty I encountered when I tried to select the little girl to perform this duty. None of the parents would allow their daughter to present the gift. They feared the evil eye.

The evil eye is the eye of envy; there would be many envious eyes, they felt, and ill luck might follow.

As a last resort Ismail Bey, who for an entirely different reason had not proposed his daughter, said, "I don't believe in the evil eye, so send Rowada with the gift."

His daughter Rowada was a beautiful child about eight years old.

The Kaiserin presented her with a diamond pin in the shape of the German eagle and a box of bonbons and spoke to her in English.

I have mentioned that the houses were illuminated at night during the royal visit. As there was no electricity in Palestine at the time, small lanterns with lighted candles inside were hung on hooks. In the late afternoon of that day Ismail Bey's manservant was lighting and hanging the lanterns on the roof. Rowada went up to watch, still wearing the thin white muslin dress that she had worn for her visit to the Kaiserin. Her dress caught fire.

I happened to be talking to Sitt Fatme, Ismail Bey's wife when we heard screams. We flew upstairs to find Rowada enveloped in flames. I threw her down and rolled her in a small but priceless rug. It put out the fire, but the mischief was done. She was burned all over her body. Doctors could do little except relieve her suffering. I sat up all night with her. The Kaiser sent his personal doctor, but there was nothing anyone could do.

Toward dawn she died.

When Mother came to condole with Ismail Bey and his wife, he said to her, "Don't ever again say there is no evil eye. I know now that there is."

The carriage road to the Mount of Olives was made for the Kaiser's visit. It passed the American Colony. At the junction of the two roads, that leading to the Mount of Olives going east and the other northwest to Nablus, there was a sharp hairpin bend. On the first trip of the imperial visitors to the Mount of Olives the whole party stopped at the hairpin bend for some time.

I remember we were all out looking over the wall of our garden to watch the important visitors pass by, and we were intrigued with their stop. We asked the Cook's representative who accompanied the imperial company on all their trips what it meant.

Mr. Heilpern told us that the Kaiser had been explaining to his Turkish hosts that the bend was far too sharp and narrow to allow cannon to pass that way.

We gave our informant incredulous smiles, but we lived to see German and Austrian howitzers and cannon roll down that widened bend on their way to fight the British.

A private service was arranged for the imperial pair on top of the Mount of Olives one Sunday afternoon during their visit. I was engaged to Frederick at the time and we had gone for a walk to the top of Olivet. As we sat beneath the cyprus trees, we noticed agitation, and suddenly Turkish police were everywhere. A carpet was spread on the cistern top in the Russian Compound; some chairs and a small prayer desk were arranged there.

Almost immediately the imperial pair, accompanied by a small entourage, took their places on the chairs.

A German officer, seeing Frederick and me, came over and asked if we would like to join them. We certainly would! We sat directly behind the Kaiser and Kaiserin and heard them sing.

The Kaiserin expressed a wish to own property on the Mount of Olives. His Excellency Von Mirbach, who was Oberhomeister Ihren Major der Kaiserin, took note of this desire, and it was he who organized the appeal to all Germans living in the Fatherland and "im Ausland," after a considerable sum had been given by a rich German lady for the purpose, and the property was bought on which the Kaiserin Augusta Victoria Stiftung was later built. The title deeds, made out in the Kaiserin's name, were given to the imperial pair on the silver anniversary of their wed-

ding day. The Kaiser and Kaiserin never saw this building.
They are represented as Crusaders in statuettes in the large open
court and painted in Byzantine style on the ceiling of the church
holding the architect's model on their knees. Until the war of
1914—16 the Stiftung was used as a sanitarium and the Kaiserswert deaconesses were in charge.

Several of the deaconesses working in the Stiftung contracted
malaria, and one wondered how they could get malaria on the
top of the dry Mount of Olives. There were no swamps on the
top of this high mountain. But there were cisterns. Here mosquitoes hatched and thrived, but as yet no one had connected one
with the other. The Kaiserin, through Freiherr Von Mirbach,
organized the commission under the direction of the great malaria
expert, Professor Dr. Möhlens, to investigate this problem. He
took drops of blood from a large number of the inhabitants of
Jerusalem. Dr. Möhlens made an interesting statement in his
report. He said that the only place in Jerusalem which he found
100 per cent free of malarial parasites was the American Colony.
Thinking more of the pest of flies, we had brought the American
custom to Jerusalem of screening our windows and doors, which
had saved our community more than we had realized.

There were frequent cholera scares, but in December 1912
cholera broke out in Palestine and spread rapidly. The fact that
there was no universal water supply proved for once a blessing
in disguise. Individual subterranean cisterns, in which rain was
collected from the roofs of the houses during the winter months,
were our only source of supply. The Turkish Government put
a cordon of soldiers around Jerusalem to prevent contamination
and keep it isolated. The Jerusalem—Jaffa railroad stopped running. We heard rumors of the spreading of the dreaded disease
through Jaffa, Gaza, Lydda, Beersheba, Jericho, and many other
villages. People were dying in large numbers with very little
medical assistance. No serious precautions, as we understand
them now, were taken against its spread.

There was a Swedish-American, I will call him Mr. Olson,
who with his wife, two daughters and a son, had come to Jerusalem with the Chicago group. He had become dissatisfied with
the life of the Colony and had left it with his son, but he couldn't
persuade his wife and two daughters to leave and go away with
him. We heard that he was working on a farm in Jericho, also,
that he was drinking heavily and behaving badly.

On the first of December, at about 3 A.M., Jacob and Frederick,

who were sleeping in a room near the front door, heard a carriage
come up the private road and stop at the Colony gate. Soon they
heard knocking. When they opened the front door, there stood
two Jews, who informed them that Mr. Olson had started with
them from Jericho. On the road he was taken ill and had died.
The corpse was in the carriage in the driveway. Jericho, being
one of the places infected by cholera, they feared that Mr. Olson
had died of that malady. I was roused to make a cup of hot tea
for the two Jews, but we refused to take any responsibily for
the body. He was an American citizen, therefore we sent the men
to Consul Merrill.

A little later Jacob and Frederick heard the carriage return
stealthily. They were up in a trice, but only just in time to prevent the Jews from dropping the dead body over the garden wall.

The men said these had been their instructions from Consul
Merrill. How these men got through the cordon at Gethsemane
can only be surmised. Thither they were taken again by the
police.

Two of our men went to Dr. Merrill. It was still early morning,
and he would not receive them. He sent out a note which said
that we were the proper people to look after the burial. Our men
replied that Mr. Olson was no longer a member of the Colony
and that we had no responsibility in the matter. They said,
however, as a Christian duty, to help the two men on whose
hands the corpse was, that the Colony would be willing to bury
the body on condition that Dr. Merrill supply the death certificate and authorize us to bury him in the new American Cemetery. We were compelled to safeguard the Colony in this way
because of a threat which Consul Merrill had made, that if he
only got the chance he would quarantine the Colony.

This was not the first time that our Consul had refused to
receive a delegation from the American Colony, so another note
was passed between the parties. Our men wrote that in view of
Dr. Merrill's refusal to put the Colony in a position which would
make it possible for them to bury Mr. Olson, who had died under
suspicious circumstances, we would notify the municipal authorities to take the proper action.

Dr. Merrill refused to read or even to receive the last note.
The municipal authorities notified Consul Merrill to take charge
of the body. Dr. Merrill referred the officials to us. We raised
no further question. We buried Mr. Olson in our recently purchased private cemetery.

A friend wrote us:

Your account of the cunning trap which Mr. Merrill set for you in the case of the dead body left at your door . . . reads, in some of its details, like a story out of the *Arabian Nights.*

Sometimes the two Consuls, in their zeal to gather derogatory testimony against the Colony, fell into ditches of their own digging. Mr. Wallace's statements to travelers about us were so gratuitous and uncalled for that they aroused suspicion, and a number of people visited the Colony who would not otherwise have done so, to find out the truth for themselves. Many wrote back wonderful letters, others were in time to raise powerful voices in our behalf. One such visitor was Judge H. Crosby of New York, who was one of the judges of the mixed tribunal in Egypt. Judge Crosby came to the Colony and asked many questions about our household, our principles, our mode of life, and was deeply impressed with our work. When he said good-by, he asked one more question.

He wanted to know if we owed anything toward the rent of our house.

When Judge Crosby got to London, he telegraphed to his banker in New York to send us a check for the amount. He became a stanch friend of the Colony.

Early in 1900 Miss, later Dr. Selma Lagerlof, Sweden's famous authoress, visited Jerusalem.

She stopped at the Grand New Hotel, which was inside the Jaffa Gate and was patronized by Thomas Cook and Son. Dr. Merrill also lived there.

He knocked at her bedroom door one day and warned her against visiting the American Colony, which, he said, included a number of Swedes. He told her that it was not a proper place for ladies to visit. He deplored the fact that it bore the name of America and said he was doing all he could to break it up. He told her that Mrs. Spafford would not allow anyone to see the Swedes alone, that she exercised hypnotic influence over them.

Miss Lagerlof felt that if this was the case she was in duty bound to deliver her compatriots from such an evil bondage.

She came to the Colony accompanied by a friend who was traveling with her. I remember their visit well. They asked for Mother, and I went to the living room with her.

Miss Lagerlof sat on the edge of her chair as though she were afraid of contamination. Mother received her cordially, as she did everyone.

When she heard that Miss Lagerlof was Swedish she said, "You have many compatriots here, and they will be delighted to see you." And Mother sent me to call all the Swedish members.

After that first visit Miss Lagerlof came many times to the Colony. She talked to the Swedish members collectively and alone; she saw us at our work, and attended our services and our social gatherings.

She had many talks with Mother. One day, I remember, she said to Mother in fun, with a bright smile on her intelligent face, "Mrs. Spafford, you are the best-looking woman I ever saw to be so wicked."

There was no Swedish Consul in Jerusalem at the time, but when Miss Lagerlof reached Constantinople she swore to an affidavit at the Swedish and Norwegian Consulate General and sent it to us, in which she told of the slanderous attacks against the American Colony and what she had found to be true.

Dr. Lagerlof wrote the novel about a colony called "Jerusalem" for which she received the Nobel prize. Mother is the heroine of her book and is called Mrs. Gordon.

At the Universal Christian Conference on Life and Work which met in Stockholm in 1925 Dr. Lagerlof gave an address which was about Mother and the American Colony. She told about Mother's experience at the time of the shipwreck. I quote:

Then in her extremity she thought no longer of her husband and children. She thought about lifting her soul to God. Is it so easy to die? she thought. Then she heard a mighty voice . . . that filled her ears with the thundering reply: "It is true that it is easy to die. That which is difficult is to live." "That which is required in order that it may become easy to live on earth is unity, unity, unity." . . . This incident and this message came into my mind when I first heard about the Universal Christian Conference on Life and Work. I fancied that after the great collision—the terrible shipwreck that had be-fallen Christianity (1914-18) many of its best members had felt themselves cast out into a bottomless deep, with the dear one lost, with aversion to life, ready to accept the threatening annihilation as a release. But out of the abyss of agony voices from another world have reached these despairing ones. They, too, have heard, amid the wild tumult and bloodshed, the cry of unity, unity, unity; and it is for this reason that they have now gathered here from the four corners of the world to create the peace and harmony that people have yearned after for thousands of years, which surely should make life easier to live. This is the first thought that came to me upon hearing about the conference.

May I relate further about the shipwrecked woman's life and work? The problem that she had to solve was the same as that of this Conference, although on a different scale. And I may well admit that when I meditated upon her life, my heart trembled. I seemed to see a message written by the very finger of God—a message of guidance, of awakening, of trust—which should be read by just this gathering. But let me say first that the young American woman, Anna Spafford, received the message that had come that terrible night as the true Word of God. She did not tell herself that it was illusion and self-deception, but interpreted it as a sacred command, which it was her task to convert into reality. Several years went by, however, before she made a serious attempt. Two daughters grew up in the home, but the sense of loss continued. At least she realized that help and consolation would not be hers until she had dedicated her life to the establishment of unity in the disunited world.

But unity—what is unity? How can it be realized? How can one live in unity with one's fellow men as they now are—selfish, self-righteous, false, dissipated, sinful? Let us go forth to meet the great difficulty. . . . Anna Spafford adopted the usual expedient. She herself, her husband and twenty of their friends, founded a community whose members pledged themselves to live in unity with each other and to serve and help all humanity. . . . While they thus sought to emulate the first confessors of Christianity, whose lives in Jerusalem were continually in their thoughts, news came to them that disease and famine were devastating the Holy City. The message that had been given to Anna Spafford seemed to them the very essence of Christianity. . . . Their occupation was to search out the sick in the narrow lanes of the Holy City, to feed the hungry, and to help and care for the orphaned. They lived a simple life, taking their meals together and performing earnest devotions. They concerned themselves but little with preaching the principles that had led them to this place. . . .

Let us stop here for a moment. Does it not seem strange that this community, which desired to spread unity throughout the world, should have chosen to proclaim its beliefs through good works? It demanded no uniformity of dogmas. It desired, like this Conference, to bring about Christian unanimity in work and modes of living.

It also came to pass that a few, through seeing the peace, harmony, and quiet happiness that prevailed in the little circle, became convinced that theirs was the right course and requested that they might attach themselves to the American Colony. The largest addition to the American Colony came, however, not from Palestine, but, strangely enough, from Sweden. A group of peasants in the parish of Nås in Dalarna had organized a similar religious cult. Through countrymen who had emigrated to Chicago they came to hear of the Americans who had settled in Jerusalem. . . . Those peasants were seized with a desire to unite themselves with the Colony. . . .

The Colony in Jerusalem was conposed chiefly of the same nations who have gathered for this Conference. To the Colony came small groups of people from far west and from far north in order to work for unity in association with a few Orientals. There, Anglo-Saxon energy met with oriental mysticism and northern sincerity.

But let us go further. From the beginning the Colony had assumed a distinct position among the many Christian communities in Jerusalem. Its members had always felt it a duty to display a Christian character toward the oriental surroundings, and to hold fast to the idea of unity. . . .

The Colonists, who were cultured, loyal, peaceful people, had always enjoyed the greatest esteem among the natives of the city, and this was not only among the poor. Such aristocratic Arabic and Jewish families as there were in the city visited the Colonists and were their true friends. But to many of the Christian communities in Jerusalem and the Orient the Colony became from the first a rock of offense. They could not understand what this lay-man's organization, which exerted a missionary activity and made itself friends among the opponents of Christianity, had to do in Jerusalem. The Colonists were accused of leading despicable lives, and attempts were made to harm them and make it impossible for them to live in the Orient.

Is there anyone present who doubts that the Conference will meet with the same fate? Is it not certain that the best among the non-Christians will greet such a Conference as this with joy and follow it with good wishes? And is it not equally certain that its worst adversaries will arise out of Chris-tianity itself, that from this quarter will come the voices that misinterpret its motives and seek to frustrate its resolution? I need hardly say it. . . . .

Despite hers and other powerful voices lifted in our behalf, six years passed between Dr. Lagerlof's visit and the end of our feud with the American Consulate. During that time a great deal happened.

John Whiting was nearing his majority, and it was considered wise to send him to the United States to make another appeal for part, if not all, of his inheritance. Jacob accompanied him to America.

Mr. Luther Laflin Mills, who had successfully fought the Whiting case in 1895, represented John, and a settlement was reached out of court. Mr. Mills succeeded in getting $100 a month for the Whiting children and $5000 for John to invest in business.

In Jerusalem, the Colony had recently purchased the store which my future father-in-law, Ferdinand Vester, had main-tained for many years for the sale of the olivewood articles made in his workshops. I have mentioned in an earlier chapter that this work was started by a Swiss-German mission. When that organ-ization ceased to function in Palestine, Mr. Vester took over the work himself. He was now old and feeble and wished to relinquish the responsibility. Frederick had been a member of the American Colony for ten years and felt this was a good opportunity for the Colony's expansion. One of the British members of the Colony had recently been left a legacy and she offered this sum to the Colony to invest in the shop. Mr. Vester made a reasonable offer in view of the fact that his son would become manager and part owner. John's money was jointly invested in the shop under the name of Vester and Co., American Colony Stores.

Frederick and I were planning our marriage at this time. I

hoped that the date could be the twenty-fifth of September, which was my parents' wedding day. But my foster brother was in the United States, and we wanted Jacob to be present. As soon as Jacob got Mr. Mills working on John Whiting's case, he left America for Palestine. Once we knew he had touched Egypt, we issued the invitations to our wedding on March 1, 1904. A storm came up and we feared Jacob would not be able to land. But he did, and all was well.

For the civil ceremony my birth certificate was necessary, but I had none. The only procurable paper of any sort to show that I was born an American citizen was Father's registration in the American Consulate in 1881, when he registered his two minor children at the same time. A statement of this from the Consul of the United States was necessary. Dr. Merrill refused to give this to me.

Frederick and I consulted the German Consul General. Dr. Merill's treatment of the members of the Colony was well known. Consul General Schmidt said to me: "Tell your mother to write a letter to Dr. Merrill asking him for a copy of Mr. Spafford's registration. He won't dare refuse when the request is in writing," and, giving a whimsical smile, he added, "invite him to the wedding."

The civil ceremony took place in the German Consulate in the morning of the first of March. After it was over the Consul General and Mrs. Schmidt invited us to their private apartment and drank our health in champagne. In the afternoon we were married by Probst Bussman in the large drawing room of the American Colony. (On August 11, 1909, he married my sister Grace and John Whiting in the same place.) We invited only a few friends to the religious ceremony, so that there would be room for all the members of the Colony to attend. Later in the afternoon a large reception was given to several hundred people. We had no honeymoon but went at once to our new-old home in the old city, which was the first abode of the Colony and the home Father knew and loved.

And so began thirty-four years of happy married life for Frederick and me, and for the Colony.

The man I married was reserved; he was a loyal friend to rich and poor, high and low. He would not compromise with evil or with error.

His temper was even and he was tolerant. It was quite impossible for Frederick to sustain a grudge. He soon forgot what the trouble had been about and would meet late enemies cordially. It was easy to work with him and a joy to live with him.

It was the most auspicious bit of good luck for the Colony that I should fall in love with the right man. He became Mother's right-hand. He took over the business management of the Colony from Mr. Rudy, who was getting old and wanted to retire.

The city was full of tourists that spring of 1904. Rain was abundant and crops were good. Very soon the shop was enlarged and doing well. The financial condition of the American Colony grew steadily brighter. But, although it was prospering, Dr. Merrill was still using his office to harass us.

Early in April of that year the Sunday-school Convention, led by our friend Mr. E. K. Warren, met in Jerusalem. We took in as many of the delegates as we could accommodate in both the old house on the wall of the old city and the new Colony house at Sheik Jerah. A huge marquee was pitched for the meetings.

When the meeting of the Sunday-school Convention started, Mr. Warren insisted that Mother and several members of the Colony should sit on the platform with the leaders of the Convention. When Dr. Merrill saw this he refused to sit on the same platform. Mr. Hartshorn and Mr. Warren challenged him and let him understand that the Colony people were going to remain and he could do as he liked. Very angry, but for the first time foiled, he decided he had better appear.

In a speech made at one of the meetings Dr. Merrill told how he had been to the villages and persuaded them "to keep their beggars and pickpockets at home" so as not to annoy the delegates. Some of the Turkish Government officials who were present were insulted and contradicted the Consul.

Before the meetings ended Mr. and Mrs. Warren invited Frederick and me at their expense to return on the ship *Grosser Kurfürst* with them and visit Egypt and Italy, returning from Naples via Athens, Constantinople, Smyrna, Beirut, and Damascus. This was their wedding present to us, and a magnificent one! No one knew but Frederick and me that we had given up our plan for a honeymoon, which was to spend a few days in Jericho, that being all we could afford at the time, in order to give an Arab woman the means of buying a sewing machine. This was a case of "casting our bread upon the water," for we certainly found it "after many days" more than doubled. I had not been away from Palestine since I returned from the United States in

1895, and we enjoyed every minute of the wonderful trip.

The meeting in Jerusalem of the Sunday-school Convention was a landmark in the history of the Colony. It was the first time Dr. Merrill had been openly and publicly challenged and his threats ignored.

There was great excitement in Jerusalem that May of 1904. Under the direction of an Englishman by the name of Kenward, a Greek engineer bored a well and struck water at a depth of one hundred and fifty feet on the Bethlehem plain or Upper Baka'a. Water meant so much to this bleak and arid mountain plateau that the people of Jerusalem were very excited.

Ismail Bey brought us a bottle containing some of the water. It was clear and sweet.

Jacob wrote:

> Great numbers of people have been out there. The Pasha, the consuls, the Patriarch, and they gave the thanksgiving sacrifice to the workmen, "zarb" (a whole sheep roasted in a primitive oven). It seems that Mr. Kenward had gone to England for improved machinery and that it was hoped an abundant water supply would be the result.

However, nothing more happened at that time, and the whole excitement died down in disappointment.

Further efforts were made to supply Jerusalem's 40,000 inhabitants with running water. It was the burning problem at the time. A writer, signing himself "The Religious Rambler," wrote:

> The mania for improvement is taking fast hold of Jerusalem. At present it has only cistern water to drink and the American Colony is considering the project of supplying the city with a water system.

Jacob had a friend, Mr. S. P. Meyers, an influential and wealthy cloth manufacturer, in Bradford, England. He appealed to him for help. A Bradford paper wrote under the title "Jerusalem and Its Water Supply":

> A charming example of municipal enterprise as understood by Turkish municipal authorities is exhibited in a correspondence which has been taking place between Mr. S. P. Meyers of Bradford and the mayor of Jerusalem. Although the casual visitor might not think so from superficial inquiry, Jerusalem possesses both a mayor and a town council, but the main functions which in our occidental views attach to these bodies—sanitation and the provision of the necessaries of life—are not matters which have hitherto troubled them much. Of late, however, there has been much discussion upon the project of establishing a city water supply.

"This (Mr. Meyers') report," the article continues, "was for-warded to the mayor of Jerusalem, and that it has been received with not a little gratitude is evident from letters of thanks." But that was all that came of the careful estimates, plans, and vast correspondence. The earmarked money was otherwise needed in Constantinople. What could a progressive Arab mayor do?

Jacob was grateful to Mr. Meyers for taking no end of trouble over procuring such exhaustive information about the proposed water supply for thirsty Jerusalem and felt chagrined that after all his labor nothing came of it.

Knowing that Mr. Meyers was a collector of quaint and unique objects, Jacob procured several grains of wheat on which a Jewish scribe had written the Ten Commandments in Hebrew. These were packed carefully and sent by registered post.

They reached their destination safely but ahead of the letter which gave Mr. Meyers a description of the unusual grains.

Much to Jacob's consternation he received a letter from Mr. Meyers thanking him. He said, "Seeing how well packed they were, I realized that they must be seeds of unusual plants, so I gave them to my gardener with instructions that they should be planted at once."

Jacob commented that if they would propagate the Ten Com-mandments, it was worth-while.

Later, under another Turkish governor, Solomon's Aqueduct was repaired, and the water to the quantity of 40,000 gallons per day was brought from Solomon's Pools and the Sealed Fountain near by to two standpipes where people could fill their jars and tin pails with water. The supply was insufficient and incon-venient. It was not until 1926 that the drought caused by the meager rainfall (twelve inches) in the foregoing rainy season crystallized the much-thought-of and talked-about plan for a water supply for Jerusalem. At a cost of £63,000 the Government of Palestine contracted with the firm of Sir John Jackson, Ltd., of London, to bring water to Jerusalem from Ein Farrah, the copious spring northeast of Jerusalem. Work was commenced on January 2, 1926, and the High Commissioner for Palestine, the late Field Marshal Lord Plumer, opened the completed work on July 17 of the same year.

Some years later this supply proved inadequate for the grow-ing city, and a larger source was tapped at Ras-el-Ain, near the coast, and was pumped 2,700 feet to Jerusalem.

One of the first actions in the Jewish-Arab struggle for the possession of Palestine was the cutting off of this water supply, causing great suffering in the newer part of Jerusalem. Old Jerusalem simply went back to its cisterns.

It was estimated that Jerusalem contained rain-water storage cisterns to the capacity of 360,000,000 gallons—about enough for a city the size of London for two days! The same "Religious Rambler" wrote about the American Colony:

> The range of activities of this community is amusing as well as amazing, extending from the baking of a mince pie to the discovery, digging, and delivery of an ancient sarcophagus. Their latest bit of enterprise is the beginning of a telephone system over the city of Jerusalem. For the first time in all its long history the Holy City hears the tinkle of the telephone bell—and it's a Bell telephone at that! The new courthouse at Jerusalem has been connected with the old serai, and the system is to be extended until first all official points and then business houses and residences will be supplied with telephones.

I remember what a novelty it was! The first telephone to be installed as an experiment was one connecting the American Colony with our store. After this proved a success, the Turkish Government allowed us to install telephones in other places.

We had some amusing experiences with those uninitiated in its use. One day some of our Bedouin friends, who since 1884 had been regular visitors at the Colony, were asked to talk over the telephone to one of our men at the store. Their comments were something like this: "This travels faster than a rifle shot— it's like pinching a dog's tail in Jerusalem and he barks in Jericho. This is even more wonderful than the telegraph, which takes three hours to get to Jericho, and then it is written in Turkish and you have to run around and find someone to translate it. This is like lightning."

Today a Bedouin telegraph or telephone operator is not unusual, but I recall how recently he acquired this knowledge.

Another of the innovations suggested by the American Colony was a steam roller to improve road making. It came from Chicago.

We were often consulted in such matters, because in the course of our life under the Turkish regime three Arab mayors had been our pupils.

I have spoken several times of Mr. Hess. He was the German Vice-Consul. Mrs. Hess was considered the best-dressed woman in Jerusalem. They were Alexandrian Germans.

Soon after our first baby was born my father-in-law celebrated the fiftieth anniversary of his arrival in Jerusalem. Tables were placed in his garden under the large almond trees and his many friends were entertained at a large garden party. There were speeches; there never was a German party without speeches.

Frederick and I, with Mother, were a bit late in arriving. All the tables were filled, but we found seats rather far away from Mr. Hess, who was making a speech. He was greatly excited, pounding his fists on the table, and shouting. We were too far off to hear what he was saying, and we didn't care anyway, but I remember how amused I was by Mother's saying:

"Whatever does Mr. Hess find so exciting in the fact that Mr. Vester has been in Jerusalem for fifty years to make such a noise about?"

Sometimes, but not frequently, the Hesses came to call at the American Colony. Whenever they did, they brought their young son with them. He was a terrific nuisance. He meddled with everything and was very inquisitive, and there was no peace when he was about. We always delegated one of our members, Brother Elijah, to keep Rudolph in charge so we could get through tea undisturbed. Brother Elijah was a converted Jew from India and the abjectly poor member of a famous family of fabulous wealth. Our Brother Elijah would take the boy to the stables and show him our cows, pigs, and horses. He had his hands full trying to entertain the nervous, mischievous boy who was to become the sinister Rudolph Hess—mysterious visitor to England and notorious prisoner of World War II.

CHAPTER NINETEEN

SOME years ago I was visiting Phillips Academy, in Andover, Massachusetts, where my sons were at school. It was late autumn and the coloring glorious. We went for a walk under the trees and I remarked that in the United States I missed the link of history; in Palestine every hill, tree, velley, and well has its ancient story.

At that moment we noticed a boulder with a bronze inscription. "Here is history!" we exclaimed, and followed a path around a pond to investigate.

On this spot, the plaque informed us, in 1810, the first students of Andover "walked and talked" and resolved that the First American Society of Foreign Missions should be started.

I thought back to the long years of heartbreak when the very mention of this mission lay like the shadow of a cross over the American Colony in Jerusalem.

I remember at the same time all that the Presbyterian Board of Foreign Missions had accomplished in the Far East. The large proportion of doctors, dentists, and chemists in the eastern Mediterranean countries received their education at one of the colleges or universities that the Presbyterian Board of Foreign Missions established and conducted, including the Robert College of Istanbul and the American University of Beirut, besides those in Greece and Turkey. The standard of life has been raised through their influence. Leading citizens in many walks of life received their education and have the Presbyterian Board to thank for their successful careers.

It is therefore with a sad heart that I write this chapter. But it is part of the history of the American Colony and the "war of the graveyard" that was to last fifteen years. It cut deeply into Mother's life, and into all our lives.

I have told in another chapter that in 1891 our American Consul was responsible for the first of the graveyard troubles. I was only eleven years old when I saw the trenches cut across the American Cemetery and my father's grave exposed.

Dr. Merrill, who considered himself an authority on archaeology, had excavated the cemetery without regard to the graves.

Seven years later our troubles began again. To explain them I must go back in history.

The first Presbyterian missionaries in Jerusalem had purchased the site of the American Cemetery "on the summit of Zion, outside the city wall," and I have in my possession a translation of the deed of sale, dated Rabch 1251 of the Hegira, and May 1838 in the year of our Lord.

Prior to the purchase of the cemetery several Americans who died in Jerusalem were secretly buried at the foot of the Mount of Olives. This must have taken place during the epidemic of plague, about 1838, when Jerusalem was shut within its walls and no one was allowed to enter or leave the city.

In 1841 a powerful foreign element had been brought into Palestine through the Anglo-Prussian Bishopric, which exercised great influence through the enterprises conducted in the diocese. Christ Church, erected by the London Jews' Society, served as the seat of the bishop. It had been erected inside the walls opposite the Citadel and near the Jaffa Gate. Consent to build this church had been difficult to obtain from the Moslem Turkish Government. It was made an integral part of the British Consulate and this facilitated permission being granted for its erection. The so-called British Cemetery on Mount Zion was held jointly by the English and the Germans. A hospital for the Jews under the auspices of the English Mission with Dr. McGowan in charge had been opened in the Old City, and later a Prussian hospital was established under the supervision of Kaiserswert deaconesses. Schools, orphanages, and other institutions giving instruction in agriculture and many kinds of industry were started by both English and German missionaries; my father-in-law, Ferdinand Vester, was one of these. There was a controversy between the different missionary societies, and it was deemed expedient that the American missionaries should leave Palestine and concentrate their labors in the Lebanon and Syria.

When the activities of the Presbyterian Mission were removed from Palestine, the walled cemetery on Mount Zion, where a number of their members had been laid to rest, was left in charge of the American Consulate, with the understanding, as we were told, that any American dying in Jerusalem should have a place of burial. The key was kept at the American Consulate.

In the course of time ten members of the American Colony

were buried there, and there were other interments as well.

The site of ancient Jerusalem is full of ruins covered over and hidden by the debris and dust of centuries. Mount Zion was important in the early history of Jerusalem as well as in Byzantine and medieval times. The site of the Presbyterian Cemetery on Mount Zion, as Mr. Robinson describes it, was "adjacent to the northwestern enclosure connected with the Mosque and Tomb of David." Tradition has it that this was the "upper room," where Jesus and His disciples ate the Passover and instituted the Lord's Supper.

Before the time of Constantine, Christians had worshiped in an old house-church on Mount Zion called variously the Church of the Apostles, the Church of Zion, or the Mother of Churches. It was traditionally on the site of the house of John Mark, where the Apostles met, and where such events as the Last Supper and the descent of the Holy Spirit were supposed to have taken place. Here some time about the middle of the fourth century (after Helena's death) a new church was erected. To it attached other traditions: the house of Saint John where Saint Mary was believed to have died, and the Tomb of David.

It was in ruins at the time of the Crusaders and rebuilt by them about 1130 as the Church of Zion or of Saint Mary. Once again it was laid waste. In 1335 the Franciscans, who, after the collapse of the Crusades and the departure of the Latins, had secured a foothold in Palestine, secured a portion of the site where tradition had located the place of the Last Supper. It was a fragment of the Crusading Church, with some pillars still standing. Here they erected a shrine called the Coenaculum, or place of the Supper. However, as it was also identified as the site of the Tomb of David, it was coveted by the Moslems, who had great respect for King David, and in 1523 the Moslems took it from them, making it the mosque of the Tomb of David. Then the Franciscans in 1551 established themselves in the old Georgian monastry now called Saint Salvatore.

The Tomb of David occupied only a small part of the old Crusading Church, the rest of the site having crumbled to the ground and been covered with the dust of ages. Here, where the American Presbyterian missionaries acquired ground for their cemetery, Dr. Merrill had suspected the existence of the old church under the ground and dug for it.

In 1897, the year before the German Emperor William II visited Jerusalem, we began to hear rumors that the American

Cemetery was to be sold. But we did not learn until the following year, when the German Emperor came, the reason for the
secrecy involved. The Emperor had arranged for a site to be
given him by his friend Sultan Abdul-Hamid. The Franciscan
Fathers, who had been expelled from almost this very spot in
1561, had long been trying to secure the site of the Dormition
de la Sainte Vierge on Mount Zion, of which the American
Cemetery was a corner. They offered the Presbyterian Board a
large sum of money for the tiny cemetery—on the condition that
it was cleared of graves—and it was a tempting offer, especially
as missions are always in need of funds.

Emperor William's father, Emperor Frederick, then Crown
Prince, had visited Palestine in 1869 and was presented by the
Sublime Porte with the ancient site of the Muristan on which
the Lutheran Church of the Redeemer was built. The consecration of this church was one excuse for the Kaiser's trip to Palestine in 1898.

As the Muristan had been given to the Lutherans, it was un-
questioned that the Dormition de la Sainte Vierge would be
given to his Catholic subjects. Although the Franciscans bought
the American Cemetery, the site of the Dormition was given to
the Benedictines, who built the modern church, which later was
to serve the Israelis as a stronghold.

When we heard of the probability that the American Cemetery
might be sold we had no objections. The cemetery was not bene-
fiting the Presbyterian Board and they had every right to sell it.
We had no legal claim to the privilege of burying our dead there
except that given us by the American Consul at each burial.

We therefore selected a suitable site and started negotiations
to purchase a small plot of ground to be used as a private burial
place. Our petition to the Turkish authorities had to go through
the American Consulate. Under Turkish law, a cemetery becomes a Pious Foundation, which cannot easily be sold. Because
of these restrictions, there is a certain amount of "red tape" to
be gotten through.

In view of our petition for purchase of a cemetery, which took
its legitimate course through the American Consulate, Mr. Rudy
received a letter from Mr. Wallace dated February 10, 1897, in
which he acknowledged the receipt of Mr. Rudy's request and
said in reply, "Permit me to state that I fear you will have great
difficulty in procuring permission to use the ground you propose
purchasing as a cemetery. An application for such purchase must

be made through the Legation at Constantinople." Then Mr. Wallace asked Mr. Rudy to call at the Consulate, which he did.

During the interview Mr. Wallace said that the matter of the sale of the American Cemetery was under consideration by the Presbyterian Board, but it would be some time before they would decide to make the sale.

Mr. Wallace asked Mr. Rudy whether the American Colony, in case of such a sale, would be willing to undertake the transfer of their dead.

Mr. Rudy replied that we would certainly be willing, but as we did not have a place of burial yet, he asked that timely notice should be given.

Mr. Rudy at this time was preparing to leave for the United States as our personal representative to Washington. Matters had steadily grown worse between the American Colony and the American Consulate. Several requests for an investigation into the actions of the two Consuls had been made, and each time they had been evaded. This time we were obdurate.

Since so much of our life at this time was subjected to protracted persecution in which enemies of our Group sought to discredit the leaders and individuals of the American Colony, I think it best that we be perfectly frank in explaining the basis of the trouble that was distorted by evil minds into charges of moral laxity. At the same time it must be remembered that the actual animus was over theological questions which in a day of fanatical dogmatism aroused the intensest passions against any who were in any way different.

Some time after my parents came to Jerusalem, Father told Mother in private that he wanted to live Matthew 19:12, "and there are eunuchs which have made themselves eunuchs for the kingdom of heaven's sake." Nothing about this resolution was mentioned at the time to any of the other members of the Group. When, finally, Mother spoke of it to Mrs. Whiting, she found that the Whitings had made much the same choice.

It was a solemn undertaking, a personal dedication which did not concern any except those who chose to live it. Celibacy was never meant to become a governing canon of the Group.

Somehow this had leaked out. It was misinterpreted and degraded by our opponents.

After Father died Dr. Merrill became less cautious in his attacks and accused us of forbidding marriage. There were no young people in the Colony at the time to get married, so we had no means of disputing this new charge. Mother went to Dr. Merrill to try to explain, saying that she believed if he knew it was false, he, being a Christian gentleman, would cease to repeat such statements. "Why don't you get married?" he demanded rudely.

Mother's reply was that she still felt close to Father.

Dr. Merrill's next accusation was that we were spiritualists who claimed communication with the dead!

The article by Mr. Wallace and the insinuations of the Alley paper had clearly pointed the way to an investigation. We made up our minds to put a legal stop to the continual slanders by the two Consuls against the American Colony.

We knew we could expect no possible redress from instituting a court procedure in Jerusalem against our persecutors, for in Turkish times American citizens held their own consular courts, and our archenemy would have been our judge.

Mr. Rudy left for the United States on September 8, 1897, to present our case to the State Department in Washington. He was armed with letters from responsible representative citizens.

Ten days after his departure one of our older Swedish members, Mr. Matsson, died. Mr. Baldwin and Mr. Olaf Larson went to the American Consulate to obtain the key to the cemetery, as had been done ten times before.

To their consternation they were curtly informed by Mr. Wallace that the cemetery had been sold and the bodies of ten beloved American Colony members, including those of my father, Aunt Maggie, and Captain Sylvester, had been removed.

We learned later that because of the Emperor's nearing visit the sale had been swiftly consummated.

We were told that the Presbyterian Mission had sent a representative to Jerusalem from Sidon, and that he had removed the bodies under the protection of the Consulate.

Mr. Matsson's death had uncovered the plot.

We were left with the dreadful problem: Where should we bury Mr. Matsson? Interment, as always, must be swift. The Greek Orthodox Patriarch, Monsignor Damianos, came to our rescue and allowed us to use the Greek Cemetery.

Four months passed before we could find out where the bodies of our American Colony members were lying. Consul Wallace sent us to the mission representative. He, in turn, emphasized his full right to sell the cemetery, which was never disputed, and sent us back to Mr. Wallace.

Our objection was that it had been done secretly and without our knowledge, and that we wanted to know where our dead had been taken, so that we ourselves might bury them decently in a cemetery of our own.

Mr. Rudy was in the United States presenting our complaints to the State Department. He also met members of the Presbyterian Board of Foreign Missions. And still we could not discover where the bodies were. At last we turned to the British Government.

We learned that the bodies were "temporarily" in a large pit in the English Cemetery.

Delay was caused by a vast amount of correspondence between the British and American Consuls and the Anglican bishop who was in charge of the English Cemetery before we received permission to open the pit. Mrs. Sylvester wrote to Lord Salisbury, H.B.M. Secretary of Foreign Affairs, in the matter of the desecration of the grave of her late husband:

without my knowledge or consent and with permission and co-operation of Mr. Edwin S. Wallace, the United States Consul for Jerusalem, who refuses to restore these remains to me or to give me any real information in the matter, disregarding my personal appeals to him and those communicated to him officially by John Dickson, Esq., H.B.M.'s Consul for Jerusalem . . .

She also requested the return of the body of Mr. Drake, whose father in England joined in the demand for his son's body.

The British Consul's efforts in our behalf were answered by a letter from Mr. Wallace, stating the American Consulate

had nothing whatsoever to do in the matter of transferring the bodies from the American Cemetery to their temporary resting place in the English Cemetery. . . .

In response to Lord Salisbury the British Consul took action and secured the number of the box containing the remains of Captain Sylvester. After this the tone of the correspondence changed. Bishop Blyth, Bishop of Jerusalem, wrote instructions to the superintendent of the English Cemetery to write Mrs. Sylvester offering "to take up the body of her husband and give it over to herself or her representative if she could identify the coffin (or box, as they call it)."

When at last permission was granted to open the pit, Mrs. Sylvester felt that because so much intrigue and quibbling had been practiced, she wanted to be present, no matter how harrowing the experience might be.

With Mrs. Sylvester that day in the English Cemetery were Mr. Hensman the cemetery superintendent, the British Consul's dragoman, and also a kavass from the Consulate, Dr. Savignoni, and several members of the American Colony. She had a plan of the American Cemetery with the graves.

Captain Sylvester's was number thirteen.

Until the pit was opened and the condition uncovered no member of the Colony had any idea of the true facts. We had been told by the workmen who assisted at the removal that the bodies had been ruthlessly dismembered in order to cram them into the boxes. We could not credit such a story.

The truth lay bared in the pit. Fifteen boxes represented the twenty-five graves of the American Cemetery. They were stacked helter-skelter, some on their sides, some on end. The boxes were not coffins, but packing cases, the largest ones about thirty inches long, sixteen inches wide, sixteen inches deep. The majority of the boxes were smaller, about thirteen inches by ten and nine.

There was no box thirteen.

Nor was there any way of telling the American Colony dead from the other American dead. One box was marked three and four, indicating that it might contain the contents of two graves.

Another had burst open, disclosing limbs severed into parts, confirming the testimony of the fellaheen workman which we had refused to believe.

This box held the remains of more than one body, and among them Mrs. Gould and Jacob made a harrowing discovery, its identity proven beyond doubt by the fact that Father had lost his front teeth in an accident when he was a boy.

Nothing could be done. The boxes were replaced in the pit and covered up. A complete report was sent to Mr. Rudy in Washington and he redoubled his attempts to extract from the State Department an answer to our request for an investigation into the cemetery affair as well as into our earlier and oft-repeated complaints against the two Consuls.

After another long delay a cable came from Mr. Rudy: "Investigation granted."

Consul General Dickenson came from Constantinople to Jerusalem to conduct it.

It was a bit of good luck that both Dr. Merrill and Mr. Wallace were in Jerusalem at the time.

Before bringing the cemetery matter before Mr. Dickenson, all signers of the notorious Alley paper were brought to prove what they had signed. One after another they said that they had not seen the whole pamphlet. Not one could substantiate any of the statements against the morals of the American Colony.

Instead, witness after witness, all respected members of Jerusalem society, came forward in our behalf.

This was the first part of the investigation. After its completion Mr. Dickenson told us that one would think it would be a pleasure to visit Jerusalem, but the atmosphere, he said, "was overburdened with crucifixion."

The next part of the investigation dealt with the cemetery.

On opening, Mr. Dickenson recorded: "Inasmuch as this plot is not a cemetery." We could not allow that to pass. We expostulated and said that it had been used as such for more than sixty years. We produced official documents to prove that as a cemetery under Turkish law no taxes had been paid on it.

A photograph of the stone slab which had stood over the cemetery gate was shown—I have it still. It showed the break caused by its removal at the time of the sale through the carved words in Arabic and English: "American Cemetery—Jesus Christ is the Resurrection and the Life."

To the Presbyterian Board the case seemed to hang on the question as to whether this plot of ground on Mount Zion was a cemetery or not. If it was not a cemetery, it could be sold privately. The moral issue, which was to us the most important, was obscured.

I have just reread all the testimony of this investigation and I am impressed with the futility of the whole affair as far as the cemetery matter was concerned.

I remember the last day very well. I was to be the first witness. We went to the Consulate full of hope and were met by Mr. Wallace, who told us that Consul General Dickenson had left that morning for Constantinople.

So this was the end!

What had been done, we knew, could never be undone. Our dead could never be restored. Victory, if it ever came, would simply be a vindication.

It was not until the end of 1906 eight years later, that the entire matter was thrashed out and vindication came.

During that time a great change had taken place in the status of the American Colony. I married Frederick Vester, and the

German Consul represented us and was friendly. Our Swedish members, who had been at the mercy of our American Consul, now had an advocate in their own Consul. We had more English members, who had their English Consul as protector. The American Colony was a prosperous and respected force in Jerusalem.

One day a friend came in haste to let us know that the representative was back in Jerusalem and at work in the English Cemetery, evidently for the second removal of the bodies he had placed there so many years before. Various members of the Colony rushed off in four different directions, some to the English Consul, others to the Swedish Consul, and others to the German authorities, who had joint control of the cemetery with the English.

Another group hurried to the English Cemetery to be eyewitnesses of whatever might be taking place there. John Whiting joined this delegation and had the foresight to take a camera along.

They found the man at the cemetery with workmen, and the pit open.

Porters waited to carry the remains away. Five of the boxes had already been removed from the pit, and the pictures John took were eloquent testimony.

The English Consul sent a protest to the English bishop for allowing the second removal without notifying him. The Swedish and German Consuls sent the same protests. After a conference between the German and English custodians of the cemetery an order was received that the remains must be replaced where they were and not molested again. But we would not allow any helter-skelter burial. We made new boxes and marked them just as they had been before placing them in the common grave.

The American Colony was given the right to this small plot in the English Cemetery and permission to put up a stone with the names of those whose bones had been so sadly disturbed. We put the inscription on the stone that had been on the American Cemetery door: "I am the Resurrection and the Life" with the names below. On each side are the names of those not belonging to the Colony but who were in the American Cemetery and now lie in this common grave. However, there was still an unsolved question. Where were the five bodies which had been buried nearest the time of the sale? I have in my possession a large number of letters dealing with the matter. Finally we were given four bodies which we buried in our newly purchased cemetery on Mount Scopus.

One body was never found.

One Sunday afternoon in 1906 a gentleman by the name of Alexander Hume Ford called on Mother. He had heard about the American Colony years before in Chicago, and I believe he had attended Father's Sunday school as a boy. In the course of conversation he expressed a wish to visit Father's grave. A look of anguish passed over Mother's face. He noticed it and tried to turn the subject, but Mother said she would like to tell him about the trouble we had had with the two Consuls and about the cemetery affair. Mr. Ford was shocked and sympathetic. He was also a newspaper correspondent. He asked for full information, which we supplied, and he wrote an article entitled "Our American Colony in Jerusalem," which appeared in the Christmas number of *Appleton's Magazine* in 1908.

This article, so completely laudatory to us and damning to the opposition, caused many of our friends in America and the Holy Land to write to the State Department. At last action was taken. This time every bit of testimony was brought out into the open.

The Rev. Edwin Wallace had left Jerusalem several years before and gone back to his old vocation. His church was in Pennsylvania, and among others, of course, his parishioners read the article. They knew their pastor had been Consul of the United States in Jerusalem, and also the article gave his name.

The indictment against him was serious. There was no alternative, the Rev. Edwin Wallace had to bring action against *Appleton's Magazine*.

I have in my possession copies of the entire proceedings. Mr. Wallace had to resign his church, he claimed, on account of the publication of this article.

By a confusing coincidence, Mr. Thomas R. Wallace, no relation, was now Consul of Jerusalem. He gathered the evidence about the cemetery, which was even worse than we had anticipated. Workmen who had been employed in the gruesome task testified under oath how they had dismembered the bodies with their pickaxes to fit them into the smaller boxes.

The lawyers for *Appleton's Magazine* wrote to thank Consul Thomas R. Wallace for so ably conducting the case and for the voluminous amount of evidence procured. The trial had undoubtedly cost Rev. Edwin Wallace several thousand dollars.

Meanwhile, in Jerusalem, Dr. Merrill had been failing in health, and finally underwent a serious operation on his throat which removed his power of speech.

Early in 1910 Mrs. Newman, widow of the Methodist Bishop Newman, came to Jeruslaem and bought property on the Street of the Prophets. She was very old, and had been a friend of Mother's for many years. She absorbed none of the Jerusalem gossip or realized the bitterness of local feuds. She gave a housewarming to which she invited Mother and me, among others, and Dr. and Mrs. Merrill.

By this time we were prosperous enough to have a handsome carriage and two beautiful grays. Dr. Merrill recognized our carriage and would not come in. Mrs. Merrill entered, but Dr. Merrill walked up and down outside in the street, hoping, I suppose, that we would leave. But mother and Mrs. Merrill were having their first conversation, and I was very much amused to see that the two ladies were enjoying each other's company. Mrs. Merrill was a friendly, comfortable American matron of portly size, who was meeting for the first time the much-discussed Mrs. Spafford and evidently not sharing her husband's estimation of her.

At last Dr. Merrill entered with some belated guests. His agonized behavior was disconcerting to witness. He wrote on a pad but was careful not to let the pad out of his hands.

The Arabs were convinced that God had punished Dr. Merrill for his persecution of the American Colony.

It must be remembered that the case brought by the Rev. E. Wallace was against *Appleton's Magazine* and not against the American Colony. For us, there was no redress other than having been vindicated.

But a persecution that had lasted twenty-five years was ended.

CHAPTER TWENTY

In the years leading up to World War I there were disturbing historical and political happenings, many of which had repercussions in Jerusalem. In 1908 the Young Turk revolution took place after Austria annexed Bosnia-Herzegovina. A series of changes in Turkish policy covering a number of years finally brought about the reviving of the 1876 constitution.

The granting of the new Turkish constitution evoked in the Empire an all-prevailing spirit of liberty.

A nation of patriots was born, with a keen sense and appreciation of freedom. To some, utterly untrained in its use, freedom meant lack of restraint and license.

In Palestine under the new regime all were now brothers; Moslems, Christians, and Jews were Turkish subjects. Heretofore only Moslems were drafted into the Army while a nominal sum exempted Jewish and Christian Turkish subjects from military service. Now all were alike drafted, and this was the first shock experienced in Palestine as to what "equality" meant.

In the first zeal of reform many obnoxious and corrupt officials were removed and in the elections of members for the new Turkish parliament the new government insisted on the return of men whose patriotism was unquestionable. The two delegates from Jerusalem were the best men that could be found.

Incidentally, both these men, Rohi Effendi Khalidi and Said Effendi Husseini, had not only been instructed in English by members of the American Colony, but had received a strong impetus in the direction of justice, progress, and democracy.

Later on there were other members of Parliament from Jerusalem, Faidi Effendi al Alami and Ragib Bey Nashashebie, both friends of the Colony.

Among the religious communities in the Holy City there was a marked rising to obtain their rights. The ecclesiastical heads of each sect had long dominated the people composing their congregations, and in case of opposition the leaders could invoke the strong arm of the secular Turkish authority, and so all dissatisfaction was silenced. The new constitution contained clauses which gave the laity in these communities the right to formulate their demands, and several more or less serious agitations occurred.

Even among the Jews there was some commotion. The official chief rabbi was removed in consequence of demonstrations. I have mentioned the halukkah, or prayer money, which was sent from Jewish communities all over the world for distribution among their co-religionists in the Holy City. Undoubtedly there were abuses.

The Armenian community showed its independence by rising as one man in a threatening manner, and would not be quieted until the government ordered the removal from his position of an obnoxious factotum of the aged Patriarch.

The Roman Catholic or Latin community remained reasonably quiet. Its administration had been lacking in what caused friction in other communities. However, demands were made for better housing facilities and these were speedily acceded to. To understand this demand it should be explained that all the larger Christian communities in Jerusalem provide house accommodation free for nearly all their members. The Roman Catholic Church was under the historic French protection, and its position, therefore, was unique. The affairs of all the other ecclesiastical bodies of Palestine were under the control of the Turkish Government. Among the smaller of the old Christian sects more or less agitation occurred with different degrees of seriousness. But nearly all were made conscious of their new and independent position.

The most serious far-reaching movements for liberty took place in the Greek Orthodox Community in Jerusalem. It soon spread to other cities, and Bethlehem, Jaffa, Gaza, Haifa, and even Trans-Jordan and smaller towns and villages in Palestine, which were under the jurisdiction of the Jerusalem Patriarchate, were affected.

The point on which the conflict turned was the discrimination in the administration of the Greek Church affairs in favor of those members who were Greek by nationality as well as religion. The Greek clergy were exclusively of Hellenic nationality and did not know the language of the country, whereas the great majority of the laity were native Arabs. All the affairs of the church including the finances, were controlled by the Holy Synod of the church. The Synod selected the Patriarch, who was then approved by the Turkish Government. This was the inner circle of the rich and all-powerful Greek convent. Under the then-existing arrangements none of the native community could ever become a member of the Greek convent or the Holy Synod. The Greek Church Theological School at the Convent of the Cross, which I have mentioned in a previous chapter,was the path of entrance into the convent, and no Arab was admitted. It was even difficult for Arabs to obtain entrance to better secular schools conducted by the Greek convent, which were attended by those of Greek birth from Greece or Cyprus.

The one exception was the Orthodox Patriarchate of Damascus, where the native element had succeeded, with Russian help, in having a Greek-born incumbent removed for misconduct and a native priest elevated to his place. The intensity of race feeling is illustrated by the fact that whereas in public church services the Patriarchs of Alexandria and Constantinople were prayed for, the native-born Patriarch of Damascus was omitted.

The prominent men of the Arab-speaking Orthodox community in Jerusalem met and discussed their grievances. They demanded equal rights, ecclesiastical and otherwise, and a share in the direction of committees which should be composed equally of clergy and laity; an increase of educational, medical, and hospital facilities and better free housing accommodation for the lay members; and a larger proportion of the immense revenues of the convent for the poor of the community. The income of the Greek convent was swelled by donations from abroad, and large sums of money were given to the many shrines or holy places by the army of pilgrims who annually came to Jerusalem from the different countries where the Greek Church was active.

A delegation of Arab laity waited on the Patriarch and laid their demands before him. The Patriarch was kindly disposed, but the intolerant Greek priests withstood making the least concession or compromise. Excitement rose to fever heat. The native churches were all closed; the people refused to attend. Even funeral services were held in open-air shrines in the cemeteries rather than in the churches.

Dissension began between the priests who favored the Patriarch and the laity on one side and the monks of the Holy Synod on the other. The Greek convent was the scene of priestly violence and bloodshed. Turkish forces were called into the precincts of the convent to protect the Patriarch.

During this time my husband and I were dining at the Grand New Hotel with the new American Consul, Mr. Thomas R. Wallace, (not to be confused with Edwin Wallace) and Mrs. Wallace, and in the arcade under the hotel, which is the property of the Greek convent and leads to the Patriarchate, a battle started between the clergy and Arab laity. Shots were fired and Turkish soldiers called to quell the disturbance.

The Consul had to send us home under the protection of the kavass of the United States Consulate.

Russia, which at that time was predominantly Greek Orthodox, was brought into the conflict. Large sums of money came to Jerusalem in particular, and Palestine in general, from thousands of Russian pilgrims. Tension grew, in Jerusalem and in the outer world.

In April 1911 the "Parker fiasco" came nearer causing anti-Christian riots and even massacre than anything that had happened during our long residence in Jerusalem.

Several years before an agent, acting mysteriously on behalf of a group of "notable Englishmen," came to Jerusalem for the acquisition of property to "build schools and hospitals for the people on behalf of the Turkish Government." According to his accounts, he enjoyed the patronage of the Grand Vizier, the Minister of the Interior, et al. Soon it evolved that the property sought was the hill situated to the south of the city, above the Virgin's Fount. It was the historic site Mount Ophel. The local authorities ordered the municipal architect to make plans of the entire hill for the purchasers, and appraised, advertised, and purchased at a nominal sum the tract desired, and handed the property over to the Englishmen at the same price.

The Englishmen came to Jaffa by yacht and, in due time, to Jerusalem.

They brought with them many cases of implements for excavation. Nothing more was said about a hospital or school. They set to work at once to excavate Mount Ophel. They also began working at the tunnel that conveys the water from the Virgin's Fount to the Pool of Siloam, in which Jaocb, as a schoolboy, had discovered the Siloam inscription.

Of course we were greatly interested and equally mystified by the activities of the Englishmen. We heard many curious and amusing reports about them from their dragoman and from Mr. Tarsha, who catered for the party, and who was our tenant. My husband and I, with a growing family, had rented a larger house and sublet the old one to Mr. Tarsha.

We heard of gay dinners given by the Englishmen, once with the Turkish Pasha as guest, and of their using oranges for target practice, with the little Jewish children from the nearby "box colony" scrambling about to gather the smashed fruit. They rode to their excavations near Silwan on donkeyback. One morning we heard unusual noises along the road, and saw the worthy archaeologists playing at being donkeyboys, running alongside the donkeys and imitating the yelling, only much louder, usually made by the Arab boys, who were mounted in the Englishmen's places.

They were certainly the oddest archaeologists ever to visit Jerusalem. Frederick and I met some of them at a reception and found them charming, but we were puzzled by their complete lack of archaeological knowledge.

My brother Jacob was particularly grieved that these men had the privilege of excavating Ophel, and were making no record of whatever they might find. He met several of the young men at a picnic given by Faidie Effendi al Alami and impressed urgently on them the harm it would do to the whole archaeological world if they carried on excavations on the most historical spot in Palestine and left no scientific records.

Finally Jacob obtained a promise that they would request Père Vincent, belonging to the Dominican Fathers and head of the Ecole Biblique et Archéologique in Jerusalem, to be present during excavations and record the findings. Père Vincent accepted the invitation, and the result is the scholarly book entitled *Underground Jerusalem, Discoveries on the Hill of Ophel* (1909—11).

The facts that have impressed people most were that not one of the party was an archaeologist; they were not familiar with the history of what had been done by previous excavators; and they were so mysterious in what they did, imparting to none what they were after, and permitting absolutely no one to visit the excavations, that naturally it was inferred that they were after treasure.

Soon all kinds of stories were afloat—that they were trying to find the royal Tomb of David and the Kings of Judah; that they sought the buried temple treasures; that they were after the Ark of the Covenant that was hidden there, et cetera, et cetera.

Two prominent members of the Turkish parliament from Constantinople attended them as imperial commissioners, also policemen, gendarmes, and a city sergeant.

They enjoyed every privilege and immunity but let scarcely any European pass near their excavation.

It should be said that in 1874, when the Palestine Exploration

Fund conducted excavations here, this was only regarded as the Hill Ophel, at one time within the city walls; but since then research has convinced almost every competent archaeologist that here stood the oldest, the Jebuzite city, which David conquered by the hand of Joab, his sister's son. In this vicinity David built his home, the kings were buried; here was the Zion, and northward from here rose the temple reared by Solomon, his son. Here it was that everything described by Warren in his researches assumed so much greater importance, as having a bearing on Zion, on the most ancient city and settlement.

Another fact which must have influenced this group should be borne in mind, and that is the suggestion made by the eminent French archaeologist, M. Clermont-Ganneau, that here by the great sweep in the tunnel of Hezekiah, that conveys the water to the Pool of Siloam, must be sought the Tomb of David.

After working for about three months the Englishmen were compelled to stop work because of the rains; so before Christmas 1909 they left to spend a few months in England.

The rumors about the Englishmen had stirred up the Jews because they were excavating the most historic spot connected with Jewish history, and presently all the land lying between their plot and the Pool of Siloam was acquired and walled up by the Jews. Then the excavators began to experience some difficulties, and obstacles were placed in their path. It appeared that Baron Rothschild had furnished the money for the Jew's purchase, and was trying to get a concession for them to ascertain whether it was possible to locate the royal tombs under the direction of one who had made the suggestion. The government, therefore, notified the Englishmen that they must bring their work to an end in three years, so that overlapping privileges might not be granted to competing parties. So it was that when the English party returned in the fall of 1910 they worked through the winter, although there was an unusual amount of rain that year.

It appears that they had a secret arrangement by which all who had part in it agreed to give 50 per cent of whatever they found to the Turkish Government, and it was whispered about that they expected this fund to amount to £40,000,000. When the two members of the Turkish Parliament were obliged to return to Constantinople to attend the sessions, the Pasha (governor of the province) and the commander of the gendarmes became their successors as inspectors and daily attended the excavations.

Just as the Mohammedan pilgrims were arriving by the thousands for the Nebi Musa (Prophet Moses) procession, which was instituted by the Turks hundreds of years ago for a political purpose, and a counterpoise to match the large number of Christian pilgrims who assemble in the Holy City for the Easter festivities, a report got abroad and spread like wildfire that the English explorers had, clandestinely, been excavating at night in the noble sanctuary of the Mosque of Omar or Dome of the Rock. It was alleged that they had penetrated even into the sacred rock and "The Well of the Spirits" through the connivance of the sheiks, who acted as guards, and the mosque attendants and the police who were in their employ. The report grew that they had carried off the Crown of David, and the genie-attended ring of Solomon, the two tables of stone containing the law, and the sword of Mohammed.

The aroused people forced the hands of the authorities, the sheiks were cast into prison, and the military attendants of the Englishmen were arrested.

The Turkish lawyer, who was brought from Constantinople in their service, was detained and put under surveillance in Jerusalem. Every bit of their baggage was opened and searched before they were allowed to go.

The Englishmen hastened to their yacht at Jaffa. After illuminating their vessel and announcing that they were going to hold a reception on board in honor of the Jaffa officials, they slipped away at night.

An admission was extorted from the son of the head sheik that the Englishmen had worked for nine nights in the Dome of the Rock, coming there wearing fezzes to avoid detection. They opened up the hitherto inaccessible "Well of the Spirits," penetrated a passage (described by M. Clermont-Ganneau about 1874) in the surface of the Sacred Rock and running downward for several meters, and discovered a basin, whose plastered interior plainly showed marks of the different levels of the liquid that had stood in it. (Could it have been the blood of the sacrifice?) They were prevented only by public indignation from going still farther. The son of the sheik confessed also that they had opened and entered the stables of Solomon through a rock-hewn passage running southward.

The exposure was caused by another mosque attendant who was not in the secret, coming there after midnight to sleep, as he had visitors at home. Finding European strangers there and work going on, he made his escape and told the story.

The wrath of the people of Jerusalem was so great and so well realized by the military authorities that patrols were posted in every street.

On Friday, the last day of the Feast of Nebi Musa, when upward of ten thousand people were assembled in the mosque grounds for the benediction and dismissal, a quarrel between two sweetmeat vendors and the hastening of the police to intervene so inflamed the imagination of the crowd that they stampeded.

A fearful panic ensued, the peasant women and pilgrims pouring out of the walls of the enclosure and running toward the city gates crying, "Massacre! Massacre!" The business places were closed up in a few minutes, every family arming itself and barricading its home.

It is said that the Russian Compound was completely shut up—a most unusual performance. It is also stated that the barracks were at once closed, lest, with the great number of soldiers absent attending the many Christian festivities, the arsenal might be seized and the soldiers kept at bay by the cannon being turned on them. The wildest reports were circulated: that the sheik had been killed, that the governor had been dealt with by the mob, et cetera. Officials were soon sent out along the roads in every direction to stop and assure the fleeing people that nothing was the matter, lest alarming reports should unsettle the country. Tradespeople were urged to reopen their stores and resume business, and soon everything was quiet.

So ended the ignoble episode. It could not have happened at a worse time of year than the time when the Greek Orthodox Easter coincides with the Jewish Passover and the Moslem political Feast of Nebi Musa. In those days there was no controversy between Jews and Arabs. That started after the Zionsit national aspirations were made public by the Balfour Declaration. Friction in those days was between "hotheads" who came with the different Christian pilgrims from many countries and got into trouble with one another or with the Turkish military and police. Many a Turkish governor lost his position because of trouble taking place in or near the Holy Sepulcher at Eastertime, as did Azmey Bey. During that crucial week the Turkish authorities kept the telegraph line free. Only urgent messages could be sent by the public. It was during this critical week that the Englishman was accused of entering the Moslem holy of holies.

Before closing this episode I wish to draw attention again to Jacob, who, with his usual modesty, never disclosed or allowed anyone to mention that it was he who made it possible for Père Vincent to give the world the benefit of the excavations on Mount Ophel by an expert mind and pen.

Many years later the plot of ground bought by Baron Rothschild on Mount Ophel, covering the great swing of Hezekiah's tunnel, which it was thought might contain the tombs of the Kings of Judah, was laid bare to the rock under the able supervision of the Department of Archaeology of the Hebrew University. M. Clermont-Ganneau's theory was proved baseless.

Mother wrote:

Our friend Abu Hassan Insari has donned the green cloak. Since the Parker episode and the disgrace and imprisonment of his uncle the great sheik, he has been made chief sheik of the Dome of the Rock in his place. He was very pleased with himself and carried a heavy staff as tall as he is.

CHAPTER TWENTY-ONE

FOR years Frederick and I had been talking about a camping trip across the Jordan and in May 1914 we planned our itinerary to cover as many historical places as possible in the time we could afford.

We told friends of our plans, and almost before we were aware of it we were a party of fifteen.

The cooks and muleteers started the evening before, after such jabbering that one might have thought they were going to cut one another's throats, but which was actually only the best natured of conversations. They would be waiting camp for us, with dinner prepared, at the Jordan Bridge.

A sirocco was blowing that morning when the party gathered before our house. The horses were fresh, and because they came from several livery stables, there was a great deal of snorting and kicking. Good-bys were many, for relatives and friends had come to watch the start of our cavalcade, and three among us who were mothers were leaving fifteen children.

We left them in the gentlest of hands. Mother, smiling, watched us go.

We rode past the familiar places—the Mount of Olives, Gethsemane, Bethany. A rest in the hotel at Jericho at noon was followed by more riding in the cooling afternoon to the River Jordan. Much sacred lore crowds around this river that boasts of so little natural beauty. On either side semi-tropical thickets of tamarisk, poplar, and dwarf acacia, hid the swift stream, which runs like a green serpent through broken, scaly formations of gray clay. Then, winding our way around one of the queer clay formations on the banks of the Jordan, we found near the ridge and tollhouse our seven white tents, with the flags of the different nations our party represented floating above them.

The friendly campfire, with the portly cook Yousef steaming above it, promised a lordly evening meal, which it proved to be.

When we left the dining tent the moon was shining brightly over the Jordan.

Two Bedouin musicians, hanging about the Bedouin camp on

the river, volunteered to amuse us. They were the professional type of singers, dancers, and jesters which every influential tribe possesses. They sang lustily, their voices sounding harsh and out of place in this quiet place. We gave them ample baksheesh to get rid of them, and they left shouting their displeasure to our muleteers for the pittance we had given for such magnificent entertainment.

Afterward we sang songs and hymns, which seemed to us more in keeping with our surroundings. I suppose the Bedouins, listening in the dark, were laughing in their turn. They not only dislike our music, but consider a mixed choir most undignified.

Long after the other tents were dark my husband and I sat on in the door of ours. The moon set behind the Judean hills, leaving us with the glow of the stars and the flicker of the camp lanterns suspended on poles to keep away jackals and hyenas.

We spoke of the feelings of the Children of Israel when they came to the "swelling of Jordan" and by God's mighty hand were permitted to "cross on dry land" and entered upon new temptations to overcome.

Here Elijah was caught up in the chariot of fire, and Elisha obtained his blessing. We rejoiced that this, too, was the scene of a greater victory, when heaven opened and God sanctioned His son.

The next day we crossed several watercourses, where pink oleanders were struggling to bloom. The winter rain having been less than usual, these streams were already dry. Where the waters of Heshbon rush across the plain toward the Jordan, and on through Wadi Sha'ib, wild flowers began to appear again, and the sides of the road were spotted with poppies, daisies, and blue chicory flowers. We regretted that the spring was too far advanced for the scarlet tulips, anemones, lilies, and wild iris, some of the varieties of which are so deep in color that they are almost black.

We stopped for lunch at Ayun Musa (Springs of Moses). This is supposed to be Nebo. "Pisgah's lofty peak" soared above us. Bedouin shepherds gathered to water their flocks "beside the still waters" and crowded round us with expressions such as we have when looking at monkeys, intrigued by our behavior. Our knowledge of Arabic enabled us to understand their comments. They marveled at our "black and yellow hands," and when we casually removed our gloves they looked shocked, as though they expected the blood to run in the skinning process. I took off my hat and they wondered why I uncovered my head before so many men. The women hid the lower part of their faces with their sleeves, as well-bred Bedouin women should when strange men are around, and they giggled with embarrassment when they saw my husband take my hand to help me over the loose stones in the brook and gently lead me to a seat. This, in their estimation, was humiliating to his lordship.

The view here was magnificent—the Jordan Valley and the Gileadian hills, blue in their distant beauty, to the mountains round Hebron, and the Dead Sea from Ain Jidy (Engedi) northward, glittering like burnished steel at the southern end. This was the view Moses had of the land that was his goal. So far he could go, but never set his foot on it. What a lesson to every Christian! This man, the meekest that had ever lived, with the murmuring of a backsliding and complaining people continually in his ears; this man who had led them so far and had spoken to God "face to face," because of his impatience at their continual faultfinding was not allowed to pass over the dividing line.

That afternoon we passed several Bedouin encampments. The dogs gave us an unwelcome challenge, but the inhabitants were always friendly, and when we greeted them with "*Salam aleikum* (Peace be unto you)," they answered "*Ou aleikum es-salam* (And unto you be peace)." It is rare in more civilized parts to have a Mohammedan use this greeting to a Christian. Mohammedans will use pleasant salutations such as "Good day," "May your day be blessed," but the "peace" is for the "faithful."

The fields became greener as we mounted the hills, and the grain, despite the meager rainfall, was surprisingly luxuriant. Here reapers were at work at the barley harvest, while in the *ghor* (the rift of the Jordan Valley) all had been harvested. The contrast between the green wheat and the golden barley made the landscape one of uncommon beauty in the long rays of the declining sun. Crude little shelters were erected out of an abayeh or two fastened on poles, helped out with an isolated *dom* tree, or some branches and straw. We did not see one of these small abodes without babies and children in them; and when we thought of the care our little ones got, and compared it to what these received, we did not wonder at the enormous death rate among infants in this country.

It is not uncommon for Bedouin women to mother eight or twelve children, of which only two or three ever reach maturity.

One of our attendants told us that his father had had three wives; each had given birth to eight, ten, or twelve children, and that out of the thirty children born, he and a younger brother and three sisters were the only survivors.

Harvest time is the hardest season on the Bedouin babies, and many must suffer greatly, because they are a stalwart race, before they finally succumb. Another interesting fact we learned about these poor harvesters is that the Bedouins consider themselves too aristocratic to do such menial work as plowing, sowing, and harvesting, their vocation being war and raids, and that the peasants, some property poor, others displaced through the Jewish invasion of Palestine, come across the Jordan and work on shares for the Bedouins. Others, who are still poorer, come as gleaners, and all that they gather, following the harvesters and clearing the corners of the fields, which are purposely left for them, they carry home for their own use. This is another relic of the Mosaic law. The Bedouins of the hills consider themselves far superior to the peasantry who live in villages.

Once on the tableland, we were not far from Madeba, and were glad to see the conspicuous mound on which that small village stands.

The modern village of Madeba, nestling among the ruins of earlier dates that speak of ancient wealth and grandeur, can boast of very little now that is attractive.

The Greek Orthodox Church, close to the old northern gate of the city, covers the only remaining bit of the much-referred-to mosaic map. We were among the first people to see this on a previous trip. It was originally a map of Palestine and Egypt and dates from the fifth or sixth century. The present church was built upon the foundations of an old basilica, and the mosaic map was the floor of the old church. It was sad to see how little of the mosaic map was left, covering two small patches in the floor of the present church, which is considerably smaller than the original basilica. Jerusalem is particularly interesting in the map. A huge column is shown at the northern gate, and from there a colonnade runs through the city to the Holy Sepulcher. In Arabic this gate is still called *Bab el Amud* (Gate of the Pillar).

In the Old Testament Madeba is considered a Moabite town, and later, when Reuben, Gad, and the half tribe of Manasseh decided to return to this fertile tableland it was allotted to Reuben. When you see the magnificent plain, just the land for the cultivation of grain, you do not wonder that the tribes were attracted by it and would have been content to remain on the east side of

Jordan without passing over and subduing the enemies before they could occupy the land of Canaan. This luxuriant land is different from Palestine, where stones and rocks give the country a barren appearance. Reuben and Gad were in continual warfare with the Moabites, who were forever molesting their territory, and in consequence Reuben disappeared from among the tribes of Israel.

We know by the "Moabite Stone" that, toward the beginning of the ninth century B.C. Madeba belonged to Israel. Moab invaded the land at that time but was driven back by Omri across the Arnon, and became tributary throughout his reign and all Ahab's. Later it became a city of the Nabataeans. John Hyrcanus, son of Simon Maccabaeus, after defeating Demetrius and succeeding in establishing the independence of Judea, turned to subdue his antagonistic neighbors, first attacking Madeba and the Jordan Valley, and then, marching on Shechem, succeeded in destroying the Samaritan temple on Mount Gerizim (120 B.C.). His alliance with Rome, which was begun by his uncle Judas and followed by his father Simon, who gave him paternal help in this work of subjugation, invested him with the needed authority.

The ruins of Madeba have been inhabited only since the year 1880 by about two thousand Christian Bedouins from el-Kerak, mostly belonging to the Greek Orthodox Church. There are a few Roman Catholics, and they, too, have a presbytery and a school occupying the highest point on the small hill. It is remarkable to see how these big, stalwart men and fine-looking women are willing to settle among the ruins with twenty or twenty-five feet of rubbish under them; without clearing the debris away they build a room or two, supplying the missing walls to a crumbling structure. Bits of exquisite mosaic floors are found in some of these miserable hovels, so dark, so dirty that candles had to be lighted and water used again, so that we could admire their unusual beauty.

Upon our arrival in Madeba we had sent a letter to the sheik of our old friends the Adwan tribe, addressing it to the "Sheik Diab, son of Fiaz, son of Ali Diab Adwan." This was the grandson of Ali Diab Adwan whom we visited in 1884, when I was six years old. On their numerous visits to Jerusalem they stopped with us, and we extended the hand of fellowship to them, contrary to the Arabic proverb that "one should change the front door of one's house if a Bedouin got to know where it was." We have found their friendship most enjoyable and our kindness reciprocated through three generations of sheiks.

On their visits they invariably disarmed themselves as soon as they came to the "house of peace" as they called the American Colony. In our large living room there was, oriental style, a long line of hooks, and on these they hung their swords, revolvers, rifles, and ammunition belts, daggers and knives. Anyone coming in at such a time, and not knowing the spirit of peace in which the weapons were put there, would have thought we were starting an armory. Once the tribesmen were in the city with grain to sell, and they brought a few hundred dollars to a Colony member to keep for them. Instinctively he started to count it, to be able to give them a receipt. They looked at him in surprise.

"What are you doing?" they asked. "Do you want to insult us? Do we not trust you?"

When they were ready to leave, they took the money without counting it.

Sheik Diab received our letter and sent three servants to escort us to Heshbon, which is only a short ride from Madeba. Crossing the ridge of the tableland was one of the roughest parts of the whole trip. Our city horses trembled on the slippery rocks, while those of our Bedouin guides skipped over them like goats.

I asked one of our three friends his name, judging from his fine sword and other arms that he belonged to the sheik's family. He answered, "I am your slave Mutlag." It was an unusual answer and I wondered at his humility. After a while I ventured another question: "Do you belong to Sheik Diab's family?" "No," he replied, "I am his slave; this is his sword; I carry it for him." Here, in the twentieth century, was the Bible made alive. An armor-bearer, like Saul's or David's, was guiding us to Heshbon.

At the spring we were met by a delegation sent by the sheik, consisting of his uncle and other notables and a number of servants. They led the way to the camp, where the black tents looked like huge spiderwebs fastened to the ground. They had chosen a small valley running north and south, where the high hills protected them from the west wind, still piercing and cold.

Sheik Diab met us cordially, looking very proud, tall, and handsome in his rich flowing robe. A reception had been arranged in a tent one hundred and fifty feet long, furnished with carpets and low lounges. It was gay with its brightly colored carpets and mattresses covered with crimson and yellow silk, green velvet, and silk brocade of many hues. The women were busy cooking the "fatted calf," in this case a lamb, on the other side of the partition that separated the women's part from the men's. We were first served with lemonade, and Mutlag's face beamed as he carried in a tray with three glasses. Contrary to their custom, but having learned it in their frequent visits to our home, it was passed to the ladies first. We drank, and without the glasses being washed, they were refilled and passed again, until all were served.

Immediately after the lemonade was served faithful Mutlag brought in the *muhbagh* which they use instead of a coffee mill. It is made of a section of a walnut tree hollowed out and roughly carved on the outside. A long handle cut to fit the cavity is ornamented with carvings and brass tacks. The coffee is put into the muhbagh, and in the presence of the visitors the coffee is pounded into a powder. Each stroke is in perfect rhythm to a song in praise of their honored guests. It is an art to be able to do this, and a special servant performs this duty. The coffeepot was brought and placed upon the ever-ready campfire, and soon our musical coffee was made.

The serving of coffee is an important item in the entertainment of guests. Those who understand the etiquette of the coffee language get many significant hints regarding their friendship and as to the mood their host is in. A few drops of the coffee were poured into a little round cup without any handle, and from that into another, and after rinsing that cup out, were poured into another, and so on, until all had been rinsed, which Mutlag then drank, showing that there was no poison in the cups.

One often hears the expression, "he died from a cup of coffee," and although it is not practiced as of old, the tradition still continues.

All sipped bitter coffee, fragrant with orange-blossom water. In about half an hour the same performance was repeated, and at regular intervals, until the midday meal was ready. Fortunately for us the cups were not filled to the top, for it shows very bad taste to refuse any.

Before lunch we made a tour of the different tents, pitched close together, and all smaller than the sheik's tents. In one we were welcomed by the sheik's aunt Fada, sister of Sheik Fiaz. She had been to our Colony and an amusing experience we had had with her. It was the first time she had seen stone buildings. We had a room ready for her on the second floor. She crawled up the stairs on her hands and knees, frightened to death, and on reaching the top, she sat down on the step and cried.

"Please take me down," she pleaded; "I am so afraid these walls will fall on me."

The fact that we had been living there for years did not convince Aunt Fada that the house would not immediately collapse and crush her. She was unhappy until we fixed a bed for her beneath a big fig tree in the garden, where she could feel safe under her familiar stars.

She took us into her confidence. She said that she had come to Jerusalem, for she had heard that there existed a wonderful doctor who could put false teeth into one's mouth, and they would renew one's youth and beauty. Aunt Fada was anxious to know if this was true. We told her it was, and to verify our statement we pointed out one of Colony ladies so equipped. She was overjoyed, and coming over to the lady, begged her to let her try on the teeth. "Just once," she pleaded, so that she might know if she could use them, then she could tell the doctor to make some for her "just like the *sitt's* (lady's)."

It was with difficulty we made the sheik's aunt understand that the doctor would have to make hers to fit her mouth, and that every mouth had a different shape. To her a mouth was a mouth, and she said she could tell the doctor to make it half the width of her finger smaller or larger, as needed.

After many visits to the Colony dentist, she returned to her people carrying with her a complete set of false teeth.

On this visit we found Aunt Fada in her tent smoking a long *ghalune* (pipe). Her husband had died, and there had been quite a fight over her, she had so many suitors. In the end she married a fine-looking man much younger than herself.

Our meal was ready so we went back to the long black tent. In the center was a wooden bowl about twenty-four inches in diameter filled with rice cooked in broth, with a good deal of melted goat's butter poured over it and roasted *snobar* (pine-cone nuts). In another bowl was roast mutton with a beautiful rich gravy, and still another bowl had mutton cooked in tomato sauce. Fifteen wooden spoons stood upright in the rice, and all around this repast was placed what looked like sheets of some very coarse material folded up for napkins. This is the Bedouin bread. The Bedouins make an unleavened dough and bake it in thin cakes over a convex piece of sheet iron. This is supported by three stones over a charcoal fire.

This must have been the bread, spoken of in the Old Testament, that Gideon baked for the angel.

We were hungry notwithstanding our many sips of coffee, and we really enjoyed the meal. There were many longing eyes watching us, and the moment we were finished the Bedouin guests and two Turkish gendarmes, who had stopped in for refreshment and rest, fell upon the remainder. The real "pitching in," however, was when the servants, slaves, and children began. Such scrambling and grabbing, snatching and smacking of lips, we had never witnessed. Some of the men made huge balls of rice and by a toss of the thumb sent them down their throats. We thought the Bedouins must be provided with gizzards, for they did not take time to chew their food. If they performed the unnecessary work of chewing, someone else might get an extra mouthful!

Afterward the entire coffee ceremony was repeated, then we bade our host good night and retired to our tents, which were pitched in one of the beautiful orchards at the spring belonging to Muthafy, the sheik's cousin.

Muthafy had been married a few months previous to our visit to Hafitha, Sheik Diab's sister, and paid an unusual price for his beautiful bride. The price was one thoroughbred mare, one modern rifle, two cows, one camel, one hundred and eighty sheep, one hundred and twenty goats, one hundred and twenty measures of wheat, eighty napoleons, which he was to pay back for the privilege of Muthafy's niece, a child about twelve years old, to be given in marriage to Hafitha's youngest brother.

They were anxious to know what my husband had paid for me, and looked absolutely horror-struck when I showed them my wedding ring. They decided that a wife with us was a cheap luxury. But I said that before I allowed my husband to put that ring on my finger he had placed his heart in my hand. They appreciated such sentimental talk.

As we sat in our own camp enjoying the beautiful moonlit evening, listening to the ripple of the water and the croaking of the frogs, we heard, in the distance, shooting, clapping, and the sound of hundreds of voices singing what might be a wedding song or a war challenge. Our unaccustomed ears could not tell the difference. We were not frightened, although our twelve-year-old traveler became excited. We were soon surrounded by the sheik and all the men of the camp, who had come to entertain us. First they sang, in their weird monotone, songs in praise of their guests. "Our eyes were like the gazelle's"; "our tongues were as sweet as honey in the comb"; "our feet brought good fortune"; and so on. Now they were singing a wedding song; now they were singing how their old sheik, Ali Diab, had subdued his enemies, who were like the dust—and the musician would take up a handful of dirt and throw it into the air. He was accompanied by an instrument made of wolf's skin, stretched over a wooden box with one gut string called *rubabi* which was played with a bow of horsehair.

I remembered that once when Ziad, the tribe musician, was at the American Colony in Jerusalem, and we had "knocked on the box" (played on the piano) for them, they were anxious to show their appreciation by giving us some of their music. The nearest we could come to a rubabi was a violin, which we gave to Ziad. After making several attempts at tuning it, he gave it up in disgust, saying, "This rubabi only speaks French; I can't make it speak Arabic." Now they had a chance to let us hear a real instrument and real singing, and they were pleased to show off.

This was our opportunity to return coffee, and our Yousef was happy to be master of ceremonies, although we could not sing or pound the coffee and praise the guests in the orthodox Bedouin style.

After the singing and dancing were over our Bedouin friends amused us by playing games.

The evolution which our games had gone through made them almost unrecognizable. Instead of "cat and mouse" it was "hyena and lamb," and all the horrible sounds that the animals made were introduced into the game. Two men dressed up to represent a wild boar dashed in among us with so much realism that we scattered.

Our fear was always met with peals of laughter. After many games and exhibitions of high jumping, target shooting, and other desert sports, the sheik rose and took leave.

This was the signal, and not one Bedouin remained seated after his lordship rose. A few minutes later we were alone in our camp, commenting and laughing over the very unusual and interesting evening. The voices we had heard a few hours before coming toward us were now dying away in the distance. They, too, sounded happy, and we knew our friendship with Sheik Diab's tribe had taken on another long lease.

We rode to Meshita, with its beautiful but mysterious castle, to Ziza, and el Humar.

We strolled through Es Salt's narrow streets.

The little shops looked gay with handkerchiefs of various designs and colors and red leather boots and slippers, regarded longingly by the Bedouins and Circassians who came from the neighboring camps and villages to barter wheat, barley, and fodder for them.

Our camp nestled under two hills in a narrow valley, and we were glad of their protection that stormy night. The wind whistled and blew and the rain poured down. Those of us who were wise enough to place everything in the center of the tent reaped a dry harvest of clothes the next morning.

Just as we started the sun came out, and we turned for a last view of Es Salt, with its vineyards emerald green with early summer and the fig and other fruit trees just putting out their leaves.

Prominent on the horizon was Jebel Osha, the supposed burial place of the prophet Osha (Arabic for Hosea). The wali on the top of the hill is known to be three hundred years old, and is visited by Bedouins from all over the vicinity. The tradition must have been handed down from Jewish times. Hosea belonged to the northern kingdom, and speaks in his prophecies of the "vanity of Gilead although they sacrifice bullocks in Gilgal." Under the big oak tree which stands near the wali the Bedouins often deposit grain and other possessions, and no one would dare steal them—their superstition about the evil which would follow a thief who had stolen from a "holy place" is sufficient to insure their safety.

On the fertile plain called el Backaa, below the clay hills, we saw large flocks of black goats, but they were not "gratefully grazing on rocks," as Mark Twain described them in *Innocents Abroad*, but availing themselves of the good pasture they were to have for so short a time. This whole country seems wonderfully adapted to the raising of flocks, with ideal pasture land and abundant springs.

We followed a roundabout way up the hills to the small Turcoman village of Umm Rummane, where our camp was waiting and we spent the night.

We were actually on our way to Jerash! The morning was clear and sparkling after the storm, and the day dazzling, appropriate to its importance. For years Frederick and I had looked

forward to this day. Along the road little plants and the buds
on the trees lifted to drink the warm rays. The sun seemed to
penetrate our souls, and we wondered how anyone could be unhappy on such a day.

Almost in answer, Hassan, our muleteer, rode alongside with a
philosophical admonishment. "Look at the land! Look at the
trees! Look at the sky! Everything is praising God for the rain
of yesterday and the sunshine of today. 'Only man is vile,' he is
not satisfied; he never thinks to lift his head to the Almighty and
return thanks as everything else does. Even a chicken, when
drinking, after each mouthful lifts its head to Allah and says
el hamdulillah. Beni Adam (son of man) is satisfied only when
a bit of soil (the grave) gets into his eye."

So saying, our Hassan cast a meaning eye in the direction of
the camp attendants and muleteers. There had been more cursing
and quarreling this morning than on any previous day.

We passed a spring on the road where were gathered the
Turcoman women from the village on the hill where we had
spent the night.

Over a fire, and supported on two good-sized stones, was a
Standard Oil tin for boiling their clothes. They were busy as bees
and happy as birds, jabbering in their quaint language which
sounded like a jargon of Turkish, Russian, and Arabic. Their
full and brightly colored bloomers, tight-fitting jackets of con-
trasting hue, broad girdles, and heavy turbans, gave beautiful
touches of color to this peaceful scene. How different was this
medley of color from the somber blue of the Bedouin women's
dress! The activity and energy of their work were also contrasts
to the slow, stately movements of the bedouweyeh. We left the
merry crowd behind us, perfectly happy in their small world.
How soon this peace was to be disturbed by World War I.

We came to the brow of a hill, and were gazing down a steep
ravine where flowed the River Jabbok, hidden from view by
oleander bushes covered with beautiful pink and white blossoms.

The memories clustering around this lonely ravine are many.
Here Jacob came from the land of Haran, with his wives and
children, maidservants and menservants, sheep, goats, cattle,
and camels, and here he allowed the whole caravan to pass over,
and he remained alone to wrestle with doubts and fears. Here
he became master over hate and revenge. Here he fought and
conquered, and was able to meet in peace the brother who had
lightly esteemed God's heritage to him and had sold it for a

"mess of pottage," then, seeing he had lost his blessing, turned
to have his revenge on Jacob. Here Jacob wrestled "till the
breaking of the day," and God met him "face to face." When
Jacob laid his sacrifice of a broken will on his altar, the dreaded
meeting on the morrow was with a friendly and gentle brother.

Just before reaching Jerash, within sight of its magnificent
Triumphal Arch, we turned to the right that we might see the
pretty waterfall in the Wadi Keirawan, or Wadi Jerash. Coming,
as we did, from Jerusalem, where our only water supply was rain
caught in cisterns and treasured to supply our needs during the
whole dry season, it is no wonder that running water green with
lichen and fern gave us so much pleasure. We passed through
wheat fields which were a delight to behold, the unripe ears
reaching to our knees as we rode. Our poor horses were tempted,
and against our efforts stole a mouthful now and then. Fortunately for us, the people of this country consider it wrong to
refuse a passing horse this privilege. These are the people who
keep up the traditions and customs of the Bible. It is among
the Arabs that we see, at the present time, remnants of the
Mosaic law in practice.

Jerash rose before us now across the plain, the entrance with
its large dome and its historical Triumphal Arch still fronting
the fabulous ruins.

Frederick and I had begun planning to go to Jerash since the
day we had heard, years before, Dr. George Robbinson, professor of Old Testament of McCormick Theological Seminary of
Chicago, and in that year director of the American School of
Oriental Research in Jerusalem, lecture on the mysterious place,
illustrating his talk with lantern slides.

His fascinating description of a city deserted of all but the past
had made us long to see for ourselves.

We stood a long time admiring the Triumphal Arch.

Its similarity to that of Trajan's in Rome dates its erection to
about the second century. To the west of this gate was the
Naumachia, to which the water from Wadi Keirawan was conducted by means of an aqueduct, and here the pleasure seekers
of Jerash witnessed sham sea fights and miniature galleys. Adjoining the Naumachia is a large circus with four rows of seats.
We had heard how excellent the acoustics were in the Southern
Theater, so we improvised a choir, which left very few of the
party to occupy the splendidly preserved rows of seats and
backs. Our soloist performed several selections, and after some

recitations, carefully chosen, we felt sure that the comedies of
Plautus or Aristophanes must have been wonderfully represented
here.

The Temple, now called Beit et Tei, with columns with
Corinthian capitals that are beautiful, more than any other building seems to speak of destruction by earthquake which archaeologists believe may be the answer to the sudden desertion of a
thriving city.

We wandered, silent, through the splendid Forum, with most
of its fifty-six Ionian colomns still standing through the Colonnade, the magnificent Temple of the Sun, the Basilica.

The monuments about us testified mutely of grandeur, a city
of surpassing beauty, a civilization complete but departed. These
ruins had held a few centuries of luxury, culture, and prosperity
for a rich and pleasure-loving populace, and then, a sudden interruption, so mysterious and final, that it left a magnificent
empty shell of a city· that had once been splendid.

What happened to Jerash, or Gerasa, is one of the mysteries
of antiquity.

Jerash is first mentioned in history when Alexander Jannaeus,
of the Maccabean line, captured the country in 83 B.C. It was
rebuilt after the Roman conquest of Syria and Palestine under
Pompey, about 63 B.C., when Jewish raids and wars had reduced
the entire northern area to ruins. The Romans drove the inhabitants out and wrecked their cities and villages exactly as the
Jews did in Palestine in 1948. The Roman conquest, therefore,
was hailed as deliverance from a hated rule. The towns and territory captured by the Jews were separated, and some of the
destroyed towns were rebuilt. Conquest ended the independence
of the free city—states which were separated from the Seleucid
Empire. They voluntarily entered upon a defensive league with
Rome for security and also because of local quarrels among
themselves, while retaining their civil rights and customs. At
first there were ten cities leagued together, called the Decapolis,
of which Jerash was one. It was one of the most important
cities of Syria, being situated on the great Roman road. Its
most prosperous period seems to have been early in the Christian era.

Jerash was captured by Baldwin II in 1121, when the Moslems
fortified the temple of Artemis. When we hear of it again it is
from an Arabian geographer named Nakut, and he speaks of it
as being deserted.

Our next camp was at Ajlun, beside a lovely stream. From Qalat ar-Rabad majestically surmounting the village of Ajlun we had a perfect view of the surrounding country. A sharp east wind was blowing from the desert, making visibility sharp and clear. Standing on the ramparts of the Saracen castle begun in 1184 on the site of a still older foundation, we enjoyed the most perfect view of Palestine it has ever been my good fortune to see.

Snow capped Mount Hermon rose to the north representing Dan, and we could see the seashore south of Gaza—representing the complete area from "Dan to Beersheba."

Qalat ar-Rabad was the most important of the Saracen fortresses in Trans-Jordan. An inscription tells that it was repaired by Saladin. It was called Arx Ayjlun by the Crusaders. It formed one of the links in the chain of beacons and pigeon posts from the Euphrates to Cairo by which the Sultan in Cairo could be notified in twelve hours of any attack on the Euphrates frontier.

In 1260 it was destroyed the Tartar invasion but was restored and inhabited until the beginning of the nineteenth century.

From Ajlun we descended to the Jordan Valley, crossed the river in a primitive ferry, and followed the valley to Nablus, in which, within so short a time after this happy trip through Gilead, General Allenby caught and destroyed the Turkish Army, the army which we were to see retreat from Jerusalem.

CHAPTER TWENTY-TWO

WE RETURNED from our trip radiant with its success and sunburned beyond recognition. Our two-year-old Louise put her finger on my cheek. "Dirty! Wash!"

With no radio, and mails still irregular—an irregularity to which we were well accustomed—it was not surprising that we took not a ripple of interest in the killing of an Austrian archduke and archduchess that summer of 1914 in the obscure town of Sarajevo, a place of which I had never heard, until, in the latter part of July, things began to move and Palestine began filling with German military personnel, engineers, and mysterious persons.

Several German students were living at the American Colony to learn to speak English. One was about to be married. The plans were all made for the wedding; the invitations were sent out; even the cakes were baked, the chickens roasted, and other goodies for the wedding breakfast prepared.

We had heard that war was to be declared, but the date was kept secret. So hush-hush was it that every effort was made by the German guests to keep it from the American Colony by acting normally. The night of the second of August they all appeared for supper. Next morning before breakfast these German men, including the intended bridegroom, had gone. They had departed secretly for Jaffa, where a German man of war took all the men of military age back to the Fatherland.

That day, we learned later, Germany invaded France.

It may be remembered that when Germany declared war on the Allies, Turkey officially declared her neutrality, but started general mobilization at once. We had often seen Turkish recruits or reserves being brought to Jerusalem tied together or hand-cuffed like criminals. Now we heard that sealed letters had been given to the muktars (headmen) of cities and villages. These were to be opened on notification and when the contents were known the threat must have frightened them into compliance, for this was the first time in our long residence in Palestine that we saw "voluntary" mobilization to troops.

Mother was spending a few weeks at the Kaiser's and Kaiserin's palace on the Mount of Olives, which was used as a sanatarium, especially for missionaries and Christian workers. It was beautifully run and inexpensive; only twenty-five piasters ($1.25) a day, including three meals as well as afternoon tea or coffee. Frederick and I drove up in our carriage and brought Mother home; in a crisis such as this we preferred all being together.

By October the foreign post offices were closed and letters, documents, and accounts were confiscated. Before this we had had to go to several different places to get our mail, to the Austrian, French, German, and Russian post offices. There was no mail delivery. We were completely cut off from the world.

After the abrogation of the capitulations and seizing of foreign post offices people were sure Turkey would soon join the conflict, and the subjects of the allied powers were advised by their respective consulates to leave the country. I cannot remember exactly when the British Consul left Palestine, but it was before the actual declaration of war by Germany. The few British nationals who remained behind were closely watched and many who had benefitted by English schools and hospitals were induced to spy on them.

One of Saint George's schoolboys (Saint George's Boys' School is a primary and secondary school conducted by the Anglican Cathedral of Saint George in Jerusalem) heard that two cannons were stationed in front of the altar in Saint George's Cathedral, a short distance from the American Colony. I saw a group of Turkish officials going toward the cathedral and wondered what the trouble could be. They had workmen with shovels and pickaxes with them. We heard later that these worthy gentlemen dug a pit in front of the altar but found nothing.

The informant had mistaken the meaning of the word "canon."

Canon Hichens, brother of Robert Hichens, author of *The Garden of Allah*, was standing at the door of his beloved cathedral, never dreaming that he was one of the "cannons" they were looking for.

Long after the war was over this pit had a carpet thrown over it and it was shown to visitors, but it has since been covered up.

Canon Hichens and Mr. Reynolds, headmaster of Saint George's School, were the last British nationals to leave, and would have been held as hostages but for the intervention of Dr. Otis A. Glazebrook our American Consul.

Dr. Glazebrook helped the British subjects in Palestine after their consul left. He told us that the most difficult person in power was Hassan Bey, the "Tyrant of Jaffa," so called because of his many cruel acts and because he desecrated three cemeteries to immortalize his memory and built the Hassan Bey mosque, in the Manshieh Quarter between Jaffa and Tel Aviv, where later there was to be so much trouble and bloodshed. Dr. Glazebrook said that he "kept his arm around Hassan Bey's shoulders" until the last British subjects, Canon Hichens and Mr. Reynolds, got away. Hassan Bey was determined to hold them as hostages.

Several years later Canon Hichens wrote in a letter in my husband's behalf: that he and several others

were in considerable danger at the outbreak of war, and I was picked out with one or two, to go to prison at Haifa, but was rescued from it by the American Consul. While in danger Mr. Vester of the Colony begged Mr. Reynolds, headmaster, and me to come and live with him that he might feed and protect us. He thus exposed himself to the anger of the German community and the Consul General at a time when all supposed that Germany would prove victorious. He also refused to fight on the ground that the war had been unjust and said that he preferred to be shot. Later on he and Mrs. Vester helped us in every way, and even hid me in their barn premises when the Turks wished to carry me off. During the war they nursed and helped British prisoners, stored property of British subjects, and openly refused to take part in any unjust or hostile acts.

Therefore it would be a great pleasure and profit if he could be naturalized.

On November 3, 1914, a telegram from the British Foreign Office to the British Consulate revealed that Turkey had declared war against the Allies and the Consulate, which had been left in the hands of the British dragoman, who was a Turkish subject, should be handed over to the Consul of the United States of America. The Turks were especially anxious to get hold of the archives of the British Consulate, but they were too late—everything had been burned. Dr. Glazebrook, took charge of British interests in Palestine. I helped Dr. Glazebrook pack away the silver, carpets, and valuables belonging to some of the English community, who had left in haste. Frederick and I took charge of the silver crosses and chalices of Saint George's Cathedral and the title deeds of one institution after another. First we took those of the property of the Dominican Fathers and the French Ecole Biblique et Archéologique, which was commandeered by the Turks, and for a time was used as government offices, then those of the enormous property belonging to the Sisters of Saint Joseph and the Notre Dame de France and others. I remember my husband saying we had the title deeds of property worth several millions of pounds.

One evening the caretaker of the house of an English neighbor who had left for safety whispered to us over the wall dividing our gardens that she had heard a Turkish officer was going to commandeer the house. Would we take charge of the silver and carpets? We consented, but as a precaution waited until evening. It was a bright moonlight night and we had the silver safely over the wall and were rolling the carpets when we heard a loud banging at our neighbor's front door. We had only just time to put the carpets on our side of the wall in the dark shadows cast by the moonlight when the officer and his entourage entered.

After the war our neighbor returned and was grateful. She was one of the few English residents who recovered all her valuables.

I have mentioned that my husband was of German-Swiss parentage; his father and mother were missionaries and he was born in Palestine. Frederick had been in Germany for only the short period covering the compulsory military service, with which every German subject, even those living outside of the Father-land, had to comply. He had been a member of the American Colony for twenty years when the war began, and the influence on him was exactly the same as though he had been living in the United States. To all intents and purposes, except legally, he was an American, and when war was declared on the third of August 1914 it was his birthday, and he was forty-five years old, the exact age to put him above the conscription limit. We realized how narrow was the margin between eligible men for the Army and those above age limit when a representative from the German Consulate interviewed my mother-in-law to ascertain the hour Frederick was born.

The accident of birth put Frederick on the wrong side of the conflict. All his sympathies were with the Allies. His religious training had unfitted him to accept a mandate which went against his conscience.

At first he thought he could just keep quiet, and his belief was no one's business but his own. We thought the war would be over in a few months, by Christmas at the latest.

The Sunday afternoon after the fall of Namours which followed so rapidly upon the fall of Liège, German *krieg geist* rose to hysterical heights. Frederick and I were convinced that we could no longer keep quiet; we decided there was only one way for us,

and that was to stand by what we thought was right. We did not
feel the invasion of Belgium was right; nor the tearing up of
treaties as a "scrap of paper" honest.

It was a terrible stand for Frederick to take. His mother,
although Swiss, was heart and soul with Germany. Both of us
hated to hurt her feelings, but we felt there was only one road
we could travel.

On that Sunday afternoon Frederick and I went to the Probst's
house. The Probst was the pastor of the German Lutheran
community. He and his wife kept open house on Sunday; it was
the chief gathering place for the Germans and we knew we
should meet many there. We intended to make a clean breast of
our feelings and take the consequence.

We had even calculated that the consequence might be death
for Frederick.

As we entered we heard excited conversation and many voices
talking at once. The German Consul General and his wife, the
German doctor, some German officers, and others were sitting at
tables drinking coffee. I was shown to a table with the Probst's
wife, and Frederick sat at the table with the Probst and the
Consul General. I had my back to them, but my heart was
pounding and my nerves tingling with expectation. I do not know
exactly what my husband said but I heard the Probst come down
on the table with his fist. All the cups and saucers clattered.
There was a scraping of chairs and everyone in the room stood
up. All present had heard the Probst's rebuke and I surmised
what Frederick had said. The men's faces blanched with fury.

I put my hand out to say good-by to my hostess, but she held
her hand behind her. We got out immediately. If they could
have annihilated us with looks, we should have been dead.
Although both of us knew the seriousness of our deed and com-
prehended what the consequences could be, we both felt happier,
as we stepped outside the front door, than we had been since
that awful third of August.

For the next few days nothing happened.

Then the German Consul General sent for Frederick; he told
him he was a fool to express himself, but he sympathized with
him, for he, too, had lived many years outside of Germany and
realized how changed Frederick's sentiments had become by his
being a member of the American Colony for twenty years. For
a time Frederick was not interfered with.

Immediately after Turkey's declaration of war all the men of military age of Turkish nationality were drafted into the Army. Theoretically, under the young Turkish regime all Turkish subjects were equal, without regard to religious beliefs, but when the test came there was a difference. Christians and Jews were not trusted to carry arms in the same manner as the Moslem subjects but were mustered into labor corps. They built roads, they even carried loads. I remember once when a contingent of Christian and Jewish men, all loaded with bundles of provisions for the fighting troops started on their trek to Beersheba, that they passed the sarai (government offices) where the Montasarif (governor of the province) had his office. To draw his attention to their ignoble and humiliating position, they all started to imitate donkeys' braying. It worked—I never heard again of human pack animals.

Women were doing men's work.

The first attack on the Suez Canal by the Turks, which was repulsed by the British, took place on the second of February 1915. The railroad was incomplete from Constantinople and the Turkish troops accomplished an almost impossible trek from Constantinople to the Suez Canal. There were long stretches which had to be done on foot. The whole Army, with its ordnance loaded on mules, donkeys, and camels, passed the American Colony. We were situated on the main artery. Grace and other women of the Colony stood for hours handing out cups of water to these tired, footsore, and weary soldiers. Often an officer would come and urge them on by using a whip.

Soon after the war started the coastal cities, Jaffa, Gaza, Haifa, and all the smaller cities and villages were evacuated, and their inhabitants came pouring into Jerusalem. Tel Aviv was then a small town, consisting of one main street and about twenty houses. The attraction to Jerusalem was the different convents, monasteries, and the American Colony with the possibility of relief coming from these institutions.

In the summer of 1915 my husband and I with the children camped on Mount Scopus for two weeks in a pine forest belonging to the White Fathers, a Roman Catholic order of Algerian missionaries who conducted a men's college for Greek Catholics inside Saint Stephen's gate. The term "forest" is applied in tree-shorn Palestine to any small wood or copse, natural or artificial. This property, which includes the ancient Pool of Bethesda and a perfectly preserved Crusader church, was a gift from Turkey to the French Government and is now the official French Cathedral. This was commandeered by the Turks, but we got permission to camp in the forest. Often as we sat in the moonlight we could hear the heavy bombardment taking place along the coast near Gaza.

On our return, with the help of our friend Dr. Koenig, editor of the *Christian Herald*, we were able to open an industry among the women whose husbands, fathers, and brothers were in the Army and labor corps. There were many native embroideries and needle-thread lace which we felt could be improved and made attractive to Western purchasers. We heard that an American vessel was coming to Jaffa, and our idea was to pack a trunkful of these articles and send them to the United States to be sold, and thus keep up an industry among the women as long as America stayed out of the European war. The vessel never came; war conditions changed plans from day to day, but the trunk was packed.

The industry was kept up, employing more than three hundred women, until they got too hungry and emaciated to work.

It was while I and other members of the Colony were giving out work to these women that I must have brought an infection to our little daughter Tanetta, now about seven years old. It was just before Christmas, that first year of the war. We had no electricity, no kerosene, and candles were very scarce. We reverted to the Biblical lamps like those used by the wise and unwise virgins, only ours were improvised out of sardine tins with two holes, one for the wick and one for oil, and filled with sesame oil. Frederick and I had five children at this time and no way of buying anything to make Christmas seem usual and normal. So I was making Christmas presents out of odds and ends.

Tanetta had come back from school that afternoon flushed and hot. I soaked her feet in a hot mustard bath and put her to bed. I was sewing on some dolls' clothes, keeping very close to the wick of the lamp. Frederick was near me and was reading Dickens's *Christmas Carol* aloud. We were trying hard to get into the Christmas spirit when the nurse came down to say that she feared Tanetta was very ill. She was exceedingly hot and seemed delirious. The thermometer showed that her fever was as high as it could possibly go; I knew it could not go much higher and she still live, but what alarmed me most was that she was cold up to her knees.

Jerusalem was under martial law. Not a soul was on the street, but we had to have a doctor. There was no telephone, so Frederick started out into that ominous darkness. He found our doctor ill and unable to come, but our friend Dr. Canaan, a Christian Arab, and a graduate of the American University of Beirut, was in the Turkish Army at the time, and was luckily home on leave. When he examined Tanetta he confirmed my fears that she had either spotted typhus or smallpox. He said that whichever malady it proved to be we must start quarantine at once.

By this time it was 2 A.M. Frederick went to the Colony, which was only two minutes' walk north of our house, and roused first Mother and then the rest of the Colony members. Our four remaining children were awakened, dressed, and taken over to the Colony. I stayed to nurse Tanetta. The plan was for Frederick to remain downstairs in our house and be the liaison between me and the outside world. The worst fear—anguish beyond words—was that the Turkish sanitary authorities would take our child away to the pesthouse, from which she would not return.

Our two loyal servants refused to leave. Next morning I told Ahmed to buy all the Turkey-red material he could find. I remembered reading that if red light was used smallpox would not pit, and before Dr. Canaan came next morning I had red curtains over all the windows and the door. He was pleased with my precaution, and Frederick and I could never cease being grateful to Dr. Canaan for pledging to the Turkish sanitary authorities that he would be responsible for the case, that strict quarantine would be observed, and that the whole American Colony would be vaccinated; so they were satisfied to leave Tanetta at home to be nursed.

It was soon certain that she had a bad attack of smallpox. Dr. Canaan prescribed the necessary ointment and we were able to fill the prescription just twice; there was no more to be had anywhere in Jerusalem.

I sat by her bed and by the hour sang very softly the hymn she loved best, "There's a Land That Is Fairer Than Day."

No one else in the Colony caught the infection, and we were a united family for Christmas, which was the best present we could have been given.

A few months after Tanetta's recovery my husband and our son John were taken ill with typhoid malaria. It was a dangerous combination. Frederick lay unconscious in one room and in another John tossed in delirium. I was expecting my sixth child.

The doctor called me aside one day after leaving Frederick's room.

"You must be brave," he told me. "You must bear up because of another life."

He was convinced that Frederick's heart was failing and he could not pull through.

When the doctor left I went into the library. Mother was there. I must have looked utterly dejected and hopeless. Mother did not know what the doctor had told me, but she came over and looked into my face.

"Bertha," she asked, in her deep, wonderful voice, "is God dead?"

"No, Mother," I answered, "God is not dead," and remembering that, I went out into the garden. I do not know how long I was there; I lost count of time. Suddenly the window of my husband's sickroom opened and Sister Lottie spoke to me. "Your husband is asking for you."

Frederick was conscious for the first time in days.

He grew rapidly better, John's fever turned, and both were quite recovered when two months later Frieda, our youngest, was born. Although I had passed through sore trials and had insufficient food, Frieda is one of the healthiest and happiest of our six children.

During these troubled wartimes, while Jerusalem was under martial law from sundown to sunrise, one night about two o'clock our doorbell rang. This was so unusual that the whole family wakened and went to find out what the matter was. Frederick, now quite recovered from his illness, opened the door to find two Jews standing there.

We recognized them as sons of a patriarchal old Jew from Bokhara who was a friend of ours. He had come to Palestine about ten years before this and built an enormous house in the new western suburb of Jerusalem. He imported Bokharan jewelry which we sold for him at our store, receiving a commission. The jewelry was crude and garish but sought after by American tourists. It was composed of uncut emeralds and rubies set in almost pure gold with pearls and diamonds and other precious stones. Necklaces, bracelets, pendants, and earrings were the most attractive bits. Some of them were enhanced with fine enamelwork.

Old Moses was devoted to Frederick. Now he was ill and on his deathbed, and he wanted Frederick to come to him before he died. I was worried to have my husband go out on the dark street unprotected at such an unusual time and under such dangerous conditions, but Frederick would not refuse the wish of a dying man.

He did not return until breakfasttime next morning, then, after a hot bath and a shave and over a cup of hot (so-called) coffee, he told me what had taken place. He said it was like seeing the Bible lived. He had found Moses with only a short time to live, "propped up against many pillows." His wife and sons and daughters with their wives and husbands and all the grandchildren were gathered round the bed, mourning and beating their bosoms and heads.

When Moses saw Frederick enter the room, he smiled and said between pauses for labored breath, "I knew you would not refuse me—as you see, I am to be gathered to my fathers."

While he spoke, the noise subsided. Everyone was eager to hear what important thing Moses was going to say to this "goy." He continued, "My children are good children. Their mother is like Sarah, a virtuous woman. She must be taken care of. But as soon as I am gone my children will quarrel over my possessions. The property is arranged for, but here"—pointing to a dirty linen serviette tied together and bulging with something inside—"is all the jewelry which I have. It is worth many thousands of pounds. This I give to you to keep. After seven days of mourning are over you will call my sons and daughters and divide it equally among them. They must abide by your division. It is final."

Frederick wanted to give Moses a receipt for the jewelry, but the old man refused. "Don't insult me," he said. "I trust you as I always have."

Frederick had carried home the valuable bundle so casually wrapped in the serviette. After breakfast he took it to the office and locked it in the safe until the seven days of mourning were completed, for old Moses died that same day. Then, just as he had been instructed, he summoned the family and divided the jewelry and they abode by Frederick's decision.

Many years after this Mr. and Mrs. Palmer, the United States Consul General and his wife, gave a fancy-dress entertainment. Frederick and I decided to go in Bokhara costumes, and he told Moses's daughter Sarah. She entered enthusiastically into our plan. She brought gorgeous garments and expensive jewelry and insisted in dressing me herself. I was afraid to be responsible for so much, but Sarah insisted upon my wearing all her beautiful gems. Some of the pieces, she said, were what she had gotten in the final division after her father's death.

We caused quite a sensation at the party.

It was while I was sitting alone for so many hours nursing Tanetta through smallpox and thinking of what was ahead of us as war progressed, knowing that with each day conditions were growing worse in Jerusalem and in the world, that I conceived the idea of writing our friend Mr. Edward F. Loud of Oscoda, Michigan, asking him if he would collect funds to enable us to maintain a soup kitchen in the American Colony.

It was unthinkable to continue aid through giving work to the women. By this time they were too hungry to work. Also, that winter Palestine had the worst locust visitation in generations, and grain was scarce. We had been giving bread and soup and other necessities to Mohammedans and Christians and Jews who came in crowds to our doors daily. Among these needy Jews were the Gadites, a large number of whom we were still helping.

All this effort was insufficient, and our funds were finished. All avenues of work or income were sealed, meanwhile the demands upon us were increasing.

I wrote a letter to Mr. Loud which he did not receive until much later. At the same time Mr. Loud in Michigan was wondering how he could help the American Colony. Through the State Department he sent word to Dr. Glazebrook our American Consul and that December, in the darkest hour the Colony had known, the Secretary of State in Washington wrote Dr. Glazebrook, instructing him in behalf of Mr. Loud to "inquire of the American Colony in Jerusalem whether they are in need of help, and if they need money, how much is required."

As Jacob wrote in answer:

When we received your letter through the Consul, it was read aloud at the table. No words can convey to you the awe that hushed us. The ram caught in the thicket did not speak more clearly with God's voice to Abraham, and no sheep could more clearly hear the sound of its shepherd's staff than we did perceive God's care and intervention.

Besides loaning five thousand dollars to Colony members,

Mr. Loud began collecting funds from other friends in Michigan to enable us to keep our soup kitchen open.

Here are excerpts from letters I wrote Mr. Loud in 1917, before the United States entered the war:

If you could stand one day at our gate, and see the pleasure on the gaunt faces, as they go away with their pails and saucepans filled with the nutritious soup, enough to satisfy their family, it would repay you for your trouble. When I last wrote we were giving soup to four hundred people daily. Since then we have every day been obliged to increase the number, until Saturday (day before yesterday) there were eleven hundred and eighty-six souls who were fed. All the last week there were from nine hundred to one thousand daily. Working among the poor as we have, in and around Jerusalem for so many years, we get to know them all personally. However, we are cautious about accepting new applicants, and several of the sisters make it their duty to visit the homes and see exactly what they need. The deplorable condition of these homes is shocking. Americans cannot conceive, even by trying to imagine, what the reality is.

Two years ago, when distributing money from the *Christian Herald*, and last year, when conducting the Industrial Relief Work, we thought conditions could not get much worse. We have learned differently. It would be impossible to carry on an industrial relief work now. The people are not in a condition to work. It is now simply keeping soul and body together. In some cases our assistance helps; in other cases it is too late. I wish I could send you some of the numerous letters of application we get daily. In the midst of the misery we have to smile when they say, for instance, that they "have the pleasure to inform us that my husband, he dead, and my children, they starving."

My husband and Mr. Whiting were fortunate in being able to buy a few tons of beans and lentils, but they will last only until Wednesday. We have spent more than the one thousand dollars, the first installment for the soup kitchen. We were very glad to see by your letter, which came last night, that we could expect about five hundred dollars more. Some may think it would be wiser to limit the number of recipients and thus make the money last longer. This one could only advise from a distance where you do not see the applicants. It is utterly impossible to refuse.

In another letter:

It is the babies and children who suffer. They have had no part in bringing about this sad state of affairs. Their appealing glances would break hearts of stone.

The Gadite or Yemenite Jews and the Morocco and Aleppo Jews are the worst cared for among that class. A large number come daily to our soup kitchen. It is a motley crowd that gathers there every day. Poverty is a class and creed leveler. I used to speak in my letters to Mr. Koenig, editor of the *Christian Herald*, about the "bashful elite" who were ashamed to come and get work at the same time as their less fortunate sisters (in social class only), and wanted to be let in through another door, or received on another day. Now they are not only willing, but consider themselves fortunate if they are granted a soup ticket.

We make no distinction in nationality or creed, the only requirement being
if they absolutely need the help. We have Syrians and Arabs, both Mohammedans, Latins and Greeks, and Armenians, Russians, Jews, and Protestants.

Our friends in the United States responded to Mr. Loud's
appeal and we were able to feed increasing numbers, until two
thousand four hundred men, women, and children were receiving food every day from the American Colony.

We borrowed from the Armenian Convent the large copper
cauldrons they used to cook food for their pilgrims during the
pilgrimage season. We started cooking the soup about five in
the morning, and refilled the large cauldrons several times. I
wrote Mr. Loud:

> It shows the increase in poverty, when last year the Jews would not take
> our cooked soup, but asked for the uncooked cereals, while this year they are
> eager and grateful to get it.

In the spring of 1917 it became apparent that America was
preparing to enter the war and Mr. Loud wrote he feared he
could not send any more funds. We were wondering how we
could carry on the soup kitchen, when a German major called
at the American Colony and announced that it must be closed.

The kitchen was American propaganda, he claimed, and to
our protests that it was nothing of the kind, but a purely human-
itarian measure, he turned a deaf ear.

The major was one of the Germans who had been a pupil
learning English at the American Colony when war had been
declared in 1914 and they had left so mysteriously and suddenly.

Some time after this call we learned he had been made German
Ambassador to Iraq.

CHAPTER TWENTY-THREE

EARLY in April 1917 Dr. Glazebrook called on Mother and advised her, as well as the other members of the American Colony, to leave Palestine and go into safety. He said we must look forward eventually to an Allied victory, and a retreating Turkish Army would be an unpleasant thing to encounter. He was giving the same advice to all the other American citizens living in Palestine.

Mother asked him if he was ordering her to leave. He replied that he could not order her to do anything.

"Americans don't order their citizens," he said. "I wish I could. But I strongly advise you and your companions to leave." Mother thought a moment and then answered that as she had left her country to be of service to the people of Palestine, she considered this her supreme hour for service; as far as she was concerned she would not leave. The whole Colony confirmed this decision; not one left.

The Friends from the Quaker Mission in Ramallah left and the other Christian American citizens. How can I describe the feeling of isolation, of being absolutely cut off, that we felt when we bade farewell to our dear friends the Glazebrooks and the Friends Mission? The only consolation was in work, and we had our hands full.

On April 6 the United States declared war on the German Reich. The inevitable breaking off of diplomatic relations with Turkey came as a matter of course, although the United States never actually declared war on Turkey, a fact we hoped would make conditions easier for us in the American Colony.

Two British attacks on Gaza that spring failed. After the first the British Army under Sir Archibald Murray retreated and the prisoners taken by the Turks were brought to Jerusalem and paraded through the streets. Many wounded, both British and Turkish, came as well. They lay on stretchers in the road outside the French Hospital, commandered and run by Turks. There seemed insufficient medical service, for when I passed by in the afternoon I noticed what seemed to be the same stretchers with the same men still in the road unattended. It was this circumstance which made us offer our services to nurse the wounded.

My husband and I went to Turkish headquarters, then housed in the Augusta Victoria Stiftung on the Mount of Olives. Djemal Pasha, Minister of Marine in the Turkish Cabinet and one of the Young Turks who had brought about the *coup d'état* in 1912 which revived and enforced the Constitution of 1876, and eventually deposed Sultan Abdul-Hamid, was Generalissimo of the Turkish-German attack on the Suez Canal.

Djemal Pasha kept us waiting in the anteroom and when he arrived his manner was not gracious. I suppose few people requested an interview with His Excellency except when they wanted to ask a favor. He was a strange man, and one to be feared. He expected such a request now, but I said, "Your Excellency, we have come to offer our services to nurse the wounded."

I must say that Djemal Pasha was taken aback.

He immediately regained command of himself and said with a look by which he meant to wither me, "Today your country has been foolish enough to cut diplomatic relations with Turkey," and then, raising himself to his full height, for he was a short, thickset man, he said, "And now, after hearing what I have said, are you still willing to nurse our wounded?" We were stunned. Hermetically sealed as we were, we had not known we were at war.

I knew that one mistake on my part would bring trouble on the whole American Colony.

It was a tense moment in which I asked for guidance. My answer was that we had offered to nurse neither friends nor foes, but humanity—and that our offer held good.

I must say this man of iron will and dual personality was touched. He accepted our offer and put the Grand New Hotel, which he had commandeered for a hospital, at our disposal. The hotel was soon ready to receive the wounded. It was neither Grand nor New, but filthy and full of vermin, and elbow grease had to fill in where soap and disinfectant were lacking. The building was filled with memories for me. Here Thomas Cook and Son had brought their tourists, among them so many who had become friends of the Colony, and here had lived for so many years Dr. and Mrs. Selah Merrill. Here Mrs. Whiting and her children, Ruth and John, had been imprisoned.

I was in charge of getting the wounded men sorted and placed in their beds. One man lagged behind the rest and I spoke to him in Arabic. By his looks I realized that he had not under-stood what I said; he asked in English, "What did you say?" His British uniform and military boots had been stolen; he was barefoot and had on some old Turkish rags, but I realized that this man was English, that he was a Turkish prisoner, and I knew he had been sent to the American Colony Hospital by mistake. Quite naturally they would keep British prisoners away from the American Colony Hospital.

That evening we had a council of war in the Colony and decided to volunteer to take over the clearing station where the wounded were brought to be deloused, shaved, bathed—or rather scrubbed—and dispersed to the different hospitals. We thought that by doing this we could get hold of the British prisoners and help them.

Our offer was accepted with gratitude by Turkish Medical Headquarters. A gruesome part of this new responsibility was that all the corpses from the different hospitals came back to the clearing-station morgue for burial. It was part of our duty there to make sure that a Jew was not buried by the Moslems or a Roman Catholic by the Greek Orthodox, and vice versa.

I happened to be present when the Moslem emam (religious leader) in charge of the morgue received the corpse of a young Turkish soldier. His hair was fair; I did not see the color of his eyes, for they were closed. His splendid physique had succumbed to blood poisoning, as so many did when gangrene set in. Instead of handling the poor dead man with respect, the emam pulled him off the stretcher as though he were a bit of wood, and he fell to the dirty floor on his face.

I was furious and took the emam to task. I said, "No wonder there are so many deserters from the Turkish Army. They make their supreme sacrifice for their country and this is the treatment they get."

Of course the emam did not like being rebuked by a woman, and by a Christian dog at that, so he answered me rudely. I went to Medical Headquarters in the commandeered Notre Dame de France, which was only a few steps from the Casualty Clearing Station. Colonel Abdulkadir Bey, a Damascene educated at the American University of Beirut and Paris, and head medical officer, heard my story. He agreed that the treatment of corpses and burials must be investigated and improved.

I then went home for lunch, where my husband joined me. Frederick was chuckling.

"I didn't know you were so bloodthirsty as to request that the poor emam at the Casualty Clearing Station should be beaten with sixty strokes." There would not be much left of him after such a beating with a cat-o'-nine-tails.

Frederick knew that I had not made any such request and he had hurried home to let me know.

We returned at once to Colonel Abdulkadir Bey to beg for leniency. It was with difficulty that we got the emam off. At last only the second part of his punishment was enforced, and that was that he should sleep in the morgue for a week. He was terribly upset by this, for he was superstitious, and I suppose he thought the many corpses he had maltreated would haunt him there. Perhaps if given his choice he might have chosen the beating.

I saw him after the week was over and he had grown thin and pale.

In July 1917 General Allenby became commander in chief of the Middle East, replacing Sir Archibald Murray. Just before General Allenby assumed this position his only son had been killed in France. We heard rumors about the new general. The nearest the Turkish soldiers got to pronouncing his name was Al nebby, which means "said by the Prophet," and that to them had a significant meaning.

During this time I busied myself with any kind of housekeeping job connected with the four hospitals now in our charge. As long as I could manage it I kept away from the harrowing sights of the operating and dressing rooms, because of my young baby.

When I got to the Casualty Clearing Station one morning, doing my round of duties, the young man from the Colony in charge announced that among the wounded who had been brought in that morning were three Gurkhas. They belonged to the Indian Gurkha infantry regiment and had been taken prisoners. They were fierce fighters and besides their usual arms they were allowed their native kukri, a heavy, curved knife which they use for all purposes, from opening tins to unmentionable things. These men should have been disarmed when they were captured, but they had a hand grenade.

As I peeked through the window at the three, I thought that I had never seen creatures who looked more like demons. They were short and thickset with dark skin, fierce, piercing black eyes, and large mouths.

Our men had wisely removed all other casualties from the room and had the door guarded. We thought the Gurkhas were waiting for a good opportunity to let off the hand grenade.

To send in an orderly or any man to disarm them would be the challenge they were waiting for.

I knew there was only one thing to do. As a helpless woman, I might appeal to them.

Quickly, before I gave myself time to argue out of it, I went into the room. I went in smiling, patted the first Gurkha on the shoulder, and held out my hand. He understood. Without resistance he took the hand grenade out of his pocket.

With signs I asked if they had any more, smiling all the time as though I were enjoying the conversation. They shook their heads. I walked out with the hand grenade. Not knowing the mechanism, I was wondering if it would go off before I got to the door. By the time I got rid of it, I was shaking all over.

After the three Gurkhas were scrubbed I took them to our hospital, to be sure they got special care. Here again Brother Elijah was useful. It was he who was often pressed into service to amuse the obstreperous young Rudolf Hess. Brother Elijah could speak Hindustani and although it was not the Gurkha language, there was enough similarity for them to make their wants understood. The men were grateful to hear something that reminded them of India. Their grim faces would break into broad grins when I made my rounds of the hospital several times a day.

We became great friends, and we were very sorry when the time came to give them up.

As fighting got nearer, food got scarcer, and there was no business. Shops were closed, and the few food shops that were open had very little to sell. Deserters from the Army increased daily. I remember one case where a Greek Orthodox Christian Arab hid for more than a year. There was a window in an upstairs room leading onto a roof, which had an enormous old-fashioned dome covering the room below. In front of the window a wardrobe was placed. If anyone came to inquire for him, as they often did, his wife had two tunes she would sing. One, meaning a friend, the other, an enemy. If it was the latter, he would immediately get through the window on the roof and pull the wardrobe in place. They searched for him, even opening the wardrobe to look inside, but they never discovered his hiding place.

After our soup kitchen was closed by the Germans it was quite terrible not to be able to help the poor people. Thousands must have died from slow starvation and disease, notably from spotted and enteric fevers. Then cholera was added. There was nothing we could do about it. Many a person came to our door and dropped from exhaustion. We cared for as many as we could. We would carry them under the olive trees, making them as comfortable as possible, while we sought for a conveyance to carry them to the hospital. Some died before we were able to procure this. Then a more serious difficulty arose: this was to get the Turkish Government authorities to bury the dead. The characteristic Turk always procrastinates. Some of our members walked miles from one official to another before these wretched bodies were put under the sod.

Many women brought their babies to us and offered to sell them for a pittance, just to be sure of a few more meals. One mother left her skeleton twin babies at midnight hanging on our front gate. The worst of all was that many, yes, very many, pitifully young girls sold themselves to German and Turkish troops.

It was about this time that the Grand Mufti of Jerusalem, Kamil Effendi al Husseini, who was half-brother of the present Mufti Hadj Amin al Husseini, came to Mother with the request that we would manage the Khaski Sultan soup kitchen called the "D'kieh." It was an old and richly endowed institution, but the Turkish Government appropriated most of the revenue. The Mufti, a tall man of mild and gentle demeanor, had often stopped at our open-air soup-distributing center and watched us give out soup, before it was closed by a German mandate, on his way to his residence on the Mount of Olives road, northeast of the Colony. Busy as we were with running four hospitals, we could not refuse. I went to investigate and found hundreds of clamoring and ragged skeletons clawing one another to reach the distributing center, and only being kept from tearing one another's clothes by police using whips.

I announced that the first thing must be to get rid of the police and their whips. The Mufti warned me that I would be mobbed. The D'kieh was situated in an old house partly in ruins in the Tyrolean Valley which divides the four hills of Jerusalem. I got up on a wall and clapped my hands and shouted at the top of my voice to attract attention. A few realized something unusual was happening and looked up. Finally I got the attention of this motley crowd, many of whom I recognized as having been among our old clientele. I announced that the American Colony was going to take charge of this soup kitchen. I reminded them of the orderly manner in which they had acted with us; I confided that we would get rid of the policemen and their whips if they would co-operate, and I promised them that there would be soup for all. Even those at the very end of the line would get their share. Two members of the Colony undertook to oversee the work. From that day until the British occupation took place the number increased from four hundred to four thousand and then to six thousand receiving soup daily. We feared that when Jerusalem fell this work would have to stop because of lack of funds. Although belonging to an Arab Pius Foundation, it was in Turkish hands, but the British came to our rescue with funds so that the soup kitchen continued to function.

One morning Djemal Pasha's naval aide-de-camp called at our house to ask if I would be willing to oversee the renovation of the Anglican Bishop's Palace for the residence of the new civil governor, Izzat Pasha. Izzat Pasha's wife was a near relative of His Excellency, and as the bishop's house had been roughly used since it was commandeered it needed considerable repairs. I was delighted to do this.

Somehow we felt it could not be very long before the British Army would take Palestine, and secretly I thought of this as getting ready for their coming. I sent for Mr. Dahud Dadis, a Palestinian Greek Orthodox Christian, who had been the bishop's secretary, and was nominally in charge of Saint George's Close and the bishop's residence. I told him that Djemal Pasha had asked me to get the house ready for the English bishop. Mr. Dadis opened his eyes wide and said, "The English bishop?" I smiled and said, "Of course he did not say for the bishop, but for the new civil governor, but you and I can think that we are getting it ready for the bishop and keep our thoughts to ourselves." When I asked where I would find furniture and other things for the house, the aide-de-camp said that the Spanish Consul would break the seals on the English school where British furniture was stored. My heart sank, for that was where Mrs. Glazebrook and I had packed all the English valuables away.

The aide-de-camp and the Spanish Consul's dragomans arrived to break the seals. I asked my foster brother if he would entertain the aide-de-camp by telling him about archaeological sites in the vicinity, and I took the Spanish dragoman, a Roman

Catholic Palestinian Arab, into my confidence.

Hurriedly I pushed the cases containing the silver and carpets into the background and took out mattresses, bedding, and other odds and ends sufficient to furnish the house. By this time Jacob and the aide-de-camp were with us, and I pointed to all the things we had removed from the storeroom. Then the doors were locked and sealed again.

When the repairs and furnishing of the house were complete, Djemal Pasha came to inspect them, and the first question he asked was, "Were there no carpets among the British belongings?" I answered, "Your Excellency, I didn't see any," and he was satisfied. Of course I had not seen any. They were all packed away carefully with moth balls. But not one thing was saved of all those left behind. The seals must have been broken later and everything was stolen. But I fear they would not have been saved even if I had taken them to the bishop's house, for when the Turks retreated they carried everything they could with them.

The Ordnance Workshops occupied the commandeered English schools near the American Colony. In the late afternoon the reckoning took place for all the imaginary or real insubordination of the Christian and Jewish laborers. They were lined up to watch their unfortunate companions being punished. The basti-nado was generally used, which is a cruel chastisement. The victim was thrown on the ground and his feet made firm by twisting a rope around a stick with the feet in between. The stick was held by two men and the beating was on the soles of the feet. We could hear the screams of these wretched men from our house. I had instructed the nurse to be sure to keep the children on the farther side of the house in the late afternoon, but I returned once and missed my four-year-old son John. By the screaming that was going on I knew that chastisement was being inflicted, so I went over to Saint Mary's School Compound.

Sure enough, there stood John looking up into the face of the commanding officer and shaking his little finger up and down, repeating over and over again in English, "You won't go to heaven!"

The officer, not understanding what the child was saying, was much amused. I grabbed John by the hand and fled.

Not long after this the director of Pius Foundations, of which the endowment of the D'kieh was one, asked Mother to take charge of his daughter, Nimette, who was about eleven years old.

Her mother had died of tuberculosis in Switzerland and the child was very lonely. Mother asked me to take Nimette into our nursery, and when I saw the wistful little face I could not refuse.

Nimette became one of our family and was never any trouble except for the fact that she had an enlarged spleen from malaria and she infected all our children with the disease. We had been free of malaria until then, but mosquitoes spread the disease among our children after biting Nimette, and my son Horatio still has a bout every now and then.

Her father was a great friend of Djemal Pasha, and one afternoon he asked if he could bring the field marshal to tea. Mother, with her innate Scandinavian hospitality, wondered what we would give His Excellency to eat with his tea, but I suggested that he could have the carob syrup gingerbread, which was the only sweet we had. Carob is made from the locust bean.

Djemal Pasha was a man of dual personality. We had heard that he was capable of lunching with a man one day and hanging him the next; yet he could say to Mother this afternoon as he held my two-year-old Louise on his knee that children were a bit of heaven and that God's richest blessing to mankind was friendship.

I told His Excellency about John's escapade at the Ordnance Workshops and how he rebuked the officer for beating the men. Djemal Pasha was considerate about it and had the workshops moved away. He said, "I shall not allow those children to witness such sights." So we were no longer harassed by the daily beatings.

A few days later our daughter Louise came home with the nurse very much elated over her "pretty-pretty," and, to my utter consternation, I recognized a diamond star decoration belonging to Djemal Pasha pinned on her dress. He had pinned it there. What could that mean? I was suspicious because of the rumors about his duplicity and cruelty. Was he trying to get us into trouble? If Louise should lose this valuable decoration, what would happen? I wrapped it up and sent it back at once.

The choir of the American Colony were practicing Handel's "Hallelujah Chorus" with a view to singing it when Jerusalem was delivered. One day I heard my four-year-old son sitting high up in an old olive tree in our garden lustily singing the tune of the "Hallelujah Chorus," but the words were his own:

> "Dje-mal Pasha Dje-mal Pasha
> Djemal Pasha Djemal Pasha
> Dje-ma-al Pa-sh . . ."

He stopped singing and got down double quick for two reasons. First, I disliked the combination of the music with John's improvised words; second, I feared someone might hear him and report us for taking the great man's name in vain.

Early in August we received several more wounded British soldiers and we realized with a thrill how very beneficial our work was going to be in regard to British prisoners of war. One of these was an officer, Second Lieutenant D:ck. Another was Thomas Morie, a very young man with a wound in his head, the bullet having lodged in his brain. An effort was made by the surgeon to extract the bullet, but without avail. His condition grew worse daily and we knew there was no hope of his recovery. I watched by his bedside, soothing his delirium by singing hymns, among them "It Is Well with My Soul."

When he died, I went again with my husband to Djemal Pasha and asked for permission to follow his body to the grave. We hoped to make a precedent by this for all British prisoners who might die in our hospital. We got a coffin through the Spanish Consul, who since Dr. Glazebrook's departure was in charge of British and American interests. This was the first death of a British prisoner, and we were determined to see to it that all British prisoners got proper burial. We wanted a Protestant clergyman to officiate, but those whom we asked were afraid. Djemal Pasha might give his consent, but that did not insure their not being taken up for it later and perhaps banished.

At last an Arab Lutheran clergyman, seeing my dilemma, consented to officiate, which he did in English. It was a very brave act on his part. Our children, who came daily to the hospitals with flowers from our garden for the wounded, made beautiful wreaths and four of us went to the funeral in the English Cemetery. We sang, "Nearer, My God to Thee" and "Jesus, Lover of My Soul" at the grave; we conveyed the coffin to the cemetery in our carriage.

The other British prisoners were very much touched. We had four deaths among the British prisoners, and each time we were allowed to follow the body to the grave. When I say every time, I must except one case for which the Turks gave their consent, but the soldier being Roman Catholic, the priest, who was called to administer the last rites and officiate at the funeral, would not allow us to follow the corpse or to sing at the grave. We were particularly sorry, for we had become very much attached to

Francis Flood.

The rest of the men were slightly wounded, and in a few weeks they were perfectly well. We endeavored to keep them as long as possible, and whenever an inspection of the hospital was made we kept them out of the way. Several of them thus were retained for several months.

During this time we tried to mark every Sunday by sending down a pork roast or a steamed pudding which we made with the carob syrup, and the choir from the Colony would go to the hospital and sing.

We knew the time must be nearing for the British to be taken away. We hated to let them go, for we could imagine what treatment they would get. We wanted them to see something of the Holy City before they left, so again I went with my husband to headquarters to get permission for us to take them to see some of the holy places. I never went to headquarters without my husband. Frederick was busy in the Izzat Pasha's Civilian Food Control Office, but he always managed to find time to accompany me.

At headquarters they wanted to know where I was going to take the men, and I replied without hesitation, "to the Mount of Olives," for we had worked out a plan which we knew would please them.

The American Colony is on the road to the Mount of Olives. When we got them to the Colony, we had the best afternoon tea prepared for them that our limited resources could furnish. We managed to get hold of some real tea. We made scones and some homemade butter (we had been saving cream off the milk for days for this) and cake made without sugar but sweetened with carob syrup.

An amusing fact was that in the black market one could not only buy sugar at an exorbitant price but one could buy it in its original English wrappings. This did not mean a successful raid on any British position, but the fact that Bedouins bartered English sugar mostly for Hebron grapes to Allenby's troops.

After tea we put recorded familiar songs on the Victrola belonging to the Friends' Mission, which we had taken to save it. This was one time when Harry Lauder's comic songs in broad Scotch made the tears come to the boys' eyes. It was so good to hear something from home, and yet they knew what lay between them and that home. They knew this was the last bit of civilization, of home and kindness that they would meet with for a long time, if ever. We were feeling sad, but we tried in every way we could to cheer them before starting on their precarious and uncertain march.

Three weeks after this a great change took place for all of us. Djemal Pasha had been absent from Palestine for some time; there were rumors that he was in Syria and the Lebanon. The immense crop of rumors circulated by the "grapevine" method increased our feeling of insecurity.

Day by day people were arrested on the slightest pretext and accused of being spies. The Mufti of Gaza and his son were hanged at the Jaffa Gate. They belonged to the Husseini family and were condemned as traitors, because someone said they were pro-British.

There were other executions at the Damascus Gate. I remember one morning going to the hospital in the carriage with my husband. We were stopped by a Moslem friend who told us to go round another way as two men, hanged at dawn, were still hanging outside the Damascus Gate. They were left there as an object lesson to other pro-British sympathizers.

We often remarked to one another our fellow feeling with Daniel about Nebuchadnezzar, "whom he would he slew, whom he kept alive, he kept alive." The executions and hangings in the Lebanon were on a larger scale than in Palestine, and the condition of people in the Lebanon was even more pitiable than those in Jerusalem. Djemal Pasha had announced that pardons were to be granted to many condemned persons, especially those from Nablus, where the notables were known to be in favor of Britain. A conference was called to meet at Abbey in the Lebanon. We had a Moslem friend, Ahmed Effendi, in Nablus whose sons were in the Colony school. He was among those summoned to Abbey. He was delayed in starting, which saved his life.

They were all under the impression that they were going to be pardoned. Arriving by carriage from Damascus to Abbey, Ahmed Effendi went into a hotel and casually took up a newspaper. There he read that the whole group who had answered Djemal Pasha's summons, his uncle among them, had been hanged the day before.

Ahmed hastily dropped the newspaper and went in search of his carriage. He bribed the driver to harness the poor, weary horses at once and start back to Damascus. He told him that he had left all his money in Damascus, and haste was necessary

to find it. In Damascus he went to a friend's house and for fear
of being betrayed, and to make sure to bind his host to secrecy,
he paid a high price for and married the daughter of the house—
thus he gave a motive to his father-in-law to protect him. He
had a wife and a large family in Nablus, but, as Mohammedans
are allowed four wives, that was no hindrance.

Conditions were not progressing well for the Turks on the
Sinai front, since the new British general—Allenby—was in
command. We heard rumors that there were jealousies and dis-
agreements between the Turks and their German allies. Incidents
arising between them were frequent, owing to the Germans'
contemptuous and overbearing treatment of the Turks. The
heavy howitzer artillery were under the command of the Austrian
contingent. They had their headquarters in Ratizbon's School
(French Roman Catholic) on the western extremity of the new
city (as it was then). The Austrians got on much better with the
Turks.

While Djemal Pasha was absent in Syria, Nimette spent a few
days with her father at Turkish headquarters at the Augusta
Victoria Stiftung. She got lonesome for her playmates, to whom
she had become attached, and asked if our daughter Anna Grace,
who was her own age, could spend the week end with her. While
she was there British planes bombed the Kaiser's palace. I was
awakened early by the sound of explosions, and looking from
our east window, I saw the Stiftung enveloped in smoke. I
thought it was on fire and was frantic with fear because Anna
Grace and Nimette were there. Several of the young men from
the Colony hitched up our carriage and galloped as fast as horses
could go to headquarters. It was a foolhardy thing to do, because
the raiders might have thought an important personage was in
the carriage and bombed it. However, in those days aerial marks-
manship was less perfect than it became later, and the planes
were flying very high for fear of attack.

Of all the bombs which were dropped on headquarters only
the church containing the Kaiser's and the Kaiserin's portraits
was hit. We were grateful indeed for the children's safe return.
They rather enjoyed the excitement.

Then one day, without the usual warning, the great Envar
Pasha came to Jerusalem. Envar with Taliat and Djemal formed
the Young Turk triumvirate who held the reings of power in
Turkey. Djemal had always been pro-French.

Envar Pasha was inspecting the Sinai and Baghdad fronts.

The Turkish policy favored the retaking of Baghdad, a former capital of the khalifs which was all-important to the pan-Islamic part of the Young Turk party. It had the backing of Berlin as well. But the argument was that if Palestine fell to the British, Iraq would, too, so Palestine became the most important issue.

It was then that we began to hear General von Falkenhayn's name mentioned in connection with Palestine. Envar Pasha came with the pomp and ceremony of a conquering hero. He visited all the properties, schools, and hospitals which had been commandeered by the Turks after the evacuation of allied nationals. Their pride in them was as though they had created them. The boys' college belonging to the White Fathers was turned into a Moslem missionary college. They seemed to feel secure, and planned for years ahead.

Envar Pasha, accompanied by Djemal Pasha, passed the American Colony several times, and we had a good opportunity to see the man of whom we had read and heard so much. Once we saw Djemal Pasha point to the Colony and tell Envar Pasha something, and we wished we could know what it was.

Transportation was one of the great difficulties which the Turks had to contend with. The railroad from Haider Pasha, the Constantinople station on the Asiatic side to Beersheba, was about thirteen hundred miles, and the Amanus and Taurus tunnels were still incomplete. The power for the Palestinian narrow-gauge railroad was supplied by wood.

Many of the ancient oak forests disappeared, ruthlessly chopped down for this purpose. The rolling stock was neither good nor numerous and the inefficiency of the Turkish officers and their propensity to bribery made the supply of equipment difficult.

In reality the Turkish Army lived and fought under indescribable conditions. Their German allies were aware of the growing discontent in the Turkish Army because of this and we heard of the continual and ever-growing friction between them.

Marshal von Falkenhayn was asked to take over the command of the Sinai front and he came out in German uniform to inspect and to have a look around.

Living conditions became steadily worse in Jerusalem, and our hopes grew proportionately higher. Rumor led us to believe Allenby's troops might be nearing the Holy City.

In the courtyard of the American Colony, circa 1900
Anna Spafford 3rd from right in back row

Eric Matsson, photographer of the American Colony

The Park Hotel in Jaffa, owned by Baron Ustinov

Camping in Jericho

Procession approaching Jaffa Gate

By the "Fast Hotel", next to Jaffa Gate

Jamal Pasha

Triumphal arch for Jamal Pasha, 1914

Louise Vester on Jamal Pasha's knee, 1915

The Locusts, 1915

Military funeral on Mount Zion, 1916

German Consulate at Haifa blown up
by French ships, 1916

Jamal Pasha's body-guard in Barracks Square

Indian guard by the Dome of the Rock

Relief work at the Colony, 1916

Vester and Whiting families, 1916

General View of Beersheba, 1917

Hassan Bey the Tyrant of Jaffa

Ruins of Gaza after the Great Attack, 1917

Standard presented to the regiment
who defended Gaza in the first attack

Camels transporting grain to Jerusalem, 1917

German military transport, Jerusalem 1917

The American Colony Nursing Corps, 1917

Bertha Vester in nurse's
uniform, 1917

Infantry lines North of Jerusalem
near Nebi Samwil, 1917

Turkish officer wounded in the Turks' attempt to recapture
Nebi Samwil, in the American Colony Hospital, 1917

Surrender of the Mayor of
Jerusalem with the white flag
Left: The white flag at the
entrance to the city

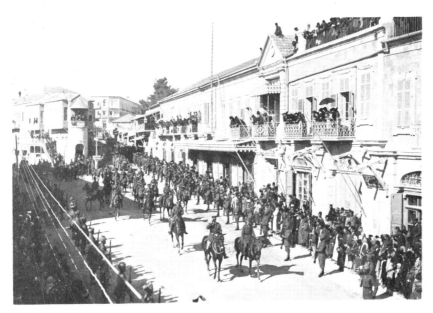

Entry of Allenby to Jerusalem

Allenby entering the Old City on foot, December 1917

Allenby's Proclamation

British military camp on Mount Scopus, 1918
with Jerusalem in the distance

Official opening of the Allenby Bridge, 1918

4th of July celebration at the American Colony, 1918;
Mrs. Spafford, Ronald Storrs and Allenby at left

The American Colony Band

Haj Amin Husseini

Anti-Zionist demonstration, 1920

Herbert Samuel arriving in Jaffa, 1920

General Allenby, Lord Balfour
and Sir Herbert Samuel

T.E. Lawrence and Abdulla

Abdulla, Samuel and Mr. & Mrs. Churchill
at Government House

The First British flag over Governement House
after the   arrival of Sir Herbert Samuel

Opening of the Hebrew University on Mount Scopus, 1925

Excavations at Ascalon by Professor John Garstang
(the first archaeological dig during the British Mandate)

The Earthquake, 1927. Total destruction of
the new "Winter Palace" in Jericho

Arabs moving away from Manshieh Quarter
(during the Riots, 1936-39)

Jews moving away from Manshieh Quarter
during the Riots

American Colony Aid Association
distributing bread, 1938

Block House near the American Colony, 1938

Search for arms, 1938

American Colony stores inside Jaffa Gate closed,
never to be opened again for business, 1948

British guards in the Bazaar

Closing Jaffa Gate to demonstrators
the day Palestine was divided,
November 29th, 1947

King David Hotel blown up by the Jews, 1946

Jewish Agency blown up by Arabs, 1948

Jewish convey of 82 cars ambushed by Arabs
at Bab-el Wad

Abdul Kadar al-Husseini in Bir Zeit

Glubb Pasha

Count Bernadotte

Arab refugees at Jericho

Aerial view of the American Colony in the thirties

Aerial view of the Old City of Jerusalem today
(Taken from American Colony direction)

CHAPTER TWENTY-FOUR

ON THE ninth of December 1917 the sun rose for the last time on the Ottoman domination of Jerusalem. It was Sunday, and the peace of Sabbath filled the air.

It had been raining but now the sky was clear and cloudless. Sunshine flooded the country that had so recently been drenched with rain. Steam was rising from the muddy roads and the trees were fresh and dripping.

In Palestine we have many such sparkling days after the first rains have washed away the accumulated dust of seven or eight months of unbroken summer, and Nature seems in tune with the joyful expectation of deliverance.

About seven that morning our doorbell rang. In those dangerous times we did not allow the door to be answered by just one person, so we trailed in a procession to the gate.

There stood Hassain Effendi al Husseini, the mayor of Jerusalem.

"Where is Mother?" he asked, meaning my mother. "I am on my way to deliver the letter of surrender to the English general, and I want her to be the first to know. I realize how eagerly you all, and especially Mother, have been looking forward to this day."

Mother was there in a moment, and we raised our voices in singing the Doxology. Hassain was a Moslem, but he had been a student at the American Colony and later a constant visitor, and he knew many of our hymns. He joined us in praise to God.

Mother warned Hassain not to go out without a white flag. One of the Colony hospital sheets was torn in two and attached to a stick, and this was the historical flag of truce which is now in the Military Museum of London.

There were several surrenders on that historic day. Before the actual arrival of the white flag of truce, crowds were going out from the city toward the position where they knew the British outposts were stationed. One of the young men from the American Colony met a complacent-looking soldier riding a pack animal. He noticed that he was unarmed and he cautioned him that as Jerusalem had not yet surrendered he had better be careful. The soldier answered that he was the mess cook and all he wanted was to buy "heggs for his hofficers."

This has been mentioned humorously as one of the surrenders.

It was the civilian crowd which first informed two privates of the 220th Battalion London Regiment, who were seeking water and had advanced to the outskirts of Jerusalem, that the Turks had retreated and they reported this information. Shortly afterward Sergeant Hurcombe and Sergeant Sedgewick of the 219th Battalion London Regiment, two of the outposts, met the mayor with the flag of truce.

It was not long before Lieutenant Colonel H. Bailey, D.S.O., Major M. D. H. Cooke, and Major W. Beck, R.A., arrived and talked with the mayor. Lieutenant Colonel Bailey, being the senior officer, reported this fact to Brigadier General C. F. Watson, C.M.G., D.S.O., commanding the 180th Brigade. Brigadier General Watson mounted an old nag, for the bridge at Kulonia had been blown up by the retreating Turks, rode as quickly as possible to reassure the mayor. Brigadier General Watson then transmitted the mayor's offer to surrender Jerusalem to Major General J. S. M. Shea, C.B., C.M.G., D.S.O., general in command of the 60th Division, who was then at Kuryet el-Enab (shortened to Enab by the ingenious Tommies). This village marks the farthest point that King Richard the Lion-Hearted reached in his advance toward Jerusalem in January 1192, and which he never saw. Allenby's army from this point went forward and completed King Richard's work.

General Shea had difficulty in crossing the muddy stream in his car, swelled by the recent rains. Hassain Effendi, with Mr. Demetri Salameh, Jerusalem's representative of Thomas Cook and Son, begged General Watson to show himself to the inhabitants because the civilian population had been looting. During the few hours between the retreat of the Turks and the entrance of the British troops there was no recognized government. The mayor and Mr. Salameh knew that if the people could see one British officer they would know that there were others not far behind.

I remember one case of looting in particular when a man who lived near the Italian Hospital, which was used for spotted typhus and other contagious diseases, appropriated some coveted mattresses. He and his whole family were blotted out by the disease he brought home with his loot.

As Frederick and I walked to the hospital that morning, not a Turk was to be seen in the streets. Everyone looked happy and hopeful. Ten o'clock arrived, every nerve was tingling with expectation, and then came a subdued shout, for people were still afraid to show their joy. "*Aju! Aju* (They've come!)!" and Brigadier General Watson was sighted escorted by Hassain Effendi, Mr. Salameh, and a crowd of followers. We were all on the balcony of the hospital, and there was not a dry eye. For us the joy of that hour was indescribable. I rushed down and kissed the general's stirrup and rushed back. I feel quite sure that he never knew who the person was who did that impulsive act.

My husband and brother-in-law then asked the brigadier to come up into the hospital and see our three prisoners of war. It would be hard to find words to describe the joy of these men at seeing their brigadier general again. Poor Roberts, in his weak mental state, upbraided the general for having left him to suffer so long. But the general soothed him with kind words.

It was only after we had given out the last meal to the sixteen hundred wounded and sick Turkish soldiers that I met Major General Sir John Shea.

John Whiting and I were summoned to the hospital in the Russian Compound by Colonel T. B. Layton, in charge of the 2d Fourth Field Ambulance. Colonel Layton wanted information about the different hospitals in the city to enable him to make his men comfortable who had been wounded in the actual taking of the last Turkish stronghold. The British troops were still in their summer clothing, without greatcoast and blankets. Until a few hours before they had been suffering from the heat of the desert and the plain. The drop in temperature as they climbed the mountains was quick and severe, and many of the men had taken cold.

I had got back as far as the old post office in front of an open space, which has since come to be known as Allenby Square, when I saw a car coming down the Jaffa Road from the west. I knew that a car could mean only British military, for there were no civilian cars in Jerusalem, and the Turks had left. There were officers in the car with red tabs on their uniforms and a good deal of gold on their caps, but these meant nothing to me. Besides, I did not care who they were or how high their station was. I was thinking about my men, and that I had no more food to give them, so I went out into the middle of the road and put out my arms. The car had to stop or run over me, so it stopped.

I got on to the running board and told the officer, whom I found was Major General Sir John Shea, divisional commander, who I was and why I had been so bold. He gave orders to his aide-de-camp to take note of what I said.

As I stood on the running board of the general's car, a crowd of people advanced toward us in the road led by Hassain Effendi al Husseini, and I introduced him to General Sir John Shea. I stood beside the car while General Shea received the letter of surrender, written by Izzat Pasha a few hours before.

In a commanding voice the general said, after reading the letter, "It is a lie, it is a lie," My knees shook, and I wondered what had roused the general. I soon found out. In the letter which the Pasha had written he said that the reason the Turkish Army had retreated was to save the holy places from destruction by British guns, and the general knew that not one English gun had been fired on Jerusalem.

The general soon followed me to the hospital, and I took him on the roof to get a view of old Jerusalem as well as the surrounding country. From there I noticed what seemed to be skirmishing on the hills north of Jerusalem very near the American Colony. I could hardly answer General Shea's questions coherently about the different sites to be seen from the roof. I was so eager to send a messenger to Mother to find out if they were safe.

Mother's answer to my note was that nine of the windows of the Colony had been smashed by bullets coming from the retreating Turkish stragglers on Mount Scopus, but that no one was hurt. She said that one of the Swedish ladies was in her bedroom when a bullet came through the window, through the dress lying on her bed which she had expected to put on, through the matterss, and into the floor. My eldest daughter and son told me later that they were so fascinated they could not leave the north window of our nursery until Mother found them there and sent them to a safer place. They described the bayonet charge which they had seen, but fortunately it was some distance away. The fighting was on the ridge of Mount Scopus, north of the city, where Titus's army had encamped before he conquered Jerusalem in A.D. 70.

That afternoon the 74th and 60th Divisions wheeled round from Nebbi Samuel to the house on Mount Scopus belonging to Sir John Gray Hill. This had been strongly held by the enemy,

and the British troops encountered stiff resistance but finally
dislodged them. Sir John Gray Hill was a member of the British
Parliament from Birkenhead, Liverpool. He had bought property
and built a house on the summit of Scopus, where he and his
family spent several months each year. Lady Gray Hill was
an artist, and often remained longer than her husband painting
in their hilltop villa. She was particularly good at catching the
atmosphere of the desert. Sir John died several years previously,
and on this fateful ninth day of December 1917 Lady Gray
Hill singed the deed of sale of her house and property on Mount
Scopus to a representative of the Hebrew University.

Very soon after General Shea left the hospital the British
senior medical officer, Colonel T. B. Layton, came and took
over the command of our four hospitals. Our men were still
frightened, and many of the Arabs threatened to jump out of
the second-story window to get away rather than be taken
prisoners. I asked Colonel Layton if he would appoint some
orderlies to help look after the men, and he said in an abrupt
manner for which he was noted, "I hold you responsible for
the men." As soon as Colonel Layton was gone I turned to
my husband and said, "What a horrid man! How can I prevent
all these men from deserting without help?"

Frederick assured me that Colonel Layton was only joking;
that he understood that no single person could prevent the
men from desertingnor did he expect it. My husband was right,
as he always was. We soon understood Colonel Layton's manner,
and our children loved him, as did one and all of the members
of the American Colony. He became and has remained one
of our trusted friends. He advised vaccinating our year-old
Frieda, but for fear she would take a dislike to him, he would
not do it himself, but brought one of his assistants.

I remember so well the next morning after meeting General
Shea. Twenty trucks arrived at the hospital laden with quantities
of food for our wounded Turks. For three years all put together
we had not seen so much food. There was OXO, Quaker Oats,
rice, beans, flour, coffee, tea, sugar, biscuits, and butter to say
nothing of bully beef and lots of other tinned food. I remember
wishing that I could take some of it home to my children.

It was like Christmas. Everyone was happy, and good will
toward men was the universal feeling.

Jerusalem was a new city. Strangers greeted and congratulated
one another. Faces we had not seen for months and years emerged

from hiding. People we had considered dead came fearlessly from concealment, their faces yellow from confinement.

It was estimated that 25,000 deserters from the Turkish Army were recorded in the Jerusalem district alone. (This number grew larger later on.) That circumstance in itself showed the sentiment of the Arab population.

Farther north the Turks were in a long series of trenches. These were taken with a rush, and the British line advanced beyond the village of Sha'afat just over the hill from the Colony. Welsh troops from the south pushed across the road east of Jerusalem leading to Jericho and thrust back Turkish reinforcements, advancing along this road to defend Jerusalem. Bad weather and stiff Turkish resistance had delayed the advance from the south. During the cold and drizzling rain of the night of the eighth and ninth of December, the 53d Division, which had been at Mar Elias, halfway to Bethlehem, came up as far as the Jerusalem railroad station. The commander's orderly knocked at the door of a nice-looking house and asked if his officer could be billeted there. The owner was a German but he spoke English fluently. It is from the landlord that I heard the following characteristic dialogue:

Orderly: "Have you place for my officer?"
German: "Certainly. Come in."
O: "What nationality are you?"
G: "German, but as an individual I like the English and your officer is welcome."
O: "NO! No, not in a German house."
G: "But we are not soldiers; we do not fight."
O: "Yes, you do, every German man, woman, child, dog, cat, and chicken are soldiers, and you all fight."

He went his way.

On December 11 the commander in chief, General Allenby, made his formal entry into Jerusalem. The great general rode on horseback as far as the Jaffa Gate. The gate had been closed for some time. Before the visit to Jerusalem of Kaiser Wilhelm II of Germany in 1898, the Turks, fearing the narrow gate would obstruct traffic, had made a breach in the old rampart wall so that carriages could enter the city. The Kaiser had entered on a white charger wearing the gorgeous white Uhlan uniform with the dazzling and burnished helmet surmounted by the German eagle, but even that was not spectacular enough for him. Whatever uniform His Majesty put on was the signal for the rest of his military entourage to copy; but as some of his suite were more imposing in stature than he was, he had made himself unique by wearing a white-and-gold kaffiyeh gathered under the spreading eagle, and over his white uniform was a white silk abayah with gold threads running through that sparkled in the sunlight. The Emperor was not only an artist in his choice of costume to impress his oriental audience, but also an actor.

How different was this solemn and dignified entrance of General Allenby, who, to do honor to his Master, walked into the Holy City as a pilhgim.

First in the procession came Colonel Barton, postmaster general of Cairo, who had hurriedly come to Jerusalem to be the first military governor.

The commander in chief, preceded by his aide-de-camp, had on his right the commander of the French detachment and on his left the commander of the Italian detachment. Following were the Italian, French, and American military attachés and a few members of the General Staff. The American military attaché was Colonel Edward Davis. Guards of honor marched in the rear.

The procession entered the Jaffa Gate, walked past the Grand New Hotel, which was our hospital, turned to the right toward Zion, and on the steps of the citadel in the shadow of the Tower of David, part of which dates from David's time, and another part which was standing at the time of Christ, the proclamation was read.

This proclamation, which was read in English, French, Arabic, Hebrew, Greek, Russian, and Italian, announced that order would be maintained and all the sacred sites of the three great religions would be carefully guarded for the full use of the worshipers—it assured the people that they might pursue their lawful business without interruption.

Throughout the ceremony no Allied flag was flown. After the short ceremony the chief notables and ecclesiastics of the different communities who were in Jerusalem were presented to General Allenby. In a photograph of this ceremony the Chief Rabbi stands beside the Grand Mufti. After the reception the commander in chief left Jerusalem by the Jaffa Gate. Outside the gate he mounted his horse and rode away. Our American Colony photographer took pictures of all. The photographs showing General Allenby leaving Jerusalem on a horse, with the city wall as a background, had difficulty in passing the censor, but it was finally released because the rampart wall at his back proved he was leaving the city, not entering.

Palestine had a so-called Christian government for the first time since the Crusaders were driven out by Saladin. As soon as the inhabitants were confident of the stability of the British occupation they expressed their gratitude for being delivered from the Ottoman yoke. Church bells rang in acknowledgment and officers were met with flowers thrown into their cars.

During the ceremony I was on the balcony of the Grand New Hotel. John Whiting touched me on my shoulder and asked whether I would mind giving my place to James McBey. Of course I minded, but I could not refuse the official artist a good place to make the sketches for his famous painting of the historical entry of General Allenby. I looked over his shoulder, and I knew I was fortunate indeed to be witnessing one of the great events in history. I realized that the whole Christian world outside of Germany and Austria was jubilant. People in the streets were crying at their deliverance. I saw a Jew embrace a Greek priest, and his tall, clerical hat went askew in the exuberance of fraternal feeling. Truly we could sing with the Psalmist, "Then were our mouths filled with laughter and our tongue with smiling . . . the Lord hath done great things for us, therefore we are glad."

I never recall this day without remembering John Finley's words:

> The earth's free nations now will bring
> Their genius to its glorying,
> And they who sat in darkness sing
> Fore'er of thee, O Allenby!

We thought then we were witnessing the triumph of the last crusade. A Christian nation had conquered Palestine!

We were still busy in the hospitals, helping to get our men off to Egypt. How different was their fate now! Instead of traveling in irontired lorries, which shook them almost beyond endurance, or on stretchers strapped either side of a camel, they were moved in ambulances and hospital trains with pillows and blankets to make them comfortable.

During those first busy days when I would be gone all day four-year-old John would stand at our garden gate craning his

neck to get a glimpse of a British soldier. At last some Tommies
were billeted at Saint George's School across the street from
our house.

One of them came over and said, "What is your name, little
boy?" Our son straightened his shoulders and answered that
his name was John. "Oh, you are a Johnny Turk, are you?"
said the Tommy. John was heartbroken. When I returned,
John told me about his encounter with the British soldier and
announced that he did not want to be called John any more.
Canon Hichens, the "cannon" the Turks had hoped to find
when they excavated in the English Cathedral, had returned
to Jerusalem as padre to the troops and was our guest. He came
to John's defense and said, "You shall be called Jock after this.
Jock is a good Scottish name and suits you!" So Jock he has
been called ever since. At present he is a captain in the American
Army, stationed at Fort Knox, Kentucky.

At once the commander in chief was faced with the peculiar
status of Jerusalem, where numerous ecclesiastical associations
demanded special rights. The inhabitants were impoverished
and half starved from the continued drain from requisitioning
by the armies and the blockade of the country. Brigadier General
G. F. Clayton, C.B., C.M.C., who was chief political officer,
was put in charge of southern Palestine and he built up a certain
measure of government for what was called "Occupied Enemy
Territory."

About April 1918 the first chief administrator of O.E.T.A.
(Occupied Enemy Territory Administration), Major General
Sir Arthur Wigram Money, K.C.B., C.S.I., arrived, and very
soon he constituted a system for administering justice, organizing
finance, and policing the country. I think it was only a few days
after the occupation that Colonel Barton was taken ill, and
Colonel Ronald Storrs, C.M.G., came as military governor of
Jerusalem. Colonel Storrs spoke Arabic fluently and was able
to converse with the populace without an interpreter, which
greatly facilitated negotiations.

Only three weeks after the surrender of Jerusalem Hassain
Effendi al Husseini was taken ill with double pneumonia. No
one had known that he had weak lungs, but in a few days he
died. His death was unexpected and unfortunate for the new
British administration because he possessed a liberal outlook,
an educated mind, and had hoped to help the new rulers whom
he welcomed. He was survived by his wife and four little sons.

The British Government honored Hassain Effendi with a military funeral. Colonel T. E. Lawrence attended in Arab costume.

Before Hassain Effendi died he had sent for me, but as I was still working in the hospital I was too late to see him alive. His wife told me that Hassain realized his serious condition and wanted me to intercede with the authorities on behalf of his wife and four small sons, who, although belonging to the powerful Hasseini family, were land poor, without any fluid income. The American Colony was able to help them at the time. Many years later, when Hassain's property was put up at auction to pay his debts to Barclay's Bank (D.C. and O), there was a duel of bidding between the Grand Mufti, Hadj Amin al Husseini, and the Zionist organization. The Mufti, also president of the Moslem Supreme Council with jurisdiction over the enormous Moslem Pius Bequests, would not let Dair Amer go to the Zionists and kept on bidding higher. It became a veritable duel, and finally the Moslem Pius Bequests paid an exorbitant price for it. This put Sitt Fatme Hassain Husseini into comfortable circumstances and enabled her to educate her four sons at Saint George's School in Jerusalem and the American University of Beirut. Dair Amer was put to good use. A modern agricultural schoolhouse was built on the hilltop and run by a progressive committee of Moslem and Christian Arabs.

Christmas 1917 was a happy one for the American Colony. Mother invited a distinguished company to partake of our Christmas dinner, which was put off until the twenty-sixth, Boxing Day. In a letter she wrote: "We had four generals and twenty other British officers to dinner."

With much planning and ingenuity we produced stuffed roast turkey with all the usual accompaniments except cranberry sauce. The proverbial plum pudding, blazing with burning brandy, was made possible, and there were Jaffa oranges. There was an abundance of friendly welcome and cheer and heartfelt gratitude for our deliverance. During dinner the band of the American Colony played, and after dinner the choir sang the "Hallelujah Chorus" we had been practicing, but, I need not add, not Jock's version.

As the evening advanced it became harder to entertain our guests. In spite of our efforts small groups of officers would form who spoke in undertones. At one minute after midnight we realized the cause of it. The guns north of us began firing, which repulsed a counterattack by the Turks. They had got back as far as Tel el Fül, which is just over the hill north of the American Colony. It was too near to be comfortable, but at dawn on December 27 the Turks were dislodged. Some of Falkenhayn's troops were among the fallen; they were conspicuous in their new uniforms and equipment. Two naval guns from the *Breslau* and the *Guben*, two German men-of-war which took refuge in Constantinople early in the war, were hauled down to Palestine. One was called "Nablus Lizzy" and the other "Jericho Jane" by the British Tommies. But they were both too late in arriving for the Turkish defense of Jerusalem.

My brother-in-law was pressed into service almost immediately. John joined the Field Intelligence under General Wyndham Deedes with the rank of captain. He had traveled all over Palestine on foot, on donkey and horseback, and by carriage. No non-Palestinian knew the country so intimately as John. His knowledge of every bypath, well, and spring of water was invaluable to General Allenby's troops in their advance north and east.

On December 29 Ramallah, twelve miles north of Jerusalem, was occupied by British troops. A modern version of Simon the tanner from Jaffa is a true story. When Jaffa was evacuated Simon, who was actually a tanner and his buxom wife with his wife's niece, a sort of foster daughter, in delicate health, came to Jerusalem. We had helped Simon for years, trying to improve his method of tanning so as to produce fine leather which could be tooled and worked up into attractive souvenirs. They arrived in Jerusalem penniless, with no hope of work. John Whiting, always resourceful, got the Turkish Military Shoemaking Department interested enough in Simon to set him up in tanning hides for military shoes at the nearest stream of water, which was Ein Senia. Later Ein Senia became no-man's land for a time, lying between British-occupied Ramallah and the Turkish lines farther north, and it was being shelled by both Turkish and British batteries.

Simon and his wife and invalid niece started walking from Ein Senia over the hills to Ramallah, where the British forces were stationed. The country they traversed was very broken and precipitous. It was not safe to travel in the daytime on roads or tracks; rain and darkness greatly increased the difficulty of their advance, and they had to dodge shells.

At last the exhausted niece could go no farther, and they left her lying unconscious in a gully. By the time they reached Ramallah there was very little life left in Simon and his fat wife. They had difficulty in persuading the outposts that they were friendly. Through an interpreter they informed the officer in command at Ramallah that they were friends of the American Colony. John Whiting went to Ramallah and brought back Simon and his wife to the Colony, where for months we nursed them back to health. Their poor bruised feet were in bad condition. A search party went to find the niece, but nothing was found except a few rags of clothing and some bones. Evidently hyenas had attacked her.

The first letters we wrote, even before permission was granted for writing, were to Mr. Loud and other kind friends who had been mindful of us in our dark hour.

A short time before the Turks retreated, to ingratiate themselves in the good graces of the Arabs, whom they had treated harshly, they announced that all political prisoners would be forgiven. Thousands of Arabs had been uprooted from their homes and sent hither and yon, mostly to Asia Minor. Among these unfortunates were an old Moslem and his wife. They were punished because their son, who was in the Turkish Army near the Suez Canal, deserted to the British. After the British occupation my husband and I heard that Hadj Ahmed and his wife, who were neighbors of the American Colony, had returned and were ill. We went to call and found Hadj Ahmed in a really serious condition. He said he would give his eyes if he could only see his son before he died. He was a prisoner of war at Sidi Bishr, near Alexandria, Egypt. He asked me to beg General Allenby to release his son, as though it was the easiest possible thing to do. I was horrified by the faith the poor man put in my ability to influence the great commander in chief and in the possibility of his seeing his son again. As luck would have it, I did meet General Allenby a few days later and I mentioned this fact. The general asked very casually if I would guarantee the young man's integrity, and I answered in the affirmative. It seemed utterly futile to consider the possibility of the son's return, and I thought no more about it.

In less than two weeks I was invited to celebrate the homecoming of the son, and the old father's gratitude was very moving. The father lived only a short time after this. It illustrated General Allenby's character and his graciousness that in the midst of leading a great campaign he had time to attend to an insignificant detail like this.

Among letters I cherish are these:

Headquarters, MHOW
Central Provinces District

MHOW C. I.
March 15th, 1922

DEAR MR. VESTER:

I have always felt that I owed both Mrs. Vester and yourself so much, not only at the time that my division took Jerusalem but subsequently, that I should like to put the fact in writing for record, should you wish, amongst your family papers. Not only did Mrs. Vester nurse the wounded British prisoners in the hospital at Jerusalem with devoted care prior to our arrival, but you yourself, at great personal risk, successfully hid three British prisoners when the Turks had decided to evacuate the town. By your action you prevented these prisoners being carried away by the Turks and you handed them over to the British on December 9th, 1917.

Further the information which you and your wife gave to me was of the greatest value to me during the time we were preparing to drive the Turks further North and East.

With my sincere thanks and best wishes
(*signed*) J. H. SHEA
Lieut. Genl.

High Commissioner for Egypt
January, 1924

Upper Nile Province
Sudan

DEAR MRS. VESTER:

I am glad to place on record my appreciation of the services to humanity rendered by Mr. Vester and yourself during the War. In devoting yourselves to the care of the wounded and sick, without distinction of creed or nationality, and in circumstances of peculiar difficulty, and even danger, I consider that you and Mr. Vester performed a task of very real value. The British wounded, among others, owe you a debt of gratitude.

Yours sincerely
(*signed*) ALLENBY,
F. M.

Mrs. Vester
   The American Colony,
      Jerusalem

CHAPTER TWENTY-FIVE

THE last of our wounded men had been dispatched to Egypt, and our responsibility at the Turkish hospitals was over. We anticipated a good long rest. However, we were not given the chance. John Whiting received a cable from Mr. Vickrey, head of the Syria and Palestine Relief, asking if he would organize the relief work in Jerualem. John asked me to take his place on the Syria and Palestine Relief Committee, because he was occupied with Field Intelligence for Allenby's army.

This was the first time Frederick and I had come face to face with our position as German subjects under the British military regime at war with Germany. I advised John that before recommending me to Mr. Vickrey, General Allenby should be consulted. The general's reply to this request was to send a member of his Intelligence Department to our house to say that Mr. Vester was going to be treated in every way as though he were an American citizen. The messenger added that there would be notices issued governing the restricted actions of German subjects, but he emphasized that Mr. Vester need not comply with any of these restrictions. And so, when General Allenby was consulted about my eligibility to supervise the relief arrangements, he gave not only his consent but his blessing.

I have mentioned in an earlier chapter that Mother gave me the benefit of her experience in organizing relief work after the Chicago Fire. I had good material to draw from in the younger group of American Colony members who had been nursing in the hospitals.

We divided Jerusalem into sections and appointed Moslem and Christian Arab and Jewish ladies to make house-to-house investigations and to report to the committee. The daughter of the Grand Mufti and a number of Moslem ladies, who for the first time in their lives were out of "purdah," did excellent work.

Mother wrote to a friend:

Bertha and fourteen others from the Colony are devoting all their time to the relief work in the clinic and in visiting the various sections of the city, going from house to house, to learn about and describe the prevailing conditions.

And in another letter:

> One of the local cinema halls was taken for the entertainment of the troops and here Jacob has given many lectures on Bible history illustrated by magic-lantern slides. This led to an extended series of talks in the outlying camps among the British and Australian troops and enabled them to appreciate the sites they would be visiting in a more intelligent and comprehensive manner.

When the personnel administering the Syria and Palestine Relief Fund were allowed to come into Palestine, Bishop and Mrs. Rennie MacInnes and many missionaries who had given years of service to Syria and Palestine were among the number. It was a marvelous reunion with former friends after nearly four years of being the only non-natives in Palestine. Bishop MacInnes had been consecrated Anglican Bishop in Jerusalem, Egypt, and the East, succeeding the late Bishop Blyth, but this was his first visit to Jerusalem after his consecration. I was put on the Executive Committee of the Relief and enjoyed the work, which was soon going with a swing.

Austrian Hospice, in the heart of the Old City, was opened as an orphanage. Mr. and Mrs. Wendell Cleland, Mr. and Mrs. Stephen Trowbridge and many others were among the workers and were kept very busy. I was asked to organize a sewing establishment for making garments for distribution. We employed eight hundred women. Sister Tilly Holmstrum and Mrs. Fred Meyres from the Colony spent the day cutting out garments and teaching the more intelligent women to help. Every garment was checked before it was sent out. After Jerusalem got its share of clothes, these garments were packed ready for the Lebanon and Syria when that part of the country was opened up by Allenby's army.

Business began to brighten, and my husband with several other men of the Colony gathered up our broken business ties and opened the American Colony stores.

Early in 1918 the Hadassah Medical Units came to Jerusalem and started relief work among the Jewish population. The name Hadassah was Queen Esther's Hebrew name—the name which her Cousin Mordecai called her. Since then medical work among the Jews of Jerusalem has grown enormously.

Infant welfare work is raising a super generation. Infants are taken care of from the cradle to the grave, nay, even before that, for prenatal work is universal and well done. Miss Henrietta Szold's work is too well known to be enumerated here. She made herself a place among the matriarchs of Israel, compared in obituaries at her death to Miriam the sister of Aaron and Moses and to Deborah. The Henrietta Szold Nurses' Training Center connected with the Hebrew University is a fitting memorial to her extensive work. I worked with Miss Szold for many years on the Social Service Association and the Woman's Council. During those early years it was still possible for Arabs, Jews, and Christians to work together on the same committee. As a matter of fact the Social Service was started by an Arab, a Jewess, and an American. Mrs. Demetri Salameh, a leading Greek Orthodox Arab, and wife of the local manager of Thomas Cook and Son; Mrs. Hoofien, a leading Jewess, and wife of the director of the Anglo-Palestine Bank; and I, started it a few days after the British occupation took place.

We asked the Syria and Palestine Relief personnel to join our efforts to clean up the city morally. Members of the American Red Cross and Hadassah Medical Units joined, and Mrs. MacInnes, wife of the Anglican Bishop, became our first president.

The foundation stone of the Hebrew University was laid several months later. Our invitation came from the Zionist Commission from Tel Aviv Jaffa. How changed is the situation of those two cities since then. At that time Jaffa was the important place and Tel Aviv was a suburb. Now Tel Aviv has swallowed Jaffa. I went with Mother, the crowd was so great that we were pushed nearer and yet nearer until finally I stood next to the speakers. I remember with what fervor Rabbi Kok spoke of their cultural rather than political aspirations.

In April 1918 Major General Sir Arthur Money, K.C.B., C.B.I., was appointed chief administrator of Occupied Enemy Territory, the O.E.T.A. He did much to improve postal facilities for civilians and introduce stable Egyptian currency which enabled commerce to revive. He also improved the old system of the dispensation of justice. Taxes were soon being paid, by which the military administration was able to hand over the management of the rich Moslem Pius Bequests to be appropriated to the needs of Moslem beneficiaries in Palestine; whereas under the Turkish regime the major part of this income had been sent to

Constantinople.

Many happy afternoons have my husband and I spent at Government House, playing tennis with General Sir Arthur Money. Government House occupied the Kaiserin Augusta Victoria Stiftung on the Mount of Olives. I was at the reopening of the Rothschild Hospital in Jerusalem when Sir Arthur Money made a speech in which he condemned the policy of creating separate institutions for different communities whether charitable or educational. The only hope for Palestine, he said, was for Christian and Moslem Arabs and Jews to co-operate in every way.

It was generally considered that Sir Arthur Money's recall soon after was connected with this attitude.

He was succeeded by General Sir Harry Watson.

Lady Watson took an active part in the revival of Palestine. She became president of the Y.W.C.A. and organized a fete in Antimus's Garden, now called Zion Square, to raise money for the Y.W.C.A. People were in the mood for having a bit of joy after four years of poverty, fear, and oppression, and it was financially successful. Frederick and I gave a moonlight picnic to Emmaus on horseback for the two daughters of Sir Harry and Lady Watson. We arranged to have supper at the Franciscan Monastery at Emmaus. On the picnic Mr. Richard Babcock became engaged to Miss Watson. The two young people lagged behind, and I had all I could do to keep John Whiting from accompanying them. He feared it was not safe for them to follow so far behind the group, but his solicitous attention was definitely not wanted. Frederick, John, and I kept within sight, but out of earshot, to protect them.

Not long after Allenby conquered the Holy City a young American came to call. Mother welcomed Lowell Thomas as though he were an old friend. He was, I believe, the first American we met after the long years of war when we had been cut off from home and friends. We had experienced so much during that time that it seemed a lifetime since we had seen people of our own race and nation. Mr. Thomas was young and handsome and full of American zest for adventure. He was in American military uniform and looked very fine in the uncomfortable stiff collar which the United States later changed for a more comfortable neckline. We took him into the family circle of the American Colony, so to speak, and there he has held an honored place ever since. His book, *With Lawrence in Arabia*, which made Colonel T. E. Lawrence a household hero in both England and America, was the result of this trip. It was in Jerusalem that Lowell Thomas met Colonel Lawrence, who was introduced to him by Colonel Ronald Storrs as the "Uncrowned King of Arabia."

The American Colony kept open house those days, and there were callers at all hours during the day and evening.

One morning Colonel Lawrence called on Mother. Mother was busy at the moment, and asked me to go up and speak to him. We had not heard much about Colonel Lawrence at that time. The war in Arabia was remote from Palestine, with the Turko-German armies between, and Lawrence's exploits had been kept a profound secret. A day or two before this I was returning from the hospital with my husband and we noticed a Bedouin coming down the steps from Fast's Hotel. Frederick said:

"Do you see that Bedouin?"

"Yes. Why?"

"He is not a Bedouin at all but an Englishman who has been among the Sherifian troops."

I thought this quite impossible, for I had never seen a European wear the Arab dress with such ease. The correct wearing of the long robe, the seamless abayah, which an Arab gathers round himself making certain folds, is difficult for a foreigner to acquire, and this, to the accustomed eye, gives him away. The Bedouin headdress, the kaffiyeh and agal, is hard to manage for a non-Bedouin, and there is an unspoken language which the Bedouin understands in the manner in which the kaffiyeh is worn. All these mannerisms were perfect in the person whom Frederick told me was an Englishman and whose name was Colonel Lawrence.

It may be that Colonel Lawrence was not pleased that Mother delayed receiving him. At all events he was curt and silent during the visit. I said something about the Bedouins, for we were on very friendly terms with the Bedouins east of the Jordan. (Had I not been initiated into the Adwan tribe as a child?) Colonel Lawrence turned his back as soon as I mentioned the word "Bedouin." I thought him rude and did not try again to create conversation. Mother soon arrived, and I left the room.

The next time I met Colonel Lawrence I found myself sitting next to him at dinner at the house of Colonel Storrs. I turned to my neighbor on the other side and conversed with him all through dinner. As I left the table with the other ladies, Colonel Lawrence turned to me and said: "We're quits," and smiled in his most engaging manner. When the men of the party joined us in the drawing room to listen to a recital of music Colonel Storrs had arranged for the entertainment of his guests, Colonel Lawrence walked straight over to the broad window sill where I was sitting. We spent the rest of the evening together, and in the intervals between music he told me about his exciting life in the most natural manner, as though it were nothing at all to lead a raid and blow up Turkish bridges, and about Auda Abu Tayi, that incredible man who was later so useful to Colonel Lawrence. At first Colonel Lawrence knew that Auda was as much a German instrument as he was a British, and Colonel Lawrence told him in feigned confidence exactly what he wanted the Germans to know. It was not until one morning when he heard something being smashed outside his tent and raised the flap to see what was going on, that he realized that Auda had really chosen his master. Auda was smashing something with a stone, and to Colonel Lawrence's question his only answer was "Don't you trust me? Am I not true to you?" Colonel Lawrence assured him that of course he trusted him, he had never doubted him. "But what are you doing?" Auda, still with his back to Colonel Lawrence and still grinding, said, "Wallah, I can't eat English food with German teeth." "So," said Colonel Lawrence, "I had to fly Auda to Egypt and get him a new set of teeth."

We saw Colonel Lawrence often after this. He was shy and reserved, and kept away from social gatherings and parties. He had suffered from conjunctivitis and his eyes were weak. One had to get behind his reserve really to know and appreciate his greatness. He rarely spoke about his achievements. We had one topic to which we could always revert in conversation, Gertrude Bell. We both admired her archaeological work, her unusual intellect, her accomplishments, and her writings. Another mutual friend was Ronald Storrs, and no conversation about him was ever dull.

Colonel Storrs, "successor of Pontius Pilate," as he liked to call himself, was military governor of Jerusalem our first Easter under the British.

The Greek Orthodox Church keeps to the old Julian calendar, which is thirteen days later than ours. However, as Easter in both calendars falls on the first Sunday after the first full moon after the twenty-first of March, it sometimes falls in a different moon from the Western Easter and maybe the same date, one or five weeks later. In 1918 the Greek Orthodox Easter fell on the fifth of May, which was that year five weeks later than Western Easter, March 31, and coincided with the Jewish Passover and Nebi Musa Procession.

The festive season had always been an anxious time for whoever was governor of Jerusalem. Colonel Storrs was desirous that the ecclesiastical differences connected with the Easter ceremonies of the many Eastern churches, which overlapped and frequently clashed in the Church of the Holy Sepulcher, should proceed with utmost tranquility. It was largely because of his personal efforts and his remarkable insight and understanding of traditions belonging to the Eastern churches that the ceremony of the Holy Fire passed off without military or police intervention inside the church. This had never happened before. There was a long tradition of riot and violence during the Turkish period of occupation, owing to the venality of the Turkish officials, who encouraged communal rivalries. Extra Turkish troops were always quartered in Jerusalem and inside the church to hold the peace which might so easily be broken by disputes over the respective rights of the various denominations using the same church at the same hour; and between Moslems, Jews, and Christians equally in flamed with religious fervor.

The new government was solicitous not to give offense and was careful in its handling of conflicting religious questions. Indian Moslem troops were guarding the Dome of the Rock and al Aksa Mosque. The commander in chief gave every possible facility to make successful the procession of Nebi Musa and the week of pilgrimage at the purported Tomb of Moses. British, French, and Italian sentries guarded the Holy Sepulcher.

Great care was taken to safeguard the Jewish pilgrimages to the Wailing Wall and the celebration of the Feast of the Passover.

One of the many improvements for which Palestine has the military government to thank was his ability to induce the Greek Orthodox clergy to remove the unsightly wall cutting off the Ikonostasis of the Church of the Nativity in Bethlehem and exposing the high altar to view from the entrance.

This beautiful basilica, founded by Constantine and rebuilt by Justinian in the sixth century, alone escaped the destruction which in the course of many wars ruined almost all the churches of that period in Jerusalem.

The old controversy between the Greek clergy and the Arab laity continued after the British occupation, and in 1921 a commission was appointed to investigate and report to the High Commissioner. It consisted of Sir Anton Bertram, M.A., K.C., chief justice of Ceylon, sometime puisne judge of the Supreme Court of Cyprus, and Mr. (later Sir) Harry Charles Luke, B.Litt., M.A., assistant governor of Jerusalem.

The breach between some of the Synod and the Patriarch made the constitution of a quorum impossible, and the Synod ceased to function. The crisis arose at a time when because of World War I the Patriarchate was temporarily insolvent. Its debts had risen to an unprecedented figure which it was unable to pay, and also unable to meet its current expenditures. All pilgrims had stopped coming, and its income from that source had ceased, and the Russian and Rumanian governments had confiscated the income-producing properties owned here by the Jerusalem Patriarch.

To supplement deficiencies in their budget, the Greek Convent had for many years made loans which paid a high rate of interest and had carried on a banking establishment.

People of all types entrusted their money to the convent. Incidentally, it gave the convent ready money for current expenses.

During World War I the convent had received no income from Russia or from pilgrims and was burdened with heavy expenses, which it met by huge borrowings. These debts it was unable to pay when peace returned because Russia confiscated its funds and property in Russia. A special moratorium was declared, which was in effect a declaration of bankruptcy.

Two Arab members of the Orthodox Community were appointed in an advisory capacity, under the chairmanship of Sir Anton Bertram, by Sir Herbert Samuel, the High Commissioner of Palestine, to make a report. The report consists of a book of three hundred and thirty-three pages of interesting material. In consequence of this exhaustive report, Sir Herbert, later Lord Samuel, promulgated an ordinance for the liquidation of the debts of the Orthodox Patriarchate by selling parts of the vast amount of land belonging to it. In this way the plots of land now occupied by the Jerusalem Y.M.C.A. and the King David Hotel were purchased from the Greek Convent.

We heard a great deal about it all at the time, because Sir Anton and Lady Bertram stopped at the Colony. It was a privilege to know them and to count them among our friends.

This commission, making it possible for the debts of the convent to be paid, did not settle the burning controversy between the clergy and laity of the Greek Orthodox Church. In

1925 Sir Anton Bertram, with the help of Mr. J. W. A. Young, was appointed to go further into the trouble. Sir Herbert Samuel in his letter to the Orthodox Patriarch wrote that he was desirous, before laying down his office as High Commissioner, "of endeavoring to find a solution to these questions, which, while preserving the essential character and the ancient dignity of the illustrious Patriarchate, will free it from disputes which have impaired its effectiveness; and I earnestly trust that in this effort I may have the support and co-operation of your Beatitude."

The second report is a book of three hundred and seventy-two pages, but as far as I know it has not brought about a better feeling between the clergy and the members of the Arab Greek Orthodox Community.

Following the advice of the Commission, the finances were supervised for years by an Englishman.

About May 1918 the American Red Cross came to Jerusalem under the able command of Colonel John H. Finley. It was a revelation to see the amount of equipment they brought. It seemed more than the whole Turkish Army had possessed. Major Lowenstein, director of Mount Sinai Hospital in New York, Major T. Waters, assistant editor of the *Christian Herald;* returning workers and missionaries; Miss Alice Jones and Mr. Edward Kelsey of the Friends' Mission in Ramallah; and others were among the personnel of the American Red Cross. I was released from my many duties connected with the relief so that I could help Colonel Finley.

To have had the privilege of knowing Colonel Finley is one of the treasured memories of my life. When he came to Palestine as Red Cross commissioner for the Near East it was on a mission that appealed deeply to every part of his being. The vision then dawning of a better order in the Near East, the belief that the United States might contribute to it, and the fact that the British cause was represented by such gifted men as Allenby, Lawrence, and Storrs, gave the great undertaking an atmosphere of hope. He entered Jerusalem as Allenby had, on foot, as a pilgrim.

Colonel Finley knew the Bible so well that his present errand was almost to repeat, in a modern way, the experience of a medieval pilgrim beholding sacred places long imagined. He walked the traditional length of Palestine from Dan to Beersheba, only he reversed the traditional journey, entering Dan only a few hours after its capture by the advancing British Army.

From his experiences in the Holy Land would come his book, *A Pilgrim in Palestine*. When he returned to New York it would be as associate editor, editor, and editor emeritus of the New York *Times* (1921-40).

Many years later, when General Allenby came to Jerusalem for the opening of the magnificent Y.M.C.A., he said to me, "In retracing my paths again I miss that great compatriot of yours, Colonel Finley—a great man!"

Colonel Finley took over the old Bergheim House as Red Cross Headquarters and some of the buildings in the Russian Compound for laboratories, workrooms, and living quarters for personnel. The whole place buzzed with activity. It was a new experience for Jerusalem to witness American efficiency, speed, and accomplishment.

It had been the custom of the American Colony to give a garden party on the Fourth of July. This had to be suspended during the war years. We found that Colonel Finley had decided to have the official opening of the Red Cross Headquarters on the same historic date, so we compromised by putting off our reception to a later time.

We sent an invitation to the commander in chief through the military governor, and Colonel Storrs wrote to say that General Allenby had accepted. No flags flew in Palestine except the Red Cross flags over hospitals, but the Red Cross Headquarters was beautifully decorated with the English and United States flags entwined. Colonel Finley made one of his choice speeches in which he spoke about this being Independence Day, the birthday of the Daughter of England, which had cost some severe pangs, and which we now celebrate as "Interdependence Day." General Allenby made a short but gracious response. The guests then all proceeded to the American Colony, where refreshments were served. The children of the Colony performed a drill in fancy dress, which received enthusiastic applause. Members of the Syria and Palestine Relief, American Red Cross, and Hadassah Medical Units were invited, besides many Arab and Jewish friends.

Colonel Storrs invited Frederick and me to bring our children to see the unfolding of the Saint George's flag in the small chapel of Saint George in the Anglican Cathedral. General Allenby and Bishop and Mrs. MacInnes were present, but they had not been allowed to bring their family to Jerusalem. We stood in a group in the close after the ceremony and Colonel

Storrs, with his usual humor, said to the commander in chief, pointing to our children, that these were the most obstreperous inhabitants of Jerusalem, and that he had more trouble in keeping them in order than any others. General Allenby was holding his huge walking stick, and he handed this to Colonel Storrs with a resounding laugh, saying, "Use this on them." I shall never forget the look of fear on the face of my four-year-old Jock. He had seen the Turkish soldiers being beaten and thought this was what was going to happen to him; however, he was soon consoled.

It was that day, when General Allenby saw our robust children, that he facilitated the MacInnes children's reunion with their parents in Jerusalem.

Less than a week after this happy Fourth of July my sense of felicity had a brief interruption. German nationals had few restrictions, but suddenly the British policy changed, and we heard that all German subjects were to be sent to Helwan on the Nile. Frederick and I wondered what our fate would be.

On July 10 we gave a dinner to Colonel Finley. I have forgotten who the other guests were, but our table held twelve and was full to capacity. I remember the majority were British officers, and that there were very few ladies—ladies were scarce articles in Jerusalem in those days. While we were at dinner an official envelope was brought me by messenger. I opened it and read a printed slip:

A notice is being sent today to German. Austrian, and Bulgarian subjects to prepare themselves for evacuation from Palestine.
This intimation will not be forwarded to you as it is not the intention of the authorities to send you away, unless you are desirous of accompanying the members of your Community to their internment camp in Egypt.
(*Signed*) R. Storrs, Colonel,
Military Governor.

Colonel Finley was the only person to sense something was wrong, and quietly asked what was the matter and could he help. I handed him the slip of paper under the table so that no one else would be attracted. He read it and understood it as I had: it inferred that while I was exempted because I was an American citizen, my husband would have to go.

Engaged, apparently, merely in dinner-table chatter, Colonel Finley and I planned. He offered to see the commander in chief, Allenby, and carry to him my request that if possible he should give permission for the children to remain with Mother, since I was determined to follow my husband into internment. Then I turned back to my other guests, and how I managed to continue conversation with them I shall never know, but I did. After fruit, I led the ladies into the laibrary for coffee, and as soon as they were engrossed in conversation I went to the dining-room door and beckoned to Frederick. He left the table and came to me. I showed him the frightening order.

Frederick smiled and took me in his arms. "I got one too," he said, "but as it came by a different messenger, and just as we were sitting down to dinner, I thought it best not to disturb you."

It would be hard to describe my relief and our gratitude at learning Colonel Storrs's message had been merely a form and means of exemption. I believe we were the only people in Jerusalem who were so exempted.

Colonel Storrs became Uncle Ronald to our six children. Many times I returned from work in the hospital to find him sitting on the nursery floor with all the children clustered around him while he read aloud to them *Alice in Wonderland* or some other of the children's classics.

Major Theodore Waters, assistant editor of the *Christian Herald* and major in the Red Cross contingent under Colonel Finley, had brought a request from Dr. Koenig that the American Colony should conduct some work in Jerusalen which the *Christian Herald* undertook to support. After debate and many consultations the consensus of opinion was that the most urgent need was for an orphanage in which to house the small neglected children wandering the streets.

Major Waters left five thousand dollars in the bank to enable us to get this started and then left Palestine. Until 1922, when my husband and I went to the United States, the American Colony conducted this orphanage in the name of the *Christian Herald*. Our friend Dr. Koenig had died and frequent changes in the editorship made the continuance of this undertaking difficult. One of the little Arab girls in the orphanage had belonged to a wealthy family before the war, but she was in a pitiable condition. We had found the mother with two small daughters nearly starved. Little Asma had a distended abdomen from starvation. She also had scald head, or favus. We did everything we could to cure the head, but to no avail. One day the mother said that if she only had ten shillings she would cure the scald head, using the Arabic way. I gave her ten shillings, and she took her little daughter away.

After some days the doctor who attended the orphanage asked where Asma was and I told him what I had done. He said if only there was an X ray in Jerusalem we could cure Asma's head as easily and painlessly as having her picture taken. Then he asked me if I knew what the "Arabic way" was. When I said I did not, he answered, "I thought as much." He explained that after cutting the hair short the remaining hair was covered with a cotton cap made fast with pitch. After several applications, making sure that every hair was stuck fast to the cap by repeated applications of pitch, several women took hold of the child and, while she was held tight, the cap was pulled off, hair and all. It was really scalping. It was efficacious, for instinct tells them that the disease is in the roots of the hair, but painfully cruel and crude.

I was so horrified to think of Asma's suffering and filled with remorse for my part in it that I made a solemn vow to collect money to buy an X-ray apparatus for Jerusalem. Through the generosity of Mr. Frederick Loesch, a prominent Chicago lawyer who came to Jerusalem on a cruise about this time and heard us tell about the need, he and some of his friends provided the necessary money to buy the latest model in X ray with a view to curing scald head, free of charge, for the poor of Palestine.

The American Colony had no hospital under its care at the time, so the X-ray machine was placed in Government Hospital under British supervision, where we felt it would do the most good.

After I was relieved from the management of the workrooms, we tried to get away to rest, but it was impossible to venture far from Jerusalem; war was still in progress. We rented a house on the Plain of Rephaim, between Jerusalem and Bethlehem, where David fought the Philistines.

The house stood alone on the plain which has since been covered with houses belonging to the better Arab class. It had large grounds with huge eucalyptus trees. At this time the whole plain was covered as far as one could see with the camps of the Australian light-horse cavalry.

We followed with keen interest the advance of Allenby's forces north and east. My brother-in-law was busy working with the largescale maps made from the survey of Palestine by the Palestine Exploration Fund. The fieldwork was done in the 1870s by Lieutenant, later Lord, Kitchener. John's work extended eastward into the uncharted desert through which he had traveled and it was his duty to bring these maps up to date from a military standpoint. This push eastward necessitated the minutest information about every source of water in that part of the country. Every spring, well, or cistern was to be marked with the amount of water available. Roads and paths and the strength of bridges were to be noted, also how to bypass them if the bridges happened to be blown up. Another of John's duties was to translate between the Bedouins who came from across the Jordan and the British officers. He could speak and understand several dialects of Arabic, and to the untrained ear they sound almost like a different language. As interpreter John was often in attendance upon the commander in chief.

On one occasion a number of sheiks came from Moab to get their final briefing. As they waited to meet General Allenby, John noticed that the sheiks were nervous. They made John promise that he would point out the "General Inglezi" (English general) to them, for fear they would make an error in precedent. But when General Allenby came forward, towering above his entire staff which followed him, his magnificent stature and physique, his amiable and friendly manner, made the Bedouin's ideal of what a general should be. "*Wallah! The General Inglezi jaddah* (The English general is a real man)," they said. After a careful briefing they were told to meet at a precise spot on the fourth day to get the final orders.

The headman among the group took John's hand in his and turned his finger down into the palm of his hand, then the second, third, and fourth. As each finger was pressed down he said, "We meet not on this day, or this or this, but on this, the fourth day." John assured him that he was correct, but the sheik was not satisfied until John had taken General Allenby's hand in his and while translating what the sheik said, turned four of the General's fingers into his palm.

The Turks made stubborn resistance across the defile of Ein Farrah, where we had spent many happy days picnicking. The boldness of the country in this vicinity made the advance of the cavalry difficult. In places they could go only single file. The Good Samaritan's Inn, halfway to Jericho, and Nebi Musa were taken sometime in February, gaining the north end of the Dead

Sea, and opened up communications with the northern operations of the Sherifian army. Djemal Pasha had made a naval base on the north end of the Dead Sea with workshops. The landing place was afterward used to advantage when the Sherifian army was near Karak.

There were heavy rains during March, and the River Jordan was in flood, but a raid upon the enemy's communications in Moab was considered. It was the Hedjaz Railroad that was feeding the Turkish forces which must be destroyed. This was the first combined action between Allenby's troops and the Sherifian forces. It was under the command of General Sir John Shea. The Jordan was unfordable because of so much flood water, and the bridge had been blown up, so a pontoon bridge was thrown across. The advance was further hindered by a feud which was being waged between the Moslem Circassians and the Christian Arabs of El Fuhais near Es Salt. There are several villages east of the Jordan inhabited by Circassians who, in the reign of Sultan Abdul-Hamid, gave land to several thousands of them who settled in the mountains of Moab. They are industrious, and their villages are a contrast in cleanliness to the Arab villages, but there is continual strife between these fair-haired, blue-eyed Caucasian Moslem Circassians and their Christian Arab neighbors. One of these feuds was in progress at this time.

The raid on Es Salt and Amman was successful but met with difficulties. The situation in Es Salt became complicated owing to Turkish reinforcements having arrived, but before the British withdrew the whole of the captured ammunition was blown up.

The civilian population had welcomed the British troops, and the fear of Turkish revenge prompted thousands of refugees to follow the British troops into Palestine.

Colonel T. B. Layton told us about this raid and the manifold difficulties encountered, in great part owing to the bad weather. He brought many wounded back to Jerusalem.

As Colonel Layton was leaving Es Salt he saw two small children, a boy and a girl of about four an two years old, sitting under an olive tree by the side of the road. He looked around to find some person to whom the children belonged. Finding no one, he imagined that they had been abandoned, so he picked them up and brought them in his car to Jerusalem. I received them with a note from Colonel Layton: "Herewith two children picked up by the side of the road in Wad es Shaib." We kept the children. Finally the mother arrived. She had been one of our needle-lace workers, who had fled to Moab with her two children in the hope of finding more food there. When she realized that the civilians were leaving Es Salt, she had carried her two children out of the city, and placing them under an olive tree, had gone back for the baby. It was while she was gone that Colonel Layton found the two children abandoned, as he thought. The mother said, "I knew the children would be brought to the American Colony; that is why I have come straight here."

The Anzac troops were stationed for some time in the Jordan Valley. As spring advanced, the heat of the subtropical valley became hard to bear, and the Australians got restless. The Rev. Stacy Waddy, later canon of Saint George's Cathedral in Jerusalem and archdeacon of Palestine, was padre to the Australian soldiers at the time. In a lecture he told us about their hardships and about one of the ways in which the troops amused themselves. They would stage a fight between a gray scorpion, which is considered more dangerous than the black scorpion of more temperate regions and the black hairy tarantula. Betting would be brisk until one or the other succumbed. The scorpion was at a disadvantage because he had to manipulate his tail to sting while the tarantula worked faster. Frequently the spider won, only to die later.

In September 1918 the commander in chief made the historic dash which caught the major part of the Turkish Army in and around Nazareth and in the narrow defile leading to the Jordan Valley. The movements of British troops had been kept so secret, so perfectly concealed in orange and olive groves near Ludd and Ramleh, that German Intelligence reported "nothing unusual to report." A bold plan had been conceived and carried out for deceiving the enemy by leaving dummy horses at the deserted camps in the Jordan Valley, and the enemy was completely taken by surprise. Marshal Liman von Sanders Pasha only just escaped in his pajamas from Nazareth. We were told that the German deaconesses held up the British officer with polite conversation while the marshal left by the back door.

The Australians came through the historic defile at Megiddo and put the Turks to flight. The commander in chief returned to his headquarters saying, "I tell you it is not only a victory, it is a rout." This victory at Megiddo is the reason the commander in chief chose the title "Lord of Felixstowe and Megiddo" when he was made a peer.

The terrorism we had feared from the retreating Turkish Army was later perpetrated on the unfortunate inhabitants of the country east of the Jordan and the Hauran, where they made an example of several villages. Women and children were butchered in revolting circumstances. The Arabs, instead of being overawed and terrorized into subjection by this, were justly incensed at this Turkish outrage, and fought with greater courage.

After the complete rout at Samaria and Galilee the advance into Damascus was rapid. Colonel Lawrence with the Sherifian forces played an important part in this campaign.

Our next Chief Administrator was General Sir Louis Bols, who later was governor of Bermuda.

To a certain extent the Arabs had confidence in the military administration, which had done its best to carry out the Hague Convention and had tried to influence the Zionist Commission to fall in with General Allenby's proclamation, but the Zionist Commission was not in a conciliatory mood. It enjoyed strong support in England and from the Zionists in the United States and it would not compromise.

By this time there had been two serious outbreaks of violent anti-Zionist antagonism.

In 1920 forty-seven Jews were killed and one hundred and forty-six wounded. Forty-eight Arabs were also killed, but mostly in the course of quelling the disturbance. A delegation of women went to headquarters of O.E.T.A. (Occupied Enemy Territory Administration) and demanded that justice be done to the Arabs. I was asked to join the procession, but I refused, because the American Colony had never taken part in any political controversy. Anti-Zionist riots continued and brought matters to a head. General Sir Louis Bols wrote to general headquarters in Cairo stating that he could not allocate the blame to any section of the community or to individuals while their case was still *sub judice*, but he stated in no uncertain terms that when the strain came the Zionist Commission adopted a hostile and critical attitude. General Bols warned headquarters that this state of affairs could not continue without grave danger to the public peace. It was no use saying to the Moslem and Christian elements of the population, who comprised 90 per cent, that the *status quo* at the time of the entrance of General Allenby was being kept. He recommended in the interests of peace and development, and even for the Zionists themselves, that the

Zionist Commission be abolished. As far as I know this was never published. The British Cabinet was not in accord with General Bols and instead of the Zionist Commission it was the military administration that was abolished. Their answer to his suggestion was to install in Palestine a civil administration with a Jewish High Commissioner.

Finding himself summarily superseded, Sir Louis Bols wished to leave at once, but he was asked to remain until Sir Herbert Samuel, the new High Commissioner, arrived. True to the best British tradition, no resentment was manifest.

When the formalities of harding the office over to Sir Herbert Samuel were completed, Sir Louis Bols, as a joke to accord with military practice, asked Sir Herbert if he would mind signing a receipt for Palestine.

On a sheet of Government House notepaper Sir Louis had written in his own hand: "Received from Major General Sir Louis Bols one Palestine complete." Sir Herbert smilingly agreed, signed, and left the room.

Later an aide-de-camp returned, asking if Sir Herbert might have the receipt back for a moment, as he wished to add something to his signature.

He had originally signed only "Herbert Samuel," but when returned the signature bore the addition of the letters "E. & O.E." to accord with civil practice.

Sir Louis Bols's son, Major General Eric Bols, kindly explained to me what this meant; the British business abbreviation for "errors and omissions excepted."

A number of British officials resigned their positions rather than remain under the new civil regime. Among these was Colonel Popham, assistant governor of Jerusalem.

Dr. Glazebrook's return to Jerusalem as American Consul was opportune for the American Colony. A custodian for enemy property had been appointed. He tried to include all the property belonging to the American Colony under this category, because it was registered in Frederick's name, as representing the American Colony, and Frederick was still a German subject. It was Dr. Glazebrook's return to Jerusalem and his certifying that Frederick had wanted to have the property put in the name of an American member, which Dr. Glazebrook had opposed, knowing that Frederick could still protect it, which frustrated the custodian's plan to get hold of it.

Dr. Glazebrook remained only a short time in Palestine and

Mother suggested that the American Colony give a garden party in his honor. Sir Louis Bols was also leaving Palestine. This was the end of O.E.T.A.; Palestine was to have a civil administration and Sir Herbert Samuel was to be our first High Commissioner. Mother asked permission to give the garden party jointly in honor of Palestine's last Chief Administrator, Sir Louis Bols, and the United States Consul Dr. Glazebrook. About five hundred people attended. Before noon of that day Mr. Burton Holmes, the renowned travelogue lecturer, called on Mother, and she promptly invited him to the party. Mr. Burton Holmes asked permission to bring his photographer and take a film of the gathering. Permission was granted by Government House and the United States Consulate.

This film shows the Greek Orthodox Patriarch and other ecclesiastical dignitaries sitting with the guests enjoying the music by the American Colony band and drills performed by the children. Camil Effendi al Husseini, the Grand Mufti, and Mrs. Norman Bentwich, wife of the Jewish Attorney General, are seen enjoying a good joke together, and Sir Ronald Storrs and Mrs. Ragib Bey Nashashebie, wife of Jerusalem's mayor, are having a confidential conversation. So we have a record of that unique gathering when British officials and civilians, with Jews and Arabs, mingled and had a good time.

Jacob wrote in a letter:

On Sunday, November 14, a service of Thanksgiving was held in the Collegiate Church of Saint George for the glorious and decisive victory of the Allies, and the termination of the war. All the Eastern Christian churches were represented by their highest ecclesiastics. Both the Grand Mufti of Jerusalem and Grand Rabbi were in the Cathedral.

And Mother wrote:

Our children, some of whom remember nothing but the war, now had the time of their life. They gathered all the bells and tin cans they could find, stripping our ten camels of their bells and making festoons of these, carried them between them running all round the house, whistling and making the greatest noise they could. They lit a bonfire and had great fun out of that. Our band went out and serenaded the Chief Administrator and Governor Storrs. On every side of Jerusalem the soldiers manifested their joy by sending up rockets and starting bonfires, red lights, etc. It was impossible to have a delirium of joy here, except inwardly, for the means available were most limited.

CHAPTER TWENTY-SIX

Not long after the end of World War I rumors began that a German Consul was returning to Palestine. It was evident that we would have to do something about my husband's nationality. Frederick felt he could no longer ask for German protection when he had failed to stand on the German side in the war. Ever since that day at the Probst's house, when Frederick made his declaration against the German invasion of Belgium, we had talked of becoming American citizens if we survived the war.

With this intention in mind, we left for the United States in April 1922, taking with us our three elder children, Anna Grace, Horatio, and Tanetta. Our plan was that when we were settled we would have the three younger children, Jock, Louise, and Frieda, brought over to us by their Swedish nurse, who was a member of the Colony. Meantime they would stay in Jerusalem with Mother and Sister Grace.

Mother came to the railway station to see us off, and it happened that a regiment of soldiers was leaving for Egypt and the military band played "The End of a Perfect Day." The plaintive strains were appropriate, for our going to the United States was the end of a chapter in our lives.

We had many letters that we hoped would speed Frederick's naturalization plans. Our friends among the British officials were eager to help us succeed. The Chief Secretary, Sir Wyndham Deedes, who, under Lord Allenby, was head of the Intelligence Department and knew more about Frederick's case than anyone else, sent the accompanying statement with a covering letter for us to use in case of need:

I clearly recollect the case of Mr. Vester which, together with the cases of the other Germans whom we found in Jerusalem when we occupied the city, it was my duty, as head of the Political Intelligence Department of the Egyptian Expeditionary Force, to deal with. We sent all the Germans in Jerusalem down to Egypt. The only exception, as far as I can remember, was Mr. Vester. His case was considered from the beginning to be on a different footing to that of other Germans.

First, by reason of his being the husband of Mrs. Vester, an American subject.

Second, by reason of the fact that he was one of the members of the American Colony and was held in high esteem by all who knew him.

And third, because it was publicly known that his sympathies, in the question of the war, were with the Allies and contrary to the policy and actions of Germany.

Finally, he, together with his wife and other members of the American Colony, had shown repeated kindness to British prisoners of war at considerable personal risk before the occupation.

Mr. Vester was never treated therefore other than as an Allied subject and so he has continued to be regarded. I renewed my acquaintance with Mr. Vester while I was Chief Secretary to the Palestine Administration and I have never had any doubt that the exceptional treatment meted out to him during the war was fully warranted both by reason of his personal character and of the general esteem in which he was held by branches of the community in Jerusalem.

(*signed*) WYNDHAM DEEDES.
Colonel Reserve of Officers

The following is an extract from a letter sent to us by Major General Sir Arthur Money:

Levington Hall
Ipswich

During the operations of the British Expeditionary Force which invaded Palestine from Egypt, Mr. and Mrs. Vester of the American Colony in Jerusalem devoted themselves to the care of the British soldiers wounded and taken as prisoners to Jerusalem by the Germans and Turks. Their care and devotion were undoubtedly responsible for saving the lives of many British wounded, and for ameliorating the condition of many more.

This action tended to make Mr. Vester unpopular amongst his German compatriots. I heard on all sides of their good work when I became Chief Administrator of Palestine after the capture of Jerusalem.

(*signed*) A. W. MONEY.
Major General
(Retired)

We went to Egypt by the newly constructed military railroad. Every mile of the road through the desert was interesting to us. It had been built by Allenby's engineers, and we had followed its progress with anxiety, knowing that our deliverance depended on its completion. We crossed the Mediterranean in the *Esperia*, built to accommodate and gratify the rich Egyptian clientele who traveled year by year to Monte Carlo and the Riviera. The lounge was all gilt and glitter but without one comfortable chair. We landed in Venice, then crossed Italy to Rome and Naples, where we caught the *Patria* of the old Fabre Line.

At last the New York skyline came into view. I saw the Statue of Liberty. My husband stood beside me. We were tremendously moved. We had at last come to the "Land of the Free" and the "Home of the Brave." What did it hold for us?

To make this break in our lives and cross the Atlantic had necessitated much planning. We would have to support ourselves while we were in the United States. We considered that a branch of our store in New York might be a good investment.

Mr. and Mrs. James Morgan were good friends. We had met them in Jerusalem. Mr. Morgan was editor of the Boston *Globe*, and they lived in Lynn, Massachusetts. We thought while we were being initiated into the American methods and mode of life, and while deciding how and where to start business, that we could not do better than live near the Morgans. They rented a furnished cottage for us in Lynn and supplemented what was lacking. Even the supper was on the table when we arrived, and we were introduced to Boston baked beans on that first evening.

Next morning I looked around for the household implements I was accustomed to having our servants use in Jerusalem. I found a black mop which I washed before using it on the floor. Later, I found it was neither dirty nor greasy, but was what people use on a parquet floor in the United States. I had no idea how to use an electric vacuum cleaner. I was frightened of a gas stove. I had heard how prevalent fires were in wooden houses. Our houses in Jerusalem are built solidly of stone, so that fires are not a menace. I telephoned and confessed my difficulties and fears to Mrs. Morgan; I can still hear her laugh.

That afternoon I was sitting on the porch, quite exhausted with the unsuccessful efforts of my first day of housework in the United States, when a car stopped at our gate and its driver got out, a lady wearing a stylish hat with a veil, a neat suit, and black kid gloves.

Who could this caller be? I extended a hand in welcome as she said, "Mrs. Morgan told me you were looking for someone to help you with the housework." I have forgotten what I said, but I know what I thought. How could I ask this superior person to work? But Mrs. Ladrie adopted us and became our friend and helper.

When necessity called, her husband proved a useful part of the family. There was nothing Mr. Ladrie could not turn his hand to. He took us sightseeing in their car to Salem to see the House of Seven Gables and to Revere Beach. He drove for us on an extended tour through the White Mountains. The New England countryside was beautiful in summer. The abundance of water, trees, and green foliage was manna to eyes accustomed to the parched Palestinian summer landscape.

Before we left Jerusalem the Colony had bought all but two parts comprising several shares each in the "Big House" as we called the main building of the American Colony at Sheik Jerah. In a preceding chapter I have explained that property administered under Sharia law is divided into twenty-four carats or shares. The remaining few belonged to Hadj Amin al Husseini and his brother.

We had no money at the time to enable us to buy up the shares, and the threat of division was real and urgent. We hoped on our trip to the United States to be able to raise a loan on the property from some of our friends. In response to several letters, the most promising was one from Mrs. Chester A. Congdon of Duluth, Minnesota. This necessitated Frederick and me taking the Great Lakes trip, and we enjoyed every minute of it.

The first question her lawyer asked us when we arrived in Duluth was what we had to show that we represented the American Colony. Frederick and I looked at each other in dismay. We did not have even a scrap of paper to identify us. We had felt so much a part of the Colony that it never occurred to us that we would need identification. The conference lasted a short time. Evidently Mrs. Congdon, her son, and their lawyer were convinced of our integrity, for they loaned us the required sum with moderate interest, to be paid back at the first possible moment. Our gratitude was unbounded. We wanted the Colony to know this good news at once, so we cabled "Thirty thousand, thank God." In Jerusalem, the Colony members were being pressed by Hadj Amin and his brother. They were increasing their threats to bring the Colony to terms. Mother, Brother Jacob, and John Whiting felt that the other members of the Colony should know about these difficulties and they called a meeting to explain them and to pray that God would facilitate our efforts to obtain the necessary loan. While the meeting was in session our telegram was handed to John Whiting. He was so moved that he felt faint. Jacob, thinking it was bad news, took the telegram and read it aloud to the assembly. All were in tears. We all believed in prayer, but it is not often that an answer comes so promptly.

We began business in a small way in New York, and one of

the young men from the Colony was put in charge. This developed into a branch of the American Colony stores in New York.

Our next most pressing duty was to go to Washington and deliver Lord Northcliffe's letter of introduction to Mr. Charles Evans Hughes, then Secretary of State, and ascertain his idea about Frederick's naturalization. While we were gone, Miss Mattoon, who conducted a girls' camp on Lake Winnepesaukee, invited Anna Grace and Tanetta to spend the time at her camp. She was a friend of American Consul and Mrs. W. Coffin, who were in Jerusalem, and she had met us at their home. Horatio went as counselor to a boys' camp in the vicinity, and they all had a marvelous time. When we returned to Jerusalem they were continually asked to sing American camp songs.

Mr. Hughes received us in his office in the State Department in Washington. He was interested in our story, but explained that to have Frederick gain United States citizenship by special act of Congress constituted a colossal transaction with endless red tape. It might arouse opposition because of creating a precedent. We had not|expected much, so we were neither cast down nor disappointed. We planned to remain in the United States for the spesified time it took for Frederick to become a naturalized citizen.

We returned to Lynn to find a cable from my sister Grace informing us that Mother had had a stroke of apoplexy and was asking for us continually. The doctor felt that her life depended upon our return. Under such conditions we could not refuse. Mother had been through so much in her life, she had been magnificently brave. Now she was old and sick and needed us. To allow selfish desires or wants to influence us was unthinkable. We gave up all plans for Frederick's naturalization to hurry back to Jerusalem. After the arrival of our cable, informing Mother that we were returning, she rallied remarkably.

On our way back to Palestine we passed through Paris. I thought it would please Mother if I called on her friend and schoolmate Mme. Ribot. M. Ribot was Prime Minister of France at the time. I wrote a note, and very soon a special messenger came to the hotel from Gare d'Orsay with an invitation from Mme. Ribot asking me to call and she sent her car and chauffeur. She was still beautiful, as Mother always said she was. She had not seen Mother since the sad days after the shipwreck, when Mother was brokenhearted over the loss of her children and

Mme. Ribot had been so very kind to her. She looked at me critically, trying to find traces of Mother in my looks, but she was too kind to disappoint me.

She spoke about their schooldays; about the Bible readings and discussions; she said Mother had given her a knowledge of and a love for the Bible which had stayed with her throughout her life.

We were distressed to see the change in Mother since we had left Jerusalem hardly seven months before.

Although Mother's mind was as clear as ever she was unable to walk. Her joy at seeing us, especially the children, was enough reward for any sacrifice we might have made. We never regretted our decision, although, as it worked out, it made many more obstacles to overcome in our course and difficulties to surmount in the years to come. Mother failed from day to day, until on April 17, 1923, the end came quietly and peacefully. It was like a candle flickering and finally going out. It was strange that during the last days of her life she spoke Norwegian.

We were determined that the only note sounded at her funeral should be one of praise for a useful life, which had been a blessing to many. There must be no mourning. There could be no regrets for such a life. Letters and telegrams poured in from all over the world. The whole of Jerusalem was stirred, from the High Commissioner to the lowliest and humblest of the inhabitants. Jerusalem had lost a real mother and hundreds attended her funeral. Our friend, Dr. A. C. Harte, general secretary of the Y.M.C.A., conducted the funeral service, and the son of Father's and Mother's old friends in Chicago, Mr. E. W. Blatchford, a man beloved in Jerusalem, read a beautiful prayer. I remember these words:

> . . . life is eternal and love is immortal;
> And death is only a horizon;
> And a horizon is nothing,
> Save the limit of our sight!

CHAPTER TWENTY-SEVEN

IT WAS in the early days of the British occupation that the Italian Consul's wife and I went to tea with the family of Aref Pasha ed Dajani at his residence on Mount Zion. As we passed my husband's office we stopped, and Frederick asked if we would like to see Lord Northcliffe, proprietor of England's largest newspaper. We said we would, so we waited, and soon Sir Ronald Storrs and Lord Northcliffe drove past. Sir Ronald had been showing him the sites of the old city. When I got home I found Lord Northcliffe's card. I was disappointed to have missed this monarch of journalism. In a short time a telephone message from Government House informed me that Lord Northcliffe would call on me the next afternoon, so I invited him to tea. I had the tea table ready in the library, but to my dismay he said he never took tea, and asked for a whisky and soda. I had to confess that I had neither in the house—a bad beginning, I thought.

Lord Northcliffe was a large, portly man with an unhealthy complexion. He was nervous and spoke jerkily and abruptly. He said sternly, "I was here yesterday." "Yes," I replied, "I found your card, and I was very sorry to miss you, but you can't guess what I was doing." And I confessed that I had been standing on my tiptoes trying to get a glimpse of him. This amused him and put him in a good humor. We discussed conditions since the British occupation; he was shocked that England was forcing an alien population on the Arabs of Palestine. We discussed my husband's ambiguous position, and I told Lord Northcliffe about the stand he had taken in the late war. I told him that our plan was to go to the United States so that Frederick could become a naturalized citizen. He was interested and said that in his estimation, because of the assistance Frederick had rendered the Allied cause during the war, he should be created an American citizen by a special act of Congress. It was then that he gave us a letter to Mr. Charles Evans Hughes, Secretary of State, asking him to assist us in this matter.

When Lord Northcliffe was due to arrive, Jerusalem was

excited because of the exposé in the London *Daily News* of the
Protocols of the Elders of Zion. Its authorship had been considered Jewish and the Jews were very angry about it. During
the exodus of Russian refugees through Constantinople the
manuscript came into the possession of Mr. Robert Graves,
correspondent for Lord Northcliffe's paper in Istanbul. It was
a bit of good fortune to come by a scoop of such magnitude.
It rocked the American and British press with comment. Here
was proof that the atrocious document, attributed to Jewish
authorship, was nothing of the sort, but written by a Russian.
Of course at the time of the disclosure Lord Northcliffe had
not exposed it for any political purpose, but because it was a
scoop, to use newspaper slang, which he had succeeded in getting
before his rivals.

The repercussion to this discovery when Lord Northcliffe's
visit was made known in Jerusalem was that the Jews announced
their intention to erect a triumphal arch to do him honor and
the Arabs proclaimed that if the Jews put up a triumphal arch,
then they would organize a counterdemonstration. It was an
anxious time for the government, and it was decided that Lord
Northcliffe had better leave the train bringing him from Egypt
at Lydda, so that his entrance could be kept secret. A captain
went to meet Lord Northcliffe accompanied by two armored
cars, one of which was disabled on the way.

Lord Northcliffe told me that at first he had been flattered
because the Palestine Government thought him important
enough to send two armored cars to escort him to Jerusalem.
He chuckled and added, "I thought that was the way I ought
to be treated." Then, he reflected, he was not quite so sure,
so he asked the captain why an armored car had been sent to
meet him. "Well, you see, sir," said the captain, "on account
of your exposé of the origin of the Protocols of the Elders of
Zion, the Jews were going to put up a triumphal arch to welcome
you and the Arabs threatened a counterdemonstration."

"So that's it," said Lord Northcliffe. "I shall let them know
I have no favorites and I don't approve of pursuing a policy
in Palestine which passes on to the British taxpayer the cost
of an armored car or two to protect a person in Palestine."
And he did let them know.

Sir Ronald Storrs had Lord Northcliffe address one of his
pro-Jerusalem meetings. Sir Ronald had succeeded in collecting

a completely representative committee of Jerusalem residents to improve the city—a creditable accomplishment. With the invited guests at this special meeting, it comprised a cross-section of Jerusalem's inhabitants. This was the only speech Lord Northcliffe made in Jerusalem.

Ever since I had been in charge of the Moslem Girls' School I had been fighting some of the worst elements in Moslem domestic life, and better to be able to advise the girls under my care I had studied the Moslem Sharia (religious) law which governed marriage, divorce, age of consent, and inheritance. In many countries the customs go ahead of the laws, but the Moslem customs in Palestine were infinitely worse than the law. The Sharia law is elastic enough for them to get around it. They have been practicing evasion for centuries exactly in the same manner as the Orthodox Jews have evaded the Mosaic law. The law says that the girl must be of an age to be capable of marriage and childbearing, which would mean after puberty. But to get around this they sometimes take an older sister before the cadi (religious judge) in her outer garment, and with her face covered by a veil, he is not able to judge her age. He sees a developed figure and gives the necessary document authorizing the consummation of the nuptial relation.

During my work at the Moslem Girls' School I often saw women come on visiting day and choose a bride from among the girls for a son or relative and sometimes even select a second wife for their own husbands. A woman's argument was that since it had to be, she had better choose the second wife herself. But the alarming thing was that these were mere children who would be taken out of school to be married, frequently to older men.

I was so incensed with the injustice of this evil custom that I made it my special duty to fight child marriage. I talked to mothers about it, and I studied the Sharia law to be able to enlighten the girls themselves and let them know that they had a right to object. They could not be married without their consent being given, and I tried to encourage them to protest and object to being taken out of school to be married. Finally, after hearing about several terrible cases of child marriage with dire consequences to the girl, I decided that the Mufti must know about these conditions. Perhaps he, who posed as a reformer, would help raise the age of marriage and consent. I invited Hadj Amin al Husseini, Hadj Said es Shawa, with several other members of the Moslem Supreme Council to dinner, the invitation being for the evening following Lord Northcliffe's talk at the pro-Jerusalem meeting.

After dinner I clenched my teeth, to go through with the ordeal of telling these men how their customs worked in actual fact. It was very hard for me to do. I had to be explicit, and I had to tell shocking details. They listened attentively, but when they spoke it was only to ask for more details about Lord Northcliffe's speech. I was flabbergasted. I felt all the painful ordeal had been wasted. They gave me the impression that they were not interested in the suffering of a few girls. But I had misjudged them. To their credit, I found the Mufti and his associates had been shocked, and they requested the government to make the legal age of marriage and consent nineteen.

Some time after this the chief justice, Sir Thomas Haycraft, asked me to serve on a committee with Colonel George Heron, Director of Health; Mr. Humphrey Bowman, Director of Education; Miss Margaret Nixon, Government Senior Welfare Worker; Mrs. Norman Bentwich, wife of the Attorney General, and Dr. Helen Kagan, a Jewish lady doctor, to revise the old Ottoman Penal Code of laws covering women and children. We met frequently during six weeks, and our recommendations were all accepted by the Colonial Office.

Later on, during the tenure of High Commissionership of General Sir Arthur Wauchope, the question of the age of consent and marriage came up again. Jewish, Moslem, and Eastern Christian churches have jurisdiction in matters of marriage, consent, and inheritance, but it was hoped that if the civil administration would not sanction the completion of marriage until the girl had reached a proper age, it would influence the judges of the religious courts. The Moslems were willing to make the age nineteen, which was too high. I felt that fifteen would be the right age, but I heard that the High Commissioner had advised thirteen.

By good fortune my husband and I were invited to lunch at Government House. As Frederick had no official position I rarely had the honor of sitting next to His Excellency, but this time I was on Sir Arthur Wauchope's left. I was not going to miss the opportunity of speaking to him about a matter so close to my heart and for which I had worked so hard. In spite of its not being an appropriate subject for a luncheon table I plunged in.

Sir Arthur affirmed his belief that as girls matured so early in Palestine, thirteen was quite old enough. I told him that in the East as soon as a child entered upon its thirteenth year, she was considered to be thirteen years old, so this actually meant twelve years of age. Even so, Sir Arthur thought, because of the hot climate, twelve was old enough. I argued against it. I knew because of careful study of the subject. Sir Arthur answered, with a good deal of feeling, that he was adamant on the subject. I looked up, and, to my utter horror, found that all the guests had stopped talking and were listening to Sir Arthur Wauchope and me quarreling over the age of consent and the age of marriage.

I learned later that the discussion had not been so futile as I had supposed. Sir Arthur was not adamant. I had been rather afraid of him. He was a real soldier and expected his orders to be executed without comment, but after this we became very good friends.

Generally, when I was invited to Government House, I was seated next to some Arab who could not speak English, because I spoke Arabic. One time I was placed beside the old cadi. After the evacuation of the Turks, the British had appointed Hadj Ahmed al Uri to that post. Heretofore the cadi had been a fellah from Bait Ur el Foka or Upper Beth Horan of the Old Testament. After the soup, the next course was mayonnaise fish. It looked attractive in the platters going round the table, and I noticed the cadi watching it go from one person to another, perhaps wondering if there would be enough left for him. Mayonnaise is an acquired taste to the natives. When, at last, the platter came to Hadj Ahmed, he helped himself bountifully. After the first mouthful, he nudged my elbow. "Tell me," he said in a stage whisper, "what I shall do with what I have in my mouth?" I always enjoyed relating bits of fun to Their Excellencies, and I kept this as a bon mot to tell them later on. "And what did you tell the cadi?" asked Sir Herbert. "She doesn't need to tell," said Lady Samuel. "I found out what happened later on."

One day she called me on the telephone to say that Mrs. Holman Hunt was visiting at Government House. She was now more than eighty and had returned to Palestine to erect a memorial to her famous artist husband who had done so much of his work there.

Her selection of a memorial was a stone seat to be placed overlooking one of Holman Hunt's favorite views. Major Ernest

Richmond, then Director of Antiquities, designed the stone seat with an appropriate inscription, and it was placed in the property of the Greek Orthodox Monastery of Saint Elias, halfway to Bethlehem. It overlooked the shepherds' fields and Bethlehem and the artificial mound called Frank Mountain, where Herod the Great was buried.

Lady Samuel said that Mrs. Holman Hunt was anxious to walk through the Via Dolorosa to the Holy Sepulcher and asked if I would accompany her. I was very pleased to do so, but on second thought I wondered if I was sufficiently informed about the traditional sites to be a good exponent, so I asked Jacob to go with us. There was not much either traditional or authentic about the Holy City that my foster brother did not know. It was arranged that we would meet Mrs. Hunt at Saint Stephen's Gate. This is the eastern gate of the old city and very likely where the Biblical Sheep Gate was situated, for just inside the gate, in the property belonging to the White Fathers, is the ancient and historical Pool of Bethesda. Jacob showed Mrs. Hunt the pool with its unusual five porches. In reality it is two pools, one for humans and the other for animals with a dividing or fifth porch.

We came out from the Ecce Homo Convent where the "pavement" is shown upon which Pilate stood when he showed Jesus to the Jews. It is one of the most impressive spots in Jerusalem. I walked next to Mrs. Hunt. I suppose she was too old to sustain interest in the present for long; her mind went back to the most glorious moment in her life. That was a ball at which she had danced with King Edward VII, then Prince of Wales. She started describing her dress. She explained that they wore stays in those days. "Mine were very tight," she said.

By this time we had reached the station, and I stopped her story to draw her attention to it.

"Oh yes," she said, giving the inscription a sideways glance, but continued her story—"and we wore hoopskirts in those days. My skirt was made from yards and yards of material...." We were climbing the steep, narrow street and had got to the station where Saint Veronica is supposed to have put a handkerchief over the Lord's face, leaving the impress on it. I looked around for Jacob to tell Mrs. Holman Hunt the story, but Jacob was nowhere to be seen. He was not interested in the taffeta dress or the ball or her dancing with the Prince of Wales, and had simply evaporated. I gave up interrupting the dear old lady telling her story. His Royal Highness had actually asked her to dance with him.

She was too tired to see much of the Holy Sepulcher, but she was profuse in her thanks of our "most inspiring walk."

Edwin Samuel, Sir Herbert and Lady Samuel's eldest son, was married to a young girl from Tel Aviv while they were at Government House. The American Colony made the wedding cake. The frosting was put on very thickly and then carved into a landscape by one of our Colony artists.

Sir Herbert and Lady Samuel spent part of one summer at the mission home at Safed. Their daughter Nancy and our Anna Grace were friends, and they asked Anna Grace to spend part of the summer with them in Safed. I was invited to go up for the week end and bring Anna Grace home. There was a macadam road as far as one of the old Rothschild colonies, and from there we rode horseback to Safed. It was a delightful change, and Anna Grace thoroughly enjoyed it. We amused the party by frequently using Americanisms in manner or speech. In the afternoons we played badminton, as there was no tennis court. One afternoon Philip Samuel came to tea in new trousers and Anna Grace remarked, "You're very fine, Philip, you have on new pants." Philip was shocked and said, "How do you know?" To the English pants are "undies."

Sir Herbert accompanied us as far as the Lazarist guest house at Tabgha on the shores of the Sea of Galilee where we had lunch. Father Tapper, the Superior, was a personality known throughout Palestine. After bidding Sir Herbert Samuel and the young people good-by, we stayed on for a bit at Tabgha with the English governor and his wife. We made several trips to Capernaum and other places around the lake so sacred in memory.

One day one of the ladies said, "I'm so sorry my gramophone is out of order or else we could take it out on the lake. There will be beautiful moonlight this evening." I was thankful indeed that the gramophone was out of order. But I realized that one has to live a normal life even if it happens to be a sacred spot.

Lord Balfour and Field Marshal Lord and Lady Allenby arrived with many representatives of European and American universities for the opening of the Hebrew University. A temporary platform was erected in front of a natural amphitheater in the grounds of the Hebrew Universiry, so familiar to us as the home of Sir John and Lady Gray Hill. Concrete steps had

hurriedly been placed, following the natural curve of the mountain. The acoustics were perfect. The speeches were easily
heard. I saw Lord Balfour, who was profoundly moved, with
tears running down his face, deliver his oration. Nebo was
at his back, where Moses viewed the Promised Land; before
him stood the Hebrew University, the emblem of Israel's new life.

When Lord Balfour followed the road through Jerusalem to
the Mount of Olives to be entertained by the High Commissioner
at Government House, he did not notice the Arab residences
and places of business draped in black with black flags flying
and women giving the death cry. He would not have understood
what it meant even if he had heard the shrill cry, for he was
surrounded by Zionists who did not enlighten him. We heard
it, and pondered what the future might hold for Palestine.

CHAPTER TWENTY-EIGHT

When the Samuels left Palestine our next High Commissioner was Lord Plumer. Field Marshal Lord and Lady Plumer were greatly beloved. He was a short man, dignified and very much the soldier; she, typically the English Victorian *grande dame*, but an absolute dear. She was so sure of her position that she could unbend and be gracious without condescension. She wore her hat on the top of her head like Queen Mary when everyone else was wearing hats which fitted one's head like a helmet. She wore strings and strings of irregular pearls.

During the four years of Lord Plumer's administration there was peace in Palestine. I remember hearing about the way in which he answered the Mufti when Hadj Amin remarked that if England continued the policy of favoring Zionism he could not be responsible for the safety of Palestine.

Lord Plumer retorted, "You responsible? Who asked you to be responsible for the peace of this place? I am!" And he answered the Zionist Commission in the same brisk manner.

The Druses were kicking up trouble for the French, and we heard Lord Plumer had asked the director of Public Works Department how long it would take to complete a road past Lake Huleh to the frontier. The answer was that it would take about six months. The astonished director was told that a steamer left in a week's time for England, and that he could take it. The road was finished in as many weeks.

Frederick and I went over the new road in our Ford car when it was completed. It took us through a part of the country I had never seen before, past the Litani River with the imposing Crusader Castle towering on the heights above.

A garden club was started in Jerusalem but was given the grandiose name of Horticultural Society. It did much to encourage gardening, which, because of the lack of water, had been neglected. Flower shows were given in spring and summer and displayed a creditable advance in market gardening of vegetables, besides flowers.

One year the spring flower show was held at the Sports Club, and my brother-in-law was exhibiting some of the twenty or more iris which grow wild in Palestine and Trans-Jordan, many of which he had discovered himself. John was exceedingly proud of this iris, and some received prizes.

However, at that special flower show Lady Plumer took most of the prizes. A French member, who spoke little English, wanted to congratulate her. He said something to Lady Plumer and she turned abruptly away, gasping: "Oh! Oh! Oh!"

The poor Frenchman was distressed. He came to John, gesticulating as only Frenchmen can.

"Monsieur Whiting, what have I say to Mme. Lady Plumer that she look red and say, Oh, Oh, Oh?"

"Well, what did you say?" asked John.

"Mme. Her Ladyship took the mos' of the prizes, and so I naturalmont wished to felicitate her. You know the English say, 'You are a lucky dog.' I could not say, 'You are a lucky dog' to Mme. Lady Plumer, so I say, 'Madame, allow me to present my felicitations, you are a lucky b—— Have I say something very bad?"

We advised the poor bewildered man not to apologize. If he had made such a mistake in offering his congratulations, what might he not say in apology!

The Plumers were in England on leave in 1927 when we experienced a severe earthquake in southern Palestine. The course of the shocks was irregular and the damage just as irregular. The quake seemed to jump from place to place. Nablus and Lydda were badly damaged, whereas Ramleh, only a few miles away, suffered little. Jerusalem felt the shocks, but the Scopus Ridge and the Mount of Olives overlooking the rift of the Jordan Valley were badly shaken.

Government House was so badly damaged that the Plumers could not go back there to live.

The Mandatory Government was paying rent to the Germans for the use of their property, and after the earthquake there was a long and hot controversy about which country was to repair the damage. It went to the World Court at The Hague, and because "Acts of God" were not included in the contract, the court ruled that Britain would have to pay for the repairs.

One of the queer jumps the course of the earthquake took was to deal gently with Bethany, whereas in Abu Dis, half a mile away, there was not a sound house left. Abu Dis depended upon rain-water cisterns for its water supply. Every cistern was cracked and the water drained out.

My husband and I toured the damaged cities and villages. We found Abu Dis sadly in need of help. Dysentery and enteric fever were prevalent; nearly everyone was suffering from sore eyes caused by the high wind which raised dust from the crumbling houses. Water was non-existent and had to be carried for several miles from the Apostles' Fountain in a deep defile, where we, as children, had witnessed the fight between two opposing Bedouin parties.

We opened a clinic at Abu Dis, which continued for several months. The sheik gave us a partially damaged room in his house and we went out every day from Jerusalem in our Ford with nurse and doctor. The sheik at this time was the grandson of the sheik who had accompanied Mrs. Buckingham and her daughter Rose on their trip to Jericho, the River Jordan, and the Dead Sea, and who had exhibited Arab horsemanship by grabbing Rose and staging a feigned kidnaping.

Dr. Bailey Willis, professor of geology at Stanford University, California, and famed as "Earthquake Willis," because he hunted earthquakes in every corner of the globe, had known Palestine was due for a quake and hastened to be in "on the kill." He missed our quake by a few hours. He had reached Cairo when the tremors shook Palestine.

He stopped with us in Jerusalem. His stories of the earthquakes he had experienced were so instructive and interesting that we asked him to give a lecture on the subject in the American Colony hostel, and among others we invited the acting High Commissioner, Colonel, later Sir, John Symes.

Dr. Willis had been awarded many of the world's highest honors for his research in seismology, but his great interest was in building to resist earthquake damage, and many of his discoveries at Stanford University had been made requirements in California building codes.

His lecture at the American Colony revolutionized building in the Holy Land. He was requested to put it into writing by the Palestine Administration. From that time on the demand was for reinforced concrete with a facing of stone. The outside held the same appearance, whereas the old-fashioned mode of walls several feet thick built of double rows of large cut stones filled in with lime plaster and rubble was abandoned. Picturesque domed roofs were also given up. Different heights in the same building were advised to be separate from the foundation up, and connected only superficially on the outside, so that each height could sway in an earthquake at its own angle. This simple but as yet uncomprehended truth was made manifest to us by the two towers on the Mount of Olives. The tower supposed to be designed by Kaiser Wilhelm and part of the Augusta Victoria Stiftung was so badly injured that it had to be taken down and rebuilt by the Mandatory Government, whereas the Russian tower, which was higher, but stood alone, and was known to be cracked previous to the earthquake, survived the shock with little damage done.

Dr. Bailey Willis's visit so influenced my family that our daughter Tanetta decided to major in geology in her college course.

Sir Ronald and Lady Storrs had invited me to join their party on a trip to Petra, that wonderful rock city of the dead. All my life I had heard about the glories of Petra and longed to go there. My husband had taken the trip several times, but I usually had had a baby to care for and had remained at home. John Whiting wrote an article about Petra for the *National Geographic Magazine* with colored pictures showing the waves of mauve, purple, rose, and deep red coloring in the sandstone. I had often heard Jacob lecture on Petra, and he was exuberant in his description. I thought I might be disappointed when I actually saw it, but actually I was to feel that not half had been told.

The company consisted besides Sir Ronald and Lady Storrs and Lady Storrs's daughter Daisy Clewes, of Mr. Benton Fletcher, an artist, Mrs. Stewart Erskine, a writer, the wife of the Director General of the Suez Canal in Egypt, and Peak Pasha and his mother Mrs. Peak. The arrangements for the trip were made by Peak Pasha, who was commander of the Arab Legion, so we were well looked after.

We approached the enchanted city through the narrow defile a mile and a quarter in length, with sides towering above at one hundred to one hundred and sixty feet in height. As we turned in the winding gorge there came to view the Khazneh, or, as the Arabs call it, the "Treasury" of Pharaoh. This temple of rose-pink and red sandstone, with the slanting afternoon rays of the setting sun shining on it and intensifying the natural coloring and beauty, is a sight worth many miles of travel. It is dated in the second century A.D., or earlier. An urn-shaped ornament, ninety feet high, adorns the top, and is dented with bullets shot from Bedouin marksmen who have tried to bring it down and reveal its hidden treasure.

From the place of sacrifice on one of the highest hills, which is the relic of earliest date in Petra, we got a magnificent view of the Araba and Mount Hor, the reputed tomb of Aaron.

We slept in rock-hewn tombs, putting up oleander branches to form screens, and used a large natural cave for our dining room. We did not stay long in our rock dwellings, for the days were spent in climbing the steep mountains and visiting the different monuments, each of which seem to be placed on the top of a different and very steep cliff.

One afternoon in Petra I saw a Bedouin woman and a child with a smaller boy on a donkey standing watching me from a distance. She called out to me, "*Ana minkum, Ana minkum* (I belong to you, or, I am one of you)." I beckoned her to come to where I was. She told me she was a Christian from Asia Minor, who, during World War I, was kidnaped and married to a Mohammedan. Her husband was unkind to her, and finally she had run away with her two sons. She was heading for one of the Christian villages in Trans-Jordan, where she hoped to get protection.

I was not in any position to help, except with a little money, and I have often wondered what happened to that poor woman in that deserted city. I hope she found refuge among the Christian Trans-Jordan population.

Such cases as hers had been cared for at Aleppo by Miss Kerin Yappe, financed by the League of Nations. For years Miss Yappe had been repatriating Christian girls who had been kidnaped by Moslem Turks and Arabs and put into their harems, but when I visited Aleppo in the 1920s the League of Nations had decided to discontinue the work, as many years had passed since the kidnapings, and the advanced age of the offspring of these marriages caused complications. Miss Yappe took me on an interesting visit to the numerous industries she was conducting to support these women. She told me that the Armenian and Assyrian men married them without imputing any blame or disgrace to their lives, because they had been forcibly taken, and at great risk had returned. She told me that she had found homes for about ten thousand such women.

As we stood saying good-by on Miss Yappe's doorstep a woman with a child about ten or eleven years old dropped at her feet and tried to kiss them. The woman, who was dressed like a Bedouin, was shaken with sobs. She said she had traveled

for more than a month on foot to get to Aleppo and to Miss
Yappe, which, to her, meant salvation.

Miss Yappe was in a quandary, because the Committee of the
League of Nations connected with this problem had decided to
shut down this special repatriation work. The poor woman in
question was not sent back to a repugnant life, but I believe she
was among the last to be rescued. The woman I had met at
Petra was just such a case.

When King Husein of Arabia was deposed by the Wahabi
hosts marching on the Hejaz, he took refuge with his son, the
Emir Abdullah of Trans-Jordan. I think it was in the spring of
1925 that the American Consul and Mrs. Heizer asked Frederick
and me to accompany them on a visit to the King at the Emir's
winter camp at Shunet Nimrin in the Jordan Valley. It was a
beautiful warm day. The sky was blue and visibility so clear that
one mistook distances. The iridescent coloring in the lights and
shadows of the mountains of Moab was glorious. Yellow chrysanthemums and white and yellow mustard grow to enormous
size in this semi-tropical Jordan Valley, and they flourished
in profusion on each side of the road. In the gardens near
Jericho orange blossoms emitted an exotic perfume. Wild
narcissus were blossoming among the irrigated wheat and
barley fields.

The camp was situated in a protected wadi, forming a slightly
elevated semicircle into the mountains. After we entered the
beautiful reception tent lined with brocade, and seated ourselves
on gilt-and satin-upholstered chairs, the deposed King entered,
majestic even in his disgrace. King Husein was short in stature
with an impressive face and piercing brown eyes which seemed
to miss no detail. His gray beard was cut short. He wore a large
white turban and a long black "jubbah," or mantle. We all rose
as he entered, and were presented to him by his son the Emir
Abdullah. I spoke Arabic to him, which pleased him. He asked
to have me brought back after the introductions were over, and
I sat next to him. He ordered his mare to be brought, and a black
attendant led in the most beautiful white Arabian mare I have
ever seen. She was too fat, if I had any criticism to make, but
as she was a special pet of the King's and fed with the best of
fodder and sweets, it was not to be wondered at. She mounted
the two steps into the tent and walked straight over to her master.
The King gave the appearance of whispering something into her

ear, whereupon the mare knelt in front of the King and putting first her nozzle on his hand, as though she were kissing it, she then touched it with her forehead. She was rewarded with sweets.

The King took only two meals a day, breakfast after morning prayers and dinner at sundown, so when luncheon was announced he did not join us. The King beckoned his son to approach him and gave instructions that he was to seat me on his right at luncheon. I saw that this command embarrassed the Emir. There were guests in the party who guarded their social standing zealously. The French Consul General and his wife as well as our American Consul and Mrs. Heizer were in the party. My husband had no diplomatic position, and by right I should have been placed far down in the social scale.

I thought I would make matters easier for the Emir, so I said in Arabic, "Your Highness, please do not bother about where I sit at luncheon."

The Emir answered, "My father's word is law," with a glance which left no doubt that I had nothing to do with it.

Our plan to return to the Unites States to live had to be abandoned on account of my sister's health. Grace needed medical attention which she could not receive in Palestine. She and John left for America. Their home there was open to our children for their holidays and this made it possible for all of them to get their education in the United States.

Frederick and I remained in Jerusalem to help with the American Colony's many branches of service and industry.

The charitable work carried on by the Colony was getting to be more than we could support without assistance, one reason being that paid professional help was necessary. This fact was brought home to us in the early days of the British occupation. I was nursing a typhoid patient. The Public Health Department was notified. The Public Health Department doctor asked where I had got my training, and I had to confess that I had only the training which a lifetime of nursing experience gave. I was promptly but kindly dismissed.

The important thing now was to make something permanent of all the numerous activities we had been carrying on which had been interrupted by World War I. Now that the British Mandate governed Palestine, much work which we had been doing would be taken care of by the Public Health Department. However, there seemed a great deal to do; the Turks had left much to be desired; the British Mandate had a colossal job on its hands. They needed help, but what should that be? Certainly not something they, in their official capacity, could do better than we.

It must be something they would or could not do, and that work, we decided, could be done by the women of Jerusalem.

I have spoken several times about the evil custom of child marriage, and although it was neither as prevalent nor consummated at so early an age as in some other Moslem countries, it was bad enough. At the root of this evil custom is an economic problem. We felt here was a chance to remedy this condition by making the small girls an asset to the family instead of a liability.

I have already mentioned the starting of the Industrial School during the early years of the war. Now we enlarged the school and added plain sewing and dressmaking classes. Instruction was given in the three R's in Arabic, and English was taught. Needle lace and embroidery, using traditional patterns characteristic to the country, were developed. Later we added knitting, crocheting, and weaving.

In a few years our Industrial School was doing excellent work. We found that in England an industrial school is a school of correction, so we changed the name to the "School of Handicrafts and Dressmaking."

The members from the Colony occupied in teaching at this school received no remuneration, but we had to engage helpers, and that necessitated the payment of salaries. Many of the beautiful tablecloths, tea cloths, dinner and luncheon sets, guest towels, handkerchiefs, babies' garments, and many other useful articles were sold at an annual bazaar. During the year ladies of many nationalities and creeds met at the American Colony and made articles which added considerably to the value of the bazaar. It became one of the social events of Jerusalem at Christmastime.

The work grew simply because the need was so obvious that it could not be ignored.

On Christmas Eve, 1925, we had given the girls of the School of Handicrafts and Dressmaking a jolly tea party, with plenty of cake, candy, and oranges, and a Christmas tree and presents followed by games. It was over, and the girls had gone off in a happy mood. I was joining my husband and the children to sing carols on the shepherds' fields near Bethlehem. It was the first time this had been done. It happened to be full moon and the weather, which is often wet and cold at Christmastime, was pleasant.

The idea had been that of our dear friend Dr. A. C. Harte of the Y.M.C.A. We wondered why we had never thought of doing it. Imagine the thrill it gave one to be singing carols on the shepherds' fields, with the stars brilliant overhead as they are in that dry climate, and looking up to Bethlehem in the distance and seeing the lights flickering in that hallowed place!

I had been asked to lead the singing, and accepted with pleasure. As I was hurrying down the hill leading from the school, I met a woman coming up. She was being helped on one side by a man and on the other by an elderly woman. This woman was carrying a bundle of filthy rags. I saw at once that the woman who was being helped was very sick. I stopped and asked them where they were going.

The man answered "Allah knows!"

I peeked into the bundle and found it contained a wee baby only a few days old.

I said, "Your wife is very sick."

"I know it," he replied. "I brought her for six hours on donkey-back to the hospital only to find it closed to out patients because they said you had a feast today."

I was greatly touched. I thought as I stood beside the mother and child that I was rushing off to sing carols in the shepherds' fields to commemorate the birth of a babe who was born in a stable and placed in a manger because there was no room in the inn, and here before me stood a rustic Madonna and babe, and, metaphorically speaking, no room for them in the inn.

A crowd gathered. I asked a woman I knew if the sick woman could rest in her house, which was near the place where we were standing, while I went to the hospital and got a stretcher. I was sure I could get her in to Government Hospital because I happened to be on the ladies' committee. We were promoting the training of Arab girls as nurses and to give maternity assistance to the Arab women. I telephoned my husband and told him what I was doing. I asked him to take the children to Bethlehem and to explain to Dr. Harte why I had failed to appear to lead the singing.

I found that what the man said was quite true: the hospital was closed to outpatients. Many of the British nurses were joining our party to sing carols, but I succeeded in getting a stretcher and two porters to carry the sick woman to the hospital. I remained and helped to get her comfortably settled in bed and the baby bathed and fed.

Christmas morning dawned bright with sunshine. The birds were singing as though spring had really come. With six children in our home, the early Christmas-morning excitement was in full swing. I must say the sick woman and her baby had slipped from my memory, when I happened to glance from a window overlooking our front gate, and there stood the man with his four-days-old baby in his arms. I went to him. He told me that his wife had died in the night.

He begged the American Colony to take his son. He said, "If I take my baby boy to my cave home he will die."

I knew it was only too true. My husband reminded me that I had no money to meet such a burden. But how could I refuse after last night's experience? Certainly these poor people had come up the hill, trusting that Allah would help them, and Allah must not fail them.

We took the baby; we named him Noel. A room in the School of Handicrafts and Dressmaking was arranged as a nursery and a trained nurse engaged. In less than a week two more babies were added to the fold. It soon became apparent how much needed just such a home was, and the School of Handicrafts was moved to other premises to make room. In this way the Baby Home was born.

About this time I wrote to Colonel—as I liked to call Dr.— John H. Finley, asking his advice about my coming to the United States to organize a committee to collect funds to help carry on our work. I received an encouraging answer.

I had met Mrs. Frederick W. Longfellow in Jerusalem. She was making a round-the-world tour with her son and daughter. They stopped at the American Colony hostel and she became interested. Dr. Finley became chairman of a small committee of personal friends and continued so until his death. Mrs. Longfellow assumed the responsibility of treasurer, which office she has ably occupied ever since. That the work has grown in scope and usefulness is owing to this faithful committee, which, for twenty-three years, has continued to send to us in Jerusalem the collected remittances from our many friends and supporters all over the United States. It has meant much labor for Mrs. Longfellow, who has done the work as secretary as well as treasurer, and who faithfully has acknowledged each donation.

The majority of the donations were in small amounts and necessitated a good deal of writing.

The committee in New York has changed with the years. At present Dr. Harry Emerson Fosdick is president, Mrs. John H. Finley and Mrs. Harold Hatch are vice-presidents. Mrs. F. W. Longfellow is treasurer. Others on the committee are Mrs. Harry Emerson Fosdick, Mrs. Fielding L. Taylor, Mrs. Kingsbury Curtis, Mr. Harold Hatch, Miss Sarah Lyon, Mr. Robert Finley, and Mr. Lowell Thomas. There is a finance committee consisting of Mr. Harold Hatch, Mr. Robert Finley with the president and treasurer, who take care of all money, especially that given for the endowment fund and for special purposes.

The Home has been enlarged and its function changed. When started, the Baby Home resembled an orphanage, and after keeping the babies for years and making them accustomed to cleanliness and regular habits, it was tragic to give these children back to their parents or relatives to live in the hovels from which we had rescued them. One parent or another relation was sure to claim them, and we had no right or authority to keep them. When the Home was enlarged through the generosity of a group of our friends in Indianapolis, Indiana, it was decided to turn it into a nursing home or baby hospital. An indisputable fact is that the babies are a nuisance in a general hospital and are hard to get admitted. They cry, and they disturb the other patients. The mothers are no less irritating, with their ignorance of the elements of hygiene and medical care, and they interfere with the hospital regime. All these contingencies were taken into consideration and met, and they ceased to be bothersome. As a nursing home or hospital it has served a larger number and wider area.

After having rented, for over thirty years, the house on the city wall of the old city where Father and Mother and their friends started the American Colony in 1881 it was bought through the generosity of Mrs. W. D. Cornish, Mrs. E. K. Warren, Mrs. John H. Finley, and others. We first named it the Anna Baby Home in memory of Mother. When Mrs. Cornish offered to help to buy the house she said she would do so on condition that the name be changed. She did not specify what the change would be, and I fancied that she might like her own name perpetuated. I asked for time to consider and consult the other members of the Jerusalem committee. I wanted so much to create a memorial to Mother in the Baby Home, but as I thought over the problem I felt Mother would say, if she were living, what does a name matter? It is the work that matters.

Strengthened by this resolution, in which the other members of the Colony concurred, I went with my answer to Mrs. Cornish. Her wish was that it should be called the Anna Spafford Baby Home! She said, "There are many Annas, but only one Anna Spafford."

Noel, our Christmas baby, who was responsible for its founding, is now twenty-two years old. He looks very handsome in his uniform, for Noel is a trooper in the Trans-Jordan Frontier Force. Colonel Montgomery said Noel was above the average and took responsibility well.

CHAPTER TWENTY-NINE

DURING our long sojourn in Palestine we continued to follow the work of archaeologists and excavators with interest. One of the compensations for living so far from our homeland has been meeting the professors and their wives who were members of archaeological missions and visiting their excavations. A number of these learned men stopped at the American Colony hostel and naturally our conversation was flavored with archaeology. Some of us took it up in an amateurish manner, while other members of the Colony, such as John Whiting and Jacob, gave much time and study to it.

When our eldest son, Horatio, finished his college course at Columbia, he joined the staff of Chicago House at Luxor, where Dr. Breasted directed the excavations for the Oriental Institute of the University of Chicago. While there Horatio studied law, and in the four months' holiday during the intense heat of the Upper Nile Valley, he went to London and joined Greys Inn.

During his later years Sir Flinders Petrie lived in Jerusalem, and we often met Sir Flinders and Lady Petrie. Sir Flinders, a pioneer excavator, is responsible for lifting archaeological work from a hit-and-miss guesswork to scientific level, and by means of the variety of potsherds found at different levels he set up a chronological order.

Frederick and I visited Dr. George A. Reisner and Dr. Clarence S. Fisher at their diggings in Samaria when the discovery of the magnificent temple built by Herod the Great was made. Under this temple the palaces of the Israelite kings were later unearthed by Dr. J. W. Crowfoot and a large number of carved ivories were found, presumably from Ahab's "Ivory House." (I Kings 22:39.) The Bible story in I Kings 22:39 was made to live when the pool where presumably Ahab's chariot was washed after bringing his body from Ramoth-Gilead was discovered at the same time. Many years later Frederick and I visited Dr. Reisner on Pyramid Hill near the Great Pyramids of Gezer. He was then totally blind and was dictating his memoirs to his secretary.

In March of 1929 Mr. and Mrs. John D. Rockefeller and their son David visited Jerusalem with Dr. Breasted, the great Egyptologist, and they stopped at the American Colony. Mr. Rockefeller had offered the Egyptian Government several million dollars to build a suitable museum to preserve the precious antiquities when the inundation of the Nile made the greater part of Cairo damp. Pressure was brought upon the Egyptian authorities over the management and disposition of funds, and they rejected Mr. Rockefeller's munificent offer.

Dr. Breasted influenced Mr. Rockefeller to supply Jerusalem with a fitting museum. True, many of the valuable antiquities discovered under the Turkish regime were now housed in the museum at Istanbul. These objects form a valuable list: the Siloam Inscription; the Temple Stone, known to have belonged to the Temple; the bilingual stone from Gezer, one of the boundary marks; the Holy Sepulcher inscription in Kufic. The "Orpheus Mosaic" found at the Damascus Gate; the remains from excavations at Gezer, Bethshean, ancient Jericho, and Samaria; the Sarcophagus attributed to have held the remains of Alexander the Great and another sarcophagus in Jerusalen holding the body of Queen Helena, from the Tombs of the Kings, are now at the Louvre. Under the British Mandate, with a Department of Antiquities to safeguard antiquities and retain finds in the land of discovery, the gift from Mr. Rockefeller was gladly accepted.

During their visit we went for a walk. Mrs. Rockefeller and Dr. Breasted were ahead and I was with Mr. Rockefeller. We were on our way to the old museum temporarily located in an old Arab rented house when Mr. Rockefeller asked me an unusual question—unusual, because so few people could ask such a question. He asked, "Do you remember, Mrs. Vester, whether it was one or two million dollars I donated toward the Jerusalem museum?"

Professor and Mrs. John Garstang were our next-door neighbors in Jerusalem. Dr. Garstang was director of the British School of Archaeology as well as director of the Department of Antiquities in the Mandatory Government. His excavations of old Jericho following those of German work in 1907-09 were of peculiar interest to Bible students. There was evidence of the fall of the Canaanite city described in Joshua 6—violent destruction was clear. I stayed for a short time at the Garstang camp in Jericho and helped dust and chart some of the precious bits of ivory and potsherds found in the debris.

It was when I went to the Jerusalem railroad station to meet Dr. and Mrs. Garstang returning from one of their "leaves" in England that I met Lady Astor. Mrs. Garstang called to me above the din of porters, hotel representatives, and the general crowd, each trying to outdo the other in noise. She asked me to come into the car. I shook my head, for I felt reticent at pushing my acquaintance on Lady Astor in this unceremonious fashion. Lady Astor had heard Mrs. Garstang, noticed my reticence, and said, "Yes, Mrs. Vester, I do want to meet you." That was the beginning of a pleasant acquaintance.

Frederick and I with our children happened to be camping at the time on the Mount of Olives, and Lord and Lady Astor with two of their children took Sunday luncheon with us. The two young people returned and spent the night with us in camp.

Sometime later, when we were in London, my daughter Anna Grace and I lunched with Lady Astor at her residence at 4 Saint James's Square. That afternoon we were having tea on the terrace with the member of Parliament representing the universities of Scotland, and Lady Astor asked us to drive to the House of Commons with her in her car. Before leaving us at the entrance she invited Anna Grace and me to spend the week end with her at Clevedon. As usual in London, it rained, so instead of having tea on the terrace overlooking the Thames and the beautiful view, we sat in the tearoom. At the next table to us was Mr. Walsh, the Labour War Lord, a Welsh miner. I was introduced to him, and we had a pleasant conversation. He was giving tea to some of his constituents. It was a historic day in the first Labour Government. While we were in the House of Commons, Prime Minister Ramsay MacDonald was impeached and the Labour Government fell. When we got back to Wimbledon, where we were stopping with a friend, Lady Astor called me up on the telephone. She explained that since we had parted, only a few hours since, a political crisis had arisen. Instead of going to Clevedon and spending a quiet week end, as she had anticipated, she must go to her constituency, which was Plymouth. She sent us tickets to see Pavlova dance, a never-to-be-forgotten memory, to the Albert Hall to hear the *Elijah*, and to see *Saint Joan* by George Bernard Shaw, which was being played in London at that time.

We followed the election with keen interest. Over the radio we listened to Lady Astor's seat in Parliament being contested

by a Labour candidate. He said Plymouth was a rural constituency and Lady Astor knew nothing about farms. "Why should
she represent it? I should like to ask her," he shouted, "if she
knows how many toes a pig has?" Quick as a flash Lady Astor
retorted, "Take off your boots, man, and count 'em."

Among the archaeologists who stopped at the American Colony was Dr. and Mrs. Cold and Dr. Elihu and Mrs. Grant.
Mr. and Mrs. Grant were with us for several seasons while he
excavated Beth Shan, where a series of Canaanite temples dating
from the fourteenth to the tenth centuries B.C. were found.
The city was probably destroyed by David. After the Philistines
had killed both Saul and his son Jonathan, they put his armor
in the house of Ashteroth, and fastened his body to the wall.
Valuable information was obtained from these excavations. It
would be quite impossible to mention the numerous expeditions
conducting excavations in Palestine. However, the one at Tell
Beit Mirsim, where Dr. Kyle of Xenia (now Pittsburg-Xenia)
Theological Seminary excavated under the direction of Professor W. F. Albright, then director of the American School of
Oriental Research, now of Johns Hopkins University, had sad
consequences for the American Colony. Dr. and Mrs. Kyle were
stopping at the Colony hostel. Other guests were there as well.
One was a missionary from Kirkuk in Iraq, who was invited to
visit the excavations. He asked Jacob to accompany him. This
was on July 19, 1932.

The missionary was driving his own car, and they went to
Tell Beit Mirsim through Hebron and Daharieh. In returning
they took the longer road, because the missionary wanted to
visit the reputed Valley of Elah, on the Jaffa-Jerusalem highway,
where Goliath was killed by David.

It was dark by the time they reached the steep descent from
Kastel to Kuloniah. The seven hairpin bends on this part of the
road were called the "seven sisters." There is a short, straight
piece of road and then comes the last and most dangerous bend.
They must have been going too fast, for they went over this
precipitantly and Jacob was killed. The missionary who was
driving did not sustain even a scratch, nor did the lights of the
car go out.

A passing Arab bus coming from Jaffa, seeing the lights in an
unusual place, stopped and picked them up. Jacob was taken to
Government Hospital in Jerusalem. The doctor who examined

him told us that his death had been instantaneous.

Through the generosity of a group of Jacob's friends in Indianapolis a new wing was added to the Anna Spafford Baby Home in
1936 and dedicated to his memory. He had always taken an active
part on the committee of the American Colony Aid Association,
and the Home was one of its activities. Since Jacob had come to
us, a mere boy, he had taken a leading part in all Colony affairs
and was respected and loved by all. Nothing would have pleased
my dear brother more than to be coupled in memoriam with his
foster parents, Anna and Horatio Spafford.

On the sixteenth of March 1936, which was Mother's birthday,
the new wing was opened with a key handed by my parents'
great-grand-child, and my grandchild, Peter Lind, to the wife of
our American Consul General, Mrs. George Wadsworth. The
dedication service was conducted by the Rev. R. S. Calderwood,
D.D., F.R.S.E., chaplain of the Scottish Memorial Church of
Saint Andrews, Jerusalem, and Archdeacon C. T. Bridgeman,
M.A., S.T.E. of Saint George's Cathedral, Jerusalem. The
speakers were Dr. John R. Mott, chairman of the International
Missionary Council for many years and general secretary of the
International Committee of the Y.M.C.A., who, fortunately, was
in Jerusalem at the time; Dr. Judah Magnes, president of the
Hebrew University; Colonel (later Sir George) Heron, director
of the Department of Health for Palestine; Consul General
George Wadsworth; Mr. Rajai Husseini; and Mr. Shucri Rassas.

Shucri was the grandson of the man who met my parents in
1881 as they walked up the hill to take up their life's work, as it
proved to be, in their new home which was now the Baby Home,
and said that he would always be their friend. That friendship
lasted through three generations and still continues.

Soon after the Baby Home was started we realized that an
infant welfare center was our most urgent need. A center where
mothers could get advice about themselves and their babies was
opened in 1927. In the United States, agitation against poorly
ventilated and overcrowded tenement houses is continual, whereas in the poor quarters of the cities of Palestine overcrowding in
the evil-smelling, sunless hovels called homes is so much worse
that Americans can hardly visualize such living conditions.

Many homes are devoid of furniture and a pallet in the corner
of the room is all the bedding there is. There is no separate kitchen
with a stove. A petroleum tin turned upside down and impro-

vised into a charcoal burner or a mud charcoal burner, or sometimes a primus stove, is the only means of cooking or heating in
winter. Generally a copper kettle tinned on the inside is used.
These are precious articles and are often handed down from one
generation to another.

In the midst of such slums we opened our Infant Welfare
Center. The women flocked to it. For some years we were able to
carry on sewing classes for expectant mothers. Portions of milk
prepared according to the doctor's formula were given the poorer
ones.

Our patients were many and varied, and we have kept our rules
and regulations elastic enough to meet unusual cases. The following is from a letter I sent from Jerusalem to our committee
in New York:

I am grateful that our help can go to the needy without all the rules and
regulations that hamper so many charitable institutions. They are so rigidly
regulated for efficiency that the heart is left out. "Jinkses' baby" dies while
lengthy investigations go on and reports are submitted. I had a case in point
the other day. A baby boy eighteen months old was brought to the Baby Home
in a deplorable state of starvation, neglect, and filth; he was covered with sores
and vermin. The story is a series of calamities that overtook the family. It
seems the mother of this child, whose name was Wardi, came from Jerusalem.
She had married a day laborer in Ramleh, about thirty miles northwest on
the Jaffa-Jerusalem road. Ramleh is the ancient Aramathea, the home of
Joseph who provided his rockhewn tomb to place the crucified Jesus in.
Wardi was ill, and her mother brought her, with the baby and two other
children, to Jerusalem, where she could get better and free hospitalization.
The mother was in the French hospital for a long time and finally died.
When the grandmother heard that her daughter had died, it brought on a
heart attack and she died too. Both women were buried by the city in the
proverbial "Potter's field." The father could not be traced. The three children
were left alone in the grandmother's room with nothing to eat. After three
days they were found in this terrible condition. The baby boy had cried so
hard that his navel was protruding two inches. He was a skeleton with an
enlarged abdomen. We took the baby into our Nursing Home and I appealed
to the Government Office for "Children and Young Persons in Need of
Protection," but I was confronted by Rule A.B.C., etc., none of which fit
my case. The children were taken by the American Colony and cared for
until homes were found for them. That is why I am thankful for the flexibility
of our organization.

In twenty-one years of work there has been a remarkable
change in the attitude of these women. We are now dealing with
"our" grand-children, so to speak.

Always superstitious, the Moslem mother is dreadfully afraid
of the evil eye. For years there was a continual struggle to persuade

the mothers to undress their babies for weighing in the presence of other women because of their fear that the "eye of envy" would harm them. All kinds of ridiculous methods and charms were used to ward off its dangers. From one child's cap I removed two long, sharp needles. They were to pierce the evil eye. Blue glass beads, bits of alum, garlic, and a fox's tooth are frequently attached to the babies' garments. Many of these are old, handed down from mother to daughter. We say when we are hoarse that we have a "frog in our throat" and imagine it is because we are croaking like a frog. There must be an earlier forgotten tradition attached, because the Arabs tie a little silver or metal frog to a baby's sore throat and believe it will help it get well. In Palestine one should never speak about a child without invoking the name of God, "Mashalla," which precedes any mention of it, especially if it is in praise.

The last record I have there were about 20,000 visits during the year of mothers bringing their babies for advice and medical aid. Home visiting by the nurse was an important part of the work, and we did as much of this as our funds allowed. Dr. Helen Kagan, a Jewish lady doctor, worked faithfully, from the start of the Home, for twenty-three years. When the work grew, we added an Arab graduate from the American University of Beirut and they worked amicably together until the twenty-ninth of November 1947 when Palestine was divided.

For several years we maintained a village center in Sharafat. The sheik of the village provided us with a room and we used our car to take a nurse and doctor there once a week. We chose this special village because it had a shrine to one of the rare female saints, revered by Moslems and Christians alike. Through the pilgrims to the shrine the news of our work spread, and we would have several hundred patients waiting on the appointed day. This village work was interrupted by World War II.

For years we had considered opening a playground in the thickly populated area near the Baby Home and Infant Welfare Center. A plot of ground adjoined our property which was overgrown with cactus and a convenient place in which to toss old tins and rubbish. It had a bad reputation as well as being the rendezvous of undesirable characters of both sexes, and was a danger spot to have so near the Baby Home.

It was with great satisfaction that we at last gathered funds to rent this plot of ground, which we cleared of cactus and rubbish and leveled. Swings, a merry-go-round, seesaws, gymnastic

poles, a sandbox, and a basketball field were installed. A hut was
built containing separate toilets for boys and girls and six shower
baths; also a firstaid room equipped with the simple but necessary articles in case of accidents.

On the opening day a gaily-colored marquee and chairs were
provided where government officials and friends were entertained.
The Hon. F. O. Lowden, sometime governor of Illinois, who was
visiting Jerusalem at the time, gave the opening address. Other
speeches were made by Mr. Keith Roach, District Commissioner
of Jerusalem, Mr. (later Sir Harry) Luke, Chief Secretary of the
Government of Palestine, and Mr. Humphrey Bowman, Director
of Education.

Ever since then, until interrupted by the civil war, there was
an average daily attendance of three hundred children. One day
was set aside especially for girls. In keeping the older boys off the
playground the older girls and married women were at liberty to
come to the playground. Their babies could amuse themselves in
the sandboxes while the mothers brought their knitting, and the
games mistress helped with suggestions and instruction. Some
of them had started as pupils in our School of Handicrafts.

In his speech on opening day Governor Lowden pointed out
the benefit such playgrounds were in building up stronger and
healthier bodies and clearer minds, and added, "Perhaps the
greatest feature is the contact the children of different nationalities
get by playing together and so coming to understand one another
better. This is one of the main ideas of the League of Nations as
a preventive of war. In this city, above every other, such a relationship is desirable, and I believe that this playground will be
a means toward that end."

As disappointed as we were that the League of Nations was not
able to prevent World War II, so we have been disappointed in
the increase of racial bitterness which grew from year to year.

Sometime after Mother's death Frederick and I had felt that
the Colony should be organized and have a constitution and by-
laws and an annually elected council to direct its management.
We talked about this idea a good deal, and all the members of the
Colony seemed to be in favor of it. It was difficult to visualize
what kind of organization it should be. The American Colony
was unique. It had grown from a few people who, in their single-
ness of heart and pure purpose, had banded themselves together
for mutual edification in administering to the wants of others.

Mother had been able to keep the ideals on a high level through her rare and unique personality, but we had come to the end of an epoch in the life of the Colony.

About 1928 I made a trip to the United States to visit our children in their schools, and while there succeeded in organizing the charitable part of our work under the American Colony Charities Association, incorporated in New York. On my way back I stopped in England and went to Canterbury to consult Sir Anton Bertram. Sir Anton and Lady Bertram had been in Jerusalem twice for protracted visits and had stayed each time at the American Colony. Sir Anton admired the Colony principles. He was a great jurist; he had been chief justice of Ceylon. He gave me the best advice he could on the matter. He told me that because we had not one written line or rule in the Colony the change would succeed only if all were in accord. But if some dissatisfied, ambitous, or selfish person made trouble, he foresaw great opportunities for troublemakers. He advised me to organize the Colony at the first possible moment.

The following summer I returned to the United States, this time with Frederick. This was while Jacob was still living, and we could leave the Colony in his charge. A New York friend, Mrs. Fowler, offered us her summer home in the Adirondack Mountains so our family could be together. With four children in American schools, it was less expensive to accept this kind offer than to bring the children to Jerusalem.

Before leaving Jerusalem we held a meeting to discuss the organization of the Colony. Since so many were to be in the United States, my sister and her husband, Frederick and I, as well as our eldest daughter Anna Grace, her husband, our son Horatio, and two younger members of the Colony who were accompanying us to take summer courses at Columbia University, it was considered advisable that we should get the best advice about organizing while we were all there. On arriving in the United States we consulted friends, who recommended a responsible corporation lawyer. We all met with the lawyer, and he was instructed to get a draft of a constitution and laws which we would carry back to Jerusalem for the whole Colony to consider. Frederick and I with our children then went to the Adirondack Mountains, where we anticipated spending a pleasant summer.

It was the first time in my life I had been part of the woods. I loved the woodsy smell, the soft, mossy, and narrow paths cut through the trees, and the wild flowers which were strange to me.

The American buttercups are graceful, as compared to our Palestinian buttercups, which have thick, stiff stems. There were two lakes in Mrs. Fowler's property, with trout in them.

Never had such an opportunity for recreation come into our lives before. We swam and rowed and paddled in canoes. In the afternoons we played tennis on the beautiful court. We broiled fish and sausages and had our supper in the clearing, especially equipped for picnics. We trekked to places of interest. It was all so novel, so different, that the days were not long enough.

To keep the larder replenished with fish I went out in the boat with Edward, Mrs. Fowler's caretaker. I loved to fish, but try as I would, I could not put the poor worm on the hook.

Rod in hand prepared by Edward, I threw the line, and as he gently rowed I opened the New York *Times*. We had taken the precaution of having it sent to us, but of course it was a day late.

In the midst of this tranquility, this peaceful beauty, I read the shocking news of riots in Jerusalem. They were especially bad near the Damascus Gate, and that was where our School of Handicrafts was situated. I drew in my line and went back to camp to show the newspaper to Frederick. A little later a cable arrived from Jacob asking us to return, as there was dissention between Colony members in Jerusalem.

Our summer holiday was over. Three weeks from that day Frederick and I were back in Jerusalem. We took the constitution draft with us, but try as hard as we could we were not able to reconcile the opposing parties. Eleven of the members left the Colony.

The remaining members went right on with our original plan of organization. We incorporated as the American Colony of Jerusalem, with an annually elected council which meets once a month or as necessity demands. The council reported to the annual meeting of the whole Colony, at which meeting the chairman and treasurer were elected.

On September 26, 1931, the Colony celebrated the fiftieth anniversary of its beginning in 1881. There was a Thanksgiving service followed by a reception. A large and representative company assembled in the large living room at the American Colony.

Mr. Corwin Knapp Linson, the well-known artist, had presented the Colony with a portrait of Mother. It was an excellent likeness, and the portrait was unveiled after the service.

We reprint, with Dr. Selma Lagerlöf's permission on this anniversary of the founding of the American Colony in Jerusalem, the address she had made to the Universal Christian Conference in Stockholm in 1925, in which the Nobel prize winner told of the shipwreck of the *Ville du Havre*, the death of my four sisters, and of Mother dedicating her life to God. The speech closed with these words:

The foundress of the community died . . . at the age of eighty-one, after having given her entire life to leading and serving the community. It has never become powerful and world-encompassing, as she had perhaps hoped in the beginning—it includes about fifty members. But on her death-bed she was able to say to herself that the Divine voice had led her aright. Unity had surrounded her life like a protecting wall. Sorrow had not been absent, but shared by many faithful and sympathetic hearts it had lost its bitterness. And the ability to help—to lighten others' burdens—had increased in a wondrous way. She could tell herself that for the former poverty-stricken Jerusalem her colony had been a great blessing. She could think of bands of Jewish refugees whom her colony had rescued, of suffering pilgrims in danger of death to whom they had ministered, of the five hundred hungry who had daily been fed. She felt that the people who had been trained in the Colony were sincere, pure-hearted, cheerful, mild, and happy in serving others. She could rejoice that the assistance of America during the war had to a large degree been given through her efforts.

Surely it was far from her thoughts to boast, on her deathbed, of worldly success; but nevertheless she considered that God, even in this way, had chosen to show that unity was the greatest blessing of human life. The Colony now owned a great palace. located not far from the Gate of Damascus, as well as six smaller buildings. It owned dromedaries and horses, cows and goats, buildings and land, olive and fig trees, shops and workrooms. Photographs of Palestine from its studio were sold all over the world, and it outfitted caravans which transported travelers far and wide in Palestine and Syria.

Her once so despised colony had become a resting place, a haven of peace, in the Holy City. In the evenings people gathered on the terraces for prayer and conference, song and music. Thoughts of peace went out from this place during the hopeless darkness of the World War. Unity is possible, unity can be attained between the peoples of different nations, unity can also reign between the government and the people. . . .

Let us hear! Let us listen! He whose voice, through the thunders of the World War, spoke to us of unity, speaks to us also through the humble creation of his lowly servant. "Unity!" she calls to us! Unity between Calvinists and Lutherans, unity between Protestants and Greeks, unity between Greeks and Catholics, unity between Christians and non-Christians, unity, unity, unity, between all the peoples of the earth!

Ten years later, on September 25, 1941, another reception was held at the Anna Spafford Baby Nursing Home. I quote from an article which appeared in the Palestine *Post:*

AMERICAN COLONY SIXTY YEARS OLD
WORK REVIEWED

The sixtieth anniversary of the founding of the American Colony in Jerusalem was celebrated at a reception yesterday at the Anna Spafford Home which is maintained by the Colony.

His Excellency the High Commissioner, Lady MacMichael, and Miss MacMichael attended. A prayer offered by the Rev. D. S. MacGillivray opened the proceedings and Mrs. Vester of the American Colony Committee spoke.

Describing the work of the Home for children of the Old City, Mrs. Vester recalled the early struggles of the Home and spoke of the work done during the Turkish regime and in the last war. She read extracts from the diary of her father, Mr. H. C. Spafford, who founded the American Colony, and the assembly then sang a hymn written by Mr. Spafford in 1873.

Reports were read by Mrs. W. D. Ward (daughter of Mrs. Vester), Mrs. Albert Scott (wife of the American Consul), Mr. W. H. Chinn, and Dr. Kagan. Shukri Eff. Rafass contributed reminiscences of the old days of the American Colony and Mr. J. D. Whiting moved a vote of thanks to the American Colony Association. After a blessing by Canon Bridgeman, the "Star-Spangled Banner" and "God Save the King" were sung, and the guests then visited the Home and the Infant Welfare Center.

Other guests included the American Consul General and Mrs. Pinkerton; the Chief Secretary, Mr. and Mrs. Keith Roach; Lady Flinders Petrie; Miss Henrietta Szold; Brigadier Hart; Mr. Justice Frumkin; Mr. Miller; Dr. Magnes; Dr. Bernard Joseph; many ecclesiastics; and prominent members of all communities.

Lord Allenby returned to Jerusalem in April 1933 for the opening of the magnificent new Y.M.C.A. in Jerusalem, the gift of Mr. James Jarvis of Montclair, New Jersey, and the American Colony gave a reception for him. In introducing His Lordship to the many friends gathered to meet him, I told about the days preceding his victorious entry into the Holy City. I told about the holy places having been dynamited and saved only through his consummate wisdom in allowing the Turks to retreat from Jerusalem. In response Lord Allenby said:

You have just listened to Mrs. Vester's thrilling and gallant speech, spoken, I must say, with great modesty. I hardly know what to say after that.

I recall the time within these walls when I had the privilege of meeting Mrs. Spafford. The important work she and her husband began over fifty years ago has been most loyally carried on by her daughters. America has indeed reason to be proud of such citizens as Mrs. Spafford and her two daughters, Mrs. Vester and Mrs. Whiting.

The important work for the youth of this land which is being done by the American Colony, the care of neglected and badly nourished babies, the teaching of mothers to care for, clothe, and feed their babies in the proper manner, the training of young girls in the simple but most essential household arts, are a great work, I say, and most nobly done.

CHAPTER THIRTY

For three years preceding World War II a serious Arab revolt was carried on against the British policy allowing Jewish immigration into Palestine. It began as a country-wide Arab strike which tied up transportation and business for six months. This greatly impoverished the Arab community. Later the struggle became an armed revolt. Constant guerrilla warfare continued all over the country. To support this, Arabs were taxed by their leaders until the country was drained. The British Mandatory Government issued passes to anyone traveling from town to town, and no one could travel or ride in busses without showing his pass. On the other hand, if the villagers showed their passes, they were persecuted by the Arab leaders. Other passes were necessary during the frequent periods when curfews were imposed.

The old custom of travel by donkey-and camel-back was resumed. I had some exciting experiences. Once Frederick and I were leaving the house when we met at our front door a man of middle age. He had a kind expression in his bright brown eyes, his gray beard was trimmed round, and he was well dressed. He was the sheik of a village near Bethel, which is supposed to be the one where the four hundred virgins were captured by the Benjamites after being nearly blotted out in Israel's punishment.

The sheik begged me to go out in our car to his village and get his ten-days-old baby boy whose mother had died in giving it birth. He told how the nursing mothers of the village had taken pity on his small son and he had been carried from one to another to be fed, but that he was not thriving on such irregular feeding.

He had heard about our Baby Home and had come to beg us to have pity on his baby and admit him, which I agreed to do at once. I told him to bring the baby along. He then disclosed his inability to do so because he was afraid to use his Palestinian pass, and his village was too far away to bring the baby on donkey-back. I explained that although we were glad to help him in his need, we expected him to help us by paying what he could toward his son's support at the Home. I could see that the man was well-to-do by his expensive clothes and abayah. He told us that he had been rich, and if Allah brought peace to this poor land he would be so again; that he had land which he tilled, but the insurgents had taken every penny he had of ready money. He said that to make certain that they had got every last pound from him they had put him into one of the ancient egg-shaped cisterns which are found all over the hilly country. Many of these are out of use, and this was one such.

The sheik, lowered into the cistern, found that its other occupant was a large black snake. He was so frightened that he had given up his last penny to the unsurgents.

Frederick and I went out in our car to get the baby. Our trip took us through country where the villagers were up in arms and guerrilla fighting against the British was in progress. It was eerie to be in the only car on the road. We were sure the hills and valleys were full of armed men and unseen eyes were looking at us, although we saw no one.

We brought the baby back to the Home, where he gained and grew. He had not as yet been named, because of the calamity following his birth, so I named him Hassain Hashim, after the mayor of Jerusalem who had capitulated to the British in 1917.

At another time we wanted to return a baby whose parents could not come in from the village to get him, for the same reason. We badly needed his bed for other sick babies. Parents were clamoring for admittance of their infants. This child was well, and there was no reason for keeping him, except that his parents could not travel. I took him and a nurse and we started on our lonely way. North of Beeroth, where Mary and Joseph missed the child Jesus in their caravan of pilgrims returning to Nazareth from Jerusalem, which then was "a day's journey" (it had taken us half an hour in our Ford), we turned east. We saw a man above us on the rocks pointing a rifle at us. We stopped and he did not shoot, but bounded from rock to rock and stood beside the car. He was in khaki uniform with the Bedouin headdress, the Kaffiyeh and agal.

He gruffly asked us who we were and what our business was. My knowledge of Arabic, using their own idioms, eased the tension, but he was still uncertain of my story and of allowing us to proceed without consulting higher authority.

We promised to remain where we were until he returned, and he made it plain that we had better not try to move.

Soon several men arrived, all in khaki uniform and Bedouin

headdress. One I recognized from posters all over Jerusalem as being the leader of the insurgents, who had a price on his head.

In response to his inquiry I gave him the same answer I had given the first man. He was insolent and accused me of being a British spy which I had badly covered up by this pretense. I argued that I knew many better ways to disguise myself if such had been my mission.

He knew about the American Colony and its reputation for charitable work. I told him more about our work and explained that we had never taken part in politics. He relented in his fierce attitude and sent one of his lieutenants along to check up on my story.

We got to Taibeh, and the joy of the parents in receiving their baby well and strong was evidence in our favor. They asked us to remain for coffee, as oriental hospitality demanded, but I could see they were relieved when we refused. The insurgents were near enough to this village to have drained it of all food. On our way back we were met again by the bold leader of the insurgents. Evidently he was now convinced that I was not a spy. He bade me "*Ma' salami* (Go in peace)," and said he had taken the number of the car and of the engine, and marked the color of the car. "Don't change its color," he warned; "wherever that car goes it will be safe. Continue your work of mercy and Allah help you." I thanked him. I never saw him again.

Frederick had one slight heart attack in our car as we were returning from a picnic to Kremzan, near Bethlehem, with Consul General and Mrs. George Wadsworth. The doctor kept him in bed for a month and after that his work was made lighter. He no longer returned to the office in the afternoons unless it was for some necessity.

But unrest was in the world and it was not conducive to a tranquil life.

Hitler had made his appearance on the public scene and a second war loomed, dark and menacing, on the world's horizon.

Once before Frederick had seen Germany turn enemy. He was still a German subject, for his efforts to become an American citizen had been frustrated by Mother's death.

Under a regenerated and republic Germany he had been advised by our British friends to retain his German nationality. Later there was talk about the *Anschluss* with Austria. A German

man-of-war came to the Palestinian port of Haifa to take the vote
on the subject from all German nationals. This happened when
I was in the United States. Frederick decided he would not do
anything on the matter, but the German Consul General called
him up and threatened that if he did not go to Haifa and vote
that it might have unpleasant repercussions for his sister Baroness
von Holbach, who lived in Berlin. He and our daughter decided
that they would go, but would vote "no." The Palestine *Post*
reported that there were only two negative votes to the Anschluss,
but, as it was a secret ballot, no one except themselves knew who
had cast those adverse votes.

When the Nazi regime grew more vicious, Frederick felt he
should once again stand against his country. He must become a
Palestinian citizen, there was no other way open for him. He had
thought that because of his advanced age no one would bother
about him, but the cruel threat about the safety of his sister made
him realize that age held no safety in Nazism.

Palestinian citizenship was granted to him at once and without
hesitation by the British Mandatory. On that awful Sunday when
World War II started Frederick and I had been to church. After
lunch we turned on the radio, and, as we had expected, a solemn
voice from London announced "War has been declared." Then
followed the British National Anthem. We both stood. I started
to cry and covered my eyes, so I did not see what Frederick saw.

Before the anthem was finished I heard people moving in the
room. I uncovered my eyes, and, to my horror, a soldier with
drawn bayonet stood at our library door. What could it mean?
Was it some mistake?

Three British soldiers with drawn bayonets were there to arrest
my husband.

My hat, gloves, and bag were still in the hall, where I had laid
them after church. I took them and stood by my husband and
said they would have to arrest me as well.

"We have no order, mum, to arrest you, only Mr. Vester,"
said the mystified soldier.

I answered that they would also have to take me.

Frederick, who never lost his sense of humor, laughed at my
intense demand to be arrested and told me he thought I could be
of greater service if I remained behind. Never shall I forget the
anguish of seeing my husband taken off by armed soldiers. I
called up Government House and got the High Commission's
aide-de-camp on the telephone, and told him what had happened.

He reported it to His Excellency and the heads of departments, all of whom were at Government House holding a meeting. The aide-de-camp came back saying that there surely was some mistake, that everyone had confidence in Mr. Vester, and he asked me to get in contact with Colonel Kingsley-Heath, who was then chief of police for Palestine. We knew Colonel and Mrs. Kingsley-Heath well; our two daughters had been their bridesmaids when they were married. I tried many times to get the number, and each time it would click off. In desperation I called Mr. Stanley Clark, director of Barclay's Bank in Palestine, and Colonel Kingsley-Heath's brother-in-law.

Mr. Clark was horrified when he heard my news, and it was only a few minutes before he telephoned back that Frederick was released and it had all been a mistake. Colonel Kingsley-Heath had given strict instructions that Mr. Vester was to be treated with the same special consideration that he had been given in World War I.

It was all over in less than an hour, but it was a horrible hour— one I shall never forget.

On the second of January 1942, we were giving a Christmas party to our staff of nurses, doctors, and social workers. Frederick received the guests himself. The dining-room table was laden with good things. It was to be a "Book Tea," and the young people were in my bedroom putting on their costumes, each of which illustrated some well-known book. I had gone to the kitchen to let the cook know that we were ready for tea and returning to call the party to come to the dining room and partake of refreshments, I saw Frederick had fallen on a chair, and our youngest daughter, Freida, who was a trained nurse, was massaging him over his heart. The end was sudden. Frederick never knew he was going. We had had thirty-eight perfect years together.

On the day of the funeral a sleet storm was raging, but many friends came, and the house was filled with flowers at a time of the year when flowers were hard to get in Jerusalem.

Tributes to Frederick's kindness came from all parts of the country.

Some years later I placed a small boy in the Home for Crippled Children and after visiting him I took a Jewish taxi to the Red Cross Headquarters, some distance away in the German Colony. It was an exceptionally cold day, and I remarked to my chauffeur that in my more than sixty years' residence in Jerusalem I had never felt such cold weather. The Jewish chauffeur turned around and looked at me. "Sixty years in Jerusalem? What is your name?" I told him. He asked if I was the wife of Mr. Vester. I answered that unfortunately I was his widow. Then he said, "I must get out and kiss your hand." I asked for an explanation for such extraordinary behavior, and he said, "Your husband saved my life and the life of my family." He told me that he had come from Austria at the beginning of the Nazi persecution. He wanted to run a taxi for his livelihood. One of the American Colony business interests was in the automobile business and we represented Dodge Brothers at the time. This Austrian Jew came to Frederick and asked to be allowed to buy a Dodge sedan car. Frederick asked him what guarantee he could give. He honestly told Frederick about his predicament and said that he had nothing but his word of honor to offer, and he added, "Mr. Vester believed me and I did not fail him." Frederick had trusted this man expelled by the Anschluss and enabled him to start life afresh in a new country. The chauffeur said he was now running two cars profitably.

The experiences of the American Colony and that of the whole of the population of Palestine during World War II were very different from World War I. The British Mandatory Government had prices of necessities under control and food was rationed. A black market existed and thrived where one could buy anything for a price. I heard that an English lady asked a policeman the way to the black market, and he answered, "When you have found it, let me know, I'd like to go there myself."

The British Red Cross, under the able chairmanship of Lady MacMichael, wife of Palestine's High Commissioner, kept everyone busy who could give time to it.

During the war, Jewish and Arab ladies sat at the same table making surgical dressings, sewing, or knitting and talking. For the time being controversy was buried.

But the moment war was over the old hatred and trouble flared again. Explosions, assassinations, kidnapings became almost every-day occurrences. When the sirens sounded two short blasts, the public was warned of terrorist activity. All traffic ceased until one long-continued blast of the siren announced that danger was over and traffic could be resumed. Under such conditions people went out as little as possible.

Ever since 1929, when the so-called *White Paper* was issued, which was the result of one of the many commissions introducing more liberal terms for the Arabs and checking Jewish immigration into Palestine, the Jewish underground element had grown and spread. The southwest wing of the King David Hotel was blown up and more than one hundred people lost their lives. The underground and secret radio regularly announced where the credit belonged for the last explosion.

We did little but attend funerals. I was planning to go to the United States to assist in raising funds for our work. A few days before my departure I received an invitation for dinner from Government House to meet Field Marshal Lord Montgomery. His Excellency's aide-de-camp, knowing how difficult it was to get taxis, especially at night, said he would send Government House's bulletproof car for me. I was dressing when a violent explosion took place not far from my house. The doors and windows shook, some panes of glass broke. My cook came running to me, saying, "Ya Sitt, please do not go out this evening." She was crying from fear. I assured her that if Government House sent the car, that would mean that conditions were safe to go out. I sat and waited. I felt like a child who was all dressed up and nowhere to go.

Soon the aide-de-camp called to say that the police would not allow anyone to go out. The dinner was off. The Field Marshal left Palestine next morning, and I did not meet him. I had met him some years before when he was regional commander at Haifa.

There was little or no recreation or diversion from work during this time, and to give our staff a bit of change I accompanied them to Christ Church in the old city opposite the citadel on the steps of which Lord Allenby had read the proclamation restoring hope in the hearts of the people and peace in the land. How sad has been the muddle that followed that glorious victory! The rendition by Dorothy Sears depicting the crucifixion of our Lord was to be broadcast. The wording of the King James's version was used as nearly as possible but spoken by different people. I had expected that many would avail themselves of this opportunity and the church might be crowded, so we went early, but the church was nearly empty.

When the part came where the crowd cried "Crucify Him, crucify Him," the sirens blared out the warning of terrorist activity. We waited, tense with fear and expectation, for the sound of an explosion, but none came. The broadcast went on, but it was so realistic that we sat and shivered and with difficulty kept back the tears. It ended, and still we waited for the "all clear," which finally sounded.

What happened we found out later. A mysterious suitcase left by the Jewish terrorists had been found in Government Hospital where the majority of patients were Arabs. All the patients had to be removed. Newly delivered babies and expectant mothers, cancer cases as well as fractures and the dangerously sick, all were moved to the garden before the engineers undertook to examine the mysterious suitcase. Nothing was found in it but some heavy bits of iron and old shoes.

This form of war of nerves continued with greater ingenuity and frequency. A telephone message would be received at the post office or Barclay's Bank or any of the government offices that a time bomb had been placed, and this message was to give them time to remove the personnel. Frequently no bomb was found after a thorough search took place, but the authorities could not ignore such warnings.

Personnel got so nervous and jittery that work was almost at a standstill. Any drastic measure by police or government to stop this was met by a volley of abuse against the harsh treatment of the Mandatory Government.

In January 1947 I was on my way to the United States. I had been on the Mediterranean two days, in a small British orange transport, when we heard over the radio about "Operation Polly": all British women and children were to leave Palestine at once.

Among them, I knew, was my youngest daughter, Frieda. She had completed her nurses' course in the Presbyterian Hospital in New York and returned to Palestine to take charge of my Baby Hospital, and had married an Englishman, Mr. William Ward of Barclay's Bank.

In London I received more complete news. Frieda, with her three children, one a baby of a few months, had gone to Cyprus. Her husband remained in Jerusalem.

All government offices were barricaded with barbed wire, I learned.

Jerusalem was a city besieged by unknown assailants.

CHAPTER   THIRTY-ONE

I RETURNED to Palestine from the United States, where I had been speaking in behalf of our charitable work in August 1947. I could not get passage by sea from England to Palestine, passenger traffic was almost cut off, so I flew. I was met at Lydda airport by my brother-in-law, and we followed a guarded convoy of vehicles to Jerusalem without incident. Conditions had grown more tense in Palestine in the few months that I had been away. Explosions were an every-day occurrence.

After two explosions outside the Damascus Gate, I picked up a basket of shrapnel blown over the city wall into the grounds of the Anna Spafford Baby Nursing Home.

Our two Lebanese (Armenian) nurses resigned. Their families would no longer allow them to remain in Palestine. On this account I had to close the Anna Spafford Baby Nursing Home. A few weeks after this the Deir Yaseen massacre took place.

I found a trained nurse and opened the Baby Home and took in forty orphans and half orphans. One little boy about the age of six, when he saw me, screamed out, "Is she one of them?" and fell in a faint. When we tried to revive him, we found he had actually died of fright.

The Baby Home and Infant Welfare Center, situated on the highest part of the old city, were hit many times by bullets and mortars. Several children and adults were killed in the vicinity. The wards on the western side had to be vacated, and twenty of our babies were moved to a safer place, although no place was really safe. The infant welfare work, with the nurses and doctors, moved to the old British center in a more protected part of the old city.

Going to the hospital in the mornings I ran zigzag to avoid bullets.

In spite of bombs and bullets, the work continued. The Infant Welfare Center was enlarged to serve all sick people, regardless of age or creed.

Our playground, where between five and six thousand children a month used to play, was occupied by Arab Legionnaires. They were repulsing attacks on the old city from Haganah troops in the Notre Dame de France. The merry sound of children's voices was replaced by machine-gun and mortar shots.

The American Colony residence was in the heat of battle, occupying as it does a strategical position on the Nablus Road, which Haganah was determined to get and the Arabs just as determined to keep. John Whiting was shot in the leg, but it was only a flesh wound. One of the ladies of the Colony was also shot, but not seriously, and three of our servants were wounded. Archdeacon MacInnes was accompanying his wife Dr. Joy MacInnes to our center when his leg was broken by a shot at our gate.

Early in 1948 Mr. Fred Meyers, one of the older members of the American Colony, died, in his eighty-third year. We made the funeral arrangements with doubts of how we would be able to carry them out. Our private cemetery is on the western slope of Mount Scopus, just below the Hadassah Hospital, which was occupied by the Haganah forces. We ordered the hearse and three cars to come to the American Colony at three-thirty in the afternoon.

The morning of the funeral I went to the office of the Moslem Brotherhood, about a hundred yards from our Colony, and told them we were holding a funeral that afternoon for one of our members. I asked them please not to shoot during the funeral, and they promised not to. I called up Dr. Judah Magnes and told him what I had done, and he, in his turn, promised to do his best to have a "cease fire" observed.

All that morning the gravediggers at the cemetery on Mount Scopus were protected by British police.

The funeral service was held in our open court, amid palms and flowering shrubs, ivy geraniums, ferns, and other potted plants. Mr. A. L. Miller, general secretary of the Y.M.C.A., crossed the city at great risk to conduct the funeral service, for stray bullets whistled in the streets.

In the midst of the service I was called to the telephone. The clerk in the motor office, said not one of the drivers was willing to risk his life by driving to the cemetery in the shadow of Hadassah Hospital. I told him I had the promise from both sides that they would respect the "cease fire" during the funeral, but he said no argument could persuade them.

I telephoned Mr. Wasson, our Consul General, and he tried every means to pursuade some driver to convey the coffin to our cemetery, but failed.

A police truck with eight police was waiting to accompany the funeral procession to the cemetery. We asked permission for the casket to be taken on the truck. The police were sympathetic and wished to help but could not allow the coffin on their truck without permission from headquarters. I tried to get the head of police on the telephone but could not reach him.

We were in a quandary. Just then two Englishmen employed by a chain grocery drove up the Colony driveway in their grocery delivery van. They came from Haifa and hoped to stay in our hostel. My sister met them and told them of our predicament.

"Won't you allow the coffin to be taken to the cemetery in your van?" Grace asked.

The poor men were dumfounded. "You know, we carry food in this van!" one protested. But when Grace explained the situation he consented to take the coffin and drive the van himself.

Finally the sad little procession started. The grocery van with the coffin inside led the way, with our English friend driving and my brother-in-law beside him on the driver's seat. Behind it followed the police car with the eight policemen. We watched anxiously from the windows of the American Colony to see if they reached the cemetery on the hill in safety.

Not a bullet was fired from either side as Mr. Meyer's coffin was carried to Mount Scopus. It was lowered into the earth, the grave filled in, and the procession returned safely to a still-silent Jerusalem. Later on the fighting started.

Some time after this a Swedish lady who lived on the slope of the Mount of Olives was shot dead while on her way to church. We had promised to give her space in our cemetery if anything happened to her. She was a robust person, and we had not thought of any such emergency in the peaceful times when that promise had been made. This time we did not even attempt to take the body to the cemetery but buried our friend temporarily in the grounds of the American Colony.

After the Deir Yaseen massacre the Arabs became frantic and on April 13 attacked a convoy going to the Hadassah Hospital. The road passes the American Colony and about one hundred and fifty insurgents, armed with weapons varying from blunderbusses and old flintlocks to modern Sten and Bren guns, took cover behind a cactus patch in the grounds of the American Colony. Their faces were distorted by hate and the lust for revenge. They were blind and deaf and fearless; only one obsession dominated them. I went out and faced them. I said the American Colony had served them for more than sixty years. Was this our reward? I told them that it was as though they were shooting from a mosque or a church to shoot from the American Colony. The American Colony had never taken sides or entered into politics.

Some of the men listened for a minute and then threatened to shoot me if I did not go away. I said, "Shoot me if you want to, but I must protest against your using the grounds of the American Colony as a cover." They did not shoot me, but they did not desist from attacking the convoy. I then went to the Moslem Higher Committee and protested to the vice-chairman. He asked what we would do if Haganah used our grounds, and I said that I would protest in the same manner. Both vice-chairman and his wife had been our pupils. I was like the importunate widow of the Bible. I did not leave until I had the promise from vice-chairman that he would use his influence to enable the American Colony to remain neutral.

One night the fighting was continuous and the mortar bombs and bullets crashed without ceasing over the Colony. We could hear the impact as they struck our walls, and kept as far as possible from the windows. I had finally gone to sleep, in the early hours of the morning, when a particularly loud crash woke me. The Colony had been struck, but where? It was still dark, bullets still flying, and it was madness to go out. I could not sleep, and I knew that not one of the other members of the Colony was asleep either. I opened the door to go to my sister's flat but shut it at once, because a bullet whizzed past my face and struck the wall near by.

I put on my dressing gown and tried to read. I could not concentrate, so I played Chinese checkers by myself, taking one side with all the rest against me. I played until the sun rose over Mount Olivet, bringing the new day and all it might hold. Then I dressed and went across to the "main house" to see what damage had been done.

What destruction met me! But at the same time I felt a sense of gratitude. It could have been so much worse. A mortar bomb had luckily come into the open court, exploded, and dropped inside the cistern! The palm tree in the corner of the court was killed and the flowering plants and shrubs were uprooted and damaged beyond all hope. Smashed flowerpots and heaped earth covered the court a foot deep. The palm had been a pot

plant given to Frederick and me as a wedding present from
Baron and Baroness Ustinov. Grand parents of Peter Ustimov.

How thankful we were the bomb had not struck the tile roof of
the big salon, with its beautiful antique Damascene ceiling, a
unique piece of hand painting, with its gilding of real gold leaf.

How much more thankful we were that no one in the Colony
was hurt.

Our electric current, telephone, and municipal water supply
had been cut. Fortunately we had been warned to have our
cisterns cleaned and filled. The American Colony residence,
being an old house, had five large cisterns, and these were all
well filled with rain water collected during the rainy season a
few months previous. The one in the court was the best of the
lot, and it not only held the exploded bomb, but, we realized
with dawning apprehension, our penicillin and antityphoid
serum supply.

My brother-in-law's wound had caused him much trouble,
and we thought penicillin would help. Hannah, our faithful
retainer, had risked his life to bring the penicillin from the
Arab hospital in the old city. We had given John a shot with
much benefit, but the remainder was difficult to keep without
refrigeration. Ice was unobtainable and our frigidaire was not
working. John had suggested that we put the penicillin in a bucket
and lower it down into the cistern, where it would keep cool.

Also in the bucket was the residue of our serum, for there
had been a typhoid scare and we had all been inoculated. All
this was now in our best cistern with the bomb.

The penicillin ampules had not broken. They were light and
floated, and we saw them on the surface of the water and fished
them out. But the typhoid-serum phials were heavy and had
sunk, and we were afraid that six meters of excellent drinking
water had been contaminated.

The doctor at the Arab Hospital heard of the strafing the
Colony had taken all night and came out to see if we needed
help. We were happy to be able to tell him no one was hurt,
but we also told him our anxiety over our water supply. He
put our minds at rest. The serum was sterile and would cause
no trouble.

Shortly before the British officials left Palestine I went to
Government House to lunch to bid Sir Alan Cunningham
good-by. He was the last British High Commissioner, and again
the bulletproof car was sent for me. I could not have gone

otherwise. Taxis were not running. How sad I was to see the
British leave Palestine. I know about the mistakes that have
been made, but I ask which government could have done a
better job?

The day I left Government House after bidding the last
British High Commissioner good-by, I went directly to the
office of Mr. Wasson, the Consul General of the United States.
It seemed to me something must be done to enable us to aid
the Jerusalem wounded, no matter on which side they might
be. I asked Mr. Wasson to help us in getting authority from
the International Red Cross to open a casualty clearing station
in the Colony's big dining room.

Mr. Wasson was delighted with the idea and promised to
help. After my conversation with him I left the Consulate General
by the same path in which, a few days later, Mr. Wasson was
shot and killed by snipers. With much difficulty I succeeded
in getting a taxi to take me home to the American Colony.

When we got within five hundred yards of my house there
was a sharp battle raging in the street and my chauffeur turned
deathly pale with fright. I paid him, and he hastily drove away.
I started out on foot, but was obliged to take temporary shelter
in a house belonging to an Armenian who manufactured what
we call Jerusalem glazed pottery. The men of the family and
some helpers were barricading the entrance with sandbags.

I went a few steps farther along the Nablus Road but had
to stop because the bullets were flying so near. In the entrance
of a friend's house who had long since left Jerusalem for a safer
place I waited for another half-hour. It seemed quieter and
I rushed to the main entrance of Saint George's Close. There
I found Bishop and Mrs. Stewart, who were seeing off the
chaplain of Christ Church, who had been detained by the battle.
They invited me in to tea, which I gladly accepted, and waited
there until the battle abated. They let me through their back
door to a breach in the wall we had made for a safer passage
between the American Colony and Saint George's Close.

When I got home I found my sister and the others had worried
about me. I had left before lunch to go to Government House
and now the sun was setting.

Battle continued in and about Jerusalem, but now the flag
of the Red Cross flew over the buildings of the American Colony.

More than seventeen thousand casualty cases, and many sick people, were treated in the Casualty clearing station.

Much of this book has been written in a room where sniper bullets at intervals struck the outer walls.

For almost seventy years the American Colony has served Jerusalem. It has kept its doors open to all who came; housed the homeless, fed the hungry, cared for the ill. It has never taken sides in political or religious issues. From its beginning it has been the meeting place and refuge of Christian, Moslem, and Jew.

If the faith that built it is kept alive the American Colony will live. As its chairman I hope to perpetuated the tradition of my father and mother, who built the American Colony out of their own spiritual need against intolerance and despair. This enables one to understand both sides of the problem completely dominating two peoples on opposite sides of a burning conflict in a city that has held the faith of many.

As I write this Jerusalem is still in sporadic conflict. Under its Red Cross flag our hospital stands over the ancient wall, and beyond, on the Damascus Road, the American Colony residence and hostel buildings, windowless and ravaged by bombs, shelter those remaining members of the Colony and continues the work.

It is my earnest hope that the American Colony which has spanned nearly seven decades of Jerusalem's life, under the Turkish Empire, the British military occupation, the British Mandate, and now, after the civil war, may still be instrumental in upholding the way to peace and understanding.

The long view of history reminds us that this is but a short though momentous period in the history of the city which has in the past four thousand years suffered half-a-hundred sieges by almost as many different nations.

Jerusalem has ever been sacred to Christians, Moslems, and Jews, and holds a place in the religious life of these peoples all over the world. Thither scores of thousands come annually as pilgrims.

Greater Jerusalem, including Bethlehem, should be made an international trust, where each and all may feel equally at home and share in a common endeavor.

The immediate future is clouded.

Human passions inflamed by nationalism and religious bigotry

are still high. But I feel confident that if external peace is enforced on a just basis the heavenly peace will again descend
into the souls of men, and the true holiness of the world's
holiest city will again be manifest.

EPILOGUE

Bertha Spafford Vester died quietly in her sleep in 1968, a short time after her 90th birthday, which was celebrated at a large reception given for her at the American Colony Hotel. The guests, both Jews and Arabs, delighted to meet again, came together for almost the first time after twenty years of separation.

When the city was divided in 1948 after the creation of the State of Israel, the American Colony Hotel and the Anna Spafford Home were both in the Jordan sector until the reunification of the city in 1967. During those twenty years, there was no communication between the two halves of the city, except for diplomats, tourists and priests and a few other privileged people who could cross from one side to the other through the Mandelbaum Gate, about 200 yards from the American Colony. Once a week a strange convoy passed the Colony from West to East - a heavily armoured truck, guarded by United Nations Forces. It contained supplies for the small enclave held by the Jews on the East side, the partly built Hebrew University on Mount Scopus. The American Colony Cemetery, just below the University, was inaccessible in No-Man's Land.

Across the road from the American Colony a wall was built, marking the border. From the upstairs windows of the Colony you could see over the wall into a wide stretch of No-Man's Land and into Israel beyond, but not enter it.

Jerusalem in Jordan was very different from Jerusalem in Mandatory Palestine. Then, there had been a large British community and a distinct flavour of the British Raj, with tennis parties and picnics, dinner and dancing at the King David Hotel (now in West Jerusalem) with the numerous army and police officers. It was a city facing both east and west.

Now, it faced east. Amman was the capital of Jordan, housing the government and the ministries and big businesses. The commercial side of Jerusalem had always developed to the west and, apart from two streets of modern shops, was virtually non-existent in East Jerusalem. There were serious water problems with the cutting in half of the water system, periodic times of crisis when water had to be brought in by tankers. As things got sorted out by degrees, East Jerusalem settled down into a quiet little town, but still a major tourist attraction, since it contained the whole of the Old City and its holy places and had easy access across the Jordan to the wonders of Petra and Damascus.

Changes took place both in the American Colony and in the Anna Spafford Baby Home. The community had begun to break up towards the end of the twenties and during the thirties, as a younger generation grew up, got married and took jobs and houses outside and began to lead independent lives. In 1948 many of those still living in Jerusalem dispersed to America, Sweden or other parts of the Middle East. Those who remained were old people. Housed in one of the buildings of the American Colony they continued in much the same simple way of life that they had followed for many years. Bertha still conducted prayers each morning.

The extensive piece of land north of the main building which had once been a self-supporting farm, retained only a fragment of its former activities. The cow byre had become the laundry but pigs were still kept until 1954. By then the city had grown up round the once isolated building and the Municipality ordered their removal.

The Anna Spafford Baby Home changed its name and function to meet a new need. There were not enough hospitals in the Arab sector and none exclusively for children. With the help of a generous donation from the Ford Foundation a surgical wing was added and the Anna Spafford Baby Home became the Spafford Children's Hospital.

The affairs of the diminished Colony community were run by Bertha's brother-in-law, John Whiting. On his death in 1951, Bertha, finding herself more or less alone to bear all the responsibility, cabled her daughter, Anna Grace Lind, who had been living in New York for many years, asking her to

come back and help. Stopping only to put her family affairs
in America in order, Anna Grace returned to Jerusalem in
1952.

While Bertha managed the hospital Anna Grace turned her
attention to the hostel. Very little modernization had been
done over the years. Bathrooms were few and far between, the
bath water being heated (on request) by an olive-wood fire
lit under a large water cylinder. Heating for the house was
supplied by a   wood burning stove in the middle of each
room. Gradually Anna Grace installed central heating and a
hot water system. Towards the end of the fifties the standard had been sufficiently raised to justify changing the
name from the American Colony Hostel to the American Colony
Hotel.

There was periodical sniping along the border which ran
through Jerusalem and alongside the American Colony. Raids
were made in the West Bank by Arab farmers whose land had
been cut off from their villages by the arbitrarily drawn
armistice line. But on the whole, life was comparatively
peaceful.

The American Colony, however, as so often before, had
problems. As Bertha grew older it became increasingly
difficult for her to climb the steep steps up to the Hospital and Anna Grace had to take over the charity. In 1963
Bertha's elder son, Horatio, gave up his legal profession in
London and came back to Jerusalem to run the Hotel. Anna
Grace was joined the following year by her youngest sister,
Frieda, a qualified nurse and recently widowed, and they ran
the Hospital between them. Since Frieda rejoined her family
in England, Anna Grace has administered the charity on her
own.

More modernization went on in the Hotel. Business was
brisk and tourism expanding every year.

But underneath the surface calm, things were working up
once again to boiling point, culminating in June 1967 with
the Six Day War. From across the border we heard of large-
scale Israeli preparation for war; the population piling up
sandbags, hospitals and cemeteries being prepared for
casualties, reservists being called up. But, in spite of
much inflammatory Arab rhetoric, Jordan remained singularly
ill prepared. There were not very thorough blackout practi-

ces, cars dimmed their headlights with blue paint and there was a half-hearted and much evaded call-up. Many who would have been prepared to fight had no arms. However, the unease in Amman was manifested on Saturday, June 3rd, by a telephone call from the head of the family of our old friends across the river, the Adwan tribe, whose sons were in St. George's Cathedral School in Jerusalem, asking us to send them home, which was duly done.

On the morning of June 5th, Anna Grace, unaware that about two hours before, the Israelis had made a pre-emptive air attack on Egypt, destroying virtually the whole Egyptian Air Force on the ground, was out in the Hospital garden planting out some seedlings. When bullets began to hit the wall just above her head, she and her sister, Frieda agreed that the war must indeed have begun. They decided to evacuate as many of the patients as possible before it was too late.

There was considerable shelling of Jerusalem by the Jordanians, but neither side fired at the Old City, where both were anxious not to destroy the holy places. The Israelis fired over it in order to catch the Jordan army when they were in retreat on the Jericho road. One shell fell short and landed on the roof of the Hospital, but, miraculously, failed to explode. The Hospital came through the conflict undamaged, except for many broken windows.

The Hotel was less fortunate. Being on the direct route to the Jewish enclave on Mount Scopus, which the Israelis were determined to hold and the Jordanians equally anxious to capture, the Hotel got the cross fire from both sides. It had two direct hits and much damage from mortars and flying shrapnel. The Israeli army came through on the second day, and, suspecting that pockets of the Jordan army might be harbouring there, went through all the rooms, opening the doors by firing through the locks. At the end of the fighting, it was a total mess, with two large holes in the roof, shattered bushes and flowers, pieces of ammunition littering the courtyard and hardly a whole pane of glass anywhere.

On Sunday, June 4th the American Colony was in Jordan. By the end of the week it was, de facto, in Israel.

While the Israelis were dancing in the streets of West Jerusalem to celebrate their amazing victory and the recap-

ture of the city, it was a different picture in East Jerusalem. What to the Israelis was liberation and unification of
the city was, to the majority of its Arab inhabitants,
defeat, humiliation and foreign occupation. At the same
time, there were many individual cases where Arabs and Jews,
who had been friends and neighbours before the partition,
were happy to be able to renew old ties and there were emotional reunions across the "Green Line".

After a surprisingly short time guests began to return to
the Hotel, but a rather dismal autumn and winter followed.
It was extremely cold with an exceptionally heavy fall of
snow. The gutters had been badly damaged and the roof
leaked. The electric wiring had suffered and the lights and
the central heating kept going off. There were evenings when
the guests had to sit by candlelight warmed by kerosene
stoves. The kitchen staff showed considerable ingenuity in
producing acceptable meals for everyone on primus stoves.

Meanwhile, the Hospital had to do some rethinking. In
Israel there were many hospitals, more sophisticated and up
to date. A survey was made and it was decided that, in the
new conditions, preventive medicine was the most important
contribution to be made. Therefore, in 1971, the Hospital
was closed and reopened as what it is today - the Spafford
Children's Center. The work actually starts with the pregnant mother, who attends the Pre-Natal Clinic and, after
the baby is born, automatically brings it to the Welfare
Center for routine checks, immunizations and advice on
feeding and hygiene. Besides a resident Pediatrician (a
Dutch lady married to a Moslem Arab) and an Arab doctor,
several Israeli specialists have volunteered their services
and hold clinics in Neurology and Endocrinology - a small
step towards Arabs and Israelis working together.

The descendants of Horatio and Anna Spafford and the
friends who came to Jerusalem with them in 1881, and of the
Swedes who later joined them still own the Colony's original
home in the Old City and the big house into which they later
moved - the former still devoted to charity and the latter
now the famous American Colony Hotel. Bertha's son, Horatio,
who ran the hotel for many years, died in 1985 but his wife
still lives there. Grandchildren and great grandchildren,
now scattered all over the world, from Europe and America to

Australia, periodically visit what was once, to many of them, their home for part of their lives.

The American Colony has shared in and been an integral part of the life of Jerusalem over a hundred years. Nearly forty have passed since Bertha Vester wrote the story of her family in the Holy Land. In that time it has felt the shock of three more wars, in 1967, 1973 and 1982.

During the last twenty years a new generation of Israelis had grown up who have never known an Israel without control of all Jerusalem and the West Bank and of Palestinians who feel they have been patient enough after twenty years under Jordan and twenty-one under Israel and want their own independence and nationhood.

In the midst of this turbulent sea of conflicting interests the American Colony remains, as it has always been, a neutral island where all can meet, divorced from politics.

Shortly before her death in 1968 Bertha was asked how she liked living in Israel, to which she replied, "I have lived under the Turks, the British and the Jordanians and we have got along well with everyone. We shall do the same with the Israelis."

The tradition is maintained.

Anna Grace Lind
Valentine Vester
Jerusalem 1988